Second Langua⌐e ⌐⌐iting
Instruction in (

NEW PERSPECTIVES ON LANGUAGE AND EDUCATION
Founding Editor: Viv Edwards, *University of Reading, UK*
Series Editors: Phan Le Ha, *University of Hawaii at Manoa, USA* and
Joel Windle, *Monash University, Australia*

Two decades of research and development in language and literacy education have yielded a broad, multidisciplinary focus. Yet education systems face constant economic and technological change, with attendant issues of identity and power, community and culture. This series will feature critical and interpretive, disciplinary and multidisciplinary perspectives on teaching and learning, language and literacy in new times.

All books in this series are externally peer-reviewed.

Full details of all the books in this series and of all our other publications can be found on http://www.multilingual-matters.com, or by writing to Multilingual Matters, St Nicholas House, 31–34 High Street, Bristol BS1 2AW, UK.

NEW PERSPECTIVES ON LANGUAGE AND EDUCATION: 76

Second Language Writing Instruction in Global Contexts

English Language Teacher Preparation and Development

Edited by
**Lisya Seloni and
Sarah Henderson Lee**

MULTILINGUAL MATTERS
Bristol • Blue Ridge Summit

Lisya: To Laila, the light of my life, my greatest teacher.
Sarah: To J, my constant source of love, laughter, and support.

DOI https://doi.org/10.21832/SELONI5860
Library of Congress Cataloging in Publication Data
A catalog record for – book is available from the Library of Congress.
Names: Seloni, Lisya, editor. | Henderson Lee, Sarah - editor.
Title: Second Language Writing Instruction in Global Contexts: English Language
    Teacher Preparation and Development/Lisya Seloni and Sarah Henderson Lee.
Description: Blue Ridge Summit: Multilingual Matters, 2019. | Series: New
    Perspectives on Language and Education: 76 | Includes bibliographical
    references and index. | Summary: "This book revisits second language (L2)
    writing teacher education by exploring the complex layers of L2 writing in
    non-English dominant contexts (i.e. English as a foreign language contexts). It
    re-envisions L2 writing teacher education by moving away from uncritical
    embracement of Western-based writing pedagogies"— Provided by publisher.
Identifiers: LCCN 2019022073 (print) | LCCN 2019981397 (ebook) |
    ISBN 9781788925860 (hardback) | ISBN 9781788925853 (paperback) |
    ISBN (kindle edition)
Subjects: LCSH: English language—Study and teaching—Foreign speakers.
Classification: LCC PE1128.A2 S343 2019 (print) | LCC PE1128.A2 (ebook) | DDC
    418.0071—dc23
LC record available at https://lccn.loc.gov/2019022073
LC ebook record available at https://lccn.loc.gov/201998139

British Library Cataloguing in Publication Data
A catalogue entry for this book is available from the British Library.

ISBN-13: 978-1-78892-586-0 (hbk)
ISBN-13: 978-1-78892-585-3 (pbk)

Multilingual Matters
UK: St Nicholas House, 31–34 High Street, Bristol BS1 2AW, UK.
USA: NBN, Blue Ridge Summit, PA, USA.

Website: www.multilingual-matters.com
Twitter: Multi_Ling_Mat
Facebook: https://www.facebook.com/multilingualmatters
Blog: www.channelviewpublications.wordpress.com

The policy of Multilingual Matters/Channel View Publications is to use papers that
are natural, renewable and recyclable products, made from wood grown in
sustainable forests. In the manufacturing process of our books, and to further
support our policy, preference is given to printers that have FSC and PEFC Chain of
Custody certification. The FSC and/or PEFC logos will appear on those books
where full certification has been granted to the printer concerned.

Typeset by Nova Techset Private Limited, Bengaluru and Chennai, India.
Printed and bound in the UK by Short Run Press Ltd.
Printed and bound in the US by NBN.

Contents

Acknowledgments   vii

Contributors   ix

Foreword   xvii

Introduction: Issues and Perspectives in Second Language
Writing Teacher Education in Non-English
Dominant Contexts   1
Lisya Seloni and Sarah Henderson Lee

1   Exploring Second Language Writing Teacher Education:
    The Role of Adaptive Expertise   13
    Alan Hirvela

2   Second Language Writing Teacher Education and
    Feedback Literacy Development: Perspectives from
    Hong Kong   31
    Icy Lee

3   English Writing Teachers' Concept Development in China   52
    Zhiwei Wu and Xiaoye You

4   Factors Influencing English as a Foreign Language (EFL)
    Writing Instruction in Japan from a Teacher
    Education Perspective   71
    Keiko Hirose and Chris Harwood

5   Teacher Preparation for Writing Instruction in Singapore   91
    Sarah J. McCarthey

6   English Writing Instruction and Teacher Preparation
    in Thailand: Perspectives from the Primary and
    Secondary Schools   111
    Tanita Saenkhum

7   Writing Pedagogy and Practice in South Asia: A Case of
    English Language Teachers and Teacher Trainers in Nepal   131
    Sarah Henderson Lee and Shyam B. Pandey

8   Scaffolding Second Language Disciplinary Writing in Qatar:
    A Case Study of a Design Teacher's Development   150
    Thomas D. Mitchell and Silvia Pessoa

9   The Role of Writing in an English as a Foreign Language
    Teacher Preparation Program in Turkey: Institutional
    Demands, Pedagogical Practices and Student Needs   173
    *Aylin Ünaldı, Lisya Seloni, Şebnem Yalçın and
        Nur Yiğitoğlu Aptoula*

10 Opportunities and Resources for Pre-service English
    Teachers to Teach Writing: The Case of Northern Cyprus   195
    Alev Özbilgin-Gezgin and Betil Eröz

11 English as a Foreign Language Writing Teacher Education
    and Development in Spain: The Relevance of a Focus on
    Second Language Writing as a Tool for Second
    Language Development   222
    *Lourdes Cerezo, Belén González-Cruz and
        José Ángel Mercader*

12 'Writing Makes Us Professional': Second Language Writing
    in Argentinian Teacher Education   250
    *Darío Luis Banegas, Marianela Herrera, Cristina Nieva,
        Luisina Doroñuk and Yanina Salgueiro*

13 Second Language Writing Teacher Education in Brazil   273
    Solange Aranha and Luciana C. de Oliveira

14 Preparing Teachers to Teach Writing in Various English
    as a Foreign Language Contexts   288
    Melinda Reichelt

    Index   305

Acknowledgments

This edited collection would not have been possible without the meaningful work of our contributors who care deeply about teacher education and L2 writing and who are actively engaged in research in their own teaching and learning communities. Therefore, we want to extend our sincere thanks to each contributor of this volume for their rigorous intellectual work and commitment to L2 writing teacher education. Their work has inspired us and deepened our understanding of different contexts of writing around the globe and the varying conditions and implications on writing instruction and teacher education.

The chapters in this collection benefited from thorough feedback provided by the following colleagues: Estela Ene, Dan Tannacito, Betsy Gilliland, Ryan Miller, Ali Fuad Selvi and Bedrettin Yazan. We are grateful for the insights and suggestions they provided at various stages of the process, which advanced the quality of our work.

We also thank our colleagues at Multilingual Matters for their support of this project. We especially extend our appreciation to Anna Roderick for her continuous encouragement and tireless work from proposal to publication. Her guidance throughout each stage of this project was unmatched.

Finally, we want to offer our gratitude to all senior and junior scholars whose work on EFL writing continues to motivate us. With this book, we attempt to address their call for more attention on how the teaching of writing works in under-represented contexts by illustrating the multifaceted and complex nature of L2 writing instruction in 12 countries. While it is not possible to list them all here, we are indebted to them for opening up the conversation, shaping our thinking, providing new frameworks and inspiring our L2 writing teacher education research and practice.

Contributors

Solange Aranha is a Full Professor in the Modern Languages Department at Sao Paolo State University in São José do Rio Preto (UNESP/ IBILCE). She teaches English and academic writing for undergraduates and methodology, genres, English for academic purposes (EAP) and telecollaboration at the graduate level. She advises graduate students on telecollaboration studies, genre analysis, and teaching and learning technologies. As a researcher, Solange investigates data on teletandem and is responsible for developing two multimodal corpora: DOTI (Data of Oral Teletandem Interactions) and MulTeC (Multimodal Teletandem Corpus). Her research is sponsored by FAPESP (Fundação de Amparo à pesquisa do Estado de São Paulo).

Darío Luis Banegas is a teacher educator and curriculum developer at the Ministry of Education in Chubut, Argentina. He coordinates an initial English language teacher education programme and facilitates professional development courses for experienced teachers. He is also an associate fellow with the University of Warwick, UK, and a visiting lecturer at universities in Latin America. His research has appeared in international journals and edited collections. Darío is the editor of the *Argentinian Journal of Applied Linguistics* and is involved in different English language teaching (ELT) teacher associations' initiatives in Argentina. His main interests are content language integrated learning, action research, curriculum development and initial language teacher education.

Lourdes Cerezo is an Associate Professor at the Universidad de Murcia, Spain. She coordinates and teaches a number of undergraduate and graduate level courses which form part of the academic development of prospective EFL teachers. She has also been involved in teacher training for in-service primary and secondary EFL teachers. As for her current research, she has participated in two consecutive state-funded research projects regarding the language learning potential of L2 writing and feedback processing and has presented the results at the EuroSLA, BAAL, and AAAL conferences. Her most recent publications are two co-authored chapters in *The Handbook of Second and Foreign Language Writing* and *The SLR Handbook of Classroom Learning: Processing and Processes*.

Luciana C. de Oliveira is a Professor in the Department of Teaching and Learning at the University of Miami in Miami, Florida. Her research focuses on issues related to teaching English language learners (ELLs) at the K-12 level, including the role of language in learning the content areas, teacher education, advocacy and social justice, and nonnative English-speaking teachers in TESOL. Luciana is the series editor of five volumes focused on the Common Core and ELLs (2014-2016) with TESOL Press. She has authored, co-authored, edited, or co-edited 10 books and has published a number of refereed journal articles and book chapters. Luciana has over 20 years of teaching experience in the field of TESOL and is the current president of the TESOL International Association (2017-2020).

Luisina Doroñuk is a teacher of English at an adult secondary school and at a college of higher technical education in Santa Cruz, Argentina. She has completed courses in teaching EFL through an online mode. Her main interests are teaching adults, English for specific pupuses (ESP) teaching and professional development.

Betil Eröz received her PhD in second language acquisition and teaching and her MA in English language and linguistics from the University of Arizona, where she taught freshman composition courses to international and American students from various backgrounds. Currently, she is an Associate Professor at the Department of Foreign Language Education at Middle East Technical University, educating pre-service English teachers in language skills and teaching methodologies and supervising TESOL professionals and prospective scholars in the field of ELT. Betil's research interests are L2 writing and speaking, teacher education (mainly focusing on reflective teaching and practicum issues) and language teacher identity development.

Belén González-Cruz obtained her degree in English studies at the Universidad de Murcia (2016), where she also compelted an MA in TESOL as part of her EFL teacher training (2017). She, currently, is pursuing her PhD in applied linguistics at the Universidad de Murcia and teaching EFL in the secondary context. Belén's current research interests focus on second language acquisition and the language learning potential of L2 writing from a cognitive and sociocultural perspective, as well as computer assisted language learning (CALL) and the use of information and communication technology in EFL classrooms. In collaboration with her research advisor, Dr. Lourdes Cerezo, she has investigated the language learning potential of written corrective feedback and feedback processing in an EFL context and presented the results at international conferences.

Chris Harwood is an Assistant Professor of English at Sophia University in Japan where he teaches composition and critical thinking. He earned his doctorate in language and literacies education at the University of

Toronto. He has over 20 years of experience in EAP, TESOL, TEFL, and ESP and has taught in a wide variety of contexts in Europe, North America, Asia and the Middle East. Chris's research interests focus on topics related to L2 writing pedagogy in online contexts, academic literacy development and language policy and planning. His current research investigates how students perceive and react to oral feedback about their English writing in a Japanese university writing center.

Sarah Henderson Lee is an Associate Professor of English at Minnesota State University, where she directs the L2 writing program and teaches in the graduate TESOL program. Sarah also recently served as an English Language Specialist in Bahrain and Nepal, where she led teacher training workshops on L2 writing. Her research focuses on L2 writing teacher education, literacy practices of refugee, immigrant, and resident multilinguals, and the intersection of world Englishes and composition. Her work has most recently appeared in *The TESOL Encyclopedia of English Language Teaching, The European Journal of Applied Linguistics and TEFL*, and several edited collections.

Marianela Herrera works as a teacher of English and is currently completing a teacher training course of EFL at Lenguas Vivas Bariloche, Argentina. Her main interests are linguistics and discourse analysis.

Keiko Hirose is a Professor in the School of Foreign Studies at Aichi Prefectural University in Japan, where she teaches EFL courses in English writing, second language acquisition, and TEFL courses at the graduate and undergraduate levels. She has taught for more than 30 years in tertiary education and is experienced in pre- and in-service English teacher education in Japan. Keiko earned her doctorate at Hiroshima University. Her research interests include L2 writing development, L2 writing pedagogy, and comparing L1 and L2 writing processes. She has published books on L2 writing and her research has been published in the *Journal of Second Language Writing, Language Learning,* and the *Asian Journal of English Language Teaching.*

Alan Hirvela is a Professor of Foreign and Second Language Education at Ohio State University. He was previously a faculty member at the Chinese University of Hong Kong. He served as Co-Editor of *TESOL Quarterly* from 2010-2013, and prior to that was the Assistant Editor of *English for Specific Purposes* from 1998-2003 and Review Editor of that journal from 2004-2008. His scholarship focuses primarily on reading-writing connections, the teaching and learning of argumentative writing, and L2 writing teacher education. He has published several books and numerous journal articles and book chapters.

Icy Lee is a Professor and Chair in the Department of Curriculum and Instruction of the Faculty of Education, The Chinese University of Hong

Kong. Her research areas include L2 writing, error correction and feedback in writing, classroom writing assessment, and L2 teacher education. She has published extensively on these areas in international journals such as *TESOL Quarterly, Journal of Second Language Writing, Language Teaching Research*, and *Language Teaching*. She is currently Co-editor of the *Journal of Second Language Writing* and Senior Associate Editor of *The Asia-Pacific Education Researcher*.

Sarah J. McCarthey is a Professor and Department Head of Curriculum and Instruction at the University of Illinois at Urbana-Champaign. She teaches literacy methods courses and graduate courses in qualitative literacy research methods and literacy research. Her research focuses on students' literacy identities, writing instruction and professional development in writing, and her most recent work examines how teachers are prepared to teach writing in global contexts. She has also worked with researchers and teachers to study the impact of an online writing environment on teachers' instruction. Her work on writing instruction has been published in *Written Communication Pedagogies: An International Journal, Journal of Writing Research, Journal of Literacy and Technology*, and *Computers and Composition*.

José Ángel Mercader completed an MA in TESOL at the Universidad de Murcia (Spain), where he previously obtained a degree in English Studies. He has recenty begun his PhD in Applied Linguistics also at the Universidad de Murcia to investigate the language learning potential of L2 writing and written corrective feedback (WCF) in computer-mediated writing environments. Alone and in collaboration with his research advisor, Dr. Lourdes Cerezo, he has presented the results of his research at international conferences.

Thomas D. Mitchell is an Associate Teaching Professor of English at Carnegie Mellon University in Qatar. His research interests include L2 writing, disciplinary writing, and the relationship between language, place, and identity. In his current research, he uses discourse analysis and SFL-based pedagogy to scaffold student writing through interdisciplinary collaborations. Thomas's publications have appeared in the *Journal of Second Language Writing, Journal of English for Academic Purposes, English for Specific Purposes*, and *Linguistics and Education*. He received his PhD in Rhetoric from Carnegie Mellon University in 2013.

Cristina Nieva is a teacher of English at secondary schools in Neuquén, Patagonia, Argentina. She has been teaching for 30 years in public schools and private institutions. She has also been running a private school of English for children and teenagers for 18 years. At present Cristina is in charge of the coordination of the English Department at a primary school in Neuquén. She has completed courses in teaching EFL in Argentina. Her main concern is professional development and learners' motivation. Her philosophy as a teacher is to promote opportunities for her students to succeed in their learning.

Alev Özbilgin-Gezgin holds a BA in Linguistics, an MA in TEFL, and a PhD in Rhetoric and Linguistics and has been an instructor, teacher educator, and researcher for more than 20 years. Currently, she works at METU, Northern Cyprus Campus. Her teaching and research interests include L2 writing, academic writing development, first year undergraduate writing teacher education, discourse analysis in teacher education, literacy-based language education, and corpus-based language learning. Alev's current research focuses on pre-service teachers' academic writing development and how pre-service teachers are prepared to teach writing in their future careers.

Shyam B. Pandey is a second language studies PhD student at Purdue University, USA, where he currently teaches professional/business writing courses. He holds an MEd in ELT from Kathmandu University, Nepal and an MA TESOL from Minnesota State University, Mankato, USA. Shyam has taught a variety of EFL, EAP, and composition courses, trained primary and secondary teachers through the Nepal English Language Teachers' Association (NELTA), and led the English Access Microscholarship Program in Nepal. His research interests include multimodal composition, multilingual writing, world Englishes and writers' identities.

Silvia Pessoa is an Associate Teaching Professor of English at Carnegie Mellon University in Qatar. Her areas of interest are L2 writing, academic writing development, and writing in the disciplines. She is currently involved in literacy intervention studies in various disciplines and her work has appeared in various journal articles and book chapters.

Melinda Reichelt is a Professor of English at the University of Toledo, where she directs the ESL writing program and teaches courses in TESOL and linguistics. She is also a member of the editorial board of the *Journal of Second Language Writing*. She has published many articles on L2 writing and is co-editor, with Tony Cimasko, of a collection of chapters on foreign language writing entitled *Foreign Language Writing: Principles and Practices* (Parlor Press, 2011).

Tanita Saenkhum is an Associate Professor of English at the University of Tennessee, Knoxville, where she directs the ESL Writing Program and teaches courses related to L2 writing and teaching ESL/EFL. Her book, *Decisions, Agency, and Advising: Key Issues in the Placement of Multilingual Writers into First-Year Composition Courses* (Utah State University Press, 2016), considers the role of students' agency in the placement of multilingual writers in U.S. college composition programs. She has published in the *Journal of Second Language Writing, WPA: Writing*

Program Administration, and the *Journal of English for Academic Purposes*, as well as several edited collections.

Yanina Salgueiro is a teacher of English at primary and secondary schools in Bahía Blanca, Argentina. She has experience in teaching in different contexts and has completed courses on different aspects of teaching English as a foreign language.

Lisya Seloni is an Associate Professor of Applied Linguistics and TESOL in the Department of English at Illinois State University. Her research explores ethnographic approaches to L2 writing, L2 writing teacher education, issues related to the sociopolitical context of English language teaching, and linguistic landscape in the city. Her publications have appeared in the *Journal of Second Language Writing, Language Policy, English for Specific Purpose, Journal of Excellence in College Teaching, Journal of Language and Politics* and several edited collections.

Aylin Ünaldi is currently working as an Assistant Professor in the Department of Foreign Language Education at Boğaziçi University. Her research interests include language test validation, academic literacy (reading and writing) in foreign language, reading across texts, and reading into writing as an integrated academic skill.

Zhiwei Wu is an Assistant Professor of Chinese and Bilingual Studies at The Hong Kong Polytechnic University. Since 2009, he has been an organizer and coordinator for a telecollaborative English writing project, engaging Chinese and overseas university students in technology-mediated communication. By 2018, the project has administered 31 rounds of exchange, involving over one thousand students from eight universities in China, the United States, and New Zealand. His recent research projects include technology-enhanced multiliteracies and L2 writing teacher development in China.

Şebnem Yalçin received her PhD in Second Language Education from the Ontario Institute for Studies in Education, University of Toronto, Canada. Her research interests include instructed second/foreign language acquisition, form-focused instruction, and the effects of individual learner differences (i.e. aptitude and working memory) in foreign language classrooms. She has been teaching in the Department of Foreign Language Education at Boğaziçi University, Istanbul since 2012.

Nur Yiğitoğlu Aptoula is is an assistant professor of Applied Linguistics at Bogazici University, Turkey. She teaches various courses on second language (L2) writing, L2 teaching methodologies, practice teaching and research methods at the undergraduate and graduate levels. Her current research focuses on the interface between L2 writing and L2 acquisition, genre-based approaches to teaching of L2 writing and L2 writing teacher education.

Xiaoye You is a Liberal Arts Professor of English and Asian Studies at The Pennsylvania State University and Yunshan Chair Professor at Guangdong University of Foreign Studies. His first monograph, *Writing in the Devil's Tongue: A History of English Composition in China*, won the 2011 Conference on College Composition and Communication (CCCC) Outstanding Book Award. His recent book, *Cosmopolitan English and Transliteracy*, arguing for ethical use of English in everyday life and for cultivating global citizens in English literacy education, received the 2018 CCCC Research Impact Award.

Foreword

Back in 2001, as part of the edited volume *Writing in the L2 Classroom: Issues in Research and Pedagogy* (Manchón, 2001), I invited Ilona Leki to contribute a critical reflection on the challenges faced by those involved in the teaching of writing in foreign language (FL) settings, an issue virtually absent at the time in disciplinary discussions on writing in an additional language (L2). The result was her thought-provoking paper 'Material, educational, and ideological challenges of teaching EFL writing at the turn of the century' (Leki, 2001). Leki started by acknowledging that 'English language teachers, particularly those teaching in non-English dominant countries [...], face a number of challenges' (p. 197), which she subsequently discussed in several groups. Of special relevance are those challenges that Leki characterized as being 'of a more ideological nature', which, she suggested, 'are perhaps less obvious but more powerful and far-reaching' (p. 197). These included:

> the need to justify the large investment required on the part of institutions and individuals in order to teach L2 writing, *the right to resist center imposed materials and methods*, the need for dialogue with students about the role of writing in their lives, and the need to make L2 writing enhance learner options rather than limit them so that for learners, writing in L2 becomes not a pointless additional burden but a powerful means of accomplishing personal goals. (emphasis added)

Some time after this publication I secured a contract with Multilingual Matters to publish an edited collection on L2 writing (Manchón, 2009a), the first book-length analysis monographically devoted to writing in FL contexts from the perspectives of theory, research, and pedagogy, later to be followed by comprehensive treatments in Cimasko and Reichelt (2011), and Yigotoglu and Reichelt (2019). In my own Introduction to this collective volume (Manchón, 2009b), I once again commented on Leki's (2001) challenge of 'the right to resist center imposed materials and methods'. My arguments was that:

> mainstream pedagogical discussions have rarely debated whether or not instructional recommendations for SL contexts apply to FL settings, or acknowledged (much less endorsed) the right of those in charge of writing policies and practices in FL contexts to question, or resist (should this be the case), pedagogies developed for SL writing. (p. 2)

Importantly, in her preface to this edited volume, Leki (2009) added another piece to the general puzzle, this time from a research-oriented perspective, when she argued that 'failing to consider writing practices in FL settings badly distorts our understanding of L2 writing' (p. xiii). These two ideas, i.e. the relevance and the right to resist center imposed, second-language-specific pedagogical practices and recommendations, on the one hand, and the theoretical, empirical, and pedagogical relevance of adding the study of writing in FL settings to L2 writing research agendas, on the other, are two central preoccupations in the present volume. If only for this dual focus, the publication of *Second Language Writing Instruction in Global Contexts: English Language Teacher Preparation and Development* constitutes a highly relevant and timely contribution to pedagogically-oriented L2 writing research. The reflections and empirical data offered in the various contributions to the book collective succeed, first, in shedding a strong and novel light on a kaleidoscope of idiosyncratic, socially-situated, and culturally-bound writing teaching practices across the globe, and, second, and rather importantly, in underscoring conspicuous common patterns, experiences, and practices across diverse geographical locales in diverse regions of Asia, the Middle East, Europe, and the Americas. Most crucially, in contrast to the widely reported defining characteristics of L2 writing practices in those contexts where mainstream pedagogical recommendations have been developed and from where they have been exported, readers will find that **teaching writing** in the myriad of geographical and cultural contexts represented in this book is **part of language teaching:** We learn in *Second Language Writing Instruction in Global Contexts: English Language Teacher Preparation and Development* that this is the situation from Nepal to Spain, from Thailand to Cyprus, from Argentina to Singapore, from Japan to Qatar, from Turkey to China, from Hong Kong to Brazil. Therefore, teachers in these global contexts are not, and do not consider themselves to be, teachers of writing; they portray their identity as language teachers. Through the detailed accounts of educational policies in the global contexts represented in the book we also learn that these teachers are usually constrained by rather fixed governmental regulations and curricular guidelines, hence adding another criterial element of the specificity of learning and teaching writing in FL settings, as fully elaborated by Reichelt in the concluding chapter.

A second outstanding common pattern easily discerned in the vivid descriptions of policies and practices offered in the various contributions to the book is that, in the global contexts in focus, teacher preparation to teach writing is either non-existent, or seldom situated close to the realities of the FL language classroom and the teacher's daily pedagogical practices and challenges. The dimension of teacher preparation in effect leads us to what I consider to be another major contribution of *Second Language Writing Instruction in Global Contexts: English Language*

Teacher Preparation and Development: While following from and adding to the above mentioned pioneering, critical works on the intricacies of what practicing, learning, and teaching L2 writing in foreign language settings entails, a most valuable contribution of the book resides precisely in putting teachers center stage. It does so from several valuable angles.

One of these angles corresponds to the collective attempt to problematize teacher education. As noted by Lisya Seloni and Sarah Henderson Lee in their editorial introduction to the volume, the reflections and empirical data contained in the book distinctively point to the relevance of opting for re-envisioning a new and 'broader understanding of L2 writing teacher education as contextually and culturally appropriate, moving away from the uncritical embracement of Western-based L1 or L2 writing pedagogies' (p. 2). This positioning echoes Christine Casanave's (2009) critical reflection on the challenges of teaching writing in FL settings from the perspective of teacher preparation. In "Training for writing or training for reality? Challenges facing EFL writing teachers and students in language teacher education programs", Casanave (2009) put forward several suggestions for teacher education programs, one of which was precisely the need to decenter L2 research from its traditional English dominant university settings, and to open it to new contexts and peoples. Ultimately, Casanave argued, it would be mandatory for 'EFL writing educators and teachers to observe closely the local needs and realities of their particular settings rather than prescribing fixed teacher education curricula for future EFL writing teachers' (p. 274), an idea that runs through most of the chapters in the present volume. For instance, in their analysis of the role of writing in EFL teacher preparation programs in Turkey, Aylin Ünaldi, Lisya Seloni, Şebnem Yalçin, and Nur Yiğitoğlu Aptoula conclude that teacher preparation programs ought to include 'courses on second language writing pedagogy where candidates reflexively think about various L2 writing issues as they apply to their own local contexts rather than focusing on the wholesale application of writing pedagogies imported from the Western world' (p. 192). In fact, together with the Editors' plea for the 'broader understanding of L2 writing teacher education as contextually and culturally appropriate' (p. 2) mentioned above, the idea of 'reflexivity' and 'critical thinking' as applied to teacher preparation programs permeates the whole book, as noted by the Editors themselves in their own Introduction. Importantly, readers are also provided with evidence of the positive outcomes that may derive from the inclusion of this critical and reflective component. A case in point is that of Nepal (Chapter 7), where we learn that 'recent research on the role of criticality in Nepali English teacher development highlights the success of reflective EFL teachers (re)negotiating the relationship between pedagogical ideals and realities' (p. 133). Importantly, the reflexivity component also applies to how teachers are envisioned to appropriate the technical knowledge and scientific concepts that may be part of the teacher education program, as argued, for instance, by Zhiwei Wu and Xiaoye You in their analysis of the situation in China: 'While scientific concepts abound in teacher preparation and development programs, they only provide decontextualized and systematic knowledge [...] without attending to contextual constraints inherent in any pedagogy. Therefore, English writing teacher education should not only mean explaining a whole set of scientific concepts, but also creating opportunities to allow teachers to use these concepts as psychological tools for thinking' (p. 67). Reflexivity is likewise called for when it comes to applying research findings to the realities of the classroom, as readers are reminded, for instance, by Icy Lee (Chapter 2) in the case of appropriating the abundant research on written corrective feedback. Being representative of other voices in the book, Lee advocates 'judicious choices' on the part of teachers, i.e. adapting, rather than adopting, any pedagogical implications or recommendations that may derive from research insights. Ultimately, the book reminds us, teachers need to reconcile pedagogical ideals and the realities of their own teaching situation, hence the relevance of the question 'Training for writing or training for reality?' originally posed by Casanave (2009).

Apart from problematizing teacher education, there is an additional, and rather crucial (in this case research-oriented) angle through which teachers are put center stage in *Second Language Writing Instruction in Global Contexts: English Language Teacher Preparation and Development:* The volume serves to expand L2 writing scholarship by underscoring the relevance of making the study of teachers much more central in current and future L2 research agendas. In this respect, the book continues the conversation initiated by Hirvela and Belcher (2007) in an attempt to redress the unbalance between the research attention paid to how L2 writers learn to write than to how teachers learn to teach writing. As Hirvela himself (Chapter 1) succinctly puts it, 'In the understandable zeal to decode students' experiences with writing, we have tended to keep teachers on the sidelines, despite the crucial roles they play in students' acquisition of L2 writing skills' (p. 13). Readers of *Second Language Writing Instruction in Global Contexts: English Language Teacher Preparation and Development* are provided with a myriad of analytic lenses to be applied to research agendas focused on teachers, in which problematizing, conceptualizing, and fostering the development of expertise, agency, and reflexivity become particularly relevant. Most of the chapters in the book additionally provides a rich portray of qualitative, empirical approaches to listening to teachers' voices, another defining feature of the collection.

In short, the publication of *Second Language Writing Instruction in Global Contexts: English Language Teacher Preparation and Development* constitutes a timely contribution to global scholarly debates on the intricacies of learning and teaching writing in an additional language, on the one hand, and, more specifically, to disciplinary discussions on learning and teaching L2 writing in FL settings, on the other. I feel truly honored to have been the first person to welcome the book to the L2 writing research community, and I express my gratitude to the Editors, Lisya Seloni and Sarah Henderson Lee, for giving me the privilege of writing this Foreword. I would like to take this opportunity to invite readers to initiate what I anticipate shall be a truly enjoyable and enlightening journey through the idiosyncrasies and challenges of L2 writing instruction and teacher preparation in global contexts.

Rosa M. Manchón
University of Murcia, Spain

References

Casanave, C.P. (2009) Training for writing or training for reality? Challenges facing EFL writing teachers and students in language teacher education programs. In R.M. Manchón (ed.) *Writing in Foreign Language Contexts. Learning, Teaching and Research* (pp. 256–277). Bristol: Multilingual Matters.

Cimasco, T. and Reichelt, M. (eds) (2011) *Foreign Language Writing Instruction. Principles and Practices.* Anderson, SC: Parlor Press.

Hirvela, A. and Belcher, D. (2007) Writing scholars as teacher educators: Exploring writing teacher education. *Journal of Second Language Writing* 16, 125–128.

Leki, I. (2001) Material, educational, and ideological challenges of teaching EFL writing at the turn of the century. *International Journal of English Studies* 1 (2), 197–209.

Leki, I. (2009) Preface. In R.M. Manchón (ed.) *Writing in Foreign Language Contexts. Learning, Teaching and Research* (pp. xiii-xvi). Bristol: Multilingual Matters.

Manchón, R.M. (ed.) (2001) Writing in the L2 classroom: Issues in research and pedagogy. Special Issue in *International Journal of English Studies*, 1 (2).

Manchón, R.M. (ed.) (2009a) *Writing in Foreign Language Contexts. Learning, Teaching and Research.* Bristol: Multilingual Matters.

Manchón, R.M. (2009b). Introduction. Broadening the perspective of L2 writing scholarship: The contribution of research on foreign language writing. In R.M. Manchón (ed.) *Writing in Foreign Language Contexts. Learning, Teaching and Research* (pp. 1–22). Bristol: Multilingual Matters.

Yiğitoğlu, N. and Reichelt, M. (eds) (2019) *L2 Writing Beyond English.* Bristol: Multilingual Matters.

Introduction: Issues and Perspectives in Second Language Writing Teacher Education in Non-English Dominant Contexts

Lisya Seloni and Sarah Henderson Lee

This book explores the intersection of teacher education and the ecology of second language (L2) writing[1] by expanding the scope of the field to include under-represented countries and regions across the globe and to provide a systematic discussion of L2 writing teacher education in non-English dominant contexts. We are particularly interested in expanding the current, but limited, dialogue on what it means to teach L2 writing in contexts where teaching writing mainly provides students with opportunities to practice newly learned vocabulary and grammatical structure and is often perceived as enhancing language proficiency. By spotlighting teacher literacy in L2 writing across 12 countries, we hope not only to move beyond the monopoly of related research conducted within the realm of English-dominant contexts (specifically in North America), but also to make the challenges and triumphs experienced around English as a foreign language (EFL) writing teacher preparation and development more visible in under-represented language teaching communities.

The overreliance on English-dominant contexts in L2 writing scholarship has been identified in the field for more than a decade now (e.g. Manchón, 2009; Manchón & de Haan, 2008; Ortega, 2004). Since Ortega's (2004: 3) declaration that 'L2 writing as a field is heavily ESL-oriented,' empirical research in EFL writing has grown in both publications and academic conferences and has addressed a wide range of theoretical and pedagogical issues prevalent across diverse teaching settings. Linking such growth to the strength and vitality of foreign language writing research, Manchón and de Haan's (2008) special issue of the *Journal of Second Language Writing* (*JSLW*), showcases articles on cognition and foreign language writing in three different contexts in an attempt to continue rectifying the 'traditional' and 'unproductive' L2 bias of the field. Similarly, both Manchón (2009) and Cimasko and Reichelt's (2011) edited collections feature chapters that reflect critically on foreign language writing theory, research and pedagogy, and position foreign language writing more centrally in mainstream L2 writing theoretical and pedagogical discussions. Regarding the role of teachers in L2 writing instruction, Hirvela and Belcher (2007) note that significantly more research has been devoted to understanding the needs and experiences of L2 writers than L2 writing teachers. In their special issue of *JSLW*, they 'initiate a process of drawing attention to the teacher education realm of the L2 writing field' (Hirvela & Belcher, 2007: 126) by highlighting the intersections of teacher education and the writing instruction areas of language, genre, response and assessment. While there is no question that the increase in L2 writing teacher education and foreign language writing scholarship in the last decade has advanced the field, research on the intersection of the two areas (i.e. L2 writing teacher education in foreign language contexts) is still minimal and predominantly limited to English as a Second Language (ESL) contexts.

By exploring the complex layers of L2 writing teacher education in non-English dominant contexts, this collection attempts to fill this gap. Such an agenda required us to push the boundaries of teacher education by specifically examining the development of teacher literacy in under-researched L2 writing contexts where L2 writing instruction is mainly perceived, by both the students and teachers, as a means to develop language proficiency, and where first language (L1) and L2 writing instruction may not even exist. Here, we re-envision a broader understanding of L2 writing teacher education as contextually and culturally appropriate, moving away from the uncritical embracement of Western-based L1 or L2 writing pedagogies. Because the training of L2 writing instruction in teacher education programs is not the norm in many non-English dominant contexts (Casanave, 2009; Leki, 2001; Manchón, 2009), language teachers in these contexts tend to provide literacy instruction based on their personal experiences with L2 writing. With this in mind, this book includes voices from contexts where the teaching of writing is not always prioritized and where language teachers often struggle with such local realities as varied language proficiency, instituted curricular requirements, limited materials and resources, and large class sizes. It is our hope that readers will journey through the complete collection and discover the subtle aspects, social experiences and local contingencies that drive English language teachers' beliefs, attitudes and practices related to L2 writing instruction in non-English dominant contexts.

An Overview of the Book

This volume presents chapters by L2 writing specialists who have worked in various regions where English is widely studied as a foreign language, including East Asia (Hong Kong, China, Japan), Southeast Asia (Singapore, Thailand), South Asia (Nepal), the Middle East (Qatar, Turkey, Northern Cyprus), Europe (Spain) and South America (Argentina, Brazil). Reporting on cases in 12 different countries, the contributors turn our attention to various theoretical and pedagogical issues related to the everyday challenges teachers face teaching writing in exam-burdened environments. While the chapters present shared issues and concerns in the ways in which teachers in these contexts learn to write and develop expertise in teaching writing, the readers will also see differences in the way resources are distributed, pedagogies are shared, courses are designed and training programs are shaped across different teaching contexts. The understanding of local variations and contingencies in relation to how L2 writing instruction works is at the heart of this volume. To better understand the characteristics of teacher expertise and to investigate how teachers transition from routine to adaptive expertise (Hirvela, Chapter 1), we take a closer look at the ecological factors that impact writing instruction and teacher education in contexts where both students and teachers may have limited opportunities to write-to-learn both in their mother tongue and in their additional language. With this in mind, the chapters in this collection carry on the work initiated by Manchón and de Haan (2008), Manchón (2009) and Cimasko and Reichelt (2011), who attest that teaching L2 writing in non-English dominant contexts carries sharp contrasts in the methods and materials used, as well as with the ideological and ethical dilemmas experienced by teachers.

Referring to L2 writing teacher education as an 'unstudied problem' (Freeman, 1996), Alan Hirvela in Chapter 1 discusses the expertise gap in L2 writing teacher education by drawing on the notion of 'adaptive expertise,' which is the understanding that teachers reflectively adopt their instructional knowledge as they work with students and constantly rely on their prior knowledge about the context. Hirvela eloquently argues for the importance of examining teachers' writing instruction and raising their awareness of the routine–adaptive expertise distinction. This chapter reminds readers that accounting for writing teacher expertise is a complex issue that requires the adoption of an analytical lens on writing instruction. Hirvela emphasizes, 'what matters most is that we take a step forward in L2 writing research by placing greater emphasis on studying writing teachers and, while doing so, exploring their writing instruction within the guiding framework of L2 writing teacher expertise instead of assuming that expertise is already a well-understood construct' (p. 27).

Another area addressed in the book is the lack of focus in the area of L2 writing feedback in EFL classrooms. Using data from two English teachers' written reflections on readings in an L2 writing course, Icy Lee, in Chapter 2, explores the feedback literacy development of English teachers in Hong Kong who challenged their earlier assumptions about conventional feedback practices after enrolling in a writing teacher education course. The chapter discusses the importance of EFL writing teachers' active role during the feedback process. According to Lee, EFL teachers' feedback literacy development can be facilitated through 'engaging teachers with relevant research literature,' 'stimulating classroom discussions' like the mini-debate described in the chapter, and 'providing opportunities for critical reflection through small-scale classroom inquiry' (p. 48). Lee reminds readers that writing teacher education on the topic of feedback should not be limited to university spaces, encouraging educators to support frontline teachers in their ongoing feedback literacy development and critical reflection on how they provide feedback to students.

In Chapter 3, Zhiwei Wu and Xiaoye You offer a powerful overview on how English writing pedagogies have been constructed and disseminated in China and present a case study of a group of teachers who negotiate in institutional and classroom contexts to develop locally appropriate writing pedagogies. Sharing the voices of seven in-service English writing teachers from three regions in China, this chapter illustrates how the norms of English writing pedagogies are established and negotiated in China and how English writing teachers shape and are shaped by academic discourse, institutional policies and classroom dynamics, thereby addressing the tensions between academic theories and professed practices, between school regulations and individual creativities, and between teachers' beliefs and students' realities.

Shedding light on another East Asian context in Chapter 4, Keiko Hirose and Chris Harwood highlight several challenges faced in L2 writing teacher education in Japan, where teachers of English generally have little training in English writing instruction. More specifically, the authors discuss how Japanese teachers' secondary and tertiary education experiences shape their perceptions and future English writing pedagogy and assess the impact of the national English education guidelines and university entrance examinations on their instructional practices. Regarding L2 writing teachers' beliefs and practices, their findings reveal that teachers in Japan see a large gap between their teaching realities and ideals of teaching. They argue that there is a need to foster more autonomous L2 writers in Japan through the adoption of new writing practices, which require a pedagogical shift from teacher-fronted grammer-translation to student-centered active learning, as well as a need to implement changes to L2 writing teacher education.

Sarah J. McCarthey, in Chapter 5, discusses the major differences that exist among teacher education programs across global contexts due to 'cultural and historical trajectories and economic global positioning' (p. 91) and stresses the need to document the impact of these trends on teacher education, something this collection aims to do. Focusing on the Southeast Asian context of Singapore, a small city state with a multi-ethnic population, McCarthey presents a qualitative study focused on understanding how English teachers are prepared to teach writing to students in primary and secondary schools. Her findings highlight the main factors influencing teacher preparation in this context, including: (1) limited English use in schools; (2) centrally controlled syllabi; (3) classroom practices that discourage learner mistakes; and (4) exam-oriented environments. In spite of the challenges these contextual factors present, pre-service teachers in this context demonstrated increased understanding of textual features and acceptance of innovative writing pedagogies through teacher educators' genre-focused lessons paired with discussions of process. Additionally, pre-service teachers were presented with several professional development opportunities to support their writing instruction thanks to a collaborative partnership between the government, teacher education programs and local schools. Such collaboration, as McCarthey notes, is 'particularly important for increasing teachers' competence and confidence in teaching writing' (p. 109).

To generate an understanding of how L2 writing pedagogy is approached in Thailand and to highlight how English teachers in this context are (not) prepared to teach writing, Tanita Saenkhum details a qualitative study of primary and secondary teachers in Chapter 6. Here, she situates English writing instruction and related teacher training within national language teaching policies before presenting her findings, which include the pedagogical prioritization of speaking, the association of grammar and vocabulary with writing, and the lack of L2 writing specific training in teacher education and professional development programs. Saenkhum concludes by posing three questions: (1) Should an L2 writing practicum be required for pre-service teachers? (2) Should L2 writing be taught as an independent class in primary and secondary contexts? and (3) Should collaboration between universities and schools be developed? While her findings support answering each question positively, Saenkhum acknowledges the context-specific factors that complicate the logistics of doing so in EFL contexts like Thailand and challenges teacher educators to move related conversations forward collaboratively.

Moving to the South Asian context in Chapter 7, Sarah Henderson Lee and Shyam B. Pandey detail a qualitative study of primary, secondary and post-secondary English teachers and teacher trainers' experiences with L2 writing instruction in the culturally and linguistically diverse context of Nepal. After discussing the country's current state of English language teaching, including teacher education specific to the teaching of writing, the authors report their findings in the areas of teacher preparation and continued development, classroom successes and challenges, and resources and support systems. They argue that the disconnect between pre-service training and in-service practice, the top-down approach to professional development, and other logistical constraints such as classroom space and students' varied linguistics abilities hamper motivated teachers' professional development in L2 writing and call for more local collaboration between teachers and trainers.

In Chapter 8, Thomas D. Mitchell and Silvia Pessoa showcase a model of collaboration between language specialists and disciplinary faculty to improve university-level students' L2 writing across disciplines in Qatar. In the EFL context of English-medium universities, increasing numbers of multilingual students are required to meet the writing expectations of disciplinary faculty who may not have any pedagogical training, especially training specific to the teaching of L2 writing. Through text analysis, think-aloud protocols, interviews, collaborative (re)development of materials and co-teaching, Mitchell and Pessoa's case study of Robert, a design professor, emphasizes the need for such collaboration in preparing disciplinary faculty to effectively scaffold L2 writing development in their teaching contexts. Additionally, their findings contribute to advancing L2 writing specialists' understanding of the writing demands multilingual students face outside of first year writing classes, as well as the language resources they need to meet discipline-specific writing expectations.

Reflecting on recent English language policy and planning changes, teacher education programs in Turkey, like many other EFL contexts, largely prioritize communicative language teaching and the development of spoken language proficiency. Aylin Ünaldi, Lisya Seloni, Şebnem Yalçin and Nur Yiğitoğlu Aptoula call attention to the importance of written communication skills for teacher candidates in EFL teacher training programs in Chapter 9, where they share a collaborative examination and revisioning of one foreign language teacher education program's first year writing sequence. The authors argue that such a critical analysis of teacher training programs is necessary to better understand the tensions surrounding L2 writing instruction in EFL contexts and the writing needs and experiences of future language teachers, who often do not see themselves as strong writers in English. To better reflect 21st century writing practices and the lives of the teacher candidates outside of school, Ünaldi *et al.* suggest broadening the scope of the first year writing sequence to include both academic and non-academic genres. Additionally, they propose a required course on writing pedagogy, where teacher candidates can 'reflexively think about various L2 writing issues as they apply to their own local contexts rather than focusing on the wholesale application of writing pedagogies imported from the Western world' (p. 192).

Alev Özbilgin-Gezgin and Betil Eröz, in Chapter 10, detail a case study of the L2 writing and writing pedagogy experiences of both teacher candidates and faculty in an English teacher education program in Northern Cyprus, a context with strong ties to Turkey. Data sources, including written artifacts and interviews, reveal an emphasis on academic writing basics such as organization and mechanics during teacher candidates' first year. This focus, according to the authors' findings, was appreciated by teacher candidate participants, who often had limited opportunities to develop such skills during their primary and secondary education, and by faculty participants, who noted the low language proficiency of incoming students. While challenging, Özbilgin-Gezgin and Eröz highlight the importance of simultaneously developing teacher candidates as L2 writers and future teachers of L2 writing in EFL teacher education contexts.

Shifting the contextual focus to Europe, Lourdes Cerezo, Belén González-Cruz and José Ángel Mercader remind readers in Chapter 11 of the distinction between *learning to write* and *writing to learn* an additional language, noting that learners in EFL contexts, unlike ESL contexts, most often engage in L2 writing for the purpose of developing their overall L2 competences. Focusing on the primary and secondary educational contexts in Spain, the authors argue that teachers who are educated and trained in the language learning potential of L2 writing are at an advantage. Moreover, they suggest that universities and teacher resource centers responsible for the preparation and continued development of teachers include opportunities for pre- and in-service teachers to develop their own language skills through writing, as well as explicit instruction in the theoretical underpinnings of *writing to learn* and the practical applications to primary and secondary EFL classrooms.

To better understand issues of motivation and identity in language teacher education programs in Argentina, Darío Luis Banegas, Cristina Nieva, Marianela Herrera, Luisina Doroñuk and Yanina Salgueiro, in Chapter 12, share findings from a study focused on their own L2 writing experiences as teacher educator and student-teachers in an online teacher education program. Analysis of student-teachers' genre-specific texts, written reflections and a post-course interview highlight the relationship between language proficiency development through academic writing and professional identity construction. The student-teachers' prioritization of language proficiency in their professional development and identity construction, as well as their increased motivation to meet the challenges of genre-specific writing with the support of teacher feedback, emphasize the need for language teacher education programs in Argentina and elsewhere to consider notions of teacher identity and motivation in curricular decisions, materials development and instructional practices. By doing so, the authors note, student-teachers will be able to 'strengthen and (re)configure their present identity as student-teachers and language learners in relation to their imagined future identity as EFL teachers' (p. 268).

In Chapter 13, Solange Aranha and Luciana C. de Oliveira explore the political, social and cultural factors impacting local teacher education programs that focus on the teaching and learning of foreign languages in Brazil. Their analysis of teacher education program sequences at five public universities in different regions of the country shows little to no focus on writing pedagogy, even in the few contexts where writing was taught as a productive skill. To address this gap, the authors propose four specific areas of writing teacher education for university programs to consider embedding in their current curricula: (1) a genre-based approach to writing instruction; (2) designing, learning and practicing teaching writing; (3) participation in the institutional program of grants for initiation into teaching; and (4) foreign language writing assessment. Noting that such a proposal is dependent on a national effort to revise curricula across the country, Aranha and de Oliveira's work aims to foster more conversations around the theme of L2 writing teacher education in Brazil.

One of the overlapping themes across chapters in this collection is how L2 writing teacher education is dependent on various contextual factors and social experiences that impact both writing instruction and teacher preparation. Melinda Reichelt, in Chapter 14, articulately discusses how local and institutional factors as well as the sociolinguistic status of English shape L2 writing teacher education in non-English dominant contexts. According to Reichelt, in order to avoid the application of inappropriate writing pedagogies, especially for teachers who attend graduate programs in Inner Circle countries and then teach EFL writing, practicing teachers need to be aware of how the sociolinguistic status of the target language in a given context affects learners' perceptions of the language and, in turn, the importance (or lack thereof) of learning to write. For example, when the target language and the students' native language(s) employ different writing systems, much attention must be paid to the beginning stages of instruction and to the writing system itself. Thus, the linguistic distance between students and teachers' L1 and the target language is seen as another shaping factor.

Moving Forward: Reflexive and Ecologically Responsible L2 Writing Teacher Education

One value of editing a collection on L2 writing and teacher education in non-English dominant instructional settings is drawing the field's attention to the wide range of contextual variations we see regarding the stages teachers move through in their professional careers, especially in terms of teaching writing to student populations with varied language proficiencies, language attitudes and literacy backgrounds in both their L1s and L2s. This collection brought together empirical research that investigates the teacher education dimension of teaching L2 writing, primarily focusing on how teachers understand and interpret their local realities around English use and the teaching of L2 writing. As many of the contributors in this collection suggest, teacher training in non-English dominant contexts suffers from three primary disconnections: (1) a disconnect between the realities of local teachers and Western pedagogies (specifically, writing scholarship emerging from the North American context); (2) a disconnect between available resources and professed practices; and (3) a disconnect between teacher training and students' language needs. Since many teacher education programs do not have courses devoted to preparing students to teach L2 writing, Reichelt (Chapter 14) encourages pre- and in-service teachers to address such disconnections by reflecting on their local teaching contexts and practices. Among the useful activities that can prepare local teachers for L2 writing instruction are engaging English teachers in English language writing in different genres, discussing case study scenarios related to teaching writing, investigating the sociolinguistic status of English in particular communities and exploring local beliefs and circumstances regarding writing instruction. We think that these practical suggestions are also useful for the preparation of Anglo teachers who plan to teach L2 writing in countries where they have little knowledge about the educational and linguistic practices of the local context. To own one's professional identity as a language teacher requires the hard work of reflecting on teacher beliefs and reasoning, which shape the ways classroom events are acted on and interpreted (Johnson & Ma, 1999; Kumaravadivelu, 2003). While reflecting on what it means to be a language teacher – and more specifically a writing teacher – in our individual contexts and making sense of our classrooms based on the locally produced peculiarities, opportunities and constraints is an inextricably complex task, more empirical and pedagogical work theorizing teachers' classroom practices would shed light on and create space for a better understanding of teacher expertise and practice in under-represented communities.

To produce robust and inclusive knowledge in the field of L2 writing, we need to move beyond perceiving L2 writing scholarship as if it only takes place in English-dominant contexts with writers who use English on a daily basis or with teachers who are trained exclusively in North American pedagogies. With this in mind, the chapters in this collection discuss how the epistemologies that guide teachers' instructional practices are highly shaped by and also shape local dynamics that play a crucial role in teaching writing in non-English dominant contexts. The ESL-bias of writing scholarship pointed out by Ortega (2004) not only limits the manner in which L2 writing is taught in global contexts, but also puts undue pressure on teachers, students, parents and institutions. As the chapters in this book illustrate, L2 writing scholarship should also include the people, contexts, pedagogies, epistemologies, institutional limitations and sociolinguistic realities of teachers who operate from a reality different from those in English-dominant contexts. To expand our understanding of local teaching practices and teacher literacy in L2 writing, we need also to be engaged in the 'dual exploration of the learning-to-write and writing-to-learn dimensions of writing in an additional language' (Manchón, 2011: 4) outside the context of North America and pay attention to how local teachers translate L2 writing scholarship in a way that makes sense for their own particular contexts. Emphasizing the crucial role teacher agency plays in advancing language learners' L2 knowledge and knowledge of writing in diverse genres, the work presented in this book showcases locally developed L2 writing pedagogies, instructional frameworks and teacher preparation models, attempting to bring a fuller understanding of the language learning function of L2 writing, as well as teachers' own practices around learning to write in their additional language. The presence of voices from non-English dominant teaching and learning contexts is an important step in creating a more inclusive body of knowledge in L2 writing teacher education scholarship.

As Henderson Lee and Pandey put it in Chapter 7, 'reflective teachers become local agents of change by critically reflecting on data from their own writing instruction' (p. 146). Reflexivity, therefore, is one of the main research agendas that we hope to promote with this book. As reflected by the empirical work presented in this collection, language teachers, especially those who are not trained to be writing teachers per se but who are expected to teach writing, should integrate reflexivity in their everyday practice in order to make sense of locally relevant pedagogies, set a realistic agenda for providing feedback (or utilizing classroom practices such as peer feedback), and identify appropriate strategies for navigating through their learning and teaching contexts. Finally, this book attempts to bring our attention to an ecological framework of teacher education (Casanave, 2009) where we acknowledge the complex, messy, interrelated and contextual nature of teaching and learning and reject the wholesale application of pedagogies in language teacher education programs and acknowledge individual expectations, needs, social experience, resources and constraints within local schooling contexts. As Casanave (2009: 257) notes, 'the main issues that writing teachers and educators of future teachers of writing face concern our need to understand, be sensitive to, and adapt to local conditions of learning and teaching.' In this vein, we need to be prepared to listen to teachers' stories and understand the complex dynamics of teaching and learning situations, as well as to critically reflect on the sustainability and appropriateness of writing instructional pedagogies, materials used and resources available for particular contexts. Keeping these ecological realities of teaching writing in mind, we want to leave readers with the following questions to consider for their unique teaching contexts and encourage them to think about research agendas that could promote reflexive and ecological L2 writing teacher education in their own particular teaching and learning situations:

- What professional identities and standards do language teachers in my context share when it comes to teaching L2 writing?
- What coursework or professional development exists or is needed for pre- and in-service teachers who want to advance their professionalization in L2 writing?
- How are pre- and in-service teachers' L2 writing knowledge base and practice assessed in my context?

- What theoretical frameworks and methodologies are prioritized in terms of L2 writing teacher education in my context?
- How do L2 writing teachers and scholars in my context theorize from localized practices?
- How do national education and local language policies impact L2 writing teacher education in my context?
- What collaborations exist or are needed for teacher educators and/or teachers of L2 writing in my context?
- What are the sociolinguistic realties of the English language and the urgency of L2 writing for students in my context?

Notes

(1) We acknowledge that the term second language writing is often used to refer to situations where writers compose texts in a language which is not their native language, but which is the dominant language of the context in which they live (e.g. non-native English speakers in the United States). The concept of foreign language writing, on the other hand, has been used to refer to 'writers composing in a language that is neither the writers' native language nor the dominant language in the surrounding context' (Cimasko & Reichelt, 2011: 3). However, given different periods of colonization as well as the global flow of Englishes, it is not so straightforward to determine whether individual writers write in their first or second language. While we recognize the multiplicity of language practices writers engage in while composing a text in their non-dominant language, for the sake of clarity we will use the term L2 writing as an umbrella term to refer to the act of writing done in an additional language (the English language, in this case). The contributors to this volume use the term *second language writing* to specifically refer to English instruction in a context where English is not the dominant language in the surrounding context.

References

Casanave, C.P. (2009) Training for writing or training for reality? Challenges facing EFL writing teachers and students in language teacher education programs. In R.M. Manchón (ed.) *Writing in Foreign Language Contexts. Learning, Teaching and Research* (pp. 256–277). Bristol: Multilingual Matters.

Cimasko, T. and Reichelt, M. (eds) (2011) *Foreign Language Writing Instruction: Principles and Practices*. Anderson, SC: Parlor Press.

Freeman, D. (1996) The 'unstudied problem': Research on teacher learning in language teaching. In D. Freeman and J.C. Richards (eds) *Teacher Learning in Language Teaching* (pp. 351–378). Cambridge: Cambridge University Press.

Hirvela, A. and Belcher, D. (2007) Writing scholars as teacher educators: Exploring writing teacher education. *Journal of Second Language Writing* 16 (3), 125–128.

Johnson, K.E. and Ma, P. (1999) *Understanding Language Teaching: Reasoning in Action*. Boston, MA: Heinle & Heinle.

Kumaravadivelu, B. (2003) *Beyond Methods: Macrostrategies for Language Teaching*. New Haven, CT: Yale University Press.

Leki, I. (2001) Material, educational, and ideological challenges of teaching EFL writing at the turn of the century. *International Journal of English Studies* 1 (2), 197–209.

Manchón, R.M. (2009) *Writing in Foreign Language Contexts: Learning, Teaching and Research*. Bristol: Multilingual Matters.

Manchón, R.M. (ed.) (2011) *Learning-to-write and Writing-to-learn in an Additional Language*. Amsterdam: John Benjamins.

Manchón, R.M. and de Haan, P. (2008) Writing in foreign language contexts: An introduction. *Journal of Second Language Writing* 17 (1), 1–6.

Ortega, L. (2004) L2 writing research in EFL contexts: Some challenges and opportunities for EFL researchers [Featured article]. *ALAK (Applied Linguistic Association of Korea) Newsletter*, Spring.

1 Exploring Second Language Writing Teacher Education: The Role of Adaptive Expertise

Alan Hirvela

Introduction

In writing research, we are understandably drawn to the writing itself and those who produce it, i.e. students. Not surprisingly, then, in both native language (L1) and second/foreign language (L2) writing scholarship, we see a dominant focus on students. But what about those who teach the students? In the approximately four decades since L2 writing scholarship began to emerge as a domain in its own right (as opposed to a subset within L1 scholarship), a relatively small body of research has focused on *teachers of writing*. Hence, we have no meaningful knowledge base regarding the epistemologies that guide teachers' instructional practices, or the practices themselves. In the understandable zeal to decode students' experiences with writing, we have tended to keep teachers on the sidelines, despite the crucial roles they play in students' acquisition of L2 writing skills. It was the recognition of this imbalance that motivated Hirvela and Belcher (2007) to issue a call for an increased focus on L2 writing teacher research in a special issue of the *Journal of Second Language Writing* focusing on L2 writing teacher education. This call aligned with what Freeman (1996) called the 'unstudied problem' of L2 teachers and their teaching, that is, the insufficient attention paid to teachers as classroom practitioners.

However, the modest focus on writing teachers in L2 writing research is only one dimension of what could be called the 'unstudied problem' of L2 writing teachers and writing instruction. Another important dimension of this 'unstudied problem' is an inadequately conceptualized notion of what to look for in such scholarship. This aspect of the 'unstudied problem' was acknowledged at a recent (2016) Symposium on Second

Language Writing (SSLW), which was organized around the theme of 'Expertise in Second Language Writing.' As Paul Matsuda (2016) observed in the Symposium's program:

> Expertise in second language writing is sometimes conceptualized as a binary – either you are an expert or you are not. In reality, there are different types and degrees of expertise that are needed depending on the context and roles – writing center tutors, teachers, teacher educators, program administrators, researchers, research mentors, editors, reviewers. Different instructional contexts also require different sets of expertise.

Thus, the SSLW sought to problematize and address what I believe constitutes an 'expertise gap,' and in doing so helped draw attention to the need to bring expertise to a more prominent place in studies concerning L2 writing teachers. As Matsuda's introductory words indicate, expertise is a complex, multifaceted construct operating within a range of contexts, a fact that makes it all the more worthy of investigation. We need to untangle this complexity, and making expertise a significant focus of L2 writing research would facilitate such an endeavor.

This chapter likewise speaks to the 'expertise gap,' first by addressing the nature of expertise itself and then by suggesting a narrowing of the focus on expertise that could be especially beneficial to scholarship regarding L2 writing teachers. In the latter regard, the chapter introduces the notion of 'adaptive expertise,' a teacher education framework that has rarely been discussed in the context of L2 writing instruction. The primary goal of the chapter is to show how the notion of adaptive expertise can add shape and meaning to L2 writing teacher education (hereafter, L2WTE) scholarship and offer a new direction for L2WTE research by illustrating a possible path towards defining and understanding L2 writing teacher expertise.

For contextual purposes, the chapter begins with a brief overview of L2WTE research. The purpose is not to show what has been learned about L2 writing teachers, but rather what patterns appear in that body of scholarship. Thus, this review sheds light on where the field stands with respect to investigations of writing teacher expertise. The next section then examines the broader notion of teacher expertise. The chapter concludes with sections that (a) introduce the adaptive expertise framework, and (b) discuss how it can be applied to L2WTE research.

L2 Writing Teacher Education Research

Noteworthy L2WTE scholarship began in the mid-1980s as pioneering L2 writing scholars began to carve out a place for L2 writing scholarship as a discipline of its own. For this chapter I identified 34 research-oriented publications that have appeared since that time where there was a focus on writing teachers. This does not mean other such scholarship does not exist. For the purposes of this chapter, though, these publications stood out, and at the very least provide a representative sampling of the work that has been conducted. These 34 articles and book chapters constitute an average of about one publication per year, a figure that pales in comparison to scholarship in other areas of L2 writing and thus signifies the lukewarm interest shown by L2 writing scholars with respect to teachers. Also worth noting, although it is not research oriented, is the book *ESL Composition Tales: Reflections on Teaching* (Blanton & Kroll, 2002); this consists of nine narrative accounts of their writing teaching experiences by well-known L2 writing scholars, and in doing so adds to our understanding of the instructional work of L2 writing teachers.

To gain a clearer picture of this collection of 34 publications and what they reveal relative to the goals of this chapter, I created a few categories into which I placed this body of work. Each category is examined briefly in this section of the chapter.

Chronology

One of the topics that interested me was how the publications broke down in terms of when they appeared and how many appeared during different time periods, with the number of publications in parentheses:

1980s: (1)
1990s: (9)
2000s: (24)

Here we can see that teachers were of virtually no research interest in the early years of L2 writing as a discipline. We then see some emerging interest in the 1990s, with a significant increase in L2WTE research-based publications in the current century. Thus, there is an indication that writing teachers are beginning to attract meaningful attention. Also worth noting here is that 12 of the studies published in the current century have appeared since 2010, suggesting some growing momentum for L2WTE research. This is an encouraging trend.

Teacher populations studied

The focus in this category is on two populations of L2 writing teachers: (a) those enrolled in pre-service teacher education programs; and (b) experienced teachers already in the field. The numbers in this category tell a very interesting story, with eight studies of pre-service teachers and 26 focusing on practicing teachers. Clearly, there is primary interest in current teachers as opposed to those entering the field. Whether this is an appropriate distribution of research attention is perhaps a topic worthy of debate in future discussions of L2WTE scholarship. However, to develop a more informative picture of expertise in writing instruction, increased research on novice teachers would seem to be beneficial.

Topics of L2 writing teacher education research

The category of greatest interest for this chapter is what is actually being studied among the L2 writing teachers. Here the teachers are broken down into two categories: pre-service and experienced.

Pre-service teachers

Among the eight publications examining *pre-service* teachers, three (Athanases *et al.*, 2013; Winer, 1992; Worden, 2015) focused on teacher attitudes or knowledge, while five (Casanave, 2009; Gebhard *et al.*, 2013; Seloni, 2013; Shin, 2003; Yi, 2013) looked at these developing teachers relative to various dimensions of their instructional behavior in the writing classroom. This breakdown, and the fact that so few pre-service teachers are explored in classroom contexts, suggests that there is a particular need to increase expertise-related research within the pre-service domain, as suggested earlier. It would be helpful to know how these newcomers to the field conceptualize writing teacher expertise as well as what their early attempts at acquiring expertise reveal about their developmental processes and experiences, especially in comparison to experienced teachers.

Experienced teachers

The results for this category, covering 26 studies, are presented in table form (Table 1.1) to generate a clearer picture of the research trends relative to *practicing teachers* and the teaching of L2 writing, especially since this is where most teacher-related research has occurred, as noted earlier.

Table 1.1 Foci of research on experienced L2 writing teachers

Focus of research	Studies (by author names and year of publication)
Teacher goals	Barkaoui and Fei (2006) Cummings *et al.* (2006)
Teacher conceptions/attitudes	Cumming (2001, 2003) Shi and Cumming (1995)
Teacher development/identity	Henderson Lee (2016) Larsen (2013, 2016) Lee (2010, 2013)
Teacher feedback on student writing	Cohen and Cavalcanti (1990) Lee (2003, 2004, 2007, 2008a, 2008b, 2011) Montgomery and Baker (2007) Zamel (1985)
Teachers' classroom instruction	Cumming (1992, 1993, 1995) Riazzi *et al.* (1996) Tsui (1996, 2003) Tsui and Ng (2010) Weissberg (1994)

Table 1.1 shows some clustering around two topics that are more directly related to expertise in teaching ('feedback' and 'teachers' classroom instruction'), with the final two topics featuring 16 of the 26 studies represented. That feedback on student writing (eight studies) was one of the topics is perhaps not surprising, as this has long been an especially popular topic at conferences and in L2 writing scholarship. This is also important from an expertise perspective, in that the ability to provide meaningful, effective feedback in oral and written form is clearly an important skill area for teachers of writing. It is a type of expertise. That an equal number (eight) of studies have looked at teachers' instructional behavior is also worth noting, as it signifies that there is some interest in what teachers actually do in the writing classroom.

However, very little of this work overtly identified 'expertise' as a means of capturing and understanding the work of these teachers. The same is true with respect to the earlier cited scholarship regarding pre-service teachers and their instructional activity in the classroom. By 'expertise' I mean, in broad terms, the instructional beliefs, knowledge and skills that may be considered as essential at a certain level of proficiency in order for teachers to guide students towards the acquisition of beneficial L2 writing ability. While these are valuable studies, they reveal relatively little about the epistemologies writing teachers hold and the instructional decisions they make in connection with their epistemologies. In this body of work, expertise is an implied notion rather than a clearly marked construct. Perhaps a major reason for this phenomenon is that a workable conceptualization of writing teacher expertise was missing when the studies were designed and implemented. It could also be the case that, as suggested earlier, expertise is being examined, but not overtly. My contention in this chapter is that this situation is a shortcoming we need to overcome in order to construct a more informed and useful picture of individuals teaching L2 writing.

The Broader Realm: Expertise and Teaching

While it is important to understand expertise, this is a challenging quest. As Geisler (1994: xi) says very succinctly: 'The concept of expertise is a difficult one.' Long and Richards (2003: ix) observe, 'While it is relatively easy to arrive at a common understanding of what we mean by expertise, it has proved a somewhat elusive concept for researchers to pin down and investigate.' Tsui (2003) elaborates on this point:

When we say people are experts in their profession, we expect them to possess certain qualities, such as being very knowledgeable in their field; being able to engage in skillful practice; and being able to make accurate diagnoses, insightful analyses and the right decisions, often within a very short period of time. However, what exactly constitutes their expertise is something that is not yet fully understood. (Tsui, 2003: 1)

Tsui (2003: 6) adds that: 'So far, there have been no commonly accepted criteria or methods for identifying expert teachers. In fact … it is highly doubtful whether it is possible to formulate commonly accepted criteria, however meaningful it is to do so.'

Long and Richards (2003: ix) note how, in the case of L2 education, this has been a problem: 'While the nature of expertise has long attracted the attention of researchers in the field of cognitive psychology, until recently it has been relatively less explored in relation to classroom teaching and even less so in the field of second and foreign language teaching.' That situation is magnified with respect to L2WTE.

From a historical perspective, the work of Berliner (1986, 1992) is particularly important in terms of foregrounding expertise and teacher education, especially relative to drawing distinctions between novice and expert teachers. As Berliner (1986: 5) explained: 'My colleagues and I … think we need to find and study expert and experienced teachers and compare those teachers with ordinary or novice teachers in order to search for more information about the tasks and teacher behaviors that our research community has revealed as important.' In his seminal 1986 article, he identified several benefits to teacher education programs and research that would accrue from the study of expertise in teaching. In particular, he explained that 'the performance of experts, although not necessarily perfect, provides a place to start from when we instruct novices' (Berliner, 1986: 6), especially when novices can explore cases of expert teaching that are 'richly detailed descriptions of instructional events' (Berliner, 1986: 6). He argued that 'beginning teachers need such cases of practice to develop their full understanding of pedagogy' (Berliner, 1986: 6).

In slightly later work, Berliner (1992) proposed a series of propositions about teacher expertise based on what studies up to that point in time had revealed, as shown in Table 1.2.

Table 1.2 Propositions concerning expertise in teaching

Proposition number	Proposition
#1	Experts excel mainly in their own domains and in particular contexts.
#2	Experts often develop automaticity for their repetitive operations that are needed to accomplish their goals.
#3	Experts are more sensitive than novices to task demands and the social situation when solving problems.
#4	Experts are opportunistic in their problem solving.
#5	Experts' representations of problems and situations are qualitatively different from the representations of novices.
#6	Experts have fast and accurate pattern-recognition capabilities; novices cannot always make sense of what they experience.
#7	Experts perceive meaningful patterns in the domain in which they are experienced.

These propositions build on the novice–expert teacher dichotomy and establish a model for comparing the two groups, with a particular focus on the characteristics of expert teachers. In L2WTE research it could be useful to compare L2 writing teachers with the propositions put forward by Berliner for the purpose of creating a new set of propositions relevant to the L2 writing field.

An alternative to the propositions-based approach of Berliner is a well-known scheme offered by Dreyfus and Dreyfus (1986), although theirs is not rooted in the field of education. Their work is, however, also based on the novice–expert distinction, and they show how expertise grows as individuals pass through various stages of development. Table 1.3 shows their model, with descriptions of the five stages generated by Tsui (2003: 10–11).

While the 'novice–expert' distinction at the heart of the work by Berliner and by Dreyfus and Dreyfus has attracted considerable attention and indeed become a key ingredient in studies of teacher expertise, concerns have been raised as well. For example, Bereiter and Scardamalia (1993: 34) argue that the distinction is too rigid: 'The issue is that an adequate description of expertise ought to span all varieties, and

Table 1.3 The progression from novices to experts

Stage	Description
Novice	'The novices' actions are guided by rules and a set of objectives and features related to the skill. There is little consideration for the context of the actions. … Novices are usually not taught the circumstances under which the rules should be violated, and they often judge their own performance by how well they follow the rules.'
Advanced beginners	'After novices have had experience applying the rules in real situations, they begin to recognize situational elements that they need to consider for their actions.'
Competent	'With more experience, competent performers learn how to cope with an overwhelming amount of information, by using both context-free rules and situational elements. They are now able to assess the situation and distinguish important from unimportant information. Their actions are goal-directed, and they make conscious planning decisions to achieve their goals.'
Proficient	'This stage is marked by the emergence of intuition, or know-how. Proficient performers are now able to act without conscious deliberation because, as a result of their experience, they can recall similar situations in the past and the course of actions taken that were effective. … At his stage, proficient performers still engage in analytical thinking and conscious decisions when they encounter information that they assess to be important on the basis of their experience.'
Expert	'This stage is marked by effortless and fluid performance guided by intuition. Experts are now totally engaged in skilled performance so that their skills become part of themselves. There is no need for conscious decision-making or problem solving. They just do what normally works on the basis of their experience. It is only when the outcomes are critical, when the situation is novel, and when time allows that experts engage in conscious deliberation before acting.'

expert-novice studies seem to fail on this count.' In their view, this framing places too much emphasis on the expert, and 'the expert becomes a kind of oracle, able to draw forth from inner knowledge an answer to anything within his or her specialty' (Bereiter & Scardamalia, 1993: 34). Hence, the emphasis is on what the all-knowing expert teacher can do and what the novice cannot, with no ground in between them. This limits the usefulness of the comparisons of the two types of teachers. Tsui (2003), in her book-length study of expertise in L2 teaching which is the most comprehensive study of L2 teacher expertise to date, adds that novice–expert teacher studies tend to focus on the cognitive processes 'that take place in their minds and are independent of context' (Tsui, 2003: 2). She sees a need, instead, for 'studies of teachers' work and teachers' lives [which] show that the knowledge and skills teachers develop are closely bound up with the specific contexts in which they work and in their own personal histories' (Tsui, 2003: 2). Under these conditions, the novice–expert dichotomy is not positioned to account for the nuances and the socially oriented factors that impact on teacher learning and performance.

Hence, while the novice–expert distinction could be useful in studying expertise among L2 writing teachers, there is also wisdom in adopting an alternative approach, one described in the next section of this chapter.

A Possible Analytic Lens for L2 Writing Teacher Education: Adaptive Expertise

Within the broader realm of teacher expertise scholarship, an intriguing narrower focus is on what is called 'adaptive teaching.' Regarding adaptive teaching, Corno (2008: 161) says in a major review of literature on the topic that adaptive teaching scholarship examines 'what practicing teachers do to address student differences related to learning. In teaching adaptively, teachers respond to learners as they work. Teachers read student signals to diagnose needs on the fly and tap previous experience with similar learners to respond productively.' Interest in such teaching dates back to Glaser (1977) and Snow (1980), although applications of the adaptive teaching idea since then have been sporadic and have not spread widely across the teaching landscape. For example, as Parsons (2012: 149) explains, 'Little research has examined how teachers adapt their instruction, teachers' reflections on their adaptations, or the instructional conditions in which they adapt' with respect to literacy instruction. As noted earlier, that is also the case with L2 writing instruction.

Some work has looked at adaptive teaching with respect to English language arts instruction, such as Athanases (1993) and Athanases et al. (2015). A core belief underlying this work is that 'adapting instruction thoughtfully is a feature of successful teaching' (Athanases et al., 2015: 84). As Athanases et al. (2015: 84) add, 'Adaptations in teaching include diversified scaffolding, tweaking lessons, tailoring to learners' needs, testing new strategies, and redesigning curriculum.' As such, they say, 'Adaptive teaching highlights response actions teachers take through planning, data-response instruction, and in-the-moment redirecting, with high-quality rationales for adaptations' (Athanases *et al.*, 2015: 86). Such activity is the work of what is called the 'adaptive expert' in teaching, as examined more recently in the context of the teaching of argumentative writing by Newell *et al.* (2017).

As for adaptive expertise and the notion of the 'adaptive expert,' Hayden *et al.* (2013) offer the following explanation:

> Expertise in teaching demands skillful balancing of deep and varied content knowledge with extensive pedagogy: synthesis and application of proven methods for successful teaching, and management of the unpredictability of people and teaching environments that can cause each day to be fraught with surprises. Teachers who achieve this are enacting reflective practice by combining thought and analysis with action in practice. They become 'adaptive experts' who can identify instructional roadblocks, then generate and enact successful responses. (Hayden *et al.*, 2013: 395)

An especially interesting application of the notion of adaptive expertise is outlined in the work of Hatano and Inagaki (1986). They suggest that 'there are two courses of expertise, adaptive and routine' and believe that it is important to identify 'the factors that differentiate them' (Hatano & Inagaki, 1986: 268). It was this differentiation between the 'routine expert' and the 'adaptive expert,' rather than the novice and the expert, that drew attention to their work among a number of education scholars and is of particular interest for the remainder of this chapter. Instead of classifying, and then studying, L2 writing teachers as novices and experts, there might be more flexibility, and thus more value, in working with the routine–expert distinction, which stresses the nature of teaching activity. In so doing, it avoids the kind of deficit orientation that might be associated with novice teachers and an overemphasis on the assumed superiority of the veteran teacher by virtue of having more experience.

In fleshing out the routine–adaptive expert categorization, Hatano and Inagaki maintain that procedures 'become automatized' over time (Hatano & Inagaki, 1986: 266), and they assert that an important difference between individuals is the extent to which they stay rooted to those automatized procedures or advance beyond them. Those they categorize as *routine experts* 'learn merely to perform a skill faster and more accurately, without constructing or enriching their conceptual knowledge' (Hatano & Inagaki, 1986: 266). In other words, they have command of the everyday procedures of teaching, but fail to develop or utilize the 'conceptual knowledge' that leads to more flexibility and creativity in teaching, especially in response to changing circumstances and emerging challenges. Conceptual knowledge can entail awareness of theories or models related to teaching more broadly or within a teacher's own disciplinary focus. It can also include deeper understanding of the context in which one teaches. *Adaptive experts* possess the same core skills as routine experts but, in contrast with routine experts, this 'relevant prior knowledge' is 'gradually enriched and integrated' due to their acquisition and use of the 'conceptual knowledge' noted earlier. As such, they adjust and adapt their teaching over time, thereby allowing for the growth of enhanced epistemologies and instructional activity. Unlike the routine expert, the adaptive expert is open to change and embraces opportunities to adapt instruction as is deemed necessary.

This routine–adaptive expert distinction is particularly appealing relative to a challenge in studying expertise in teaching that Berliner (1986: 9) calls the 'confounding of experience and expertise,' especially in comparisons of novice and expert teachers. On the one hand, he says, 'Expertise, it should be remembered, is a characteristic that is ordinarily developed only after lengthy experience' (Berliner, 1992: 227), and so experience is prioritized in measuring expertise. On the other hand, he points out, an experienced teacher is not necessarily an expert. The routine–adaptive expert distinction, as an alternative model, diminishes the importance attached to experience and instead leaves room for other factors that may account for differences in the performance of routine and adaptive experts. I maintain that this would be a productive way of exploring the combination of beliefs and practices among L2 writing teachers.

Applying the Notions of Routine Expertise and Adaptive Expertise to L2 Writing Teacher Education Scholarship

If the routine–adaptive expertise framework is to be applied in L2WTE, how should this occur? The overarching development that must first take place is the foregrounding of expertise as a tool for studying writing teachers, rather than operating as an underlying assumption of such research. In other words, prioritizing a quest to delineate the features of expertise as it applies to L2 writing is a necessary prerequisite to making use of a tool like the routine–adaptive expertise model.

Once the L2 writing field has fully acknowledged the 'expertise gap' and has made a commitment to eliminating that gap, as suggested by the 2016 SSLW, a useful concrete step is to identify the core features of routine and adaptive writing teacher experts. Such an approach would entail carefully examining SLW teachers in their classrooms and compiling detailed data lists of the features of their instruction that mark them as routine or adaptive experts. This can be done deductively by first gathering input from L2 writing specialists so as to create a priori categories of both routine and adaptive expertise. This step can be followed by studies of teachers that compare them to those categories in an effort to revise them as necessary. Conversely, teacher beliefs and practices can first be studied, with the aim of inductively arriving at detailed depictions of routine and adaptive expertise after analysis of the research findings. Whichever of these approaches is adopted, the core principle is the same: generate detailed descriptions of the primary characteristics of routine and adaptive writing teacher experts.

Another approach, and one that can be tied to the first, is to conceptualize routine and adaptive expertise along a continuum, with routine expertise at one end and adaptive expertise at the other. Drawing from studies of writing teachers in action, various stages of expertise could be depicted between these two poles of the continuum, just as the poles themselves could be described in detail. Such an approach would make use of a developmental notion of teaching which acknowledges that teachers change over time, as seen earlier in the stages of expertise reflected in the work of Dreyfus and Dreyfus. Research could be conducted that seeks to portray each of these stages of expertise as related to L2 writing instruction. Discussions of these stages could then take place in teaching methods courses for pre- and in-service teachers.

Also worth considering, from the perspective of application in teacher education courses or professional development workshops, is work by Hedgcock and Lee (2017) that builds upon 'teacher knowledge believed to be necessary for effective classroom performance' to occur (Hedgcock & Lee, 2017: 18). They envision three types of such knowledge. One is *subject matter knowledge*, which they describe as 'explicit familiarity with instructional methods, learning theories, and language structure' (Hedgcock & Lee, 2017: 18). Then there is *pedagogical content knowledge*, which includes 'familiarity with curriculum development, teaching methods, and classroom management' (Hedgcock & Lee, 2017: 18). The third, they say, is *procedural knowledge*, which 'involves a teacher's repertoire of technical competence, such as lesson planning, pedagogical reasoning, and observational strategies' (Hedgcock & Lee, 2017: 18). These three types of knowledge could be used as lenses through which to study writing teachers and draw helpful distinctions between them from the routine and adaptive expertise perspectives. That is, writing teachers could be examined from the vantage point of their possession and use of each of these types of knowledge, leading to a delineation of the combinations and degrees of such knowledge that mark routine and adaptive experts. The advantage of this approach is that it establishes categories from which to work, and these categories account for both the epistemological and pedagogical domains.

An additional option worth considering is viewing the routine–adaptive classifications relative to different instructional contexts, such as pre-college and college settings, or English for academic/specific purposes courses and general academic writing courses. What constitutes routine and adaptive expertise could vary considerably depending on the context in which writing instruction is taking place, and it would be helpful to know what we consider a routine and an adaptive expert relative to these different circumstances in which L2 writing instruction takes place.

An important underlying point relative to each of these potential schemes is that, unlike the novice-expert dichotomy, the routine–adaptive expert model does not have to be used as a judgement of teacher quality. In writing teacher education courses and programs, in particular, it is not necessary to declare that one type of teacher is bad and the other is good, although it is probably difficult to avoid the assumption that the adaptive expert is the better teacher. Stigmatizing the routine expert and glorifying the adaptive expert achieves very little, especially in working with pre-service teachers. For them, becoming a routine expert may be an appealing initial prospect or an alluring goal relative to their developmental trajectory. Introducing novices to the features of the adaptive expert in order to establish a long-term professional goal could be a valuable tool in a writing education course, but not in the sense of tainting the necessary step of first acquiring routine expertise. Helping such teachers understand both routine and adaptive expertise will equip them with knowledge of the options awaiting them as they ease their way into the world of L2 writing instruction. Here is where the continuum idea mentioned earlier could be useful.

Likewise, practicing teachers participating in in-service writing teacher courses or programs could benefit from an awareness of the routine–adaptive expert distinction as a developmental concept rather than a tool for judging them, similar to the approach adopted in the previously cited work of Dreyfus and Dreyfus. In-service teachers, especially in the case of L2 writing, may lack relevant experience or prior professional development work and thus may benefit from knowing about routine and adaptive expertise as stages of expertise to pursue. Anecdotally speaking, it is not uncommon for individuals to enter L2 writing instruction after acquiring teaching experience in another content area or discipline, or to have received little or no training about teaching writing in an L2 teacher preparation program, as Larsen's (2013, 2016) research has shown. Hence, they, like novice teachers, may need the initial comfort zone of routine expertise as a realistic first step towards later professional growth. Here, again, routine and adaptive expertise can be viewed as a continuum of expertise rather than a dichotomy that, in essence, relies on a 'bad teacher–good teacher' dichotomy.

To augment the routine–adaptive expert model in both research and teacher education settings, a construct from teacher agency scholarship that was introduced by McNeil (2000) and developed in depth recently by Johnson and Golombek (2016), that of 'growth points,' could be useful in looking at L2 writing teachers along the routine–adaptive continuum. Johnson and Golombek (2016: xii) describe growth points 'as a moment or series of moments when teachers' cognitive/emotional dissonance comes into being.' Working from the routine–adaptive expert framework, writing teachers' movement from routine to adaptive expertise could be charted via 'growth points' they encounter over time, such as through instructional experience or engagement in professional development opportunities like workshops or in-service teacher education courses or programs. Identifying such growth points could enhance understanding of transitions in L2 writing teacher expertise, and these could in turn be used in future preparation of L2 writing teachers.

There are no doubt other ways in which the notions of routine and adaptive expertise could be used in both studying and developing L2 writing teachers. However it is employed, the routine–adaptive expertise model has the advantage of providing a degree of flexibility not available in the more common novice–expert distinction. That flexibility should hold appeal in the process of making expertise itself a more visible and important component in L2WTE work.

Conclusion

What this chapter has sought to do is, first, to make a case for overt, focused exploration of the notion of 'expertise' in L2WTE scholarship. This is the 'unstudied problem' that confronts us, especially relative to teacher education courses and programs that seek to develop L2 writing teachers. As teacher educators, an important goal in our work is to produce experts who can better serve the needs of L2 writers. Having visible, concrete knowledge of what constitutes expertise would help greatly in that regard, and here the routine–adaptive expert model could be especially beneficial. This situation is akin to the vexing problem of knowing exactly what we mean when we speak of 'good writing.' To paraphrase Ilona Leki (1995) and her 'good writing: I know it when I see it' statement which captures the challenge of pinning down the features of good writing, we appear to have a similar situation with respect to L2 writing teacher expertise: 'Expertise: I know it when I see it.' This is not an adequate way of accounting for teacher expertise. We need to move meaningfully beyond that vague stage. Studying L2 writing teachers through the lens of routine and adaptive expertise is one way of solving the 'unstudied problem' and overcoming the 'expertise gap,' as this characterization provides the kind of focused analytic lens currently lacking. We will have concrete grounds on which to say that we know what we mean when we discuss writing teacher expertise.

Thus, as we move forward in studying L2 writing teachers in action, we need to have at our disposal a belief that understanding what expertise entails matters. While beneficial to a certain point, it is not sufficient to know what teachers believe about L2 writing and writing instruction as well as what they do in their classrooms. It is also important to understand what signifies different levels or types of expertise, as in the case of routine and adaptive expertise. As Berliner (1986), cited earlier, pointed out, novice teachers in education preparation programs or courses need an understanding of expertise to help them frame their goals and expectations for teaching. Likewise, those who teach novices in pre-service programs or experienced teachers in in-service programs or courses will benefit from having clearly delineated notions of writing teacher expertise to work from. Seeing these notions through the lens of routine and adaptive expertise could be especially beneficial in such work, as comparisons between routine expertise and adaptive expertise might help developing L2 writing teachers better understand the parameters and possibilities of L2 writing instruction. There can be an enormous gap between the novice teacher and the expert teacher and so, for teachers in preparation, a realistic pathway to expertise may be difficult to grasp. By contrast, comparisons between routine and adaptive experts may be far more productive from their perspective, especially when each type of expertise is seen as having value, as opposed to positioning one as bad and one as good.

However, establishing well-defined notions of writing teacher expertise requires a framework or model of expertise to work from. In this chapter I have suggested that the notion of adaptive expertise meets this need, especially within the routine–adaptive expert model described earlier. Specifying what characterizes routine expertise and what characterizes adaptive expertise, as well as what can promote the transition from routine to adaptive expertise, would provide both writing teachers and writing teacher educators with an important tool to use in helping pre-service and in-service teachers visualize their journey through the acquisition of writing teacher expertise. Thus adopting, and adjusting, Higano and Inagaki's model of routine and adaptive expertise for the purposes of writing teacher education is a move worth making as we continue to conceptualize and implement writing teacher education and writing teacher research.

In writing teacher education courses, 'how to' books aimed at preparing teachers of writing help articulate ideas about and suggestions for what L2 writing teachers should know, and thus can be used in conjunction with descriptions of routine and adaptive expertise. Such books provide beneficial declarative and procedural knowledge about writing instruction, as well as reviews of writing theory and epistemology, which can augment portraits of expertise. In the case of a recent publication of this type, Ferris and Hedgcock's (2014) important volume, *Teaching L2 Composition: Purpose, Process, and Practice*, the authors briefly use the term 'deep professional expertise' (Ferris & Hedgcock, 2014: 2) in introducing their book and thus suggest a notion of expertise that could be connected to discussions of routine and adaptive expertise. To supplement valuable instructional resources of this kind, we need to complement them with knowledge of the features of writing teacher expertise, especially through a continuum that draws from key constructs such as routine and adaptive expertise.

Meanwhile, there is also a research agenda to pursue, one that focuses on foregrounding and demystifying the notion of expertise as it applies to writing instruction. This is the work we have not yet seen performed much in L2 writing research, and which is a noteworthy aspect of the 'expertise gap' in the field's scholarship. Such an agenda aimed at addressing the 'expertise gap' would be facilitated by the creation of research questions worth pursuing, and here I will put forward three that are adjusted versions of questions that drove Tsui's (2003) case studies of expertise among four ESL teachers cited earlier:

(1) What are the critical differences between routine and adaptive experts in L2 writing instruction? That is, what are the characteristics that distinguish the routine expert from the adaptive expert?
(2) How does a writing teacher become an adaptive expert? What are the phases that s/he goes through in the process of transitioning from routine to adaptive expertise in L2 writing instruction?
(3) What are the factors that shape the development of adaptive expertise among L2 writing teachers?

Two additional questions worth addressing are these:

(4) What are the 'growth points' that facilitate teachers' transition from routine to adaptive expert?
(5) Based on explorations of routine and adaptive expertise among L2 writing teachers, what is a useful operational definition of L2 writing teacher expertise?

No doubt there are other research questions worth addressing, and the routine–adaptive expertise model is not the only one worth using as an analytical lens for studying L2 writing teachers in action. What matters most is that we take a step forward in L2 writing research by placing greater emphasis on studying writing teachers and, while doing so, exploring their writing instruction within the guiding framework of L2 writing teacher *expertise* instead of assuming that expertise is already a well-understood construct. We also need to analyze and interpret teachers' beliefs and actions as reflected in their practice so as to arrive at a deeper, more profound understanding of L2 writing teachers and teaching, especially by establishing a common understanding of what constitutes expertise in L2 writing instruction.

References

Athanases, S.Z. (1993) Adapting and tailoring lessons: Fostering teacher education to meet varied student needs. *Teacher Education Quarterly* 20, 71–81.

Athanases, S.Z., Bennett, L.H. and Wahleithner, J.M. (2013) Responsive teacher inquiry for learning about adolescent English learners as developing writers. In L.C. de Oliveira and T. Silva (eds) *L2 Writing in Secondary Classrooms: Student Experiences, Academic Issues, and Teacher Education* (pp. 149–165). New York: Routledge/Taylor & Francis.

Athanases, S.Z., Bennett, L.H. and Wahleithner, J.M. (2015) Adaptive teaching for English Language Arts: Following the pathway of classroom data in preservice teacher inquiry. *Journal of Literacy Research* 47, 83–114.

Barkoui, K. and Fei, J. (2006) Students' and instructors' assessment of the attainment of writing goals. In A. Cumming (ed.) *Goals for Academic Writing: ESL Students and their Instructors* (pp. 90–107). Amsterdam: John Benjamins.

Bereiter, C. and Scardamalia, M. (1993) *Surpassing Ourselves: An Inquiry into the Nature and Implications of Expertise.* Chicago and La Salle, IL: Open Court.

Berliner, D.C. (1986) In pursuit of the expert pedagogue. *Educational Researcher* 15 (7), 5–13.

Berliner, D.C. (1992) The nature of expertise in teaching. In F.K. Oser, A. Dick and J.-L. Patry (eds) *Effective and Responsible Teaching: The New Synthesis* (pp. 227–248). San Francisco, CA: Jossey-Bass.

Blanton, L.L. and Kroll, B. (eds) (2002) *ESL Composition Tales: Reflections on Teaching.* Ann Arbor, MI: University of Michigan Press.

Casanave, C.P. (2009) Training for writing or training for reality? Challenges facing EFL writing teachers and students in language teacher education programs. In R.M. Manchón (ed.) *Writing in Foreign Language Contexts: Learning, Teaching, and Research* (pp. 256–277). Bristol: Multilingual Matters.

Cohen, A.D. and Cavalcanti, M.C. (1990) Feedback on compositions: Teacher and student verbal reports. In B. Kroll (ed.) *Second Language Writing: Research Insights for the Classroom* (pp. 155–177). Cambridge: Cambridge University Press.

Corno, L. (2008) On teaching adaptively. *Educational Psychologist* 43 (3), 161–173.

Cumming, A. (1992) Instructional routines in ESL composition teaching. *Journal of Second Language Writing* 1, 17–35.

Cumming, A. (1993) Teachers' curriculum planning and accommodations of innovation: Three case studies of adult ESL instruction. *TESL Canada Journal* 11, 30–52.

Cumming, A. (1995) Fostering writing expertise in ESL composition instruction: Modeling and evaluation. In D. Belcher and G. Braine (eds) *Academic Writing in a Second Language: Essays on Research and Pedagogy* (pp. 375–397). Norwood, NJ: Ablex.

Cumming, A. (2001) ESL/EFL instructors' practices for writing assessment: Specific purposes or general purposes? *Language Testing* 18, 207–224.

Cumming, A. (2003) Experienced ESL/EFL writing instructors' conceptualizations of their teaching: Curriculum options and implications. In B. Kroll (ed.) *Exploring the Dynamics of Second Language Writing* (pp. 71–92). Cambridge: Cambridge University Press.

Cummings, J., Erdősy, U. and Cumming, A. (2006) A study of contrasts: ESL and university instructors' goals for writing improvement. In A. Cumming (ed.) *Goals for Academic Writing: ESL Students and their Instructors* (pp. 50–69). Amsterdam: John Benjamins.

Dreyfus, H.L. and Dreyfus, S.E. (1986) *Mind over Machine.* New York: Free Press.

Ferris, D.R. and Hedgcock, J.S. (2014) *Teaching L2 Composition: Purpose, Process, and Practice* (3rd edn). New York: Routledge/Taylor & Francis.

Freeman, D. (1996) The 'unstudied problem': Research on teacher learning in language teaching. In D. Freeman and J.C. Richards (eds) *Teacher Learning in Language Teaching* (pp. 351–378). Cambridge: Cambridge University Press.

Gebhard, M., Chen, I.-A., Graham, H. and Gunawan, W. (2013) Teaching to mean: SFL, L2 literacy, and teacher education. *Journal of Second Language Writing* 22, 107–124.

Geisler, C. (1994) *Academic Literacy and the Nature of Expertise: Reading, Writing, and Knowing in Academic Philosophy.* Hillsdale, NJ: Lawrence Erlbaum,

Glaser, R. (1977) *Adaptive Education: Individual Diversity and Learning.* New York: Holt, Rinehart & Winston.

Hatano, G. and Inagaki, K. (1986) Two courses of expertise. In H. Stevenson, H. Azuma and K. Hakuta (eds) *Child Development in Japan* (pp. 262–272). New York: W.H. Freeman.

Hayden, H.E., Rundel, T.D. and Smyntek-Gworek, S. (2013) Adaptive expertise: A view from the top and the ascent. *Teaching Education* 24, 395–414.

Hedgcock, J.S. and Lee, H. (2017) An exploratory study of academic literacy socialization: Building genre awareness in a teacher education program. *Journal of English for Academic Purposes* 26, 17–28.

Henderson Lee, S. (2016) Bridging the in-and-out of school writing practices of ELLs through postmethod pedagogy: One elementary teacher's journey. In L.C. de Oliveira and T. Silva (eds) *Second Language Writing in Elementary Classrooms: Instructional Issues, Content Area Writing and Teacher Education* (pp. 153–171). New York: Palgrave MacMillan.

Hirvela, A. and Belcher, D. (2007) Writing teachers as teacher educators: Exploring writing teacher education. *Journal of Second Language Writing* 16, 125–128.

Johnson, K.E. and Golombek, P. (2016) *Mindful Teacher Education: A Sociocultural Perspective on Cultivating Teachers' Professional Development.* New York: Routledge/Taylor & Francis.

Larsen, D. (2013) Focus on pre-service preparation for ESL writing instruction: Secondary teacher perspectives. In L.C. de Oliveira and T. Silva (eds) *L2 Writing in Secondary Classrooms: Student Experiences, Academic Issues, and Teacher Education* (pp. 119–132). New York: Routledge/Taylor & Francis.

Larsen, D. (2016) Pre-service teacher preparation for L2 writing: Perspectives of in-service elementary ESL teachers. In L.C. de Oliveira and T. Silva (eds) *Second Language Writing in Elementary Classrooms: Instructional Issues, Content Area Writing and Teacher Education* (pp. 172–190). New York: Palgrave MacMillan.

Lee, I. (2003) L2 writing teachers' perspectives, practices and problems regarding error feedback. *Assessing Writing* 8, 216–237.

Lee, I. (2004) Error correction in L2 secondary writing classrooms: The case of Hong Kong. *Journal of Second Language Writing* 13, 283–312.

Lee, I. (2007) Feedback in Hong Kong secondary writing classrooms: Assessment for learning or assessment of learning? *Assessing Writing* 12, 180–198.

Lee, I. (2008a) Understanding teachers' written feedback practices in Hong Kong secondary classrooms. *Journal of Second Language Writing* 17, 69–85.

Lee, I. (2008b) Ten mismatches between teachers' beliefs and written feedback practice. *ELT Journal* 63 (1), 13–22.

Lee, I. (2010) Writing teacher education and teacher learning: Testimonies of four EFL teachers. *Journal of Second Language Writing* 19, 143–157.

Lee, I. (2011) Feedback revolution: What gets in the way? *ELT Journal* 65 (1), 1–12.

Lee, I. (2013) Becoming a writing teacher: Using 'identity' as an analytic lens to understand EFL writing teachers' development. *Journal of Second Language Writing* 22, 330–345.

Leki, I. (1995) Good writing: I know it when I see it. In D. Belcher and G. Braine (eds) *Academic Writing in a Second Language: Essays on Research and Pedagogy* (pp. 23–46). Norwood, NJ: Ablex.

Long, M.H. and Richards, J.C. (2003) Series editors' preface. In A.B.M. Tsui (2003) *Understanding Expertise in Teaching: Case Studies of Second Language Teachers.* Cambridge: Cambridge University Press.

McNeil, D. (ed.) (2000) *Language and Gesture.* Cambridge: Cambridge University Press.

Matsuda, P.K. (2016) *Introduction to Symposium on Second Language Writing.* Conference program.

Montgomery, J.J. and Baker, W. (2007) Teacher-written feedback: Student perceptions, teacher self-assessment, and actual teacher performance. *Journal of Second Language Writing* 16, 82–99.

Newell, G.E., Goff, B., Buescher, E., Weyand, L., Thanos, T. and Kwak, S.B. (2017) Adaptive expertise in the teaching and learning of literary argumentation in high school English Language Arts. In R.K. Durst, G.E. Newell and J.D. Marshall (eds) *English Language Arts Research and Teaching: Revisiting and Extending Arthur Applebee's Contributions* (pp. 157–171). New York: Routledge/Taylor & Francis.

Parsons, S.A. (2012) Adaptive teaching in literacy instruction: Case studies of two teachers. *Journal of Literacy Research* 44, 149–170.

Riazzi, A., Lessard-Clouston, M. and Cumming, A. (1996) Observing ESL writing instruction: A case study of four teachers. *Journal of Intensive English Studies* 10, 19–30.

Seloni, L. (2013) Understanding how pre-service teachers develop a working knowledge of L2 writing: Toward a socioculturally oriented postmethod pedagogy. In L.C. de Oliveira and T. Silva (eds) *L2 Writing in Secondary Classrooms: Student Experiences, Academic Issues, and Teacher Education* (pp. 166–189). New York: Routledge/Taylor & Francis.

Shi, L. and Cumming, A. (1995) Teachers' conceptions of second language writing instruction: Five case studies. *Journal of Second Language Writing* 4, 87–111.

Shin, S.J. (2003) The reflective L2 writing teacher. *ELT Journal* 57 (1), 3–10.

Snow, R.E. (1980) Aptitude, learner control, and adaptive instruction. *Educational Psychologist* 15, 151–158.

Tsui, A.B.M. (1996) Learning how to teach ESL writing. In D. Freeman and J.C. Richards (eds) *Teacher Learning in Language Teaching* (pp. 97–119). Cambridge: Cambridge University Press.

Tsui, A.B.M. (2003) *Understanding Expertise in Teaching: Case Studies of Second Language Teachers*. Cambridge: Cambridge University Press.

Tsui, A.B.M. and Ng, M.M.Y. (2010) Cultural contexts and situated possibilities in the teaching of second language writing. *Journal of Teacher Education* 6, 364–375.

Weissberg, R. (1994) Speaking of writing: Functions of talk in the ESL composition class. *Journal of Second Language Writing* 3, 121–139.

Winer, L. (1992) 'Spinach to chocolate': Changing awareness and attitudes in ESL writing teachers. *TESOL Quarterly* 26, 57–80.

Worden, D. (2015) Developing writing concepts for teaching purposes: Preservice L2 writing teachers' developing conceptual understanding of parallelism. *Journal of Second Language Writing* 30, 19–30.

Yi, Y. (2013) ESOL teachers as writing teachers: From the voices of high school pre-service teachers. In L.C. de Oliveira and T. Silva (eds) *L2 Writing in Secondary Classrooms: Student Experiences, Academic Issues, and Teacher Education* (pp. 133–148). New York: Routledge/Taylor & Francis.

Zamel, V. (1985) Responding to student writing. *TESOL Quarterly* 19, 79–102.

2 Second Language Writing Teacher Education and Feedback Literacy Development: Perspectives from Hong Kong

Icy Lee

Introduction

A decade ago, Hirvela and Belcher (2007) cautioned about the lack of attention to the preparation of writing teachers in second language (L2) contexts. Against this backdrop is even 'less teacher preparation in writing assessment' (Crusan *et al.*, 2016: 44), in which feedback plays a significant role. All over the world, L2 writing teachers spend a huge amount of time responding to student writing, yet surprisingly teacher education on feedback is underdeveloped. This is particularly so in non-English dominant contexts (e.g. English as a foreign language – EFL), where writing teachers are found to simply repeat the feedback practices their own teachers used when they were students. Given massive concerns about the ineffectiveness of conventional feedback practices, it is understandable that research efforts have mainly focused on the efficacy of teachers' feedback practices (including written corrective feedback). However, lying at the heart of the matter is the issue of teacher preparedness, as well as their feedback literacy (or lack of it) – i.e. 'teachers' ability to use feedback effectively to support student learning' (Lee, 2017: 150). It is important that attention should be paid to writing teacher education on feedback to find out what teachers know and think about feedback, how they give feedback, why they give feedback in the ways they do and, above all, how teacher education may effect positive change so as to prepare L2 writing teachers to give feedback effectively – and to enhance their feedback literacy as teachers of writing.

This chapter focuses specifically on feedback literacy as a central component of classroom assessment literacy for L2 writing teachers. Using feedback literacy, or teachers' lack of feedback literacy, as a point of departure, this chapter explores the feedback literacy development of two English teachers in Hong Kong who, after attending a writing teacher education (WTE) course, began to challenge their previous assumptions about conventional feedback practices. I begin the chapter by providing a holistic view of writing teacher education in Hong Kong, which reveals insufficient attention to feedback in the writing classroom. I then provide information about the above-mentioned WTE course that I taught, before I chronicle the two teachers' feedback literacy development. I conclude the chapter with implications for L2 writing teacher education and teachers' feedback literacy development.

Writing Teacher Education in Hong Kong

Role of writing in Hong Kong

Since Hong Kong was handed back to China in 1997, the postcolonial city has witnessed a gradual decrease in the use of English in different sectors, including the government. Nonetheless, English is still officially the dominant language of written records in the civil service and the business sector and has continued to play an important role in education.

Children in Hong Kong begin to learn English in pre-school, and simple writing at the sentence level usually starts in the final year of kindergarten. Primary children learn to consolidate their sentences and construct short paragraphs and essays at different grades. At Grade 3, for example, they are expected to write short paragraphs of about 30 words (e.g. based on pictures), and at upper primary level students begin to write longer essays from 50 words at Grade 4 to 100 words or more at Grade 6. At the end of Grade 12, students are expected to write two essays within two hours during the university entrance examination – 200 and 400 words, respectively. The objectives of such writing are to assess the students' ability to write for different purposes, contexts and audiences, to use language accurately and appropriately to convey meaning, to present ideas effectively and coherently, and to use appropriate tone, style and register for the target genre (Curriculum Development Council and Hong Kong Examinations and Assessment Authority, 2007). The genres high school students are expected to write range from recounts and stories to letters of complaint, letters of advice, argumentation and discussion.

Writing teacher education in Hong Kong

In Hong Kong schools, writing classrooms tend to be dominated by conventional approaches that put a premium on the teaching of grammar and vocabulary, with writing being treated primarily as a product, and students following the textbook with mainly grammatical input from teachers (Lo & Hyland, 2007). Despite the range of more 'innovative' (not necessarily innovative in the L2 writing literature but perhaps innovative in the local context) strategies recommended in local curriculum guides, such as multiple drafting, peer evaluation and portfolio assessment, traditional approaches preponderate in local writing classrooms, characterized by a focus on the written product, a strong emphasis on written accuracy and a summative orientation to classroom writing (with a heavy focus on scores).

WTE, unfortunately, is underdeveloped in Hong Kong. In general, local undergraduate and professional teacher education programs do include a focus on the teaching of writing, whereas master's programs for practicing English teachers may not include a course on second language writing. In the university in which I am working, for example, the undergraduate BA and BEd teacher education program has a 39-hour course on the teaching of reading and writing, with half of it devoted to the teaching of writing but limited coverage on writing assessment and feedback (about three hours maximum). The Postgraduate Diploma in Education program, on the other hand, provides only 50 hours on English language teaching (ELT) methodology which covers the whole range of areas related to ELT, with writing possibly covered in a couple of hours. In the two-year part-time MA in ELT program for in-service teachers (requiring teachers to complete a total of 24 units/eight courses), there is a 42-hour elective (three units), 'Teaching of reading and writing,' with half of it on writing. I teach this course (referred to as 'the WTE course' thereafter), but can devote only a maximum of six hours to feedback and assessment in writing. Overall, in my own institution, pre-service and in-service teachers receive input on writing that ranges from three to 21 hours, depending on the program they are taking.

In other teacher education institutions in Hong Kong, while the amount of input students receive on writing may be similar at the undergraduate and postgraduate teaching training (i.e. Postgraduate Diploma in Education) levels, there are greater variations across the master's programs for in-service English teachers. An informal survey of the course offerings shows that only three out of a total of 10-odd master's programs offer L2 writing – only as an elective rather than a compulsory course. Language testing and assessment courses (usually offered as an optional course), on the other hand, address a wide range of testing and assessment issues without necessarily delving into feedback in writing. Even where feedback might be a focus, again the input is likely to be limited given the host of issues a language testing and assessment course has to address.

The large amount of time writing teachers spend on feedback, therefore, is not paralleled by the attention it receives in local teacher education programs. In fact, local teachers have expressed concern about their lack of training (Lee, 2008), being aware that in the absence of guiding principles and training, the way they respond to student writing is largely based on how their own teachers gave feedback on their writing. This is the apprenticeship of observation (Lortie, 1976), the danger of which is that unproductive and undesirable practices can be perpetuated without being critically challenged. This seems to be the case in feedback in writing among Hong Kong teachers (or in other similar contexts).

Against this backdrop of the underdevelopment of writing teacher education in general and feedback in writing in particular, this chapter examines the experiences of two in-service English teachers in Hong Kong to show how WTE can develop their feedback literacy. Before turning to the study, I examine the notion of feedback literacy and what it means for writing teachers to be feedback literate.

Feedback Literacy for L2 Writing Teachers

In this section I elaborate on the notion of feedback literacy with respect to teacher written feedback in general and written corrective feedback (WCF) in particular. Due to the scope of the chapter (which becomes clear when I chronicle the two teachers' feedback literacy development – which pertains mainly to teacher feedback and WCF), I do not include written commentary, conferencing, technology-enhanced feedback and peer feedback in my characterization of feedback literacy.

Effective feedback in general

When writing teachers possess feedback literacy, they are able to deliver effective feedback and enable students to use it productively to improve their writing. Effective feedback in the writing classroom should have balanced coverage on issues about content, organization, language, genre and style. It is best seen as an important part of classroom assessment that integrates teaching, learning and assessment (Lee, 2017); in other words, feedback should be aligned with the learning goals and success criteria teachers share with students at the instructional/pre-writing stage. Multiple drafting is crucial to facilitate learning transfer, where students are given opportunities to apply what they have learnt from feedback to another draft, and diagnostic feedback that gives information about both strengths and weaknesses in writing is essential. Above all, effective feedback should promote assessment for learning, involve and empower students (e.g. through self- and peer assessment), promote student motivation and self-esteem (Nicol & Macfarlane-Dick, 2006), and enable students to close the gap between current and desired performance, helping them to improve their future performance (and hence feedback is also feedforward) (Carless *et al.*, 2006).

To sum up, feedback literate teachers plan and deliver feedback in the context of the entire teaching-learning-assessment process, aligning it with instructional goals and making sure that it is purposeful, involves students in active learning and helps them improve their writing.

Effective written corrective feedback in particular

Given that L2 writing teachers spend an inordinate amount of time responding to written errors, much of the feedback literature has addressed WCF. Effective WCF is often discussed in terms of two areas: (1) the amount of WCF; and (2) the WCF strategies adopted. In terms of the amount of WCF, focused WCF (i.e. responding to errors selectively) is in general considered more beneficial to L2 students (except for advanced writers who make few errors in writing). It is less overwhelming and more manageable for L2 students than unfocused WCF (i.e. responding to errors comprehensively) as the latter can easily lead to 'information over-load' (Bitchener, 2008: 109). When a small number of error categories are targeted, students are more likely to notice and understand the feedback given (Ellis *et al.*, 2008); therefore, focused WCF can enable L2 students to develop a better understanding of the errors they make in writing (e.g. Ferris, 1995; Hendrickson, 1980). In this chapter, focused WCF and selective WCF are used interchangeably, and so are unfocused WCF and comprehensive WCF.

As for WCF strategies – i.e. whether teachers should use direct WCF (providing correct answers) or indirect WCF (not providing correct answers) – and whether codes should be provided alongside indirect WCF (i.e. coded WCF), research evidence is inconclusive. In general, indirect WCF can engage students in 'guided learning and problem solving' (Lalande, 1982: 143), enabling them to reflect on their existing knowledge or partially internalized knowledge (Bitchener & Ferris, 2012), which can improve written accuracy in the long run. On the other hand, direct WCF is 'preferable if learners are unable to correct their own errors' (Shintani *et al.*, 2014: 105) and may be more effective long term (Bitchener & Knoch, 2010; Van Beuningen *et al.*, 2008, 2012). In the absence of conclusive research findings, teachers should experiment flexibly with a range of WCF strategies, and vary them according to student needs (e.g. their proficiency and motivation). For instance, coded WCF can be confusing and frustrating in L2 school contexts where students do not receive explicit grammar instruction, and it can be discouraging and cumbersome if it is over-used (Ferris, 2011; Robb *et al.*, 1986).

In the main, feedback literacy in WCF entails teachers' understanding of the pros and cons of focused and unfocused WCF, and delivery of an optimum amount of WCF that suits the students and the teaching context, as well as a judicious choice of WCF strategies that cater for the specific needs of the students.

Realities of feedback in L2 writing

Amid the limited literature about teachers' feedback literacy, there is research that shows that L2 writing teachers lack feedback literacy – i.e. they are not using feedback effectively to promote student learning. The pre-service ESL teachers in Guénette and Lyster's (2013) study were found to overuse direct corrections at the expense of indirect feedback strategies. The secondary teachers in Lee's (2004) survey study reported that they used a limited range of error feedback strategies, and the error correction task they completed showed that only slightly over half of their corrections were accurate. Bailey and Garner's (2010) study showed that teacher feedback did not generally have the intended positive effect, and teachers themselves were ambivalent about the value of feedback. In EFL contexts, the majority of teachers adopt unfocused WCF (Furneaux *et al.*, 2007) even though it is advised in the feedback literature that teachers should respond to errors selectively. Also, when teachers fill student papers with red ink, their feedback is unlikely to promote students' confidence in and motivation for writing.

It is clear from the above that L2 writing teachers' feedback literacy generally falls short. What role can WTE play to impact positively on teachers' feedback literacy development? In the next section, I first describe the WTE course that I teach in my university and then examine the feedback literacy development of two in-service teachers who attended the WTE course.

A Writing Teacher Education Course Offered to Hong Kong Teachers

The WTE course I teach consists of six sessions on writing, with one session devoted to feedback in writing (three hours in total). The objective of the feedback lesson is to critically examine conventional feedback practices among teachers in Hong Kong and consider more effective ways to go about responding to student writing. The lesson begins with a lead-in feedback task which helps teachers problematize conventional practices. It then moves on to WCF, during which I engage teachers in a mini-debate on the pros and cons of focused and unfocused WCF. After that, I introduce different WCF strategies and ask teachers to consider the pros and cons of each WCF strategy in their own context. I then broaden the teachers' perspectives by asking them to discuss the purposes of feedback in writing, and consider effective strategies, including the role of students in feedback. Before wrapping up the lesson, I engage teachers in a task based on one of my articles (Lee, 2009), encouraging teachers to take a new look at some possibly taken-for-granted assumptions about feedback. Finally, I put forward the possibility of a feedback revolution in their own teaching context and invite teachers to share their views and concerns if they are to implement innovation in their feedback practices. Throughout the lesson, my focus is on fostering critical reflection and helping teachers think outside the box. In another lesson on writing assessment, I spend at least half of the session on classroom writing assessment geared towards assessment *for* and *as* learning, helping teachers understand the interconnectedness between assessment, teaching and learning, as well as the pivotal role feedback plays in classroom writing assessment.

At the end of the WTE course, teachers submit one major assignment (60% of the total assessment score) which requires them to undertake a mini-classroom inquiry project on a self-selected topic, and to reflect on the experience. They also turn in a small assignment (10%)[1] which required them to write reflections on five readings out of a total of 12 assigned. Both assignments are designed to help teachers consolidate their knowledge, crystallize their thoughts and foster critical reflection.

Two teachers, Joyce and Susan (pseudonyms), were selected for the study because of the high quality of critical reflection demonstrated in their assignments. At the time of the study, Joyce and Susan were both first year students taking the WTE course in the first semester of the MA program. Joyce was a secondary teacher and Susan a primary teacher, with seven and nine years of teaching experience, respectively, each serving as head of the English department in their school (the first year for Joyce and the third year for Susan). Joyce was born in Hong Kong but completed high school and university in Vancouver, Canada, whereas Susan was born and educated in Hong Kong. Both teachers have a non-English bachelor's degree and a teacher training qualification majoring in English.

Data for the study include the classroom inquiry assignments (i.e. the major assignment) for both Joyce and Susan (of about 2300 and 2700 words, respectively). As Joyce opted to write reflections on one of the assigned readings on feedback in writing, this small assignment of hers (of 690 words) was also collected as a data source. For Joyce, excerpts from the major assignment and her written reflections on the assigned reading are referred to as #1 and #2, respectively, in the section below.

To analyze the data, the written reflections were read a few times in order to identify the teachers' beliefs and practice about feedback, as well as the problems/challenges they faced and how the WTE course influenced their beliefs and practices. The data were coded as per the above focuses – i.e. beliefs, practice and problems/challenges in respect to different phases of their career, with a specific focus on the influence of the WTE course, if any. Consent was sought from the two teachers for me to cite their written reflections in this chapter.

Joyce's Feedback Literacy Development

Before WTE: Learning how to give feedback in a painful way

Joyce recalled that as a student in Canada, her teachers did not respond to her written errors comprehensively, and when she first began her teaching career she followed suit – and hence did not mark all the errors in her students' writing. However, pretty soon after she had started teaching, Joyce was forced to unlearn what she had learnt from her previous teachers in Canada 'in a painful way' (#2). In her first secondary school (where she taught for five years), as a new teacher, her written feedback was heavily criticized as inadequate and not up to scratch by her department head. The first 'book inspection'[2] was a shocking experience to Joyce:

> I was surprised by how many post-it notes I got from my department head in the students' writing folders. Each note was a student's error that I had missed while I was marking the writing. My appraisal was negatively affected by how many post-it notes I got. (#2)

This humiliating experience changed Joyce altogether, making her forge a new belief that 'grammar was everything' (#2). After the first book inspection, Joyce tried to be more careful in her WCF, spending more time on it and doing the job more slowly so as not to get caught by her department head again. Much to her chagrin, however, she still got post-it notes in the second book inspection in her first year of teaching.

As Joyce continued to recount her beginning teaching experience, she underscored the preponderant role of grammar in her approach to feedback; she not only marked all errors comprehensively, but also flagged them with error codes:

> I was told to underline the mistakes and write marking codes above them, a way of indirect coded feedback. ... I believed this way of marking is not that bad, because students have to think. (#1)

Gradually, grammar became a very important part of her feedback, even in peer editing:

> As time passed by and more writings were marked, I started to mark grammar automatically and put a lot of focus on it. ... Even when I asked my students to do peer editing, the focus was on finding grammatical errors. In short, grammar was everything. (#2)

The 'grammar was everything' syndrome had taken a toll on Joyce, exhausting her and burning her out:

> I sometimes feel so stressed seeing the pile of unmarked writing in my shelf that I would avoid starting the marking because I know it would take long hours to finish. (#1)

Joyce found marking student writing a highly stressful enterprise; on the one hand, she was aware that returning timely feedback to the students is essential; on the other, she wished she could evade this tedious task which would take her hours to complete. Thus, she was entangled in a vicious cycle of feedback with no way out.

In her second year of teaching in the same school, Joyce continued to get post-it notes from her department head. The experience was frustrating but revealing, as it made Joyce realize that catching all errors in student writing without any omissions or mistakes is, in fact, an illusory goal:

> I was convinced that no matter how careful one tries to be, there will still be errors that are missed. I am not a machine. I cannot mark all error in students' writing. (#2)

Even though Joyce was coerced into adopting a comprehensive approach to WCF, her experience with unfocused WCF reinforced her skepticism of such a practice. She began to consider unfocused WCF not only from her own perspective but also in terms of its negative impact on her students:

> Doing intensive marking is horrendous because students make all kinds of mistakes: crisp white paper turns blood red after marking. (#1)

Feeling discouraged and frustrated, Joyce left the first secondary school, with tons of questions about how best to approach written feedback.

During WTE: Grammar is not everything

Joyce's breakthrough came when she quit her first secondary school and joined a new one. A year after teaching in the second school, Joyce began to attend the WTE course. The new experience (from her second school and the WTE course) gave her time and space to reflect on her previous feedback practice, with her critical reflection triggered by the WTE course:

> It did not take long until I started questioning myself on whether underlining and coding all grammatical mistakes is an effective way for my current students to see their errors and learn from their mistakes. I seem to be marking the same types of error in every piece of assignment, so that means they have not learned from their mistakes. Should I focus on only one or two types of errors each time instead? (#1)

Seeing the futility of underlining and coding the same mistakes again and again, Joyce began to wonder if responding to a smaller number of error types might be more helpful. Then she learnt about the benefits of focused WCF from the WTE course, which made her cast further doubt on the usefulness of unfocused WCF. Through reading the research literature on feedback in writing, Joyce came to the following conclusion:

> A lot of research has pointed out that it is not a very effective practice when teachers locate and code all errors in students' writings. (#1)

Joyce's own first-hand experience with unfocused WCF in her first school, as well as the stimulation provided by the WTE course, was instrumental to her feedback literacy development.

In addition, Joyce came to realize that she had been working way too hard, without sharing responsibility with her students. Her feedback literacy development saw her question the assumptions behind an approach to WCF where all errors were underlined, located and coded for the students. Through her perceptive observation and critical reflection as a teacher, she realized that unfocused WCF had failed to help her students avoid errors. Instead, she found herself marking the same errors again and again, suggesting that the students 'have not learned from their mistakes' (#1). Secondly, using error codes for each and every single error is not manageable for the students as they 'cannot handle so many marking codes in one piece of writing' (#1). Joyce realized that effective WCF has to be manageable. Also, conventional feedback approaches fail to prepare the students for independent editing and writing. Since teachers locate all errors in the students' writing, the students do not have a chance to develop self-editing skills by identifying their own errors. Joyce thus concluded that her feedback practice failed to help the students 'develop into competent writers' (#1).

The WTE course also broadened Joyce's perspectives by helping her consider feedback in the context of the entire teaching and learning process in the writing classroom:

> Students can only correct errors that they have learned about. If the students have received explicit grammar instruction, identifying the errors for them might help elicit their knowledge and hence allow them to self-correct successfully. (#1)

Joyce felt that even when errors are located (or coded) for the students, the WCF would only be effective if it is aligned with the pre-writing grammatical input. Through the WTE course, Joyce was able to look beyond the teachers' act of feedback per se and reflect on the relationship between feedback, teaching and learning in classroom writing assessment.

Taste of success in small-scale classroom experimentation

As part of her written assignment, Joyce conducted two little experiments with her Grade 7 and 12 students, as a result of which she further enhanced her feedback literacy. In her Grade 7 class, Joyce experimented with indirect WCF without using codes (her previous school had made her use coded WCF for every error unthinkingly). What happened in class was that the students who finished writing early brought their texts to her. When she spotted an error in a line she asked the student to read it aloud. Through this approach, the students were able to spot more than half of their errors; it was found that they were also able to locate the same types of errors more easily in other parts of the text without the use of codes.

Although this experiment was small scale, Joyce learnt some important lessons from it. First, she realized that the students are able to locate errors if 'the area is narrowed down' – and hence there is a place for a more focused approach to WCF. Secondly, Joyce learnt about the importance of empowering the students and making them play a more active role in the feedback process: 'If their schema about a certain type of grammar item is activated, they can locate other problematic items of the same categories more easily' (#1).

In her Grade 12 class, Joyce conducted another little experiment, which reinforced her growing belief about a focused approach to WCF. In the past, Joyce used to ask the students to proofread the entire essay before submission. In her experiment, she gave the students very specific instructions about self-editing – e.g. asking them to focus on only verb tenses. The outcome wowed her:

> I saw those students using their correction tape to correct their errors. I stood beside some of them to observe their editing process, and they were able to spot their mistakes! Although not all their corrections were correct, they were at least able to locate the problems. (#1)

From this small-scale experimentation, Joyce realized the importance of empowering the students through involving them in the feedback process. Even though they were not always accurate in their error corrections, they were able to locate their own errors, which was considered a big improvement, especially given that the students had generally low English proficiency compared with their counterparts in Hong Kong.

Impact of WTE on Joyce's feedback literacy development

Indeed, the WTE course impacted on Joyce's feedback literacy development in several important ways.

One at a time; less is more

Joyce learnt that self-editing can be much more achievable when the task is broken down into manageable bits – one at a time – and that less is more:

> When teachers ask students to do self-editing, there should be only one or two grammar focuses that are explicitly stated, and not just 'Check your grammar please!' When there is a focus, their mind is activated for a particular grammar item and can locate problems more easily. (#1)

Grammar is not all

Related to the above is the need to focus less on grammar in the writing classroom. Joyce wrote:

> Local teachers should stop spoon-feeding students, and we should not put the wrong focus on errors when we teach writing. (#1)

Believe in your students

The greatest insight Joyce gained from the WTE course relates to the student role in the feedback process and writing classroom:

> The most important thing I have learned from this course is that teachers really need to believe in their students; they are capable of more than we think. (#1)

Through her small-scale experimentations in the Grade 7 and 12 classrooms, Joyce discovered the power of the self-fulfilling prophecy: when she believes that the students can do it, they can. She tried alternative feedback approaches that entailed more active student involvement, and they worked. She reiterated this new belief as follows:

> Through my experience, students are able to locate errors when the area is narrowed down. (#1)

For weaker learners, Joyce assigned specific focuses in self-editing and found that her students were capable, whereas before she thought that her students were too weak to edit their own writing.

Long-term goal of feedback

The WTE course also made Joyce reflect on the ultimate, long-term goal of feedback. Increasingly she questioned the value of pointing out all errors for the students:

> We should think about the long-term benefits for students and not forget that the purpose of teaching writing is to help students develop into independent and competent writers. (#1)

However, conventional feedback practices are producing passive learners who are reliant on the teachers, and unable to edit and develop real competence in writing.

Distribute expertise

At the time when Joyce was attending the WTE course, she was head of the English department at her school – so it was her turn to conduct book inspections. She found the same problems in her colleagues' feedback – i.e. some errors were unmarked: 'That's fine. I didn't use post-it notes' (#2). Instead, Joyce shared her experience and insights with her colleagues. Her feedback literacy development culminated in her attempt to distribute her developing expertise in feedback with her colleagues.

Concluding Joyce's case

Joyce's experience shows that the WTE course facilitated her feedback literacy development. Through critical discussion and reflection in and outside class, engagement with academic literature, experimenting with alternative approaches, and observing and reflecting on student learning, she challenged her previous feedback practices and developed new perspectives on feedback in writing. Because of the limited scope of the assignments, however, the written reflections collected are mainly related to WCF; this limitation has to be noted.

Susan's Feedback Literacy Development

Before WTE: No one dared to challenge unfocused WCF

Being educated in Hong Kong, Susan was used to conventional feedback approaches – i.e. spending the bulk of her time on unfocused WCF. In her school, no teacher ever brought up the issue of feedback, and life went on as usual – until she took the WTE course.

To elaborate on the feedback practices in her school, Susan described the form-focused written feedback practice as a given that no one would challenge:

> It's a searching game for teachers as they need to find out as many errors as possible.

Such a practice reveals some fundamental assumptions about what good writing is:

> Accuracy of the language use is believed to be more important than anything else in the writing.

Susan ascribed the primacy of written accuracy to the examination culture in Hong Kong, where grammaticality in writing is affiliated with high scores in examinations:

> For the public examinations, writing with very few grammatical mistakes can score higher marks.

Susan confessed that she was one of those teachers 'who believed that comprehensive error feedback is a must' for both students and teachers.

During WTE: Unfocused WCF may not improve written accuracy

During the WTE course, Susan engaged in critical reflection and began to challenge her own feedback practice. In the WTE class there was a mini-debate on the effectiveness of unfocused WCF; to her it was a most stimulating activity that enabled her to question its negative impact on the students:

> Most students tend to dislike writing as they can gain very little encouragement and sense of achievement, but lots of judgement and disappointment instead. Writing seems to be a battle between students and teachers.

Through the WTE course, Susan began to problematize the feedback practices she had been adopting for nine years. Giving feedback on student writing is not only time-consuming but is ineffective since the students repeatedly make the same mistakes. To the students, receiving papers inundated with red ink is demoralizing, frustrating and demotivating, while making few or no errors is almost an impossible goal.

From the WTE course and the course readings, Susan's challenge first began with her question about the efficacy of unfocused WCF:

> There is no research to prove that comprehensive error feedback may improve students' writing accuracy. However, it will definitely cause teachers' burnout. It is suggested that students' performance in grammar accuracy takes time to improve under appropriate instruction (Ferris, 2003). In other words, students need clear and explicit instruction so that they can make improvement in their writing.

Susan cited the research she had read – i.e. there is as yet no established evidence that demonstrates the effectiveness of unfocused WCF. However, its negative effects are obvious, such as teacher burnout. More importantly, Susan came to the realization that written accuracy takes time to develop and that effective feedback has to be supported by explicit instruction.

Small-scale classroom inquiry on focused WCF

During the WTE course, Susan undertook a small-scale classroom inquiry in her Grade 6 class, where she tried out focused WCF on two of the five essays the students wrote in the first semester. She told her Grade 6 students the two target error types for WCF before writing. The students produced two drafts, with the first draft being subjected to peer evaluation; at the same time she delivered feedback on content and organization in the first draft. In the second draft, she responded to the target error types instead of pointing out all errors for the students. At the end of her try-out, she surveyed her students (24 in total) and reflected on the experience.

Susan designed a simple questionnaire for her Grade 6 students, asking them whether they preferred focused or unfocused WCF, and eliciting reasons from them. The results showed that 42% of her students preferred unfocused WCF (10 out of 24), and 54% preferred focused WCF (13 out of 24) (with one student not expressing a clear preference). The students' open-ended responses (translated from Chinese) are illuminating, suggesting that unfocused WCF was perceived to be more damaging than beneficial. A number of students pointed out the deleterious effect of unfocused WCF on their motivation and confidence, suggesting its negative emotional impact on the students. Some of the responses are as follows:

> I feel bad and sad because I need to correct a lot.

I feel disappointed when I receive my writing full of red marks.
I feel worried because I need to check too many things and lower down
the marks.

One student admitted that in spite of teacher feedback she would make
the same mistakes again, which made her feel embarrassed:

I think the teachers will be 10 times more tired because there are always
silly mistakes such as 'frie' → 'fire.' I will feel embarrassed.

Having scrutinized the students' comments and reflected on her experience, Susan concluded that unfocused WCF, which she had adopted for
nine years, is undesirable. The experimentation with focused WCF
enabled her to see the various opportunities writing can offer to the
students:

The rationale behind is to return the ownership and the right of writing
to students. Instead of being a judge or an evaluator, a teacher can be a
facilitator, a motivator or even simply as reader to their students' writing.
The primary task of a teacher is to encourage students to write, get them
involved more, invite them to express themselves freely, guide them to
appreciate the others' writing, help them to develop their own ideas
openly and enjoy the process of thinking and writing.

As a result of her small-scale classroom inquiry and her ongoing critical
reflections afforded by the WTE course, Susan broadened her perspectives
on writing; although her inquiry concerned WCF only, the insight she
gathered from the results was beyond feedback per se. She came to realize
that unfocused WCF had prevented teachers from seeing the wide variety
of purposes that writing serves: it makes teachers dominate the entire
feedback process, playing the role of a judge or evaluator; it turns students
into passive and reliant writers; and it deprives them of the opportunity
to enjoy the writing process and learn from it. Additionally, as pointed
out by a student, with focused WCF, 'the teachers can focus on some
important or specific items such as format and content,' with which
Susan agreed.

Impact of the WTE course on Susan's feedback literacy development

Thanks to the WTE course, Susan became determined to implement
focused WCF. As she pondered the possible switch from unfocused to
focused WCF, she came up with some concrete ideas for change, which
contributed to her feedback literacy development. Specifically, two key
issues, according to Susan, would warrant attention, both of which were
examined in the WTE course, namely: in the session on feedback, where
teachers were invited to consider the possibility of a feedback revolution
in their own context; and in the session on classroom writing assessment,

where teachers examined the inter-relationships between teaching, learning and assessment.

Feedback as part of effective planning

First, instead of simply homing in on WCF itself, Susan believed that WCF innovation should be part of effective planning in the writing classroom. The successful implementation of focused WCF would require careful planning which emphasizes effective writing instruction in not only grammar but also content and organization at different stages of the writing process:

> To benefit students the most in writing, selective error feedback is one part of the planning only. First, in the pre-task stage, teachers need to give enough input to the students. It is necessary to explain the grammar rules thoroughly and give them opportunities to apply them by conducting learning activities or doing exercise.

The 'planning' that Susan was considering, more importantly, pertains to the other stages of the writing lesson – e.g. pre-writing:

> After introducing the writing topic, teachers need to encourage students to brainstorm ideas freely and openly. It is important to emphasize the content, the ideas and the thinking process. Before writing the first draft, students should be clearly informed about the marking criteria and be reminded to apply the grammar rules taught before carefully.

Susan also emphasized the alignment between feedback/assessment and teaching and learning, as the students should be clearly informed about the assessment criteria, including the grammar items taught before writing. In the during-writing stage, where peer evaluation is adopted, the same principle should apply:

> After the first draft, the same marking criteria should be mentioned again for peer evaluation.

For teacher feedback, it should not be restricted to language but cover content, organization and other areas; WCF should be focused:

> Teachers then mark the error selectively and it's more important to give written feedback regarding to the content, structure and other elements of the writing.

Susan believed that focused WCF can give teachers more time and space to respond to all important dimensions of student writing, which she was unable to in her previous feedback practices.

The post-writing stage is important too to further help teachers intertwine assessment with teaching and learning:

> In the post-task stage, to facilitate students' improvement in specified grammar items, it is suggested teachers point out the common mistakes that most of them have made. It can be in the form of a written exercise

or oral feedback in class. Follow-up work should be included maybe in the next writing or other form of learning activities.

Overall, Susan's experimentation with focused WCF had transformed her original belief about the primacy of unfocused WCF, enabling her to view assessment and feedback, teaching and learning from an integrated perspective.

A whole-school approach to change

Also key to the successful implementation of WCF innovation (i.e. focused WCF) is the need for a whole-school approach to change:

> To change one well-accepted policy at school is no easy task at all. Without learning the rationale or seeing the positive outcome of the change, teachers who give selective error feedback would be regarded as lazy (as mentioned by one student in the survey), unprofessional and non-productive ...

Given that unfocused WCF is an established practice in school, marking less can cause misunderstanding that its sole purpose is to help teachers 'save time and energy.' Teachers may then be perceived as 'doing less,' and hence be considered lazy and irresponsible. When the students receive less feedback, parents may worry that this will adversely affect their examination or writing performance, making them 'suffer in the examination or when they further their study in the future.'

To prevent possible misunderstanding, Susan believed that concerted efforts at the school level are necessary:

> It is necessary to seek the support of the head of English department, the curriculum development officer and the headmaster of the school. ... To ease the anxiety of different parties, teachers need to have a strong standpoint and argument to justify what they are doing. Long term planning, a complete analysis of student performance, on-and-off modification of the curriculum are also needed.

Indeed, Susan was fully cognizant of the challenges of focused WCF, which would require long-term planning and collaborative efforts, as well as compelling arguments to justify the change, preferably backed up by evidence based on student performance. This suggests that systematic classroom-based research rather than small-scale classroom inquiries (such as that conducted by Susan) is needed to gather concrete evidence to support the benefits of focused WCF.

Concluding Susan's case

When Susan left the WTE course, she developed a conviction about the need to push forward WCF innovation that advocates a focused approach:

> As an English teacher in Hong Kong, I truly believe that selective error feedback is the right way to go. I will carry on the 'experiment' in my own

classroom and gather more evidence to convince the others. Most of all, it is the ultimate goal to develop students as an independent and effective writer.

Like Joyce, Susan's feedback literacy development resided in the emphasis she put on the students and student learning: the ultimate goal is to develop them into independent and effective writers.

Conclusions

The cases of Joyce and Susan suggest that WTE can have a positive impact on teachers' feedback literacy development. Incidentally, both Joyce and Susan focused mainly on WCF in their assignments, which may suggest that the need to respond to all written errors in Hong Kong (and similar contexts) is an area that greatly vexes writing teachers. From their reflections, it is clear that conventional feedback practices that prize unfocused WCF are ingrained and not amenable to change. Even a Westernized teacher like Joyce, who returned to Hong Kong from Canada with a clear preference for focused WCF, was brainwashed by her first school and began to embrace unfocused WCF in her writing classroom. Susan, throughout her teaching career, felt that unfocused WCF was a practice that no-one, novice or experienced teachers alike, dared to challenge. Indeed, the sociocultural context does impose rigid requirements on teachers, with which they have to comply. Without attending the WTE course, it was likely that Joyce would not have found answers to the conundrum of WCF arising from her experience in the first school, and Susan would have never challenged the taken-for-granted assumptions about unfocused WCF. There are clear implications about how WTE can be designed, and what teacher educators and professional development leaders in similar contexts can do in order to facilitate teachers' feedback literacy development – e.g. through providing professional input on salient areas about feedback, engaging teachers with relevant research literature, stimulating classroom discussions like the mini-debate described above, and providing opportunities for critical reflection through small-scale classroom inquiry.

The small-scale classroom inquiries undertaken by Joyce and Susan have yielded tremendous insight for the two teachers, with resonance for teachers in similar contexts, although two caveats are in order. First, the written reflections of the two teachers were linked to assessment on the WTE course and selected because of the high quality demonstrated. It appears that the other teachers who attended the same WTE course did not reach the same level of awareness of feedback literacy as Joyce and Susan did. To draw teachers' attention to feedback literacy, it is important that teacher educators/professional development leaders encourage practicing teachers to problematize and challenge conventional feedback practices and involve them in collaborative professional learning in order to bring about more effective feedback practices that suit their own contexts. Hopefully, teachers like Joyce and Susan can take the lead in initiating change, taking on the role of a trainer or mentor in their own work context. The second caveat relates to the sustainability of the teachers' feedback literacy development after they have completed WTE. In the study, the WTE course may only mark the beginning of teachers' journey of change and feedback literacy development. How Joyce and Susan sustain and further develop their feedback literacy after the WTE course is beyond the scope of this chapter, but it is likely that they will be faced with myriads of challenges in their own work contexts. They will need to take account of these specific challenges, and to involve colleagues and other key stakeholders in collective feedback literacy development. L2 writing teacher feedback literacy, as part of classroom assessment literacy, requires knowledge that is 'contextualized in the realities of teachers' contexts of practice – as pedagogical or practical and experiential knowledge' (Scarino, 2013: 316), and the development of teachers' feedback literacy needs to take account of the multifarious contextual factors that influence their feedback practices. Just as teacher assessment literacies are understood as 'contextualized and culturally responsive practices' (Xu & Brown, 2016: 154), teacher feedback literacy has to take into consideration a contextualized perspective.

To provide stronger evidence of the impact of feedback on student learning and writing and to showcase writing teachers' feedback literacy development, systematic, robust, school-based research based in authentic classroom contexts, preferably of a longer duration, is needed. It is noteworthy that writing teacher education on feedback in writing need not be university based (as in the study); it can be also be school based, where teacher educators support frontline teachers in their ongoing feedback literacy development. Irrespective of the site, form or mode of writing teacher education, the emphasis on critical reflection and a contextualized perspective is crucial to help writing teachers bridge the gap between theory and practice regarding feedback, and to further their feedback literacy development in their specific work contexts.

Notes

(1) The other assignment, taking up 30% of the total assessment score, is about the teaching of reading.
(2) 'Book inspection,' as part of teacher appraisal, is a common practice in Hong Kong schools, whereby school leaders such as department heads 'inspect' the students' compositions and exercise books on a regular basis. One of the focuses of book inspection is the amount of teacher written feedback.

References

Bailey, R. and Garner, M. (2010) Is the feedback in higher education assessment worth the paper it is written on? Teachers' reflections on their practices. *Teaching in Higher Education* 15, 187–198.

Bitchener, J. (2008) Evidence in support of written corrective feedback. *Journal of Second Language Writing* 17 (2), 102–118.

Bitchener, J. and Ferris, D.R. (2012) *Written Corrective Feedback in Second Language Acquisition and Writing.* New York: Routledge.

Bitchener, J. and Knoch, U. (2010) The contribution of written corrective feedback to language development: A ten-month investigation. *Applied Linguistics* 31 (2), 193–214.

Carless, D., Joughin, G. and Liu, N.F. (2006) *How Assessment Supports Learning: Learning-oriented Assessment in Action.* Hong Kong: Hong Kong University Press.

Curriculum Development Council and Hong Kong Examinations and Assessment Authority (2007) *English Language Curriculum and Assessment Guide (Secondary 4–6).* Hong Kong: Hong Kong Government Printer.

Crusan, D., Plakans, L. and Gebril, A. (2016) Writing assessment literacy: Surveying second language teachers' knowledge, beliefs, and practices. *Assessing Writing* 28, 43–56.

Ellis, R., Sheen, Y., Murakami, M. and Takashima, H. (2008) The effects of focused and unfocused written corrective feedback in an English as a foreign language context. *System* 36 (3), 353–371.

Ferris, D.R. (1995) Student reactions to teacher response in multiple-draft composition classrooms. *TESOL Quarterly* 29, 33–53.

Ferris, D.R. (2003) *Response to Student Writing: Implications for Second Language Students.* Mahwah, NJ: Lawrence Erlbaum.

Ferris, D.R. (2011) *Treatment of Error in Second Language Student Writing* (2nd edn). Ann Arbor, MI: University of Michigan Press.

Furneaux, C., Paran, A. and Fairfax, B. (2007) Teacher stance as reflected in feedback on student writing: An empirical study of secondary school teachers in five countries. *International Review of Applied Linguistics in Language Teaching* 45 (1), 69–94.

Guénette, D. and Lyster, R. (2013) Written corrective feedback and its challenges for pre-service ESL teachers. *Canadian Modern Language Review* 69 (2), 129–153.

Hendrickson, H.M. (1980) The treatment of error in written work. *The Modern Language Journal* 64 (2), 216–221.

Hirvela, A. and Belcher, D. (2007) Writing scholars as teacher educators: Exploring writing teacher education. *Journal of Second Language Writing* 16, 125–128.

Lalande, J.F., II (1982) Reducing composition errors: An experiment. *The Modern Language Journal* 66, 140–149.

Lee, I. (2004) Error correction in L2 secondary writing classrooms: The case of Hong Kong. *Journal of Second Language Writing* 13 (4), 285–312.

Lee, I. (2008) Understanding teachers' written feedback practices in Hong Kong secondary classrooms. *Journal of Second Language Writing* 17 (2), 69–85.

Lee, I. (2009). A new look at an old problem: How teachers can liberate themselves from the drudgery of marking student writing. *Prospect: An Australian Journal of Teaching/Teachers of English to Speakers of Other Languages (TESOL)* 24 (2), 34–41.

Lee, I. (2017) *Classroom Writing Assessment and Feedback in L2 School Contexts.* Singapore: Springer.

Lo, J. and Hyland, F. (2007) Enhancing students' engagement and motivation in writing: The case of primary students in Hong Kong. *Journal of Second Language Writing* 16, 219–237.

Lortie, D. (1976) *Schoolteacher.* Chicago, IL: University of Chicago Press.

Nicol, D.J. and Macfarlane-Dick, D. (2006) Formative assessment and self-regulated learning: A model and seven principles of good feedback practice. *Studies in Higher Education* 31 (2), 199–218.

Robb, T., Ross, S. and Shortreed, I. (1986) Salience of feedback on error and its effect on EFL writing quality. *TESOL Quarterly* 20, 83–93.

Scarino, A. (2013) Language assessment literacy as self-awareness: Understanding the role of interpretation in assessment and in teacher learning. *Language Testing* 30 (3), 309–327.

Shintani, N., Ellis, R. and Wataru, S. (2014) Effects of written feedback and revision on learners' accuracy in using two English grammatical structures. *Language Learning* 64 (1), 103–131.

Van Beuningen, C.G., De Jong, N.H. and Kuiken, F. (2008) The effect of direct and indirect corrective feedback on L2 learner's written accuracy. *International Journal of Applied Linguistics* 156, 279–296.

Van Beuningen, C.G., De Jong, N.H. and Kuiken, F. (2012) Evidence on the effectiveness of comprehensive error correction in second language writing. *Language Learning* 62, 1–41.

Xu, Y. and Brown, G.T.L. (2016) Teacher assessment literacy in practice: A reconceptualization. *Teaching and Teacher Education* 58, 149–162.

3 English Writing Teachers' Concept Development in China

Zhiwei Wu and Xiaoye You

Introduction

When English entered the Chinese education system in the mid-1800s, it was considered a practical tool to quick-fix China's losing streak in battling against foreign powers. English was a linguistic gateway for the Chinese to learn Western science and technology, which they hoped could boost China's military power and enable the nation to defend itself from foreign invasion. This state policy was captured in the slogan '*zhong xue wei ti, xi xue wei yong*' (Chinese learning as essence; Western learning as application). This *ti-yong* dualism has traversed more than a century and is still reflected in education documents and guidelines for teaching English in China (You, 2010). The presence of the *ti-yong* dualism in the English pedagogies in contemporary China is partly caused by the colonial thinking that the West represents the advanced, scientific and effective, while China represents the old-fashioned, unscientific and ineffective. However, as Sampson (1984: 20) cautions, this colonial thinking commits 'the fallacy of the unidimensionality of development.' While it may be true that the West is advanced in science and technology, they may not be so in social development. Since education is a social domain, it is unwarranted to assume that developed nations can provide ready-made solutions to the social (i.e. educational) problems in less developed nations.

English writing instruction in China is not immune from this fallacy. Although it has gone through multifarious changes in its treatment of themes, modes of discourse and language style, and its pedagogical procedures (You, 2010), its central goal has remained largely unchanged over the last century: students' acquisition of the standard rule-based norms as practiced by native speakers. As such, Chinese English writing instructors, influenced by 'native speaker prejudice' (Ruecker, 2011) and *the West is better* discourse (Pennycook, 1994), has looked to the West for the correct, scientific and effective pedagogy. However, educational theory is laden with values and cultural implications. Some pedagogical procedures deemed effective in English-speaking countries might prove to be less so in other contexts (Hu & Lam, 2010; Sun & Cheng, 2002). This is particularly true when English writing teachers try to enact Western pedagogical approaches in their local contexts (Carson & Nelson, 1996; Tsui & Ng, 2010; You, 2004).

Given the situatedness of any pedagogy, writing teacher education should alert trainees to the possibility that a pedagogy might be productive and effective in the West but counterproductive and ineffective in other locales. This awareness is particularly important in China, where most English writing instructors are not trained before they take on writing courses (Reichelt, 2009). Second language (L2) writing courses offered, if they are offered at all, in MA and PhD programs reflect an imbalance noted by Hirvela and Belcher (2007); that is, more attention is devoted to understanding how students learn to write than how teachers learn to teach writing. Although teacher development workshops have grown in both number and scale in China over the past five years (see 'subsection on "Teacher development workshops"' for details), they can only help a limited number of in-service teachers. This stands in stark contrast to a sizable population of English writing teachers, who habitually turn to the West for a pedagogical solution to their problems.

It is in this educational context that we begin our quest for English writing teacher education in China. Specifically, we hope to understand what resources are locally available for teacher development and how teachers use these resources to develop their English writing pedagogies. In the following sections, we will first frame the discussion in two Vygotskian constructs: scientific concept and everyday concept. We then survey locally valorized resources for Chinese English writing teachers' concept development, focusing on their features and affordances. With these resources in mind, we will report on interviews conducted with seven teachers from three institutions in China, and examine how they drew upon different resources to develop everyday and scientific concepts about English writing pedagogies. Finally, we discuss the implications of the present study for English writing teacher preparation and development, with a view to unifying the two types of concepts.

Sociocultural Theory of Concept Development and English Writing Teacher Education

In the sociocultural theory of learning, concept development is manifested in two constructs: scientific concept and everyday concept (Vygotsky, 1987). Scientific concepts are usually taught and learned at school and are often structured systematically. Everyday concepts (also known as spontaneous concepts) are intuitive and tacit, emerging from our day-to-day experience. For Vygotsky, concept development is an ongoing process, whereby a learner, scaffolded by more capable peers or experts, 'integrates everyday concepts into a system of related concepts and transforms the raw material of experience into a coherent system of concepts' (Howe, 1996: 39). Everyday concepts and scientific concepts are not dichotomous but are reciprocal to each other. Everyday concepts provide an experiential basis for the development of scientific concepts which, once developed, can enable learners to organize their everyday concepts. In Vygotsky's words, everyday concepts give scientific concepts 'body and validity,' while scientific concepts 'supply structures' for everyday concepts (Vygotsky, 1966: 109).

In teacher expertise scholarship, scientific concepts are equivalent to expert knowledge – 'knowledge that is prepositional, written down, codified in textbooks and publicly accepted as a principled way of understanding phenomena within a particular discourse community' (Johnson, 2009: 15), and everyday concepts are tantamount to experiential knowledge, which 'emerges through [teachers'] own lived experiences as learners of teaching' (Johnson, 2009: 15). Specific to the context of English writing teacher education, we define scientific concepts as the systematic pedagogical content knowledge (Shulman, 1987), including content knowledge (e.g. English writing and writers) and pedagogical knowledge (e.g. how to teach English writing and why). By everyday concepts, we mean teachers' experiences, beliefs and practices derived from concrete pedagogical activities, both as learners and teachers of English writing. For example, a teacher might observe her colleague's teaching practice and discover that having students peer review one another's work is a useful activity. She decides to replicate this activity in her own classroom. This decision is driven by her everyday concept, developed from her positive impression of the activity. However, she may not understand the underlying scientific concepts (e.g. process approach, mutual scaffolding, etc.) of this practice.

For English writing teacher education in China, Vygotsky's distinction between scientific and everyday concepts is particularly relevant. First, the distinction is a powerful tool to tease out the potential conflict experienced by English writing teachers between their concept immaturity and the expert knowledge required by the profession. Dictated by a composite view of language as four core skills (reading, writing, listening and speaking), Chinese universities assume that an English teacher can teach any language skill course, regardless of her specialty. In fact, many writing teachers have not been trained, and their scientific concept development is immature. The void left by concept immaturity is usually filled by teachers' everyday concepts, formulated when they were language learners. They draw on their own experiences, histories and impressions to assemble instructional practices, which may not be theoretically or pedagogically sound. Their unexamined, episodic everyday concepts might be 'detrimental in the development of teachers' expertise' (Johnson &

Golombek, 2011: 2). Secondly, shaped by the *ti-yong* dualism and 'the West is better' ideology, teachers with underdeveloped expert knowledge might simply transfer Western pedagogies into their classrooms without examining whether they are locally appropriate. As scientific concepts are usually context neutral, there is a need to move scientific concepts from the decontextualized and abstract to the contextualized and concrete (Vygotsky, 1987). Therefore, Vygotsky's distinction is useful to alert English writing teachers to the contextual constraints in China when they enact scientific concepts from the West.

Research Design

Research questions

Our study is guided by two questions:

(1) What resources are locally available for English writing teachers' concept development in China?
(2) How do teachers use resources to develop their English writing pedagogies?

Data collection and analysis

We adopted a qualitative design and collected data in two stages. In the first stage, to address the first research question, Zhiwei contacted five experts who had three decades of experience in teaching and researching English writing in China. They were known by their dedication to developing home-grown pedagogies for teaching English writing. As the organizer of an in-service teacher training workshop, Zhiwei invited the five experts to independently construct a list of resources that could be shared with the workshop participants, based on the criteria of accessibility, quality and relevance. Zhiwei then combined the five lists into a master list and sent it to the experts, who were requested to rate the resources based on the three criteria (from 1 to 9). Based on the rankings, four types of resources were judged by the experts to be of high accessibility, quality and relevance (with an averaging rating over 7): journal articles, academic conferences, teacher development workshops and National Excellent Courses. With this four-category framework, Zhiwei conducted literature and document searches to locate specific instances of these resources available in China. The expert judgement and survey results have enabled us to sketch the 'resourcescape' for English writing teachers' concept development in China.

In the second stage, Xiaoye interviewed seven English writing teachers (all females) from three universities, based on an interview outline prepared by both of us. The first part of the interview solicits basic information about the interviewee, such as educational background, the

Table 3.1 Profile of the seven interviewees

Participant (all pseudonyms)	Education background	Years of teaching English writing	University (all pseudonyms)	Geographical location
Huang	PhD	20	Shanshui University	Southwest China
Deng	MA	4		
Kang	MA	10	Kaifang University	South China
Zheng	MA	9		
Cui	PhD	10		
Pan	MA	17	Fengshou University	East China
Guo	MA	7		

number of years teaching English writing, the types of students taught (undergraduate versus graduate, English majors versus non-English majors). The second part focuses on how prior education experiences or pre-service training have affected the interviewee's pedagogy. When the interviewees alluded to a concept to characterize their writing pedagogies, we regarded this as an act of 'active mention.' The third part inquires about the resources the interviewee drew upon as an in-service teacher. Finally, the interviewee is asked whether she recognizes five pedagogical concepts (selected on the basis of frequency obtained in the literature search). When the interviewee acknowledges that she has heard of the concept, we regarded this as 'passive recognition.' After the interviews, we compared the frequencies of active mention, passive recognition and literature representation. We tried to balance our participants by education background, seniority and location of their institution (see Table 3.1). It is important to note that we do not aim for generalization of English writing teachers in China, because institutional contexts vary to a great extent in the country. We hope that insights from the seven interviewees can reveal how they used and negotiated resources when developing a local pedagogy for English writing, thereby addressing the second research question.

We independently analyzed the interviews by breaking down the participants' answers into idea units and tentatively assigning labels to them. We also made memos, noting our interpretations and impressions of each participant. We then exchanged our notes and discussed each case and the seven cases as a whole. During this process we were able to identify the conceptual resources they drew upon to develop their pedagogies.

Resources for Concept Formation: The Survey Results

As explained in the previous section, five experts agreed upon four types of resources for English writing teachers to develop concepts in the

Chinese context: journal articles, academic conferences, teacher development workshops and National Excellent Courses. These resources cut across research endeavors and teaching practices, and are important sites for concept development. In the following subsections, we will report their features, themes and affordances in the Chinese context.

Journal articles

According to the experts, reading journal articles published in China is one of the most efficient ways to understand how everyday and scientific concepts are developed and applied in local contexts. Almost all Chinese universities subscribe to the China National Knowledge Infrastructure (CNKI) database, through which journal articles, graduate theses and dissertations, and many other reference materials are readily accessible. To ensure the quality of the journal articles, we focused on articles published in CSSCI journals. CSSCI stands for Chinese Social Sciences Citation Index, a citation index covering about 500 journals in the social sciences and humanities. We conducted article searches in the CNKI database, using the search terms '二语写作' (L2 writing), '英语写作' (English writing) and '外语写作' (foreign language writing). A total of 4159 articles published between 1998 (the earliest year available in the database) and 2016 (the most recent year available) were returned. Of these articles, 3394 (or 81.61%) directly or indirectly alluded to writing pedagogies. We then read the abstracts and narrowed down to 578 articles with English writing pedagogies as the research object. These articles can be divided into three groups.

The first group discusses the efficacy of applying Western pedagogical approaches to the Chinese context. Four approaches are recurrent: product approach, process approach, genre approach and task-based approach. The second group borrows theories from the general education discipline and repurposes them in English writing instruction in China. For instance, Ding and Liu (2011) explained how they developed a project method based on Dewey's notion of 'progressive education' and applied it to teaching English writing. The third group is dedicated to developing home-grown pedagogies tailored to the Chinese context. Wang's 'Length Approach' is a case in point. Back in the late 1990s, Wang and his colleagues noticed that Chinese students were apprehensive about making mistakes and wrote very short passages. They then designed writing tasks tapping into the students' interests and encouraged them to write long passages, hence the name 'Length Approach.' The teachers refrained from correcting language mistakes and focused on identifying strengths in the texts. Evidence showed that this approach boosted the students' confidence in writing and improved their writing abilities (Wang, 2005; Wang *et al.*, 2000).

These articles are considered important resources for concept development for two reasons. First, they either empirically or conceptually argue for the effectiveness of a particular teaching method. Teachers can familiarize themselves with scientific concepts that characterize different approaches and develop a systematic knowledge framework about English writing instruction. Secondly, these articles have detailed the instructional designs. Teachers can follow these steps and apply them in their pedagogical context. Mindful application may connect scientific concepts and concrete activities, and create opportunities for teachers to use scientific concepts as mediational tools to reflect upon their daily practices (Johnson & Golombek, 2011).

Academic conferences

Academic conferences are another site for exchanging insights, ideas and information. They enable researchers and teachers to keep up with the development in a discipline. They are also a landmark indicating the autonomy, specificity and vitality of a discipline. In China, the first conference on English writing instruction was organized in 2003. Ever since, almost every year, one conference featuring English writing teaching and research is held. We were able to obtain the conference themes over the past decade and identified two strands. The first strand directly addresses issues in writing pedagogies and teachers as a profession. For instance, in 2007 and 2008, the themes were 'Teaching and Researching English Writing across Curriculum in China' and 'Teaching and Researching English Writing as a Profession,' respectively. The second strand examines the situatedness of English writing in a local context. For example, 'Regionalized Research on Chinese English Writing in the Global Context' was the 2014 conference theme. Themes of this strand, although not directly dealing with writing pedagogies, can increase the participants' knowledge about student writers' texts and their composing processes. They can inform teachers about the importance of contextualizing students' writing, without uncritically importing and enacting Western pedagogies. Overall, these academic conferences provide opportunities for participants to internalize scientific concepts.

Teacher development workshops

Although Richards and Lockhart (1996: 2) criticized in-service workshops for having 'only short-term effects,' they constitute a crucial part of teachers' professional development. In China, in-service training for English teachers became customary in the late 2000s, with national and provincial in-service workshops being regularly organized for English writing teachers. We were able to access information about six in-service workshops for English writing teachers between 2014 and 2017. Two features were identified. First, the workshops almost always address both pedagogical and research issues. For instance, a two-day workshop organized in Jinan, Shandong Province in 2017 covered the following topics (FLTRP, 2017):

(a) status quo of and reflections on English writing instruction in China;
(b) syllabus design and teaching plan for the course, 'Practical English Writing';
(c) L2 authors' misunderstandings in academic writing;
(d) dialogue with journal editors: writing and publishing papers;
(e) teaching and learning academic vocabulary for writing;
(f) teaching L2 writing with research-based construction techniques;
(g) new developments and outdated fashions in international L2 writing research;
(h) L2 writing research status quo in China and its ecological integration.

As this list shows, topics (a), (b), (e) and (f) deal with L2 writing instruction, while topics (c), (d), (g) and (h) deal with L2 writing research. Combining teaching and research is the pre-eminent feature for writing teacher development workshops in China, because teachers are increasingly pressured to produce research output while simultaneously fulfilling a heavy teaching load. The dual focus of the in-service workshops is beneficial for English writing teachers to merge scientific concepts and everyday concepts.

As a second feature of these workshops, the trainer line-up is composed of domestic and international experts. For example, the Jinan workshop was co-delivered by Eli Hinkel (United States), Junju Wang (Chinese Mainland) and Xuesong Gao (Hong Kong). Another two workshops offered in 2016 and 2017 were co-delivered by Paul Kei Matsuda (United States) and Fang Xu (China). The juxtaposition of the domestic and international perspectives may sensitize English writing teachers to the importance of context, thereby affording rich opportunities for teachers to develop expert knowledge to determine whether a pedagogy is locally appropriate.

National Excellent Courses

National Excellent Courses are perhaps a resource unique to China. To improve the teaching quality in undergraduate programs, the Chinese Ministry of Education (MOE) launched the National Excellent Courses project, setting up exemplary courses in major disciplines so that university teachers could learn from the best practice in syllabus design, course delivery and team-building (MOE, 2003). When the title is conferred to a course, all course materials and teaching videos must be made available online. The purpose is not to require all universities to conform to the exemplar, but rather to offer resources and opportunities for them to improve their course quality. Between 2003 and 2010, a total of 3909 courses have been given the title. Among them, only two English writing courses have been recognized. One is hosted by Guangdong University of Foreign Studies (GDUFS) and the other by Xi'an International Studies University (XISU).

As the MOE project purports to set up one role model in a particular course, it may seem redundant to enlist two English writing courses. However, the two courses are divergent in their teaching philosophies. The XISU course is primarily designed along the current-traditional rhetoric model. The syllabus progresses from writing error-free sentences to writing coherent paragraphs, from writing full-length passages in three modes of discourse (narrative, expository and argumentative) to academic writing. The GDUFS course follows what Ur (2013: 470) calls 'a situated methodology' by drawing on concepts from current-traditional rhetoric, expressivist pedagogy, process approach and multiliteracies. Although correct language use is featured in the syllabus, it is complemented by other pedagogical procedures. For instance, the course begins with a heavy emphasis on expressivism. The students are encouraged to write stories in as many words as they can, echoing the 'Length Approach' described above in the subsection on 'Journal Articles.' They are told not to worry about grammar but to focus on expression of feelings and emotions. In addition, the students go through multiple drafts and peer review before handing in their stories for grading. Teachers provide minimal feedback on grammar and focus on content. Towards the end of the course, the students are assigned to conduct surveys on a social issue and report their findings in a newspaper feature article. In addition, the students are tasked to present their findings in self-made videos, mimicking the news reporting style of major Anglophone news networks (such as the BBC and CNN).

These two National Excellent Courses are a fruitful site for writing teachers to form everyday concepts. Teachers can watch teaching demos, read course materials and browse students' sample assignments (written or multimodal). As such, they can experience the pedagogical procedures and compare them with their own. Additionally, these two National Excellent Courses can contribute to the synergy between scientific concepts and everyday concepts because MOE requires the named courses to disseminate their teaching philosophies and pedagogical models to a wider public. Two dissemination channels are possible. First, the host university organizes week-long open campus activities, inviting teachers from other universities to experience the teaching procedure. Teachers can sit in on course sessions and then attend lectures delivered by the instructors explaining the pedagogical design. GDUFS has organized three open-campus workshops over the last five years. Secondly, every year MOE offers online training for teachers who are unable or unwilling to travel. Teachers can log on to an online platform and listen to lectures by course designers and instructors. XISU has been responsible for giving online training lectures since 2011. Both the physical and virtual activities provide opportunities for pre- and in-service teachers to understand how English writing is taught in these two National Excellent Courses. Better still, teachers can compare and analyze the two courses in terms of pedagogical procedures and teaching philosophies. This can further contribute to the synergy between systematic knowledge and intuitive experience.

Concept Formation in Writing Pedagogies: The Interview Findings

The previous section discusses four types of resources judged by experts to be beneficial for English writing teachers' concept development in China. With this 'resourcescape' in mind, we want to understand how writing teachers use conceptual resources to develop their pedagogies.

Everyday concepts

Our interviews found that few of the writing teachers had received any training in teaching writing before they taught English writing, which corroborates the observation made by Reichelt (2009). Although some of them went through TESOL programs in the UK or applied linguistics programs in China, they took no courses devoted to English writing instruction. Usually, writing was 'embedded in the course of English Language Teaching, along with reading, speaking, and listening' (Pan). Only one teacher (Cui) stated that she had received training in English writing pedagogies. In lieu of systematic training, teachers relied on everyday concepts developed from two resources to guide their pedagogical design: their own undergraduate writing experience and the National Excellent Courses.

All of our participants noted that their undergraduate experience had a strong impact on their writing pedagogies, especially when they were a novice teacher. They largely modeled after their undergraduate writing teachers in syllabus design, teaching content and feedback method. For instance, in her undergraduate years (back in the 1990s), Huang took writing courses delivered by exchange teachers from Yale University: 'They did not focus on language, and they emphasized multiple drafting [...] Writing courses were organized by topics, not by modes of discourse.' Huang regarded this teaching method as 'transformative and reformative,' so when she became a writing teacher she did almost the same: 'I did not use any textbook ... I organized the four-month course in four topics: education, culture, economy, and environment.'

Similarly, Guo shared how her undergraduate writing experience had shaped the focus of her teaching: 'When I was an undergrad, the teacher valued shining sentences over correct sentences [...] By shining, she meant well-phrased and well-thought-after sentences. She encouraged us to note down these sentences from our readings and use them in our writing.' When Guo became a writing teacher, she also required her students to take note of shining sentences: 'I checked students' notes twice one semester. I even showed them my notes and some students' notes to demonstrate how we collected these shining sentences.'

Some writing teachers tended to perpetuate the teaching methods they experienced as undergraduate students even though the experience was negative. Kang recalled that her undergraduate writing course was 'horrific.' The course was delivered by a native speaker who solely focused on language form: 'we wrote only one draft, and the teacher singled out language mistakes. If the mistakes were serious, he would throw chunks of chalk at the students [...] So to me, writing class was equivalent to corporal punishment.' When Kang became a writing teacher, due to her lack of teaching experience she 'thought about what [her] undergraduate writing course looked like' and she followed the same practice – focusing on language accuracy: 'I assigned students a topic and asked them to write in class. I collected their papers and corrected mistakes.' She added that 'I did not throw chunks of chalk because I did not have the audacity to do that. I was not a native speaker; I was not sure whether I was qualified to help the students correct their mistakes.'

The second resource for everyday concept formation is the National Excellent Courses. For instance, Deng explained how she capitalized on one of the National Excellent courses:

> I watched the lectures in XISU's National Excellent Course. I was inspired by one teacher, who had a literature background. She combined literature and writing [...] I also had a literature background, so in one lesson, I analyzed the form and content of the poem *I wandered lonely as a cloud*. I then asked students to comment on the theme of the poem and express different opinions as their assignments.

The National Excellent Course inspired Deng to draw on her training in literary studies, enabling her to perceive the connections between literary criticism and the teaching of writing.

These extracts show that in-service teachers develop everyday teaching concepts by observing the instructional practices of their undergraduate writing teachers or their colleagues from other universities. They then re-enact the practices in their own classrooms. One potential problem in applying the context-embedded everyday concept in another context is that the teachers might only imitate how it is taught but not understand why it is taught that way. It might be counterproductive to transfer everyday concepts to other contexts without examining the underlying scientific concepts (Howe, 1996). For instance, although Kang differed from her undergraduate writing teacher in not practicing 'corporal punishment,' her ontological perspective on the role of a writing teacher was exactly the same: it is the writing teacher's job to correct language mistakes. In essence, she unwittingly perpetuated a monolingual ideology in teaching English writing (You, 2016).

Convergence of everyday concepts and scientific concepts

In the interviews, we were able to identify how English writing teachers engaged in reflective practices (Farrell, 2007) and connected their everyday concepts with scientific concepts. For instance, Kang recounted her experience in a teacher development workshop:

> One of the trainers demonstrated how she organized a writing lesson. She treated all the trainees as her students and asked us to write whatever came to our minds in five minutes. She then asked some of us to read out our writings and related them to the focus of her teaching [...] Throughout the lesson, she improvised a lot, depending on students'/trainees' outputs and responses.

This episodic experience led Kang to marvel at the flexibility afforded by this teaching technique, but she did not stop at the experiential knowledge of 'improvising in English writing instruction.' Rather, she went on to reflect that 'this practice was student-centered, not teacher-centered. I used to structure my writing lesson according to the teaching plan and tried to control my students. Now, I realized my practice was too teacher-centered.' In the workshop, the trainer did not talk about the scientific concepts of 'student-centered' and 'teacher-centered.' Kang was able to connect her experience as a trainee to such concepts she had learned elsewhere and examined her own instructional practices through self-reflection, thereby transcending the 'improvising' practice and reaching the scientific concept of 'student-centered.'

Perhaps the most revealing example is Cui's recursive trajectory of concept development in English writing instruction. Cui pursued her PhD studies in education at an American university. There, she took a course entitled 'critical thinking assessment,' in which students were guided to connect their daily activities with the concept of 'critical thinking':

> In class, students were asked to first write from experiences and observation [...] Students would write about their church-going experiences and how these experiences shape their characters [...] The purpose of these assignments is to invoke critical thinking through reading and writing.

This institutional training helped her develop the scientific concept of 'critical thinking.' In the interview, Cui expounded her view on the concept:

> Every human being is an independent human being with his [sic] own philosophical ideas that need to be respected. What you come across, you don't take it for granted; you have to ask why; you have to challenge it. It is an attitude towards life and things.

When she returned to China, Cui tried to instantiate the concept in her English writing class, but she was confronted by sociocultural difficulties: 'Chinese students are passive listeners. They are not accustomed to arguing or critical thinking.' This reality prompted her to design activities to encourage students to speak up and think aloud:

> Even if students are poor with language, they can still express their ideas in simple language. Ideas matter! [...] I encourage them to write whatever interests them [...] for example, I ask them to write about Michael Jackson's songs. Why do you think he wrote that song? What do you make of the song?

To effectuate such a teaching philosophy, she tolerated language errors and focused predominantly on students' ideas:

> In the first two months [in the writing course], I did not care about language at all. I only focused on ideas. This way, I hoped to pique students' interest and to encourage them to write [...] I had ten items in my writing assessment criteria to gauge whether students' writing reflects critical thinking.

Later on, Cui's critical thinking focused pedagogy was connected to other scientific concepts. For instance, she attended a teacher development workshop organized by GDUFS and was exposed to the concept of the 'Length Approach' (see subsection on 'Journal Articles'): 'In the workshop, Professor Wang Chuming said, "Compositions are written up, not cleaned up." [...] I think this makes sense, because writing abilities are developed through writing, not through correction.' This concept reaffirmed her belief in focusing on ideas and sparsely correcting mistakes in students' assignments.

In the trajectory of concept formation, Cui assumed an agentive role in applying, adapting and affirming the scientific concepts in her pedagogical procedures. Her reflective practices epitomize 'the transformative process of making sense of everyday experiences through the theoretical constructs of the broader professional discourse community and vice versa' (Johnson & Arshavskaya, 2011: 170).

Disjunction between everyday and scientific concepts

In the second part of our interview, we asked the interviewees to explain their day-to-day instructional procedures in their own terms. Remarkably, the ranking of concept frequency in CSSCI journal articles was exactly the same as that in the interviewees' active mention. That is, 'peer review' is most frequently referenced in literature and by the teachers, followed by 'process approach,' 'genre-based approach,' 'five-paragraph essay,' and finally 'current-traditional rhetoric' (see Table 3.2). The paralleled rankings may indicate how scientific concepts are internalized by the teachers as psychological tools for thinking (Johnson & Golombek, 2011).

Table 3.2 Frequency of five concepts in literature, participants' active mention and passive recognition

Concepts	Frequency in literature (N = 4159)	Frequency in active mention (N = 7)	Frequency in passive recognition (N = 7)
现时-传统修辞 (current-traditional rhetoric)	4	0	0
五段式作文 (five-paragraph essay)	11	1	7
体裁教学法 (genre-based approach)	35	4	7
过程写作法 (process approach)	70	5	7
同伴互评 (peer review)	367	6	7

The rankings also demonstrate the power of locally valorized scientific concepts in structuring teachers' everyday concepts. In Vygotsky's (1966: 109) words, scientific concepts 'supply structures' for everyday concepts.

In the interviews, we also noticed that although the participants actively used a concept, their understanding might be based on their everyday concepts and divorced from the meaning codified by the academic community. 'Genre-based approach' is one such case. As an academic concept, genre is defined as 'a class of communicative events, the members of which share some set of communicative purposes' (Swales, 1990: 58). Accordingly, genre-based approaches teach 'the ways language is used in specific contexts' and 'exploit the expressive potential of society's discourse structures' (Hyland, 2007: 150). That is why genre-based pedagogies usually focus on the structural and linguistic realizations of a genre in a particular communicative context. However, in the interviews, of the four participants who mentioned this term, two of them used it to mean 'modes of discourse.' For instance, Huang said, 'I followed a genre-based syllabus: exposition, argumentation, etc.' Similarly, Zheng noted that 'in our new textbook, we have four genres: narration, exposition, argumentation, description.' What Huang and Zheng meant by 'genres' were the four hallmark modes of discourse that typify current-traditional rhetoric (Young, 1978). Their remarks represent a mismatch between the 'genre-based approach' as an academic concept and as teacher beliefs.

Discussion and Implications

Our study surveys the 'resourcescape' for English writing teachers' concept development in China and focuses on how in-service teachers, not institutionally trained to teach English writing, used resources to develop their pedagogies. We find that all the interviewees, in the absence of scientific concepts of English writing instruction, tapped into their deeply ingrained experiential knowledge obtained when they were students. This phenomenon has been described as 'the apprenticeship of observation' in general educational research (Borg, 2004; Lortie, 1975) and has also been reported in English language teaching studies (e.g. Richards & Pennington, 1998). As Lortie (1975) rightly points out, this apprenticeship results from (pre- and in-)service teachers' partial knowledge of the teaching profession. They only see the 'teacher frontstage' but do not see the 'backstage.' In Vygotskian terms, they develop their everyday concepts of what and how to teach, but may not understand the scientific concepts of teaching English writing. As in our study, six of the seven writing teachers, when they entered the profession, modeled the way they had been taught in their undergraduate writing courses. They did not examine the rationale behind their everyday concepts: topic-based syllabus in Huang's case, or 'shining sentences' in Guo's case, or error correction in Kang's case.

Although everyday concepts are experiential, unsystematic and intuitive, they can contribute to scientific concept development. A comparison of Deng's and Kang's cases might illustrate this point. Deng listened to a lecture from a National Excellent Course and found it enticing to link English literature with the teaching of writing. She then transported this practice into her classroom and asked her students to write a response paper on a poem. In Kang's case, she found free writing in a training workshop intriguing. Unlike Deng, Kang did not simply transplant free writing into her class. Rather, she reflectively compared the trainer's pedagogical design and her own. This reflection prompted her to realize that her class was teacher centered and the trainer's was student centered. In Deng's case, the everyday concept remained episodic, while in Kang's case the everyday concept provided a concrete foundation for her reflection, eventually leading to her deeper understanding of two scientific concepts: student-centered and teacher-centered teaching. The two cases show that contextual resources (e.g. National Excellent Courses or training workshops) are situated possibilities for concept formation; the level of conscious reflection may lead to the development of different types of concepts.

Our study also contributes to the scholarship that examines the resources available to and used by teachers to develop writing pedagogies (Johnson, 2015; Worden, 2015). Similar to existing research findings, 'the apprenticeship of observation,' as an unanalyzed concept, proved to be an important source (Borg, 2004). Different from previous research, our study further identifies four types of resources that are of high accessibility, quality and relevance for concept development in China. In the interviews, the writing instructors reported that they used and negotiated resources in training workshops and National Excellent Courses for concept development. Even though they did not allude to journal articles or academic conferences, we can infer that they may indirectly use these resources. For instance, the same rankings of literature representation and the teachers' active mention of five scientific concepts (see Table 3.2) may be indicative of the tacit impact of journal articles on teachers' concept development. These four types of resources are valuable sites for *praxis*, 'the integration of conceptual knowledge and practical activity with the goal of stimulating change or [concept] development' (Lantolf, 2009: 272).

To facilitate praxis-oriented concept development, one must take into account situated possibilities in a pedagogical context. While scientific concepts abound in teacher preparation and development programs, they only provide decontextualized and systematic knowledge (Vygotsky, 1987), without attending to the contextual constraints inherent in any pedagogy. Therefore, English writing teacher education should not only mean explaining a whole set of scientific concepts, but also creating opportunities to allow teachers to use these concepts as psychological tools for thinking (Johnson & Golombek, 2011). For pre-service teachers, it is necessary to observe and practice-teach writing classes in a particular context in order to understand the instructional and institutional constraints. Then they can reflect on their observations and practicum in reference to the scientific concepts. For in-service teachers, ongoing and self-initiated reflective practices are beneficial to the synergy of everyday and scientific concepts, as demonstrated in Cui's and Kang's cases. If teachers leave their concepts unanalyzed, they may risk misunderstanding scientific concepts and failing to connect their day-to-day teaching practices with systematic pedagogical content knowledge. The 'genre-based approach' reported by Zhang and Huang is one example of unexamined assumptions of a scientific concept. Therefore, teacher education programs need to train teachers to engage in effective reflective practices.

A three-stage sequence, including descriptive reflection, comparative reflection and critical reflection (Jay & Johnson, 2002), can be followed in order to understand the dialectical relations between experiential knowledge and expert knowledge. Specifically, in the first stage, teachers can describe the particulars of an instructional context (such as the expectations, proficiency and difficulties of the students) and create a problem space. In China, for instance, one potential problem space arises from the clash between the process approach endorsed by teachers and the product-based approach fueled by the exam-oriented culture (Tsui & Ng, 2010). In the second stage, teachers can compare how the problem is represented in the local resources for concept development and how these representations confirm or disconfirm their experiential knowledge. In the Chinese context, the teacher may ask: How is the process approach discussed in journal articles? Do the National Excellent Courses enact a process approach or a product approach? In teacher training workshops and academic conferences, what themes are featured? How do the discourses in these resources compare with day-to-day pedagogical routines in the local context? In the third stage, guided by the scientific concepts, teachers critically review the alternatives in response to the instructional constraints.

They may ask: How can the process approach be instantiated in a pro-product approach environment (Tsui & Ng, 2010)? How can the pedagogical designs in the National Excellent Courses be adapted to the particulars of an immediate instructional context (Ye, 2011)? Do we create unnecessary binaries underpinned by seemingly opposing scientific concepts, and deprive ourselves of the opportunities to explore pedagogical possibilities that accommodate conceptual dissonance?

Finally, we need to train (future and present) teachers to be sensitive to and skillful in managing contextual constraints, and promote teachers' (critical) awareness and use of resources as situated possibilities for concept development. Due to logistical constraints, we were unable to triangulate the participants' reported use of contextual resources with their teaching practices. Future research can focus on how teachers perceive, evaluate and negotiate different resources, and examine their negotiation of contextual resources, concept development and classroom practices. These findings can inform English writing education programs on how to train teachers to be agentive, reflective and critical users of contextual resources, prepare them to be sensitive and adaptive to the ever-changing pedagogical contexts, and enable them to 'materialize and enact theoretically and pedagogically sound instructional practices within the instructional contexts in which they work' (Johnson, 2015: 516).

References

Borg, M. (2004) The apprenticeship of observation. *ELT Journal* 58 (3), 274–276.

Carson, J.G. and Nelson, G.L. (1996) Chinese students' perceptions of ESL peer response group interaction. *Journal of Second Language Writing* 5 (1), 1–19.

Ding, Y. and Liu, H. (2011) Exploring the application of 'project method' to English writing instruction: On the publication of Writing as Communication (Books 5–6). *Foreign Language World* 2, 11–13.

Farrell, T.S.C. (2007) *Reflective Practice for Language Teachers: From Research to Practice*. London: Continuum.

FLTRP (2017) Exploring writing pedagogies and paper writing: Jinan workshop on English teaching and research. See http://teacher.unipus.cn/workshopnew/detail.php?WorkshopID=365.

Hirvela, A. and Belcher, D. (2007) Writing scholars as teacher educators: Exploring writing teacher education. *Journal of Second Language Writing* 16 (3), 125–128.

Howe, A.C. (1996) Development of science concepts within a Vygotskian framework. *Science Education* 80 (1), 35–51.

Hu, G. and Lam, S.T.E. (2010) Issues of cultural appropriateness and pedagogical efficacy: Exploring peer review in a second language writing class. *Instructional Science* 38 (4), 371–394.

Hyland, K. (2007) Genre pedagogy: Language, literacy and L2 writing instruction. *Journal of Second Language Writing* 16 (3), 148–164.

Jay, J.K. and Johnson, K.L. (2002) Capturing complexity: A typology of reflective practice for teacher education. *Teaching and Teacher Education* 18 (1), 73–85.

Johnson, K.E. (2009) *Second Language Teacher Education: A Sociocultural Perspective*. New York: Routledge.

Johnson, K.E. (2015) Reclaiming the relevance of L2 teacher education. *The Modern Language Journal* 99 (3), 515–528.

Johnson, K.E. and Arshavskaya, E. (2011) Reconceptualizing the micro-teaching simulation in an MA TESL course. In K.E. Johnson and P.R. Golombek (eds) *Research on Second Language Teacher Education: A Sociocultural Perspective on Professional Development* (pp. 168–186). New York: Routledge.

Johnson, K.E. and Golombek, P.R. (eds) (2011) *Research on Second Language Teacher Education: A Sociocultural Perspective on Professional Development*. New York: Routledge.

Lantolf, J.P. (2009) Knowledge of language in foreign language teacher education. *The Modern Language Journal* 93 (2), 270–274.

Lortie, D. (1975) *Schoolteacher: A Sociological Study*. Chicago: University of Chicago Press.

MOE (Ministry of Education) (2003) Notice of the Ministry of Education on starting the construction of excellent courses for teaching quality and teaching reform in higher education. See http://old.moe.gov.cn//publicfiles/business/htmlfiles/moe/s3843/201010/109658.html.

Pennycook, A. (1994) Incommensurable discourses? *Applied Linguistics* 15 (2), 115–138.

Reichelt, M. (2009) A critical evaluation of writing teaching programmes in different foreign language settings. In R. Manchón (ed.) *Writing in Foreign Language Contexts: Learning, Teaching, and Research* (pp. 183–206). Bristol: Multilingual Matters.

Richards, J.C. and Lockhart, C. (1996) *Reflective Teaching in Second Language Classrooms*. Cambridge: Cambridge University Press.

Ruecker, T. (2011) Challenging the native and nonnative English speaker hierarchy in ELT: New directions from race theory. *Critical Inquiry in Language Studies* 8 (4), 400–422.

Sampson, G.P. (1984) Exporting language teaching methods from Canada to China. *TESL Canada Journal* 1 (1), 19–32.

Shulman, L. (1987) Knowledge and teaching: Foundations of the new reform. *Harvard Educational Review* 57 (1), 1–23.

Sun, G. and Cheng, L. (2002) From context to curriculum: A case study of communicative language teaching in China. *TESL Canada Journal* 19, 67–86.

Swales, J. (1990) *Genre Analysis: English in Academic and Research Settings*. New York: Cambridge University Press.

Tsui, A.B. and Ng, M.M. (2010) Cultural contexts and situated possibilities in the teaching of second language writing. *Journal of Teacher Education* 61 (4), 364–375.

Ur, P. (2013) Language-teaching method revisited. *ELT Journal* 67 (4), 468–474.

Vygotsky, L. (1966) Play and its role in the mental development of the child. *Voprosy psikhologii* 12 (6), 62–76.

Vygotsky, L.S. (1987) Thinking and speech. In R.W. Rieber and A.S. Carton (eds) *The Collected Works of L.S. Vygotsky, Vol. 1. Problems of General Psychology* (trans. N. Minick) (pp. 39–285). New York: Plenum Press.

Wang, C. (2005) The length approach to foreign language learning. *China Foreign Language* 3, 45–49.

Wang, C., Niu, R. and Zheng, X. (2000) Improving English through writing. *Foreign Language Teaching and Research* 3, 207–212.

Worden, D. (2015) Developing writing concepts for teaching purposes: Preservice L2 writing teachers' developing conceptual understanding of parallelism. *Journal of Second Language Writing* 30, 19–30.

Ye, H. (2011) Contextual deconstruction and reconstruction: A postmodernist critical framework for the 'Write to Learn' Approach. *Modern Foreign Languages* 34 (4), 420–426.

You, X. (2004) 'The choice made from no choice': English writing instruction in a Chinese university. *Journal of Second Language Writing* 13 (2), 97–110.

You, X. (2010) *Writing in the Devil's Tongue: A History of English Composition in China*. Carbondale, IL: Southern Illinois University Press.

You, X. (2016) Historical knowledge and reinventing English writing teacher identity in Asia. *Writing & Pedagogy* 8 (3), 409–431.

Young, R.E. (1978) Paradigms and problems: Needed research in rhetorical invention. In C. Cooper and L. Odell (eds) *Research on Composing* (pp. 29–47). Urbana, IL: National Council of Teachers of English.

4 Factors Influencing English as a Foreign Language (EFL) Writing Instruction in Japan from a Teacher Education Perspective

Keiko Hirose and Chris Harwood

Introduction

Japan has a long and complicated history of neglect regarding English as a foreign language (EFL) writing instruction in secondary and tertiary education. This is due, in large part, to the perception by teachers, students and other key stakeholders that writing instruction is too time consuming and extraneous to student needs. These perceptions regarding English writing have been influenced greatly by the educational policies of the country, and the local constraints English teachers face in trying to implement these policies. In order to meet the challenges faced by and needs of second language (L2) writing teacher education it is necessary to understand the severe impact of these policies and constraints on the English teachers in Japan's high schools and universities.

This chapter presents a comprehensive overview of the context of English writing instruction in Japan by reviewing prior research on English writing practices and teacher education. More specifically, the chapter focuses on three key factors that influence the teaching and learning of English writing in secondary schools and subsequently tertiary education: (a) the Japanese Ministry of Education, Culture, Sports, Science and Technology (MEXT) Course of Study (CoS), (b) university entrance examinations, and (c) local constraints of English writing practices (for example, class size and teacher workload) especially at secondary school level, from the viewpoint of teacher education. As shown in Figure 4.1, these three factors are interrelated and are discussed throughout the chapter.

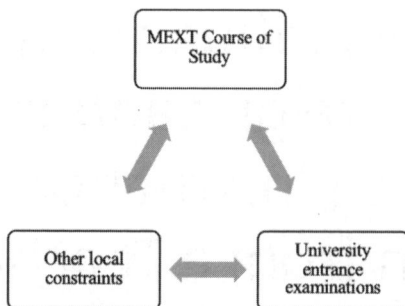

Figure 4.1 Key factors influencing writing practices in Japan

To situate English writing instruction in Japan, the chapter begins by providing an overview of the Japanese English education context and examines the MEXT CoS. Next, the washback from the university entrance examination system is explored, and its impact on the teaching of written English and teacher education is considered. This is followed by a review of the other local constraints faced by Japanese teachers of English (JTE). Finally, the chapter discusses the potential impacts of the new MEXT CoS alongside the changes to the university entrance examination and the implications of these changes on teaching writing and teacher education, providing recommendations for future writing practices and teacher education.

English Education and English Writing in Japan

The English proficiency of the Japanese is notoriously low. According to TOEFL iBT 2018 score data, the Japanese ranked third from bottom for total scores, second from bottom for writing scores and at the bottom for speaking scores in Asia (Educational Testing Service, 2019). Despite these figures, there has been an increase in the use of English in Japan's business communities. For example, Rakuten and Fast Retailing (a parent company of the international clothing retail chain Uniqlo) employ English as the in-house official language and conduct business meetings and correspondence in English. Other Japanese companies such as Honda have announced plans to do the same. However, social interactions in English are generally limited in everyday life in Japan.

A recent nationwide survey on Japanese secondary students' perceptions towards English revealed a gap between students' perceived social needs for the use of English and their personal needs for its use (Benesse Educational Research and Development Institute [hereafter Benesse], 2014). More specifically, the majority of secondary school students (90%) perceived that the Japanese would use English in the future, whereas approximately 50% did not perceive themselves as using English in their future. The gap between societal and individual needs for English was also found in JTE perceptions of social needs, as opposed to their students' personal needs, for English use (Benesse, 2016). It is also noteworthy that 90% of the student respondents in Benesse (2014) considered being able to speak English as 'cool,' which suggests that Japanese students may have a high level of motivation for learning to speak English. These findings concur with previous surveys of Japanese university students' views of studying English. For example, Koike *et al.* (1985) conducted a large-scale survey and found that 61% of university students wanted English speaking instruction, whereas only 3.1% wanted writing instruction (N=10,095). Existing survey results show that writing is the area that concerns Japanese students of English the least (see Hirose, 2005).

The Japanese students' low level of motivation for learning to write English displays a sharp contrast with learning to speak English. Therefore, a lack of need for English writing and low motivation characterize the Japanese context for English writing teaching. Although the perceived need for English writing proficiency remains peripheral for many students, the continued spread of English as a lingua franca necessitates that Japanese students now, more than ever, need to acquire written English skills to express themselves in personal social media interactions, academic term-papers and examinations, and future workplace communication such as emails and materials for meetings.

Writing has never been center stage in English language teaching in Japan, where the grammar-translation method has traditionally been used (Nishino, 2011). Surveys conducted over the past four decades (e.g. Hirota *et al.*, 1993; Yasuda, 2014) show that Japanese students' English writing instruction history is characterized as follows: (a) translation from Japanese to English; (b) accuracy-focused writing to learn vocabulary and structures; and (c) limited opportunities for students to produce their own ideas and thoughts in English. When writing is used in English classrooms it is employed as a service activity, i.e. practice/reinforcement of structures and vocabulary learned. Translation from Japanese to English at the sentence level is still a familiar activity in Japanese high school classrooms (Yasuda, 2014). Classes dedicated to English writing per se do not usually occur until students enter university, and writing courses are not required for most university students.

Furthermore, the writing activities in university classrooms do not seem to be substantially different from those mentioned above. Examining Japanese students' English writing instruction backgrounds, Yasuda (2014) conducted a survey for second year university students (N=481) and found that 'writing on a given topic using a paragraph consisting of several sentences' (Yasuda, 2014: 166) was the most frequently experienced writing activity and writing summaries of materials read was the most frequent genre. Writing term papers and reports was highly limited in their English writing experience.

A cross-country survey of tertiary English writing teachers' beliefs and practices in the Asia-Pacific region found that English teachers working in Japanese higher education perceived the biggest gap between the realities and their ideal views of teaching, suggesting that the local constraints were more severe than in other countries (see Pennington *et al.*, 1997). For example, the teachers in Japan employed process-oriented writing pedagogies such as peer feedback the least. This is partly because those teachers are not necessarily specialized in or familiar with English writing teaching.

Subsequently, JTEs in both secondary and tertiary education have little instructional English writing experience, not to mention training in English writing instruction. Hirose (2007) examined Japanese graduate students' perceptions of the English writing instruction they had received as undergraduates. All the participants of the study had an English teacher's license at secondary school level and their mean year of university English writing instruction was 1.47 years. In other words, they had taken an English writing course once a week for one and a half years. The participants reported having almost never experienced such writing procedures as pre-writing activities (e.g. brainstorming and discussion of topics), peer feedback and teacher–student conferences. Most of the participants majored in English education in the Faculty of Education, although students of other majors can obtain an English teacher's license in Japan.

As has been discussed in this section, the Japanese English writing teaching and learning context is characterized by discord. This discord appears to be closely related to such macro factors as national English education policy decisions made by MEXT and university entrance examinations in Japan.

The MEXT Course of Study

The MEXT CoS guidelines describe national English education policies in Japan. The guidelines explain the overall objectives for English teaching in secondary school education and specific goals for each subject area of English as well as a brief overview of the contents and how they should be treated. There are, however, no national guidelines for English teaching at tertiary level. The MEXT guidelines have a great influence on actual teaching practices in the Japanese classroom at the secondary school level. Furthermore, MEXT-approved textbooks are written in tandem with the guidelines and these textbooks heavily influence how teachers organize their classes. It takes several years to implement a revised CoS after it has been officially announced.

The first CoS was announced in 1947, and in 1958 the CoS, with legal influence over textbook production and curriculum organization, was announced by the Minister of Education. The guidelines are revised approximately every 10 years, as MEXT attempts to incorporate new ideas and practices into education that consider social changes as well as changes to student circumstances, which have occurred since the previous CoS was introduced.[1]

The course of study for English education

Although a number of changes have been made to the objectives and contents of English education in the guidelines, over the three decades the revision of CoS for English teaching has been oriented to the communicative approach. The 1989 version used the word 'communication' for the first time in its overall objectives and included the statement that foreign language education should foster a positive attitude towards communication through foreign languages (MEXT, 1989). In response to advances in internationalization, the following CoS version went further, stating that education should develop practical communication abilities in its overall objectives (MEXT, 1999). This version was then implemented from 2003 at high school level, and in 2003 MEXT issued a five-year 'action plan to cultivate Japanese with English abilities' (MEXT, 2003), and the plan was implemented between 2003 and 2008 (see Butler & Iino, 2005, for a critical examination of the plan).

The action plan set the goals of 'English language abilities required for all Japanese people,' not only for students but also for JTEs to improve communication abilities. To improve English education, the plan set specific score objectives for English teachers to attain in external proficiency examinations: TOEIC 730, TOEFL PBT 550, Eiken[2] grade pre-first level or over. For achieving these goals, the plan included in-service intensive training for *all* English teachers in Japan to improve their English abilities and teaching skills in order to conduct English classes to realize the objectives of English education. The training was planned and operated by each local government board of education, and its content as well as its period differed according to its organizing body. Although MEXT funded the training, it was discontinued after five years. Questions need to be asked as to the effectiveness of the training. Regarding JTE general English proficiency levels, according to the most recent data (MEXT, 2019), 68.2% of high school English teachers have achieved the set goals; concerning the use of English, 12.5% of them conduct English classes in English over 75% of the class time and 38% use English 50–75% of the class time. However, these data do not disclose the teaching methods actually employed to conduct these English classes. Both JTE English proficiencies and the ratio of English use in Japanese classrooms are on the rise, although these test results did not specifically show that teachers had improved their English writing proficiency.

The advent of communicative language teaching (CLT) has resulted in writing taking a back seat in English classrooms because both teachers and students are preoccupied with oral, rather than written, communication abilities. The current 2009 version of the CoS refers to writing in one of the objectives of English teaching as follows: 'To develop students' communication abilities such as accurately understanding and appropriately conveying information, ideas, etc.' (MEXT, 2009: 1). Subsequently, the next high school CoS was announced in 2018 and will be due in 2022 (MEXT, 2018).

The current and the next CoS for secondary school English teaching promote the enhancement of communication abilities and specifically advise integrative teaching of the four skills (listening, speaking, reading and writing). The next CoS also emphasizes developing productive skills (speaking and writing). Furthermore, the guidelines espouse the principal use of English as the medium of instruction in English classes and active learning, through the employment of student-centered activities. Active learning is defined by MEXT as 'proactive and cooperative learning and instruction methods focusing on the discovery and resolution of issues' (MEXT, 2014: 2).

The course of study guidelines and textbooks for English writing

The guidelines for writing instruction and its contents are a list of statements about what to teach, not how to teach. The following statements are examples from the present guidelines for high school level writing (the 2009-released CoS):

- Writing brief passages on information, ideas, etc., based on what one has heard, read, learned and experienced.
- Writing coherent and cohesive passages on information, ideas, etc. based on what one has heard, read, learned and experienced.
- Writing brief passages in a style suitable for the audience and purpose.
- Writing with due attention to phrases and sentences indicating the main points, connecting phrases, etc. and reviewing one's own writing.

Although these statements are comprehensible, they are quite abstract and vague. With no models or guidance given, they are open to interpretation. For example, 'writing brief passages in a style suitable for the audience and purpose' does not provide guidance regarding the content, context, length or genre of writing. Furthermore, the guidelines do not provide JTEs with techniques or methodological suggestions to facilitate their students practicing this type of writing. Nor do they appear to consider the many local constraints JTEs face regarding the implementation of these practices. Without guidance, teachers are prone to rely on textbooks that have been designed to adhere to the guidelines and approved by MEXT.

Nevertheless, past studies reveal that the textbooks appear to encourage or reproduce translation and drill instructional methods. For instance, Kobayakawa (2011) analyzed the English textbooks designed for writing classes reflecting the guidelines in the 1999 CoS.[3] The writing tasks in all of the textbooks she analyzed were dominated by translation and controlled practice activities. Translation comprised the largest percentage (41.42%), followed by controlled writing (e.g. conversion, sentence-combining, reordering; 33.18%), free composition (13.10%) and guided writing (e.g. fill-in-the-blank without translation, question-answer; 6.93%), implying that students' English writing experiences are limited. The results also showed that the writing tasks did not require students to write for an audience or revise their compositions.

In another study, Gorsuch (1999) analyzed activities in six MEXT-approved high school textbooks (four-skill integrated subjects) to examine whether or not the textbook activities included an explicit call for students: (a) to exchange information; (b) to use language according to their own purposes (i.e. unscripted language); and (c) to focus on meaning beyond the sentence level. Gorsuch found that none of the reviewed activities contained either one of them and concluded that 'the textbooks are a hindrance to teachers who want to teach students how to communicate in English' (Gorsuch, 1999: 9). Furthermore, every textbook has 'a teacher's manual that has detailed lesson plans emphasizing translation and drill-focused teaching techniques' (Browne & Wada, 1998: 105), with little or no time given to the teaching of writing. If teachers use such textbooks they take on the demanding task of adapting activities to make them communicative or of creating writing activities on their own.

Inconsistencies between the course of study guidelines and writing instruction

Despite the expected influence of the CoS, discrepancies have been noticed between the objectives and the actual practices of English education (e.g. Yoshida, 2003). Past surveys have revealed Japanese students reporting not having experienced the kind of teaching proposed by the CoS, including those of English writing (e.g. Benesse, 2014; Kikuchi & Browne, 2009; O'Donnell, 2005). Examining student perceptions of classroom pedagogies, Kikuchi and Browne (2009) found a substantial gap between the MEXT guidelines and actual teaching practices. They found that 'students didn't feel that the goals of the CoS Guidelines were being effectively implemented by their teachers in the classroom' (Kikuchi & Browne, 2009: 187). As for the writing classes, they reported: 'not one of the communicative objectives related to writing was actually being implemented in the classroom' (Kikuchi & Browne, 2009: 187). Regarding what was actually implemented in the classroom, students' open-ended responses indicate that the primary focus of the writing classes was 'the memorization of grammatical structures and long explanations by the teacher on usage' (Kikuchi & Browne, 2009: 187). A more recent Benesse survey (2014) showed that Japanese students rarely have to write English passages related to what they have heard, read, learned and experienced, for example (recall this is one of the writings specified by the guidelines quoted above). Therefore, although the guidelines have a significant role in English education, they seem to play a very limited role in what actually happens in Japanese school classrooms.

This mismatch between the MEXT guidelines and actual writing instruction practices is not new. JTE implementation of CLT has suffered a similar fate (Humphries & Burns, 2015). Although more than two decades have passed since the endorsement of CLT in the CoS, most JTEs still revert to what they are most familiar with, the grammar-translation method, and perceive CLT as unattainable (e.g. Nishino, 2011; O'Donnell, 2005; Sakui, 2004). Examining JTE beliefs about and practices of CLT, Nishino (2011) found a gap between their positive beliefs about and inconsequential use of CLT. A lack of confidence in implementing CLT, a lack of practical training in CLT, non-optimal classroom conditions such as class size, and a lack of exposure to CLT in their own education were regarded as reasons for the substantial gap. This last point is particularly salient. The fact that JTEs have similar classroom experiences to their students means that they lack experience with CLT themselves and cannot draw on their own experiences as students in their teaching practices. This is a significant factor in the grammar-translation method continuing to be the established teaching method in Japanese secondary schools (O'Donnell, 2005). As Tahira (2012) reasons, the mismatch between the proposed guidelines and the actual practices is due to the lack of commitment by MEXT to provide support and training for JTEs.

Not surprisingly, various survey results have shown that JTEs have found it difficult to embrace the MEXT guidelines. For example, the Benesse (2016) nationwide survey of teacher perceptions revealed JTE lack of confidence in implementing the kind of English teaching recommended by the CoS. Practicing JTEs have voiced their concerns over the application of teaching practices advised in the guidelines, as well as their need to receive teacher training for writing instruction, along with speaking instruction and integrated four-skills teaching. The survey also found that over 70% of JTEs felt torn between the need to develop students' communication abilities and to prepare them for entrance exams. A major problem lies in the fact that university entrance exams do not directly test productive skills.

The University Entrance Examination System

While there are basically two types of university entrance examination in Japan – the national test and individual university tests – the system is very complex. Under the purview of MEXT, the National Center Test for University Admissions (known locally as the Center Test) is produced by the National Center for University Entrance Examinations (NCUEE). In cooperation with participating universities, it is administered at over 700 sites throughout Japan on the same days, using the same test items. The Center Test is a computer-scored test of multiple-choice questions. Each year approximately half a million students take the Center Test, which includes an English test with written and listening components. It is a very high stakes exam because national, public and private universities all use the test scores to filter applicants. Although students generally have to take the Center Test to obtain admission to national and public universities, those who apply for private universities can often take individual university tests only.

The university entrance English examinations in Japan

The English component of the Center Test focuses on reading and listening skills, with writing restricted to word order rearrangement tasks (Watanabe, 2016). The exam is used by universities to vet course applicants, usually in conjunction with an interview and/or another local exam prepared by the specific university the applicant has applied to. The local university exams are prepared by the professors at the individual universities. They typically consist of reading texts with multiple-choice and cloze items which are designed to test grammatical, lexical and reading comprehension and the relationships between different parts of the text. There are also likely to be separate grammar, lexis and translation questions (Kitao & Kitao, 2014). In addition, these exams sometimes have writing components including free composition, conditional composition and summary writing (Watanabe, 2016).

Examination washback on English teaching and learning

Over the last 20 years the effects of the Center Test on teaching and learning (washback) in Japanese high schools have been periodically discussed. A number of studies argue that the university entrance examinations greatly influence the teaching and learning of English in Japanese high school classes. High school English classes conducted by JTEs tend to be university entrance examination oriented and focused on receptive skills (reading and listening) or translation skills (Brown & Yamashita, 1995; Kikuchi, 2006; Kikuchi & Browne, 2009). Consequently, they give little attention to productive skills such as speaking and writing (Brown & Yamashita, 1995; Butler & Iino, 2005).

On the other hand, in his preliminary study of the washback of the Center Test, Watanabe (1996) suggests that the Japanese university entrance exam washback on JTE teaching practices is limited, and that teachers' educational histories, personal beliefs and teaching experience play a more important role in their classroom pedagogy. He argues that because of this, even if question and task types were changed, it would not necessarily result in teachers changing their teaching practices. Indeed, studies have highlighted that changes to the Center Test do not always have the intended consequences on teaching and learning. For instance, Sage and Tanaka (2006) found that, although the introduction of the listening component to the Center Test in 2006 may have promoted more listening and speaking instruction in Japanese high school classrooms, there were issues with the construct validity of the multiple-choice questions in the listening exam. They concluded that the exam was an unreliable measure of listening proficiency.

Although some local university exams do have productive writing components, the positive washback on the writing task appears to be negligible. Kowata's (2015) comprehensive doctoral thesis on the 'washback effects of university entrance examination writing tasks on learning and teaching' investigated 239 local entrance exams administered at 177 universities in 2007.[4] The results found about half (48.1%) of the exams had no writing components, whereas 29.3% had free composition, 28.9% translation from Japanese to English, and 2.5% summary writing. Of the free composition writing tasks, 80% were of essay type, with examinees required to state and to clarify the writer's opinions, although they were not required to write for a specific audience. Furthermore, only 11% of the writing exams provided English texts for reading, whereas listening was not integrated at all. Regarding the quantity of free composition, 31.8% set a word limit of 100 words and 44.4% less than 100 words.

Subsequently, Watanabe (2016) analyzed 50 writing tasks (free compositions) in the university entrance exams in 2013 and found only a limited range of micro-genres (i.e. expositions, personal reflections, discussions and sequential explanations). Kowata (2015) also found writing composition was not integrated into the high school curricula. The 33 freshman students he interviewed began preparing for the writing component of the university entrance exam in the third grade of high school, and they usually studied at cram schools (known locally as *yobikos* or *jukus*), in supplementary classes at their high schools or at home. The extracurricular writing study usually involved the students producing a text, and the teacher correcting the text. No other exercises or writing practices were employed to help students improve their writing skills. Negative washback of this kind is well documented. Leki, Cumming and Silva (2010) provide an accessible and comprehensive review of the research and argue that if 'tests define the construct of L2 writing too narrowly or simply, they may elicit pedagogical practices, or even coaching, that simply involve test preparation rather than legitimate writing development' (Leki *et al.*, 2010: 90). These issues and lack of attention towards writing in

Japanese school classrooms are also the result of the constraints JTEs face when planning and conducting their English classes.

Other Local Constraints

Local factors that influence the teaching and learning of English writing include teacher training, time and resources, class size, and established attitudes and motivation towards L2 writing (Hyland & Hyland, 2006; Leki, 2001). Previous research has identified these constraints in English writing contexts in Asia and Europe (e.g. Lee, 2008; Reichelt, 2005; You, 2004). English writing instructors have to modify their pedagogic practices to accommodate such contextual constraints. There are a large number of local constraints that impact the amount and quality of writing instruction in Japan. Chief among these are class size, the lack of JTE teacher training in English writing, and student (de)motivation.

Class size and time management

Japanese classes usually have a maximum of 40 students of mixed-level proficiencies in each class, and this has long been considered a critical issue in the teaching of English in Japan (see Nishino, 2008). From a JTE perspective, the central problem large class sizes cause is the impact that the number of students has on the teacher's time. This is because marking and providing feedback on students' written work is labor intensive, particularly for busy teachers who often have additional school responsibilities and duties such as managing a homeroom class, supervising club activities and preparing for school events such as culture festivals. All these problems are also shared by teachers of L1 Japanese writing (Kobayashi, 2002).

The consequences of teachers being overloaded with work are that they spend less time on lesson preparation and therefore are less likely to seek professional development (Browne & Wada, 1998; Nishino, 2008). A survey conducted by Kowata (2015) revealed a link between the busyness of JTE schedules and the paucity of writing instruction. Completed by 129 JTEs in 33 high schools in Japan, the survey revealed that many teachers had little time to provide instruction for university entrance exam writing tasks.

JTE teaching and learning culture

The issues of class size and time management are compounded by the school learning culture and professional development activities for JTEs in many Japanese high schools. For example, in their one-year qualitative study into the beliefs and practices of JTEs in a private high school in Japan, Sato and Kleinsasser (2004) found that most teachers were heavily influenced by their personal experiences of learning English and teaching. This is problematic because most Japanese learn English through grammar-translation, and pre-service JTE teacher training usually takes place at the school the teacher attended as a student. In many instances, this initial training involves not only observing how classes are taught but also being mentored by the teacher who taught the practicing student teacher. This apprenticeship model for teacher training is flawed because experienced teachers generally mentor the novice teachers with the moribund teaching practices that were handed down to them in their initial teacher training. This has led to a cyclical pattern of novice teachers observing their own high school teachers and being socialized into the grammar-translation methods and exam-orientated classes they experienced as students. Moreover, there is a strong pressure to adhere to the existing teaching practices and routines in Japanese schools (O'Donnell, 2005). If novice teachers do not conform to the expectations and norms of their school culture they are likely to make their workplaces awkward, which in turn may impede their career development (Cook, 2010; Sato & Kleinsasser, 2004).

Indeed, in her longitudinal study of the effects of in-service teacher education, Cook (2010) found that the MEXT-sponsored high school JTEs who studied CLT in Canada abandoned many of the new methods and practices they had learned when faced with the constraints of teaching in Japanese high schools. The teachers reverted to traditional teaching methods such as grammar-translation because of 'a perceived need to conform to the practices of colleagues' (Cook, 2010: 60). Similar observations are made by Casanave (2009), who described how working JTEs who studied in a US university TESOL graduate program reacted to such methods as communicative and process-oriented teaching, in other words, their dilemmas of not being able to apply the newly learned methodological ideas in the local realities of Japanese classrooms.

Student motivation towards English learning

These local constraints impact student motivation. Kikuchi's (2009) study of the factors that demotivate Japanese high school students found that the grammar-translation method, lessons that focused on tests and university entrance examinations, the rote learning of lexis, and dated, uninteresting and incomprehensible textbooks all demotivated students studying English. Hamada's (2011) study concurs with Kikuchi's findings and stresses the impact these demotivators have on student self-confidence, and especially how poor test results can increase student anxiety and demotivate them 'more than being unable to understand lessons or English' (Hamada, 2011: 32).

Clearly, the university entrance exam exerts a strong influence over the learning of English in Japan. It provides students with English learning aims and objectives and, because passing the entrance exam can open the door to other opportunities, many students invest heavily in their English studies. In short, as Yoshida (2003) notes, the exam provides a motivation to study English. Next, changes to the entrance exam and its possible impacts on teaching English, especially writing, are examined.

The Future: Changes to the University Entrance Examination

Japan's university entrance exam system is currently being reassessed and large-scale reforms regarding the exam's content will be introduced in the 2020 academic year. These proposed reforms are intended to disrupt the status quo of English education in Japan. The new national Center Test (now referred to as the University Entrance Common Test) will include new English exams to measure productive skills in addition to receptive skills, in order to make the assessment congruent with the CoS objectives. Importantly, the new English university examination system requires universities to shift their focus away from individual reading and listening test components towards an integrated four-skills test. In 2017 MEXT announced that, transitionally from the 2020–2023 academic years, NCUEE will continue to produce a computer-scored test of multiple-choice questions of reading and listening, just like the present Center Test. In addition, to test students' speaking and writing skills, MEXT will allow universities to make use of the scores of external commercial English examinations such as Eiken, TOEFL iBT and IELTS. From 2024 onwards, however, only certified external English exam scores considered to be consistent with the CoS will be used.

Proposed English writing tests

In order to illustrate the impact of the proposed new English exam on writing instruction, it is useful to consider the proposed new writing component for the exams. One certified exam worthy of consideration is the new Test of English for Academic Purposes (TEAP) because it is specifically tailored for Japanese university entrants. The exam is currently being redesigned to support the next MEXT CoS due in 2022, which proposes an ambitious shift in teaching methodology towards active learning. It is proposed that there will be two writing tasks in the new TEAP exam (Weir, 2014). The first task, which is designed for most examinees, is likely to include summarizing a critique or an expository text in approximately 70 words and is expected to be accessible to and achievable by students with a B1 Common European Framework of Reference (CEFR) assessment level of proficiency (see Table 4.1).

The second task is expected to be accessible to and achievable by students with a B2 CEFR assessment level of proficiency (see Table 4.1) and will be designed to 'discriminate among high-level test takers as

Table 4.1 CEFR descriptors for writing assessment proficiency B1 and B2

B1 Writing	B2 Writing
• I can write simple connected text on topics which are familiar or of personal interest. • I can write personal letters describing experiences and impressions.	• I can write clear, detailed text on a wide range of subjects related to my interests. • I can write an essay or report, passing on information or giving reasons in support of or against a particular point of view. • I can write letters highlighting the personal significance of events and experiences.

Source: CEFR (https://www.coe.int/en/web/language-policy/home).

appropriate for the future TEAP test-taker population. The second task would be at this higher level but it still should be accessible to candidates at the B1 level' (Weir, 2014: 10). It is likely to involve reading multiple texts, graphs and charts, summarizing main points and writing a 200-word opinion essay (Eiken Foundation of Japan, n.d.). These changes have significant implications for students' and teachers' perceptions of the role and importance of English writing instruction in the curricula of compulsory and subsequent tertiary education. Teachers will have to prepare students for these types of writing. Students will have a concrete reason to focus on their writing and may see the value of writing instruction intended to prepare them for these tasks. For the first time, JTEs will be required (as a minimum) to provide instruction on summary writing, which will include differentiating between important information and minor details, taking notes and identifying key supporting points, as well as how to use synonyms, referents and cohesive devices, all while listening to and reading related English texts.

There are a large number of pedagogic challenges for JTEs in responding to the new exam changes. The changes are intended to provide opportunities for improved English writing instruction and learning; however, they could actually provide greater obstacles given the considerable constraints teachers will have in implementing them. In order to turn the changes into opportunities, the constraints of class size, time and current teacher training practices will need to be addressed. How are the tens of thousands of JTEs going to be trained how to teach English writing, and above all in English? Who is going to train the teachers to teach this integrated skills approach to writing? Which active learning writing instruction methods will be employed? Will the chosen writing methods incorporate strategies to alleviate the constraints? How do JTEs already overloaded with work find time to introduce and manage writing instruction for classes of 40 students used to a teacher-fronted transmission method of learning? How do they cope with the increased workload of providing feedback on written compositions? There are no easy answers to these questions, particularly when many JTEs are lacking in confidence regarding their own English abilities (Benesse, 2016). Although the structural and institutional changes of the kind required by the new university entrance examination may be difficult to implement, they must be addressed in order to actualize the objectives. Sufficient teacher training will hold the key to achieving the objectives.

JTE teacher training

The current structure and process of JTE teacher training programs have fundamental drawbacks for the wide-scale introduction of radical English curriculum changes that include integrating writing with other skills and the introduction of summary writing instruction and practice. Generally, trainee JTEs are often English literature or linguistics majors who are not normally required to take courses in ESL/EFL methodology, second language acquisition theory or language assessment (Browne & Wada, 1998; Lamie, 2001; Nagasawa, 2004). Moreover, although a small minority of teacher trainers at Japanese universities have international postgraduate qualifications in EFL and applied linguistics, many JTE teacher training programs have required courses that are taught in Japanese by unlicensed teachers, with little knowledge or experience of contemporary language learning practices and methods (Nagasawa, 2004; Nagatomo, 2011). In fact, because many of these teachers have had the same English education as the students they teach, most teacher trainers and in-service teachers have had little experience in writing texts of the kind needed for the new exam themselves.

Even though we are now in a post-process era (Atkinson, 2003), process writing approaches have yet to become widespread in Japanese classrooms (Hirose, 2007). However, a number of studies have been conducted assessing the suitability of process writing instruction methods with Japanese high school and university students. For example, Andrews (2016) reported the positive effects of process-oriented writing instruction with Japanese high school students, noting how his students became actively engaged in their writing and perceived it as relevant and meaningful. Indeed, the use of peer feedback is becoming more common and its effects are being investigated in university and high school classrooms (e.g. Kamimura, 2006; Kurihara, 2014). Previous studies seem to consistently indicate the positive effects of peer feedback on revisions. After comparing compositions before and after peer feedback, Kamimura (2006) revealed improvements in both high- and low-proficiency Japanese university students' English writing. Exploring the effects of written-plus-spoken peer feedback in English, Hirose (2012) found students enhanced their motivation and engagement in English writing in addition to improving both in quantity and overall quality after a semester-long writing course. Examining the effects of self-regulated learning strategy instruction on writing revision, Tando (2015) found the instruction had rich possibilities for facilitating the writing process and enhancing the ability of

English writing revision by Japanese university students. These studies examining the effects of new writing pedagogies suggest that they could be introduced and utilized more widely in Japanese high school and university classes. The use of other current writing pedagogies in the Japanese EFL context such as the genre approach (Yasuda, 2011) and collaborative writing (Storch, 2013) should also be developed and exploited.

Implications for Teacher Education

This chapter has detailed the current context of English writing teaching in Japan as well as the coming changes and considered how the constraints and challenges could impact writing teacher education in the country. The new CoS and changes to the university entrance system are an opportunity to reconfigure the teaching and learning of English, particularly English writing. Evidently, JTEs require extensive training in the teaching of writing, but first they need to be able to demonstrate their own writing ability and practice in English. In order to carry out the changes in the next CoS it is essential that JTEs be provided with professional development opportunities in order to gain experience of writing for a purpose and audience themselves. Such experience is crucial as it will inform how teachers interpret the English writing guidelines of the CoS as well as their assessments of the writing needs of their students. Moreover, professional development opportunities should be facilitated by highly trained writing instructors who use (model) writing instruction methods that epitomize how the objectives of English writing teaching guidelines in the new CoS can be achieved. This will enable JTEs to experience the pedagogic value of the kind of writing instruction they will be asked to use from a student perspective, as well as to provide a foundation from which to build their own understanding of new instructional methods and techniques.

JTEs face monumental new challenges to teach writing practices integrated with other skills in English. The proposed pedagogical shift from teacher-fronted grammar-translation to student-centered active learning requires teachers to reconceptualize English writing teaching as 'dialogic mediation' (Johnson, 2009). In order to support their students' writing development, JTEs require theoretical and practical training in the purpose and use of appropriate English writing pedagogies. The efficacy of English use in writing instruction should be justified to the teachers. The use of peer feedback and revision, which has been shown to be effective in Japanese EFL classrooms, should be exploited. Feedback practices should move away from dominant instruction techniques that emphasize grammar error correction towards content-based comments that support students through the drafting and review processes. However, new methods and techniques need to acknowledge the contextual constraints of class size, teacher workload and student proficiency and motivation, and be adapted accordingly to find their rightful place in the Japanese EFL writing classes. How this last crucial point is achieved is uncertain, but these issues must be thought through prior to the introduction of the new CoS, if it is to be successful.

The challenges described above will not be met unless teacher training is ongoing. The teaching and learning culture of JTEs has to become more dynamic and flexible. JTEs have to share best practices, problems and other experiences regarding writing instruction in regular professional development workshops, seminars and conferences. In these professional development sessions new ideas and pedagogical experimentation have to be encouraged. The redeployment of existing resources could alleviate some constraints, for example. Since the introduction of CLT, the team teaching of JTEs and non-Japanese English speaking teachers known as assistant language teachers (ALTs) has been widespread in high school English oral communication classes in Japan. The role of ALTs in high schools could be increased to support the teaching of writing. This could ease the workload of JTEs, especially regarding feedback on student writing. However, ALTs would also require specialized writing teacher training, which would in turn require further commitment and investment from MEXT and the Japanese government.

Notes

(1) Therefore, teachers need to adapt to the new CoS and corresponding textbooks and curriculum every 10 years. It takes approximately five years to change the mentality of teachers to adapt to a new CoS and textbooks (K. Yoshida, personal communication, 10 June 2017).
(2) Eiken is a public-interest incorporated foundation in Tokyo, Japan. Eiken produces and administers English-proficiency tests to over 2 million test takers a year.
(3) The existing published studies concerning English textbooks and students' classroom experiences mostly provide information about those under the previous 1999 CoS, which was implemented during the previous 10 years from the first year students in 2003. The present CoS has been implemented since 2013.
(4) The number of exams exceeds that of universities because some universities prepare and administer multiple exams for applicants to different departments.

References

Andrews, R. (2016) Process writing and its relevance to Japanese high school students. In P. Clements, A. Krause and H. Brown (eds) *Focus on the Learner* (pp. 99–106). Tokyo: JALT.

Atkinson, D. (2003) Writing and culture in the post-process era. *Journal of Second Language Writing* 12, 49–63. doi:10.1016/S1060-3743(02)00126-1

Benesse Educational Research and Development Institute (2014) *Chûkoôsei no eigo gakushû ni kansuru jittai chôsa 2014 [Survey of Students' Views of English Language Learning at Junior and Senior High Schools in Japan 2014]*. See http://berd.benesse.jp/global/research/detail1.php?id=4356.

Benesse Educational Research and Development Institute (2016) *Chûkô no eigo shidô ni kansuru jittai chôsa 2015 [Survey of English Language Teaching at Junior and Senior High Schools in Japan 2015]*. See https://berd.benesse.jp/up_images/research/Eigo_Shido_all.pdf.

Brown, J.D. and Yamashita, S.O. (1995) English language tests at Japanese universities: What do we know about them? *JALT Journal* 17, 7–30.

Browne, C.M. and Wada, M. (1998) Current issues in high school English teaching in Japan: An exploratory survey. *Language, Culture and Curriculum* 11, 97–112. doi:10.1080/07908319808666543

Butler, Y.G. and Iino, M. (2005) Current Japanese reforms in English language education: The 2003 'Action Plan'. *Language Policy* 4, 25–45. doi:10.1007/s10993-004-6563-5

Casanave, C.P. (2009) Training for writing or training for reality? Challenges facing EFL writing teachers and students in language teacher education programs. In R.M. Manchón (ed.) *Writing in Foreign Language Contexts: Learning, Teaching, and Research* (pp. 256–277). Bristol: Multilingual Matters.

Cook, M. (2010) Offshore outsourcing teacher inservice education: The long-term effects of a four-month pedagogical program on Japanese teachers of English. *TESL Canada Journal* 28, 60–76. doi:10.18806/tesl.v28i1.1060

Educational Testing Service (2019) *Test and Score Data Summary for TOEFL iBT® Tests: January 2018–December 2018 Test Data*. See https://www.ets.org/s/toefl/pdf/toefl_tsds_data.pdf.

Eiken Foundation of Japan (n.d.) *Mondai kôsei [Sections of the TEAP]*. See http://www.eiken.or.jp/teap/construct/.

Gorsuch, G.J. (1999) Monbusho approved textbooks in Japanese high school EFL classes: An aid or a hindrance to educational policy innovations? *The Language Teacher* 23 (10), 5–15.

Hamada, Y. (2011) Different demotivators for Japanese junior high and high school learners. *Journal of Pan-Pacific Association of Applied Linguistics* 15, 15–38. See http://files.eric.ed.gov/fulltext/EJ939938.pdf.

Hirose, K. (2005) *Product and Process in the L1 and L2 Writing of Japanese Students of English*. Hiroshima: Keisuisha.

Hirose, K. (2007) Japanese EFL students' perceptions of English writing instruction compared with their ideal views. In *Studies in English Language Education: A Collection of Essays Published in Commemoration of Professor Shogo Miura's Retirement from Office* (pp. 33–52). Hiroshima: Nishiki Purinto.

Hirose, K. (2012) Comparing written-only and written-plus-spoken peer feedback in a Japanese EFL university context. *Asian Journal of English Language Teaching* 22, 1–23.

Hirota, T., Okada, T., Okumura, K. and Tokioka, Y. (1993) *Daigaku ni okeru eisakubun shidô no arikata: Eisakubun jittai chôsa no hôkoku [Writing Instruction at University: Survey of Students' Writing Experience]*. Osaka: JACET Kansai Chapter.

Humphries, S. and Burns, A. (2015) 'In reality it's almost impossible': CLT-oriented curriculum change. *ELT Journal* 69, 239–248. doi:10.1093/elt/ccu081

Hyland, K. and Hyland, F. (2006) Feedback on second language students' writing. *Language Teaching* 39, 83–101. doi:10.1017/S0261444806003399

Johnson, K. (2009) *Second Language Teacher Education: A Sociocultural Perspective*. New York: Routledge.

Kamimura, T. (2006) Effects of peer feedback on EFL student writers at different levels of English proficiency: A Japanese context. *TESL Canada Journal* 23, 12–39. doi:10.18806/tesl.v23i2.53

Kikuchi, K. (2006) Revisiting English entrance examinations at Japanese universities after a decade. *JALT Journal* 28, 77–96.

Kikuchi, K. (2009) Listening to our learners' voices: What demotivates Japanese high school students? *Language Teaching Research* 13, 453–471. doi:10.1177/1362168809341520

Kikuchi, K. and Browne, C. (2009) English educational policy for high schools in Japan: Ideals vs. reality. *RELC Journal* 40, 172–191. doi:10.1177/0033688209105865

Kitao, S.K. and Kitao, K. (2014) An analysis of Japanese university entrance exams using corpus-based tools. See http://www.jlet.org/~wcf/proceedings/d-053.pdf.

Kobayakawa, M. (2011) Analyzing tasks in Japanese high school writing textbooks. *Annual Review of English Language Education in Japan* 22, 137–152.

Kobayashi, H. (2002) L1 Japanese high school literacy training: Student and teacher perspectives. *Language and Culture Study (Hiroshima University, Integrated Arts and Sciences)* 28, 1–29.

Koike, I., Ando, S., Furukawa, S., *et al.* (1985) *Daigaku eigo kyôiku ni kansuru jittai to shôraizô no sôgôteki kenkyû (II): Gakusei no tachiba [General Survey of English Language Teaching at Colleges and Universities in Japan: Students' View].* Tokyo: Research Group for College English Teaching in Japan.

Kowata, T. (2015) Daigaku nyûsi ni okeru jiyûsakubun mondai no gakushû to shidô eno hakyûkôka [Washback effects of university entrance examination writing tasks on learning and teaching]. Unpublished doctoral dissertation, Tokyo University of Foreign Studies. See http://repository.tufs.ac.jp/bitstream/10108/80582/1/dt-ko-0191.pdf.

Kurihara, N. (2014) Adoption of the process-oriented writing approach in a Japanese high school classroom. *The Language Teacher* 38 (5), 31–36.

Lamie, J.M. (2001) *Understanding Change: The Impact of In-service Training on Teachers of English in Japan.* New York: Nova Science.

Lee, I. (2008) Understanding teachers' written feedback practices in Hong Kong secondary classrooms. *Journal of Second Language Writing* 17, 69–85. doi:10.1016/j.jslw.2007.10.001

Leki, I. (2001) Material, educational, and ideological challenges of teaching EFL writing at the turn of the century. *International Journal of English Studies* 1, 197–209.

Leki, I., Cumming, A. and Silva, T. (2010) *A Synthesis of Research on Second Language Writing in English.* New York: Routledge.

MEXT (1989) *Kôtô gakkô gakushû shidô yôryô [The Course of Study for Upper Secondary School].* See http://www.mext.go.jp/a_menu/shotou/old-cs/1322571.htm.

MEXT (1999) *Kôtô gakkô gakushû shidô yôryô [The Course of Study for Upper Secondary School].* See http://www.mext.go.jp/a_menu/shotou/cs/1320179.htm.

MEXT (2003) *'Eigo ga tsukaeru nihonjin' no ikusei no tame no kôdôkeikaku [Action Plan to Cultivate 'Japanese with English Abilities'].* See http://www.mext.go.jp/b_menu/shingi/chukyo/chukyo3/004/siryo/04031601/005.pdf.

MEXT (2009) English section of the course of study for upper secondary school (Temporary English version). See http://www.mext.go.jp/a_menu/shotou/new-cs/youryou/eiyaku/__icsFiles/afieldfile/2012/10/24/1298353_3.pdf.

MEXT (2014) On integrated reforms in high school and university education and university entrance examination aimed at realizing a high school and university articulation system appropriate for a new era (Report). See http://www.mext.go.jp/en/news/topics/detail/1372628.htm.

MEXT (2018) *Kôtô gakko gakushû shidô yôryô [The Course of Study for Upper Secondary School].* See http://www.mext.go.jp/component/a_menu/education/micro_detail/__icsFiles/afieldfile/2018/04/24/1384661_6_1.pdf.

MEXT (2019) *Heisei 30 nendo eigokyôiku jissi jyôkyô chôsa (kôtô gakko) no kekka [Survey results of the status quo of English education in the 2018 academic-year (upper secondary school)].* See http://www.mext.go.jp/component/a_menu/education/detail/__icsFiles/afieldfile/2019/04/17/1415043_04_1.pdf.

Nagasawa, K. (2004) Teacher training and development. In V. Makarova and T. Rodgers (eds) *English Language Teaching: The Case of Japan* (pp. 280–295). Munich: Lincom Europa.

Nagatomo, D. (2011) A case study of how beliefs toward language learning and language teaching influence the teaching practices of a Japanese teacher of English in Japanese higher education. *The Language Teacher* 35 (6), 29–33.

Nishino, T. (2008) Japanese secondary school teachers' beliefs and practices regarding communicative language teaching: An exploratory survey. *JALT Journal* 30, 27–50.

Nishino, T. (2011) Komyunikachibu apurôchi ni kansuru nihonjin kôkô eigo kyôshi no sinjyô to jissen [Japanese high school teachers' beliefs and practices regarding communicative language teaching]. *JALT Journal* 33, 131–155.

O'Donnell, K. (2005) Japanese secondary English teachers: Negotiation of educational roles in the face of curricular reform. *Language, Culture and Curriculum* 18, 300–315. doi:10.1080/07908310508668749

Pennington, M., So, S., Hirose, K., Costa, V., Shing, J. and Niedzielski, K. (1997) The teaching of English-as-a-second-language writing in the Asia-Pacific region: A cross-country comparison. *RELC Journal* 28, 120–143.

Reichelt, M. (2005) English-language writing instruction in Poland. *Journal of Second Language Writing* 14, 215–232. doi:10.1016/j.jslw.2005.10.005

Sage, K. and Tanaka, N. (2006) So what are we listening for? A comparison of the English listening constructs in the Japanese National Centre Test and TOEFL® iBT. In T. Newfields, I. Gledall, M. Kawate-Mierzejewska, Y. Ishida, M. Chapman and P. Ross (eds) *Authentic Communication: Proceedings of the 5th Annual JALT Pan-SIG Conference* (pp. 74–98). Tokyo: JALT.

Sakui, K. (2004) Wearing two pairs of shoes: Language teaching in Japan. *ELT Journal* 58, 155–163. doi:10.1093/elt/58.2.155

Sato, K. and Kleinsasser, R. (2004) Beliefs, practices, and interactions of teachers in a Japanese high school English department. *Teaching and Teacher Education* 20, 797–816. doi:10.1016/j.tate.2004.09.004

Storch, N. (2013) *Collaborative Writing in L2 Classrooms*. Bristol: Multilingual Matters.

Tahira, M. (2012) Behind MEXT's new course of study guidelines. *The Language Teacher* 36 (3), 3–8.

Tando, H. (2015) The effects of instruction in self-regulated learning strategies on English writing revision. *Annual Review of English Language Education in Japan* 26, 365–380.

Watanabe, H. (2016) Genre analysis of writing tasks in Japanese university entrance examinations. *Language Testing in Asia* 6, 4. doi:10.1186/s40468-016-0026-8

Watanabe, Y. (1996) Does grammar translation come from the entrance examination? Preliminary findings from classroom-based research. *Language Testing* 13, 318–333. doi:10.1177/026553229601300306

Weir, C.J. (2014) *A Research Report on the Development of the Test of English for Academic Purposes (TEAP) Writing Test for Japanese University Entrants*. See Eiken Foundation of Japan website: https://www.eiken.or.jp/teap/group/pdf/teap_writing_report.pdf.

Yasuda, S. (2011) Genre-based tasks in foreign language writing: Developing writers' awareness, linguistic knowledge and writing competence. *Journal of Second Language Writing* 20, 111–133. doi:10.1016/j.jslw.2011.03.001

Yasuda, S. (2014) Issues in teaching and learning EFL writing in East Asian contexts: The case of Japan. *Asian EFL Journal* 16, 150–187.

Yoshida, K. (2003) Language education policy in Japan: The problem of espoused objectives versus practice. *The Modern Language Journal* 87, 290–292.

You, X. (2004) 'The choice made from no choice': English writing instruction in a Chinese University. *Journal of Second Language Writing* 13, 97–110. doi:10.1016/j.jslw.2003.11.001

5 Teacher Preparation for Writing Instruction in Singapore

Sarah J. McCarthey

Preparing teachers to work in classrooms across the globe is an increasingly important goal (Darling-Hammond & Lieberman, 2012). In the United States, Darling-Hammond (2006) has noted three critical components of effective teacher education programs: 'coherence and integration among courses and between course work and clinical work in schools, extensive and intensely supervised clinical work integrated with course work using pedagogies that link theory and practice, and closer, proactive relationships with schools that serve diverse learners' (Darling-Hammond, 2006: 300). At the same time, the National Commission on Writing (2003) has suggested that not enough time is devoted to preparing pre-service teachers to teach writing to K-12 students. Dismuke and Martin (2016) found in their national survey in the US that few universities or colleges offer stand-alone methods courses in the teaching of writing. Instead, instructors attempt to embed writing within reading methods courses. However, many teacher educators stated that they did not feel confident in teaching writing methods.

Scholars suggest that we look to countries outside of the United States to understand how they prepare teachers. Furlong *et al.* (2013) have noted that across the globe governments are paying more attention to the recruitment, preparation and retention of teachers. Shifts in teacher education programs include: (a) government influence over teacher education to link national curricula, assessment and scientifically based practices; and (b) the development of a common framework for teacher education with a focus on quality and standards. However, major differences exist as to how teacher education programs are implemented based on cultural and historical trajectories and economic global positioning. Thus, research needs to document the impact of these trends on teacher education in specific, global contexts.

In the United States there is widespread agreement that teachers need professional development (PD) to increase their knowledge and skills after their initial preparation and throughout their careers (Wei *et al.*, 2010). In their review, McCarthey and Geoghegan (2016) report that PD has taken the form of (a) large networks, (b) professional learning communities, (c) interventions, (d) literacy coaching, and (e) online networks and technology resources. The National Writing Project, a large network of teachers with over 200 US sites and two international sites, has had a major impact on teachers' philosophies of writing, willingness to take on leadership roles, efficacy, agency and autonomy. Investigations of professional learning communities (PLCs), small groups of teachers who meet regularly to engage in problem solving and inquiry, can transform their views of writing and students and help teachers solve problems. Intervention studies that focus on training teachers to use specific cognitive strategies in writing with children and school-wide workshops associated with writing pedagogy influence teachers' practices and affect student achievement. Studies of coaching in which trained individuals observe and provide feedback to teachers about their instruction indicate a positive impact on teachers' practices, decision making and interactions with colleagues. Finally, online PD affords teachers opportunities to work on their own time and communicate with a variety of peers.

Given the recommendations to look to other countries for examples of teacher education and research on effective PD in writing, the current study focused on teacher preparation practices in Singapore. The site was selected due to Singapore's high ranking on international measures such as the 2015 Global School Ranking by the Organisation for Economic Cooperation and Development (Tay May Yin, 2017), the existence of a national curriculum, and the emphasis on learning English within a multilingual context. The focus of the study was on how teachers were being prepared to teach writing in primary and secondary schools in English.

The Singapore Context

Singapore, a small city-state, gained its independence from Malaysia in 1965; it has grown from a small fishing town with no natural resources to a world-class financial center in a few decades. It is one of the top-performing countries by many educational indices, including PISA, TIMSS and PIRLS. Its success is often attributed to macro sociocultural factors, the high quality of organization of its schools, family-level support and socialization (Bautista *et al.*, 2015). With a multi-ethnic population of 74.3% Chinese, 13.3% Malay, 9.1% Indian and 3.2% from other ethnic groups, Singapore has designated English, Mandarin, Malay and Tamil as official languages (Singapore Department of Statistics, 2015). However, all instruction in state schools has been in English (except for mother tongue languages for a period of the day) since 1987 (Hanington & Pillai, 2016).

Teacher preparation

Teacher preparation in Singapore has been influenced by its colonial heritage and immigrant roots. Initially, the Teachers' Training College reflected a colonial educational policy, but it evolved into a strong relationship between government, the Ministry of Education (Ministry) and the National Institute of Education (NIE), situated as an autonomous unit within Nanyang Technological University. NIE has autonomy from the Ministry and the university in curricular matters, and is the only degree granting institution for teacher preparation; instruction is in English (Gopinathan et al., 1999).

There are three routes for pre-service teachers at NIE: (a) Postgraduate Diploma in Education, a one year-program after degree, focusing on secondary school teaching; (b) a four-year undergraduate program for teaching in primary school to attain a BA/BSc and Diploma; and (c) a traditional Diploma in Education, a two-year route, allowing specializations in art, music and physical education. The programs combine courses with practicum in local schools and incorporate a critical and reflective attitude. Courses include prescribed modules as well as some electives (Gopinathan et al., 1999).

Professional development

In addition to initial teacher training, in-service education and continual PD are integral aspects of teacher training. The Ministry through the Academy of Singapore Teachers (AST) has six centers to provide PD; additionally, NIE provides PD, and school-based PLCs exist within schools (Bautista et al., 2015). The Ministry provides 100 PD hours per year and the opportunities include a continuum from previously developed modules for ad hoc requests. To support PD, the Ministry has developed three tracks for providing support: the teaching track, the leadership track and the specialized track. Gopinathan et al. (1999) report that this continuum of training is effective. Challenges include some mismatch between training and employment as well as typical tensions between theory and practice and concerns about the practicum disrupting coursework.

The English Language Institute of Singapore (ELIS) is one of six centers of AST that brings together teachers from different schools in a networked learning model to share innovative practices or engage in teacher research or lesson study. The mission of ELIS is 'to be a premier English Language institute anchored in professional expertise and research and leading in the professional learning of teachers.' They strive to 'cultivate pedagogical expertise, facilitate the growth of networked learning communities, build effective communication skills in English, develop expertise in research for teachers and staff, and establish partnerships and networks to build ELIS's professional capacity to drive excellence in teaching and learning' (https://www.elis.moe.edu.sg/about-us/vision-n-mission). Writing and representing is one of the key areas of PD with courses offered throughout the school year. Recent offerings focused on the relation between talk and writing for both primary and secondary teachers and classroom inquiry. In an interpretive, qualitative research project focused on lesson study, Goh and Fang (2017) found that teachers in a primary school engaged in deliberative processes, built a common inquiry stance towards children's reading and writing, embraced curriculum-based deliberation and challenged previous assumptions about teaching and learning. The study also showed how teacher talk within the group context supported novice teachers.

ELIS offers extended support including co-teaching and lesson demonstration, classroom inquiry and special interest groups; these occur through three phases: engaging in professional conversations, inquiry into professional practice and continuing to grow (http://www.elis.moe.edu.sg). An example of a six-week course for secondary teachers focusing on teaching writing and representing included understanding writing as a complex linguistic, cognitive and social process, as well as providing formative assessment tools and strategies for teaching purpose, audience, context and culture (ELIS, 2017). An example of a special interest group for primary teachers drew from Elbow (2008) and Flower and Hayes (1981) to consider free writing and the writing process cycle; they added an 'Opening Read' and 'Opening Write' and developed norms for a supportive learning environment. Teachers then documented that students were more engaged in writing about their own experiences and generating ideas through these activities (Latiff *et al.*, 2017).

NIE provides stand-alone courses in content, pedagogy, curriculum development, assessment and student learning. Delivery modes include specialists working with teachers, workshops and university–school partnerships for research projects (Bautista *et al.*, 2015). School leaders and heads of departments lead the school-based PLCs; they are intended to be inquiry based on specific topics with a plan-analysis-reflection cycle. The sessions occur eight to 10 times (for two hours) over an academic year. The most successful are aligned with principles identified by Desimone (2009): subject matter specific, intensive and ongoing, have collective participation, coherent, and provide opportunities for active learning. Hanington and Pillai (2016) reported on their work with pre-service teachers using a process approach to writing with a blended format of face-to-face and online instruction in a short, intensive course. Ten of the original 66 students were studied in depth to determine changes in their skills and awareness as writers. Using a network analysis, the researchers found that participants benefited from experiencing process writing themselves and shifted their beliefs from the pre-course survey about process writing. The researchers noted that the course provided pre-service teachers with tools and approaches they could adapt to their teaching; they were able to challenge and build on their own beliefs and link course concepts to their own practices.

However, challenges for any of the PD offered include limitations such as attending to only those content areas teachers teach (yet primary teachers teach the spectrum of subjects), the overwhelming amount of work including administrative duties many teachers have, and the high-stakes exams for which parents request additional worksheets for practice (Bautista *et al.*, 2015). The expanded roles and duties of teachers appear to be significant in schools. In a study of 646 teachers in 14 Singapore schools, Tay-Koay (1999) found that some teachers coped well with the additional responsibilities, while a few struggled. Recommendations to address the stress of taking on additional duties included new teachers having a lighter load and a mentor, more collaboration and professional sharing. Their recommendations fit with Bautista *et al.*'s (2015) recommendations of providing opportunities to understand assumptions behind reform efforts in non-threatening environments, varied opportunities to work with colleagues, and learning in ways consistent with reform efforts.

Methods

The qualitative study focused on understanding how teachers in Singapore were being prepared to teach writing to students in primary and secondary schools. Thus, both initial teacher preparation and PD were considered as environments for learning to teach writing. Data sources included interviews with faculty, meetings with personnel and document analysis.

The researcher and author, an English-speaking professor with expertise in teacher preparation and PD in writing, interviewed seven professors at NIE, met with four members of the ELIS group who focused on writing instruction, and analyzed documents from NIE and ELIS. The researcher also met with directors of practicum experiences, the department head and other faculty, as well as visiting a primary school to understand the larger educational context.

Participants in the interviews included professors who taught across programs (undergraduate, diploma, postgraduate diploma and masters of education in English). Three focused on secondary English language or literature instruction, two focused on primary grade teacher preparation, one focused on English as an international language and one prepared students for teaching Chinese literature. Their research interests varied from classroom discourse to critical literacy, to literature, to writing pedagogy. The four participants from ELIS were lead teachers who worked closely with classroom teachers.

The analysis consisted of transcribing interviews verbatim, selecting relevant artifact data primarily from the website, categorizing data and identifying themes across data sources. The researcher analyzed each participant's interview data by category (e.g. background; course goals, materials, approaches to writing; perceptions of national and local policies; perspectives on classroom practices), and examined artifact data (programs, degrees, assessments). Next, the researcher identified cross-cutting themes including: (a) factors influencing writing instruction; (b) preparing pre-service teachers to teach writing; and (c) PD to support writing instruction.

Findings

Analyses of interview and artifact data suggested that there were several factors that influenced teacher preparation in writing, including language use, national curriculum (the Syllabus), classroom contexts and exams. While teacher educators at NIE focused on pre-service education, they also collaborated with the Ministry in their delivery of PD and engaged schools in collaborative research.

Factors influencing teacher preparation

Four important aspects of the context were particularly relevant to teacher preparation: language use, the Syllabus, classroom contexts and exams.

Language use

Professor Wong (all names are pseudonyms) characterized Singapore as 'both East and West' and noted, 'We lived for 200 years under the British Raj and our English is fluent enough for us to be able to understand the nuances of first language speakers.' However, she and Professor Chen agreed that historical changes in language use and proficiency had occurred. Professor Wong found that speakers tended to be dominant in one language over another:

> English is the working language, so many of our students here are, shall we say, either you are better in Mandarin or worse in English or you are good in English and not so good in Mandarin. Rarely do I find one that is good in both.

Professor Chen, reporting historical changes that had occurred, believed that speakers were not necessarily dominant in one language. He expressed his views on language proficiency:

> In the past in Singapore we used to have Chinese medium school and English school ... it's almost like an M shape, where you have a lot of people who are very good in Chinese, not as good in English, you have a lot of people who are very [good] in English, not as good [in] Chinese. It's two big groups. So now it seems that we have the U shape maybe – more

people in the middle. Not too bad in Chinese, not too bad in English, but maybe not very good in one language.

Several instructors noted that Singapore is not the same as an English as a second language context, but that a particular type of spoken English was preferred. Despite the fact that mother tongue languages were offered in the schools, the faculty members reported that the languages were offered as separate courses and there was very little integration of English and mother tongue instruction in schools.

The Syllabus

A branch of the Ministry, the Curriculum Planning and Development Division, determines the Syllabus, which includes the content, specific activities and number of days a week spent on activities. This national curriculum was intended to be, 'holistic, catering to students' moral, intellectual, social, physical and aesthetic development' (Tay May Yin, 2017, presentation). The Ministry consults with teachers and school leadership to plan and revise the Syllabus with the intention of encouraging 'school-based curriculum innovations that are aligned to the goals of the national curriculum, and at the same time tailored to meet the learning needs of their own students' (Tay May Yin). Faculty reported that the Ministry was often engaged in revising the curriculum, but most felt that it was a curriculum that must be followed. Mr Ito said, 'They're going through another process of re-writing the new syllabus and I think they have about 16 people here engaged in the revision of that.' Dr Gold explained that no-one ignores the national curriculum, but schools may decide to change aspects of it, not individual teachers. Everyone in the same grade level teaches the same content and activities and the Head of Department (HOD) observes classrooms. Professor Chen said, 'It's all very centrally controlled and centrally initiated.'

Classroom contexts

Instructors commented on the nature of classrooms and students in Singapore that contributed to making change difficult. For example, one instructor stated, 'I think for Singaporean students, they tend to – they're more comfortable within a boxed in approach. They don't like to try new things.' She believed it was part of a larger cultural issue, saying, 'We are indirectly encouraged not to experiment, not to be creative, not to think.' While she mentioned that managing a classroom was not difficult because the students tended to be obedient, she also made note of the 'crowded curriculum, lots of work. … There's no time.' Professor Chen added to the perception that students did not seek to change the status quo affecting their writing; he said, 'a lot of our students in Singapore fear making mistakes, you see. So, they don't really like argumentative writing because it forces them into a decision making process they're not comfortable with.' Even though some classrooms encouraged peer work, instructors stated that many students were reticent in talking in front of the entire class and teachers tended to ask 'display questions' rather than open-ended ones. Professor Zhang pointed out that teachers need 'to be responsive to all these different contextual factors that obviously would have a bearing on the way they teach writing.'

Exams

All of the teacher educators interviewed indicated that exams had a major impact on their teaching of writing. Exams were taken at the end of six years of primary school (the primary school leaving examination), and at the end of 4–6 years of secondary school (GCE O-level/N-level or GCE A-level depending on the type of secondary school attended and the post-secondary experience sought, e.g. university, junior college or polytechnic) (Tay May Yin, 2017, presentation). Exams included a speaking and writing portion. The writing portion had two tasks: Task 1: Situational Writing (200–300 words); and Task 2: Short Expository Essay (450 words). Criteria for evaluation were the following: (a) how closely the responses fulfill the task requirements; (b) how adequately ideas are developed and how appropriately organized to meet the purpose of the writing; (c) the ability to create coherent, logical connections between ideas at the sentence and paragraph levels, and the text as a whole text; (d) the use of appropriate words and expressions for the purpose, audience and context of the writing task; and (e) the appropriate use and accuracy of a range of vocabulary and grammatical structures (https://www.moe.gov.sg/careers/teach/entrance-proficiency-test/english-language-entrance-proficiency-test).

Teacher educators were familiar with the types of questions and criteria for evaluation. Professor Gold explained that at the primary level the exam asked for 'situational writing' with three pictures and a prompt. She felt that the reality was that students needed to pass the exam and it was important for teachers and teacher educators to prepare students for the exam. Mr Ito elaborated:

> One is called situational writing and that's basically a scenario-based writing task. They're given a kind of scenario: Write to your uncle who's coming to visit Singapore. Suggest some places where he can bring his family and they give a profile of different family members, ages and what their interests and inclinations are.

He noted that the response requires problem solving and addressing the visual component:

> We have a visual text component where students have to talk about the features of images and words in the visual text. Then we get a narrative passage and the students have to look at the effects of the language in the narrative and talk about what created the effect and what kind of effect. … It's still very much prescribed. And the third section is an expository text and that's all to do with argumentation.

For the secondary exam, the stakes were high because students' performance determined their post-secondary future. Thus, teachers in Singapore focused on preparing students for the test while educators at the university felt compelled to prepare future teachers to consider the consequences of the exam. Professor Toh noted the pressure, stating, 'Singapore teachers are very driven by the examination … we try to push students to look beyond – but a lot of what happens in school is shaped by what the final paper will be.' She provided information on the type of questions:

> There are essay questions, right, and then there's an unseen. So that's a typical pattern. The unseen in Singapore tends to follow the format where the first question addresses what's in the passage. So, it's a close reading of the passage. Second passage is related and it looks at outside of the passage to the book.

She explained the genres and expectations as well: 'One of them has to be from a Singapore source … this is the prose passage and you've got two questions.' Professor Toh noted that the Ministry encouraged personal responses in the syllabus; however, the exams had an underlying New Criticism emphasis, which affected the teachers' emphasis:

> If you look at the literature curriculum, so again, the official syllabus that the Ministry of Education has, personal response or response is a big thing. But in reality, if you look at how the examination questions are progressing, essentially, we're doing New Criticism. … it's a particular kind of criticality you're looking for – criticality of the text.

Mr Ito discussed the writing portion of the secondary exams and referred to the focus on the visual prompt:

> Situational writing encompasses a visual text stimuli and a set of instructions about what you're supposed to argue. It's becoming less and less predictable because it used to be normally letter writing or speech writing … they're asking you to write reports or articles, things that they haven't been asked to do in the past.

While noting that the exam structure is less predictable than in the past, he discussed the larger focus on personal experience:

> The essay writing section I believe is trying to help students answer according to their own personal experiences. So, there's a lot of questions that frame questions in terms of what a teenager is likely to know. They'll ask about what is the difference between the food court as opposed to hookah centers, for example, and how and why are they important to teenagers.

Mr Ito believed that the exams were not totally constraining: 'There's also an element of creative writing, because, you know, you can make up whatever you like to boost your argument towards a certain direction.'

Professor Zhang also discussed the exam context and the pedagogy that he labeled as 'assessment driven kind of pedagogy that happens in schools.' He suggested that even at the lesson planning level, many of the activities were driven by the exams; he said, 'Even if they are not talking about the exams explicitly or specifically, a lot of the activities, a lot of what goes into the planning of the lesson or unit of work is very much influenced by the exam.' Exams were important at every level, not just the final exam that determines entry into post-secondary education. Professor Zhang stated:

> You know, every exam is high stakes in Singapore. So even if it's just a school exam, even if it's just a test, it's still taken very seriously. And everything seems to revolve around that and be driven by that as well.

However, he acknowledged that while the exam was important, it was not the only focus of the teacher preparation programs:

> We try to therefore tell them that yes, if you really want to be faithful to the principles and the spirit of say the process approach, you have to have time. You have to give students the time and the space to think about what they want to write and to experience the pleasures of writing, to allow their voice to develop.

Educators shared the view that ignoring the exams would be a disadvantage for the students. Mr Ito stated:

> In Singapore the exams are very high stakes. In order to do best for the school and do the best for the students, I think teachers would definitely feel pressure to try and teach to the exam. This kind of teaching to the test culture is very predominant and very hard to escape as well because even if you're an innovative teacher and you want to do innovative things in the classroom, you still have to balance it with this kind of exam practice because that's the bottom line in terms of how student success is measured.

Most educators believed the evaluation criteria were clear but also limiting, especially with the reading aspect of the exam. For example, Mr Ito said:

> Even though some of the questions sound open-ended, they're actually very closed-ended. It's all about being precise and marked according to standardized procedures. The answer scheme is very fixed and cannot be deviated from very much. It's a very mechanical thing but that's how reading comprehension is done.

The interview data suggested, then, that exam preparation is an essential aspect of the Singapore context and drives much of the instruction in both primary and secondary schools. While the teacher educators were aware of the high stakes nature of the exam and believed it was important for pre-service teachers to be cognizant of the testing environment, they also pushed for their students to go beyond teaching to the test to consider other aspects of literacy.

Preparing pre-service teachers to teach writing

Although specific courses on writing were not compulsory for all students, NIE offered a range of courses to prepare primary and secondary teachers to teach a set of skills comparable to English language arts in the United States. For example, for the Advanced Diploma in Primary English Language Education, students took a course called 'Reading, viewing, writing, and representing.' Students preparing to be secondary teachers selected a focus on either English language or English literature; the teaching of writing was embedded in these courses. Masters students had more electives focused on writing, including 'Research in teaching written discourse' and 'Culture and conventions of academic writing' (http://www.nie.edu.sg/our-people/academic-groups/ell/programmes/initial-teacher-preparation-programmes).

The participants described their courses, topics and pedagogy in preparing students to teach writing, providing their own training and philosophies as context. Professor Lee taught courses on writing. One was more theoretical; she described it as 'Like writing as thinking, writing as social interaction, genre theory in writing, sociocognitive approach to teaching writing, writing to learn.' She taught second language academic writing 'to introduce them to ESL writing, needs analysis, process approach, genre-based teaching and writing, coherence, cohesion in writing, intercultural perspective on teaching writing, resources for teaching writing, assessing writing.' She expanded on the content, stating:

> We touch on many important topics in ESL teaching. For example, individualism in academic writing, differences between native speaker and non-native speaker composition, genre in three traditions. Genre is not just about the structure. Genre is a social action. Genre can be understood from three different traditions, like ESP tradition, new rhetoric tradition and another tradition, right? And researching first and second language genre learning, how we learn genre from practice, often in classrooms. We also go into the interface between second language writing and second language acquisition.

Professor Lee taught a course on academic writing focused on composing a research paper. She believed that the latter course was particularly important for undergraduates:

> [In] every school, they need to do an action research project. And after that they need to write up a report. This is important training for them. And also, they can apply the skill they learn in this course to other modules because other modules, they also need to write a research or term paper. It's more for them to improve their writing skills, right? I mean, in order to be a good teacher, you need to be a good writer as well, right?

Embedded within her courses was her philosophy that prospective teachers needed to be able to write well in order to teach students: 'You need to write well, okay, so that you can expect your students to do the same. But you need to be fully equipped yourself first.'

Both she and her students used critiquing student work as a pedagogical technique:

> They bring in the student writing, for example, where they work on the term paper. They want to show me how they teach grade one student or grade two student, how to develop coherence and everything.

Professor Lee also embraced facets of a process approach in her instruction, saying, 'I talk about writing process and writing as nonlinear. And we need to revise it many times before we submit the final paper.'

In her classes preparing secondary teachers, Professor Toh provided models of expectations for the exam. Yet she also provided opportunities for students to try out new ideas:

> I tell them they have to write an answer scheme and I teach them how to do it. ... I let them experiment. But the idea is that they need to write a short paragraph to say what they expect to see in the answer. This is what a good answer would look like. This is what a mediocre answer might look like.

Professor Toh also wanted to move her students beyond the point-evidence elaboration (PEE) template. She described her approach as she analyzed a secondary student's writing:

> One of the things I want to do is to get student teachers to think about other than PEE – what other ways are there to think about writing. So, if you look at this paragraph, what this student does is that he gives a point. And then he actually talks about – I mean, he actually gives three different interpretations.

Using students' scripts (examples of student texts) was one of the major pedagogical strategies she used: 'I like using this because it gives me the material, each of the scripts and the comparison provides the material to talk about things.' She elaborated:

> We usually map only about six to eight scripts. But each of the scripts allows me to talk about something. For example, there are some scripts which look very lengthy. Like this, the handwriting's really neat. And it's very lengthy but it's actually very thin.

She discussed one of the essays, noting that it followed the PEE format but was limited with regard to exploring character. She said:

> And this follows what you call the PEE format because there's the point, there's the evidence and then there's the elaboration. And this paragraph, the father has plenty of experiences with planes. And then we talk about why; this follows the PEE format but I don't think it's a really good paragraph, because when you think about literature, you're talking about character analysis. And you're not going for the superficial ... But

you're talking about character complexity. And that's really what you're looking for.

Mr Ito continually balanced his desire to assist students in passing the exam with his own goals and methods. He acknowledged that students and practicing teachers were always concerned about the tests, 'Even if they (students) don't tell you directly, that is at the back of their minds.' However, he wanted students to be able to internalize 'what it means to write an essay.' He valued argumentation in his teaching of writing and wanted his students to look beyond the step-by-step process of the template:

> How do we help these students improve in their writing? The current nature of writing instruction in Singapore is all about make sure you follow these steps. Make sure your paragraph looks like this, which is all about how they look on the surface. But one of the things I notice is the need for a progressive argument to underscore all paragraphs. It's not enough for each paragraph to be organized according to one of their favorites, PEEL. P-E-E-L. It's not enough to organize a paragraph like that. There must be a larger argument underneath it to drive the writing, which is not always present because the students are just thinking PEEL, PEEL, PEEL.

Like Professor Toh, he also used samples of student writing as part of his pedagogy:

> They're quite recent examples because I worked with a school quite recently, with a JC, and they were having trouble with students who were plateauing basically at the B level. They're wondering, 'what can we do to help these students level up towards an A?' They sent me their problematic B scripts. I looked through them and saw what the common issues were and then I decided to help them guide their students towards progress.

Mr Ito went beyond the traditional curriculum to focus on what he called 'a bit unorthodox ... using the pedagogy of multi-literacies to teach writing.' He explained:

> And I use the example of the photograph, you know, the family holiday snapshot. In a typical family snapshot you have Notre-Dame in the background and then you have the happy family smiling in the foreground. So how would you describe this picture is what I start talking to them about, because no one in their right mind is going to say 'this is a picture of Notre-Dame,' right? They'll say 'this is a picture of a family who is posing in front of Notre-Dame.' So similarly, you can't say that this essay topic is about education. You have to say that this is about the word failure in the context of education. What you foreground in terms of the picture and what you foreground in terms of the essay are similar.

Teacher educators' descriptions of writing reflected their own training (many were educated in the United States or Australia), their knowledge of writing theories and common practices, as well as their understanding of the Singapore context. While they recognized the pressure for students to pass tests, they also integrated more innovative ideas into their practices. Of particular note was the emphasis on using students' texts to discuss ideas, organization and elements of argumentation. The Ministry's emphasis on 'representing' was instantiated in educators' incorporations of multimodal features of text in their courses.

Professional development to support writing instruction

Professors at NIE not only prepared pre-service teachers, but they were actively engaged in PD. They offered courses to teachers in the field and short workshops. The research focused on teacher practices in the schools and many studies involved teachers as active partners.

Professional development at NIE

Dr Zhang's course on writing is an example of a longer term commitment and partnership with ELIS. He offered a 16-hour course for the subject and level heads who had not completed a degree in English language to provide a 'course that equips them with what we call subject content knowledge in terms of grammar, listening and speaking, reading and writing.' He worked with personnel in the secondary schools to offer writing content:

> We decided that we would take the three main approaches to teaching writing, so that's the product approach, the process approach and the genre approach. The genre approach being the most current as far as Singapore's context is concerned because our Syllabus is very much influenced by the genre-based approach. Although it does also incorporate aspects of both the product and the process approaches.

The course focused on the theoretical assumptions as well as the pedagogical practices associated with each approach. A major focus was 'to get the participants to evaluate the value based on the kinds of students that they work with ... different approaches might suit different kinds of students.'

In addition to the longer course, NIE professors also partnered with ELIS to provide shorter workshops. For example, Professor Lee organized a short course on writing:

> I taught an in-service course to the teachers. It was a very short course comprising only four lessons – giving them some teaching ideas and activities for explicitly teaching expository writing, coherence, cohesion in your writing.

Dr Toh provided an example of a workshop she taught on writing and assessment:

> The aim of the exercise is to get them to look at what is good writing. So basically, I give a script to them with 'Winter Syntax' which is quite a

difficult poem because this is essentially A levels. You're talking about grade 12 paper, right? And I ask them to look at it and I ask them to tell me what makes this a good piece of writing.

She reported that the Ministry recognized the importance of writing, but there were not many workshops offered. She was surprised when she had a large turn-out:

When I first started running it, I wasn't quite sure that people would attend. And sometimes I get entire departments. That means you'll have five teachers from the same school, along with the head of department or the subject, head for literature, they'll say my whole team is here. ... It's just at least an avenue for them to talk and then to learn from each other.

Professor Toh encouraged attendees to set up a writing plan to consider multiple aspects of the writing process. She found that some teachers took up the challenge while many did not:

I also encourage my students to try, set up a writing plan ... some of them take up the challenge and they actually have quite clear writing lessons along the way. Most of them don't. I mean, it's quite a lot for them to cope with just coming out with this. It's just the idea that you have to think about writing right from the beginning. You don't set the test paper and then give the students a script, mark it, return it to them and then say 'this is what went wrong with your writing' and then leave it for the rest of term until it's time for writing again.

The examples above demonstrate the close connections between ELIS and NIE. Besides the courses and workshops offered, the professors at NIE had strong partnerships with local schools where they conducted research projects.

Research projects

Research studies varied from projects on classroom discourse and reading comprehension, to using iPads for creative writing, to a study of the effects of a sociocognitive model on students' writing. Dr Gold found that the teachers were continually welcoming the researchers back to provide advice and additional strategies after the project was completed; her project subsequently became part of the school's 'learning circle' or school-based PD.

The iPad project focused on creative writing rather than composition writing or writing for the exams. Students produced DVDs and PowerPoints for different skills and concepts. The results of the research showed 'that the students love the freedom of getting new ideas from outside their classroom, from getting onto the internet and so on. And we found that their work has become much more creative ... they're definitely better than the control group.'

A research project in primary schools focused on the sociocognitive approach to teaching writing and emphasized thinking processes. The researcher noted that the teachers were 'very good in mastering the genre approach. The genre part, there's the socio part. But not so much the cognitive part, the thinking processes that involved in planning, writing, organizing and re-writing, right? So last year I trained a teacher in exercising this approach.' Her data showed 'improvement in writing in terms of the number of words being used, in terms of class complexity, class density which is an indicator of syntactic complexity. And students include all the elements that's required in the story.' She planned on extending the project to four schools to include examining motivation using collaborative learning with technology to include 21st century skills. The project was closely aligned with the goals of the 2010 Syllabus, emphasizing 'the importance of rhetorical situation, meaning the importance of purpose, audience and context in writing.' Teachers modeled writing and thinking and the use of graphic organizers. The project considered the Singapore context and getting students to ask 'why?' The researcher elaborated:

> We need to keep asking yourself, 'why do you have this character?' For example, in the Singapore context it's very common to have a character called Mary Tan because Tan is a common sir name, right? If you say Michael Jackson then we'll be asking 'why do you have this character?' If you mention your teacher's name, then teachers may not like it as well. You have to ask yourself why you have this character.

Professional development using videos with the participating teachers was a major part of the project. The researcher explained, 'I want to empower the teachers, train them so that they will be able to do it in subsequent years.' She realized that the teachers needed practice to gain confidence and 'move outside a comfort zone.'

Mr Ito was also involved in a PD project and noted that it was difficult to move teachers out of old paradigms in writing, whereas they seemed more comfortable bringing in culturally relevant reading materials. He said:

> In terms of writing, teachers are still not really able to move out of the old paradigms. In terms of reading and viewing, I think teachers are much more comfortable bringing in different types of material into the classroom. ... And what we discovered was that they're bringing a lot of interesting material, which were culturally rich, but they weren't using it in their writing. ... Writing, when it came down to it, was still very prescriptive, was still very much template-based. And even though teachers understood that the text they were getting the students to write were not very real world examples of actual texts, they felt that they had to pursue this model for teaching and writing because they felt that the students were too weak to initiate their own writing.

Mr Ito reported that teachers often undervalue students' abilities, and are uncomfortable; thus, students continue to rely on templates:

> Teachers are uncomfortable with moving away from the traditional writing instruction because they don't know how to do an alternative way of

teaching. And then students become reliant on these prescribed templates and they don't know how to deviate.

He elaborated on his own view:

> Writing, I believe, must operate within a meaningful context and a meaning making frame that the students can own, you see. If you don't do that I think it's very difficult to help improve writing. And I think that's not really being done right now in the classroom.

English Language Institute of Singapore

The efforts to shift teachers' perceptions of writing, especially as a process, were echoed by participants from ELIS. They had outreach efforts to schools where leaders modeled writing and sent leaders to the United States to learn about the National Writing Project (nwp.org) and other PD efforts in writing. They had begun the Singapore Writing Institute, bringing together teachers from different schools into a network and received advice from NWP staff on adapting the project to the Singaporean context. Master teachers from ELIS worked with classroom teachers on writing as well. The challenges they encountered included teachers' discomfort with the idea of writing as a process, especially producing multiple drafts, since teachers were accustomed to the one-draft marking system embedded in the national exams. They also reported that teachers had challenges with the frequency of assessment demanded by their schools and their large workload of 35–40 students in each class. Teachers had raised questions about how to keep students interested in revising the same piece more than once rather than writing a new text. However, the meeting participants reported that some teachers had shifted their thinking, were conducting conferences with students about their work, and were asking students to revise their drafts (ELIS meeting, March 2017).

Discussion and Implications

Reflecting on Furlong *et al.*'s (2013) argument that we have much to learn from investigating global perspectives, the lessons from Singapore are both cautionary and hopeful. The findings pointed to several contextual factors that influenced the preparation of teachers to teach writing: language use, the national curriculum (Syllabus), classroom contexts and exam pressure. English was the medium of instruction in schools, but several professors believed that the students were not necessarily fluent English speakers. Mother tongue instruction occurred in schools, but separately from other subjects. The concerns with English fluency and the isolation of mother tongue instruction from other curricular areas pose challenges for preparing students to successfully navigate Singapore's multilingual context with the ability to write in more than one language

(Canagarajah, 2011). Thus, educators in Singapore and across the globe might consider ways to integrate mother tongue instruction, especially in writing, into the everyday curriculum.

The influence of the national curriculum on the preparation for teaching writing was clear. It was well accepted by university faculty that teachers would stick to the Syllabus and that their work with pre-service and practicing teachers would reflect the goals, objectives and lessons embedded within it. They raised few objections to its content, perhaps because the 2010 revisions focused on problem solving and training for a 21st century citizenry. However, there was a disconnect between the ambitious goals of the Syllabus and the educators' perceptions of its implementation, which reflected traditional practices. The advantages of a Syllabus include a shared vision and coherent objectives and strategies; yet, the implementation of any national curriculum in a lock-step manner can lead to narrowing topics and approaches as well as undermining innovation. Even with a writing curriculum that embraced a genre-as-social action approach, the standardization resulting from a prescribed curriculum was evident in the use of templates. Therefore, educators across contexts should be cautious about the limitations of a prescribed curriculum as they adopt standards and methods for teaching writing (McCarthey & Woodard, 2018).

The focus on exams that was so pervasive in Singapore schools and was discussed by students, parents and educators acts as a cautionary note to the United States as states ramp up the pressure to align curricula and require students to pass the PARCC or other mandated tests. The extreme pressure students experience has huge tradeoffs for their mental health even as Singapore continues to rank highly on multiple measures (Teng, 2016). Additionally, the test preparation resulting from exam pressure raises questions about realistic goals for changing writing practices in schools (McCarthey, 2008).

NIE instructors knew the components of the writing tests well and believed it was important for pre-service teachers to be cognizant of the testing environment. They suggested it would do a disservice to the teachers to downplay the importance of the tests. However, focusing on a genre approach but including discussions of process, the teacher educators pushed pre-service teachers towards more innovative approaches and understanding text features. The most promising practices for the teaching of writing were the focus on using students' texts to discuss effective writing and the opportunities for students to use technology and try out 'creative writing' outside of the classrooms. Using students' texts focuses attention on what writers do well and can lead to in-depth conversations, while the use of technology allows students to go beyond the constraints of typical genres and preparing for the exams. Thus, teachers in a variety of contexts, especially multilingual classrooms, should consider using students' texts as a pedagogical tool for increasing the understanding of effective writing.

The PD opportunities provided by NIE and ELIS were numerous, rich and coherent. These were facilitated by the partnership among government, colleges that prepare teacher educators, and local schools. Interview data, published articles and more informal assessments indicated that the partnerships were having effects on teachers' understanding of writing and were supporting changes to classroom practices. The collaboration between NIE and schools to conduct research was particularly striking and a practice worth emulating on a global level. These collaborations as well as the outward look towards other countries and institutions are in sync with the practices recommended by Darling-Hammond (2017) in her efforts to understand how best to prepare teachers around the globe. These collaborations for professional development are particularly important for increasing teachers' competence and confidence in teaching writing.

References

Bautista, A., Wong, J. and Gopinathan, S. (2015) Teacher professional development in Singapore: Depicting the landscape. *Psychology, Society and Education* 7 (3), 311–326.

Canagarajah, S. (2011) Translanguaging in the classroom: Emerging issues for research and pedagogy. *Applied Linguistics Review* 2, 1–28.

Darling-Hammond, L. (2006) Constructing 21st century teacher education. *Journal of Teacher Education* 27 (3), 300–314.

Darling-Hammond, L. (2017) Teacher education around the world: What can we learn from international practice? *European Journal of Teacher Education* 40 (3), 291–309, DOI: https://doi.org/10.1080/02619768.2017.1315399

Darling-Hammond, L. and Lieberman, A. (eds) (2012) *Teacher Education around the World: Changing Policies and Practices.* New York: Routledge.

Desimone, L.M. (2009) Improving impact studies of teachers' professional development: Toward better conceptualizations and measures. *Educational Researcher* 38, 181–199.

Dismuke, S. and Martin, S. (2016) What about writing: A national study of writing instruction in teacher education programs. *Literacy Research and Instruction* 55 (4), 309–330. doi:10.1080/19388071.2016.1198442

Elbow, P. (2008) *Writing About Media: Teaching Writing, Teaching Media.* Northampton, MA: Media Education Foundation.

ELIS (2017) *Professional Learning Opportunities.* See https://www.elis.moe.edu.sg/professional-learning.

Flower, L. and Hayes, J.R. (1981) A cognitive process theory of writing. *College Composition and Communication* 32 (4), 365–387.

Furlong, J., Cochran-Smith, M. and Brennan, M. (2013) *Policy and Politics in Teacher Education: International Perspectives.* New York: Routledge.

Goh, R. and Fang, Y. (2017) Improving English language teaching through lesson study: Case study of teacher learning in a Singapore primary school grade level team. *International Journal for Lesson and Learning Studies* 6 (2), 135–150.

Gopinathan, S., Ho, W.K. and Tan, J. (1999) Teacher education and teaching in Singapore: Recent trends. *Asia-Pacific Journal of Teacher Education & Development* 2 (1), 3–14.

Hanington, L.M. and Pillai, A.D. (2016) Using a skills development course to foster teacher professional growth. *Journal of Asia TEFL* 13 (4), 294–312.

Latiff, A., Fung, L.S., Kamis, N., Albert, A., Subramanian, Y. and Damodaran, S. (2017) The joy of writing in the English language classroom. *EL Classroom Inquiry, ELIS* 9, 3–15.

McCarthey, S.J. (2008) The impact of No Child Left Behind on teachers' writing instruction. *Written Communication* 25, 462–505.

McCarthey, S.J. and Geoghegan, C. (2016) The role of professional development for enhancing writing instruction. In C. MacArthur, S. Graham and J. Fitzgerald (eds) *Handbook of Writing Research* (2nd edn) (pp. 330–345). New York: Guilford.

McCarthey, S.J. and Woodard, R. (2018) Faithfully following, adapting, or rejecting: Teachers' curricular enactments in elementary writing instruction. *Pedagogies: An International Journal* 13 (1), 56–80.

National Commission on Writing (2003) *The Neglected 'R': the Need for a Writing Revolution*. College Entrance Examination Board.

Singapore Department of Statistics (2015) See https://www.singstat.gov.sg/-/media/files/publications/reference/sif2018.pdf

Tay-Koay, S.L. (1999) Teacher development: Understanding the struggles of classroom teachers. *Asia-Pacific Journal of Teacher Education & Development* 2 (1), 15–28.

Teng, A. (2016) Exam stress among the young: When grades define worth. *Straits Times*, 30 October. See http://www.straitstimes.com/singapore/when-grades-define-worth.

Wei, R.C., Darling-Hammond, L. and Adamson, F. (2010) *Professional Development in the United States: Trends and Challenges*. Dallas, TX: National Staff Development Council.

Yin, T.M. (2017) Curriculum development in a multicultural setting. Presentation to University of Illinois Writing Project, Champaign, IL, June. Singapore: English Language Institute of Singapore, Ministry of Education.

6 English Writing Instruction and Teacher Preparation in Thailand: Perspectives from the Primary and Secondary Schools

Tanita Saenkhum

Introduction

Tony Silva (2013), in his 'Second language writing: Talking points' published in the *Journal of Second Language Writing*'s Disciplinary Dialogues, pointed out that the field of second language (L2) writing 'has been dominated by work done in the West, specifically in North America and has been dominated by work at institutions of higher education.' Furthermore, the field 'has neglected work done in primary and secondary schools' (Silva, 2013: 433). This chapter responds to Silva's important calls by examining English writing instruction at the primary and secondary levels in a non-English dominant context. Specifically, the chapter reports on a qualitative study of English writing instruction and teacher preparation in primary and secondary schools in Thailand. The goals are multifaceted: to generate an understanding of what and how writing is taught/ approached; to shed light on how teachers are (not) prepared to teach writing; and to reveal teachers' professional development needs.

I begin with a discussion of the current situation of English writing instruction, considering various national policies on English language instruction and education in Thailand. Then I review relevant scholarship in English language education, writing instruction and teacher preparation. Finally, I present my research into English writing instruction in primary and secondary schools and teacher preparation. The primary data came from in-depth interviews with 32 Thai English language teachers from 16 schools across the country. The findings address teachers' writing

111

instructional approaches and their preparedness to teach writing, as well as issues and challenges faced and their perceived resource and professional development needs. I conclude by asking relevant questions about English writing instruction and teacher preparation for teacher educators and teacher education programs to consider.

Context: English Writing Instruction in Primary and Secondary Schools in Thailand

English writing instruction has never been a primary focus in the context of teaching English in Thailand, especially at the primary and secondary levels where students spend 12 years learning English. Students study writing combined with other skills in an integrated English classroom with an English language teacher, who is expected to be able to teach all four skills. While the majority of primary and secondary Thai teachers of English are not specifically trained to teach writing, they manage to cover writing in their classrooms, but only minimally.

Like in the context of US higher education in which writing had been neglected, particularly in the mid-20th century (Matsuda, 2003), in the context of Southeast Asian educational settings, especially in Thailand, English writing has long been seen as the least important skill and writing instruction has also received little attention. In order to have a better understanding of Thailand's current English language teaching (ELT) in general and writing instruction in particular, I examined various educational policy documents. I closely looked at the country's 1999 National Education Reform Act, which detailed desired educational outcomes. The act placed the emphasis on Thai language development while the English as a foreign language (EFL) policy was not explicitly stated. Later, the Ministry of Education's Curriculum Reform Committee (CRC) urged that English education should start as early as possible. As a result, four years of English education were added to the national curriculum, which meant that students started learning English in the first grade. In the past, formal English instruction began in the fifth grade. Changes responding to the CRC's appeal included theme-based instruction implemented in some elementary schools. In these theme-based classrooms, listening was paired with speaking and reading was also paired with speaking.

Thailand's educational system had been through educational change when the Ministry of Education called for reform and subsequently announced an experimental application of a 2001 Basic Education Curriculum (BEC). This application was implemented in pilot schools across the country. Later, in 2003, a mandatory implementation of the 2001 BEC was effective in all schools providing basic education. In the 2001 BEC, the focus of learning EFL was threefold: communication, education and business. Specifically, the 2001 BEC promoted teaching approaches that utilized communicative methods, student-centered learning and critical thinking skills. Additionally, it proposed a *Course of study* for language courses, which should include the following four components:

- communication, which emphasized listening and speaking;
- culture, which referred to knowledge of and sensitivity for others;
- connections, which meant connecting learning foreign languages with other subject content; and
- community, which encouraged project work and its applications outside the classroom (Mackenzie, 2005: para. 7).

In the *Course of study*, priority was given to listening and speaking in the communication component; writing was not even listed, implying that it was not as important as listening and speaking where communication was concerned.

The 2001 BEC presented some shortcomings, as stated by the Office of the Basic Education Commission (OBEC), which included:

> … confusion and uncertainty faced by practitioners in educational institutions in preparing school curriculums; the majority of schools were ambitious in prescribing learning contents and expected outcomes; measurement and evaluation did not correlate with the standard set, with negative effects on certification and transfer of learning achievements. Furthermore, issues of learners' quality resulting from acquisition of essential knowledge, skills, capacity and desirable characteristics and attributes were quite disconcerting.[1] (Samudvanijja, 'Preface,' 2008)

In an attempt to continue to improve the quality of Thai education, the OBEC led by the Basic Education Commission revised the 2001 BEC and launched a 2008 Basic Education Core Curriculum (BECC), which was also partly guided by the country's 10th National Economic and Social Development Plan (2007–2011) (Samudvanijja, 'Preface,' 2008). The 2008 BECC, which is currently being used in Thailand, places English in an area of foreign languages – one of the eight primary learning areas, including: Thai language; mathematics; science; social studies, religion and culture; health and physical education; arts; and occupations and technology.

According to the 2008 BECC, English is the only foreign language that is a required subject. As the document states, while 'the foreign language constituting basic learning content that is prescribed for the entire basic education core curriculum is English' (OBEC, 2008: 252), institutions may offer other foreign language courses as they wish. Suggested languages include French, German, Chinese, Japanese, Arabic, Pali and other languages of neighboring countries. Specifically, the 2008 BECC describes why learning foreign languages is necessary as follows:

> In the present global society, learning foreign languages is very important and essential to daily life, as foreign languages serve as an important tool

for communication, education, seeking knowledge, livelihood and creating understanding of cultures and visions of the world community. Foreign languages enable learners to be aware of diversity of cultures and viewpoints in the world community, conducive to friendship and cooperation with various countries. They contribute to learners' development by giving learners better understanding of themselves and others. The learners are thus able to learn and understand differences of languages and cultures, customs and traditions, thinking, society, economy, politics and administration. They will be able to use foreign languages for communication as well as for easier and wider access to bodies of knowledge and will have vision in leading their lives. (OBEC, 2008: 252)

The ultimate goals of learning foreign languages, as described in the 2008 BECC, are for students to be able to use the target language(s) for communication in different situations. Subsequently, students are expected to 'have knowledge and understanding of stories and cultural diversity of the world community and will be able to creatively convey Thai concepts and culture to the global society' (OBEC, 2008: 253). In order for students to accomplish these goals, the 2008 BECC specifies four major areas that must be covered in foreign language courses:

- *language for communication*: use of foreign languages for listening, speaking, reading and writing, exchanging data and information, expressing feelings and opinions, interpreting, presenting data, concepts and views on various matters, and creating interpersonal relationships appropriately;
- *language and culture*: use of foreign languages harmoniously with the culture of native speakers; relationships, similarities and differences between languages and cultures of native speakers; languages and cultures of native speakers and Thai culture; and appropriate application;
- *language and relationship with other learning areas*: use of foreign languages to link knowledge with other learning areas, forming the basis for further development, seeking knowledge and broadening learners' world views;
- *language and relationship with the community and the world*: use of foreign languages in various situations, both in the classroom and the outside community and the global society, forming a basic tool for further education, livelihood and the exchange of learning with the global society. (OBEC, 2008: 252–253)

During the 12 years (Grades 1–12) in schools, students are expected to be able to perform certain skills after their completion of each grade level. For example, Grade 3 graduates should be able to communicate about themselves, their family and their schools by using listening and speaking skills. Grade 6 graduates should be able to speak and write for the purposes of interpersonal communication. For Grade 9 graduates, it is expected that students both converse and write about themselves, and use the foreign language to conduct research, collect data and draw conclusions. Finally, Grade 12 graduates are expected to master all four skills for communication in various situations.

While writing has been included in the English curriculum as seen in the 2001 BEC and 2008 BECC, the priority has been given to listening and speaking. I sought to understand how this neglect of English writing instruction has impacted the theoretical and pedagogical insights of teachers as well teacher preparation in Thailand. Additionally, my examination of these educational policies has led me to ponder about several questions related to English language teaching and learning in this particular context. Who teaches English, especially writing? Based on my experience as a Thai student first learning English in Grade 5, I was wondering whether writing has still been covered only minimally in English classrooms. How is writing currently taught in Thailand? To address my preliminary questions, I synthesized relevant research into English instruction and education in primary and secondary schools in Thailand (see below). I should note that since the primary focus of my study is on writing instruction and teacher preparation, I in fact intended to present a discussion of relevant research. What I have found and discussed below, however, mainly deals with English language teaching in general, except for a survey of teacher perceptions of problems relating to English teaching that revealed some helpful results about English writing instruction (Noom-ura, 2013). This implies that writing instruction and teacher preparation in teaching writing in Thailand, like in other non-English dominant contexts, has been under-researched.

Literature Review

English language education and teacher preparation

Even though Thailand has never been colonized and Thai has been the country's official language, English has played an important role in Thai education since the 18th century, a growing period of the British Colonial Empire in South East Asia (Foley, 2005; Methitham & Chamcharatsri, 2011; Wiriyachitra, 2002; Wongsothorn, 2004; Wongsothorn *et al.*, 2004). As suggested by World Englishes scholars (e.g. Bautista & Gonzalez, 2006; Chamcharatsri, 2013), English language teaching in Thailand has one of the longest histories in the region. Nonetheless, English, at the highest level, is considered to be a required foreign language in schools (Wongsothorn, 2004). As in other EFL contexts, in typical English classrooms students learn to master four skills. Thai, as the native language, is used as the medium of instruction in most schools, except for international schools and schools providing English programs. In an integrated English classroom, speaking is the focus of instruction, and writing has always been the last skill that teachers cover.

Current studies examining English teaching and learning in Thailand's primary and secondary schools[2] have found that learning outcomes are unsatisfactory (Khamkhien, 2010, as cited in Teng & Sinwongsuwat, 2015). Specifically, Noom-ura (2013: 139) argues that learning results are 'questionable', despite students studying English in primary and secondary schools for 12 years. The factors and/or causes of this lack of success identified include the following: 'unqualified and poorly-trained teachers, poorly-motivated students, learners of mixed abilities in overly large classes, and rare opportunities for student exposure to English outside of class time' (Dhanasobhon, 2006, as cited in Noom-ura, 2013: 139). What has been discovered about the teaching of English in the context of Thai education is very typical in non-English dominant contexts and/or EFL settings (e.g. Ene & Mitrea, 2013; Manchón, 2009).

Although research into English language teaching and learning has provided insights into various issues related to teaching English in Thailand, research focusing on writing instruction in particular is scarce. A study by Noom-ura (2013), which investigated secondary school teachers' English-teaching problems, revealed that Thai English teachers ranked teaching writing as the principal problem involved in teaching English. Since this was a survey study and writing instruction was not its focus, explanations as to why teaching writing was one of participants' major problems were not discussed. Other results from this same survey study showed that participants' problems related to teaching English had to do with 'students having problems with writing' and 'students thinking in Thai before translating [in]to English' (Noom-ura, 2013: 143). Problems related to the assessment of writing were also mentioned by the teacher participants. Again, no detailed discussions were provided as to why the teachers mentioned such problems relating to writing instruction.

Since students' learning success largely depends on teachers, L2 writing researchers (e.g. Casanave, 2009; Ene & Mitrea, 2013; Hirvela & Belcher, 2007; Lee, 2010) have investigated issues related to teacher education and preparation for teaching writing. Some major findings in this research area have demonstrated that teaching approaches are influenced by teachers' knowledge and prior training (e.g. Casanave, 2009; Ene & Mitrea, 2013; Lee, 2010); teaching is also influenced by external factors, such as national entrance examinations, large class sizes, students' motivations and teachers' limited training in teaching writing (e.g. Noom-Ura, 2013; Reichelt, 2005; You, 2004). In the context of Thailand, research related to writing teacher preparation is also scarce. The same survey study by Noom-ura (2013) revealed some professional development needs perceived by secondary school English language teachers. They indicated some areas that were problematic and needed to be addressed, including 'their own English proficiency development, especially in listening-speaking and writing skills'

(Noom-ura, 2013: 144) and their teaching of writing. These results imply that Thai teachers of English were uncertain about their own writing skills and had inadequate preparation in teaching English writing.

In order to expand the discussion about writing instruction in non-English dominant contexts and issues related to teacher preparation in teaching writing in the field of L2 writing, this current study aims to examine English writing instruction and teacher preparation at the primary and secondary levels in Thailand. The research questions are as follows:

(1) How is English writing taught/approached at the primary and secondary levels in Thailand?
(2) To what extent are teachers prepared to teach writing?
(3) What resource and professional development needs do teachers perceive in the teaching of English writing?

The Present Study

To address the above research questions, I conducted a qualitative interview study of 32 Thai teachers of English who teach at the primary and secondary levels in Thailand. This study took place in Thailand in summer 2016.

Participant selection

I selected participants who were currently teaching in various primary and secondary schools located in four different regions (central, northern, northeastern and southern) of the country. This homogeneous sampling strategy, according to Dörnyei (2007), allows researchers to select participants who share some background and experiences relevant to their studies. In my case, I was interested in examining English writing instruction in Thailand's K-12 school context, and this strategy helped me obtain in-depth data about and identify K-12 school English teachers' writing instructional approaches, their preparedness to teach writing, and their perceptions of resource and professional development needs.

Thailand has 77 provinces and four regions.[3] First, I selected two provinces (Bangkok and Nonthaburi) from the central region, two provinces (Phitsanulok and Uttaradit) from the northern region, one province (Mahasarakham) from the northeastern region and one province (Songkhla) from the southern region. Secondly, I selected primary and secondary schools (see Table 6.1) from the provinces mentioned above. Then I emailed an invitation to participate in the study, including both Thai- and English-informed consent forms, to heads of the English departments of the selected schools in summer 2016. The total number of

Table 6.1 Participating schools ($N = 16$) and teachers ($N = 32$)

Level	Central region	Northern region	Northeastern region	Southern region
Primary	Bangkok ($N = 2$ schools)	Uttaradit ($N = 2$ schools)	Mahasarakham ($N = 2$ schools)	Songkhla ($N = 2$ schools)
	Participants: one teacher from each school	Participants: one teacher from one school and three teachers from the other school	Participants: one teacher from one school and two teachers from the other school	Participants: five teachers from one school and three teachers from the other school
	P1 School P2 School	P3 School P4 School	P5 School P6 School	P7 School P8 School
Secondary	Bangkok ($N = 1$ school)	Uttaradit ($N = 1$ school)	Mahasarakham ($N = 2$ schools)	Songkhla ($N = 2$ schools)
	Nonthaburi ($N = 1$ school)	Phitsanulok ($N = 1$ school)		
	Participants: one teacher from each school	Participants: three teachers from each school	Participants: one teacher from one school and four teachers from the other school	Participants: one teacher from each school
	S9 School S10 School	S11 School S12 School	S13 School S14 School	S15 School S16 School
Total	4 schools 4 teachers	4 schools 10 teachers	4 schools 8 teachers	4 schools 10 teachers

participating schools across the country was 16; for instance, in the central region, two primary schools in Bangkok, one secondary school in Bangkok and one secondary school in Nonthaburi participated in the study. In each participating school the number of Thai English teachers taking part in interviews varied, ranging from one to five, yielding a total of 32 teacher participants.

To protect the participating schools' and teachers' identities, I used the following names to refer to each primary and secondary school in the 'Findings' section: Primary schools – P1 School, P2 School, P3 School, P4 School, P5 School, P6 School, P7 School and P8 School; Secondary schools – S9 School, S10 School, S11 School, S12 School, S13 School, S14 School, S15 School and S16 School. However, not every school was mentioned in the 'Findings' section. Table 6.1 provides detailed information about the participating schools and the number of teachers. For the teacher participants, I referred to them as a teacher from P1 School or P5 School's teacher, for example. Information about some teachers' educational backgrounds and their experience teaching English is provided in Table 6.2.

Table 6.2 Some teachers' educational backgrounds and experience teaching English[a]

Teacher	Degree earned	Experience teaching English
P1 School teacher	BA in elementary education (Major: English) MA in elementary education	18 years
P7 School teachers Teacher I	BA in English MA in TEFL	20 years
Teacher II	BA in English MA in education management	22 years
S10 School teacher	BA in education (Major: English)	37 years
S12 School teacher	BA in Education (Major: English) MA in English	36 years
S15 School teacher	BA in primary education MA in secondary education (Major: English)	25 years

Note: [a]While the total number of the teacher participants is 32, I included some of the teachers' educational backgrounds and experience teaching English in this table.

Data sources and data analysis

I conducted a one-time semi-structured interview with the teacher participants from different schools in May–July 2016. The participants were given a list of questions (see Appendix) before the interview. The interviews, each of which was conducted in Thai and lasted between 45 and 75 minutes, focused on how the teachers approached the teaching of English writing, their perceptions of teaching writing, and their professional development needs. Using the interview questions, I asked follow-up questions in order to, for instance, encourage the participants to provide some specific examples and to clarify some information that was unclear. Each interview was audio-recorded with permission from the participants.

Each interview was transcribed in Thai. As I coded the interview transcripts, specifically identifying patterns based on the research questions, I translated them into English. Later, I established the three main themes I wanted to address: (1) teachers' approaches to writing instruction in primary and secondary schools; (2) teachers' preparedness for teaching writing and challenges and issues faced; and (3) teachers' perceived resource and professional development needs.

Findings

I present the findings of the study based on the three established research questions that I aimed to address: teachers' writing instructional approaches; their preparedness to teach writing and challenges and issues faced; and their perceived resource and professional needs in the teaching of English writing.

Teachers' approaches to writing instruction in primary and secondary schools

While I was interested in writing instructional approaches in primary and secondary schools in Thailand, I appreciated that English writing skills were one part of other English communication skills promoted at these levels. It was very rare that primary and secondary schools provided a separate writing course for their students. In an English classroom, an English language teacher teaches four skills. Based on my interviews with the English language teachers from the participating 16 schools, they all said that their English curricula were designed based on guidelines and requirements found in the 2008 BECC. For example, the participants teaching Grades 1–3 all said that they followed the 2008 BECC when teaching English. In these English classes, listening and speaking skills were taught together, plus grammar lessons. A teacher from P6 School said as follows: 'We emphasize listening and speaking skills in our first, second, and third grade classes.' A teacher from P2 School explained that expectations for first graders included English for communication, in which students should be able to both understand and give commands. My interviews with the participants suggested that during the first three years of students' learning English, writing was covered only minimally (e.g. in a grammar lesson).

Although the participating schools primarily relied on the 2008 BECC when designing and revising their English curricula, they were able to make some adjustments to meet local needs and circumstances. For example, P7 School incorporated some signature characteristics (e.g. places of attraction and local food) of southern Thailand into their English curriculum for fifth grade. One teacher from P7 School shared with me that her lessons were designed using a concept of southern Thai food as her course theme. Her lessons always started with a listening activity, followed by speaking, reading and writing. She said that 'sometimes we did not have time to cover a writing activity in a 50-minute class. We had to use the next class period to go over the writing activity, but it was very brief.' This same teacher, who taught fifth and sixth grade, discussed her writing instructional approach as follows:

> I begin with some vocabulary words, followed by grammar instruction. I teach vocabulary and grammar together so that students learn different sentence structures and patterns at the same time. I assign them to write a paragraph introducing themselves using various sentence structures and patterns learned as the point of departure.

From what this teacher explained, students learned to write from grammar lessons. They learned from sentence samples, especially how to put vocabulary words into sentences. Then they wrote their own stories using the grammar patterns they had learned. This suggests that the participants associated grammar instruction with the teaching of writing.

In other primary schools (Grades 4–6) students learned to write from a reading-writing lesson. The students were assigned a short text or passage to read. Then the teacher and students analyzed the text. To illustrate, a teacher from P5 School shared what she did in her reading-writing lesson:

> I assign them to read a short passage. Then we practice writing using sentence structures learned from the reading. The selected reading helps my students understand English writing better. Then I assign them to compose their own writing. Topics vary, ranging from family members to favorite sports.

In the context of the secondary schools, especially in Grades 7–9, the four English skills are still integrated in the classroom, emphasizing speaking, listening, reading and writing, respectively. Like at primary school level, grammar is the focus in the teaching of writing. The majority of the secondary school teacher participants agreed that grammar was one of the most essential components in students' ability to write. A teacher from S11 School said as follows:

> Students in Grade 7–Grade 9 learn paragraph writing by reading a sample text. For example, we analyze how each sentence from the sample text was formed. Then the students are assigned to compose a piece of writing, such as a profile, using sentence patterns they learned from the text.

Writing instruction, however, is the focus in an integrated English classroom in Grades 10–12, the last three years of their secondary school studies. Writing activities and/or processes, including freewriting, brainstorming, drafting and editing, are clearly seen in the writing instruction. Some schools assigned journal writing and diaries. A teacher from S15 School said she assigned a comparison essay in her Grade 11 class, and students were allowed to choose what they wanted to compare. Another teacher from S12 School said she used a theme-based writing activity when teaching and discussing writing with her students. She elaborated:

> I always come up with different themes and encourage my students to write about them. For example, we did my pet, my favorite food, and my favorite restaurant. They should be able to write a short paragraph of 200 words.

A teacher from S14 School discussed how she utilized freewriting activities in her English class for Grade 11 students:

> I usually assign freewriting on the first day of classes in order to find out how my student writing is like so that I can make some adjustments to my teaching. For example, if the majority of students have a problem with sentence structures, I may provide a mini lesson on simple sentences, compound sentences, and complex sentences before moving forward writing instruction.

Some secondary schools that provide an intensive English program specifically for Grade 12 students offer separate writing classes taught by faculty members who specialize in teaching writing. For example, S12 School invited faculty members from a nearby university to teach writing to their Grade 12 students. A teacher from S12 School explained as follows:

> We offer a writing course called English for Academic Purposes. This class is designed to prepare Grade 12 students to write in the university setting. The focus of the class is on organization of ideas and some grammar lessons to help students master writing.

In addition to their approaches to writing instruction, I was also interested in how the participating teachers responded to student writing, given the fact that English writing classes in EFL contexts enroll 40 students or more. A teacher from S14 School said: 'Providing oral feedback is almost impossible because we have too many students [45–46] in our classes.' The same teacher added: 'I require my students to revise and resubmit after I mark their papers.' Keep in mind that the student–teacher ratio at this school is 300:1. To mitigate the class size issue, this teacher utilized peer review in her class, asking her students to provide feedback on their classmates' drafts, using the questions she provided. However, she admitted that the feedback her students provided to one another focused on grammar and vocabulary. Like S14 School's teacher, S15 School's teacher also provided feedback on her students' writing; she focused on sentence-level issues by circling and asked students to revise and resubmit. Sometimes she even 'corrected grammar for my students. For example, I wrote "you were supposed to use a past tense here."' This practice was also evidenced in a class taught by S10 School's teacher who provided only grammar comments on her students' assignments.

Teachers' preparedness to teach writing and issues and challenges faced

All the teachers interviewed had at least received a bachelor's degree in teaching, majoring in English (see Table 6.2 for some teachers' educational backgrounds and teaching experience). P8 School, for example, had a very strict policy that an English teacher must graduate with a teacher education degree majoring in teaching English. Some of the English teachers interviewed had also earned an MA in TEFL or secondary education. Most of the primary and secondary teacher participants identified themselves as language teachers. None of them was specifically trained to teach English writing, and they did not consider themselves as writing teachers. Specifically, P5 School's teacher said: 'We [Thai English language teachers] are not trained to teach writing.'

When asked how well they were prepared to teach writing, the responses from the teacher participants varied. First, some teachers were not confident in their English writing skills. To illustrate, the same teacher from P5 School said: 'We (English language teachers) can't write well [in English]. When teaching writing, I feel more comfortable marking grammatical errors. It's something I know.' Then she added, 'I don't blame my students if they are not able to master English writing.' This same teacher also pointed out that the students did not like to write, explaining 'they tend to think writing is difficult, and they don't want to write.' These responses suggest that when teachers are not prepared and/or trained to teach writing, they feel that they are not qualified to teach students how to write. However, as English language teachers, they feel that they know more about grammar, and they use their grammar knowledge as a tool when teaching writing. In addition, what P5 School's teacher mentioned about students not liking writing resonated with what Thai teachers of English in previous studies had perceived as one of major problems of English teaching. Specifically, in these English teachers' perceptions, 'students having problems with writing' (Noom-ura, 2013: 143) was also their problem when teaching English. These particular results may suggest that teachers' minimal preparation for teaching writing as well as their perceptions of their own English writing skills affect their English writing instructional practices in the classroom.

Secondly, some teachers primarily relied on textbooks when teaching writing. For example, P16 School's teacher said: 'We use all exercises in textbooks for writing activities. We follow exactly what the textbooks say. We also sometimes ask students to write based on their personal experiences.' There is nothing wrong with using textbooks to teach writing. However, it is worth discussing why textbooks play such a significant role in this teacher's writing instruction. In EFL contexts, it is typical that teachers are required to use the same textbooks and the same exercises when teaching the same course. This also means that teachers may not have much freedom to design their own lessons.

Thirdly, controlled composition was frequently mentioned by the participants when responding to this question. For example, all three teachers from S11 School agreed that their students were able to write better when using controlled composition as a guide for writing. The three teachers went on to explain that their students' writing skills were weak because the students did not have enough vocabulary. The three teachers explained that learning to write from controlled composition could help students to develop their vocabulary and fluency as well as to control their errors.

Additionally, accuracy in student writing seemed to be the major focus of the writing teaching in these primary and secondary schools. The teacher participants found that accuracy in student writing was their major challenge when teaching writing. It seemed that accuracy was prioritized. According to some teacher participants, the students needed to master grammar in order to produce good writing. A teacher from S12 said as follows: 'Students can't form sentences. They also have limited vocabulary words.' In sum, in my interviews with the teacher participants, I seldom heard them mention the content and organization of student writing.

Furthermore, another challenge faced by the teacher participants when teaching writing was that Thai students tended to translate directly from Thai into English. P2 School's teacher said: 'Students think in Thai and translate it into English. Their sentences are awkward.' This teacher, who taught Grades 2 and 6, gave several examples of her students' writing as follows:

> My family have four people.
> In the classroom has a teacher and student.
> This is 10 a.m.
> My teacher is sitting back in the class while the students reading book.
> In the living room has mom and dad.
> Today is Saturday 2 p.m., mom is cooking food while dad reading newspaper.

One last concern about teaching writing pointed out by S15 School's teacher was that students rarely used what they learned about writing in the classroom in their real life. They studied writing for standardized testing or entrance examinations. 'When students don't see its benefits, it's difficult to motivate them,' this teacher explained, adding that the students might realize its usefulness when entering college. 'Our job is to motivate them, explaining to them that writing is the most important skill; it demonstrates our ability to express in English.' In responding to this same concern, S16 School's teacher commented that 'English writing is not tested in an entrance exam.' She added that in such examinations, grammar and vocabulary are the two major areas on which students are assessed.

Teachers' perceived resource and professional needs in the teaching of writing

The responses from my interviews with the teacher participants revealed that they were not specifically trained to teach writing. With their academic and training backgrounds as language teachers, the teachers wished to attend workshops on teaching writing. However, the workshops that were made available for primary and secondary school teachers did not always focus on teaching writing. For example, the teachers from P7 School mentioned that the workshops they had attended in the past were organized by textbook companies and publishers. The goal was to advertise textbooks and to demonstrate how to use them in a classroom. The teachers said 'we learned new teaching techniques for teaching speaking and listening.' Like P7 School's teachers, P8 School's teachers had attended workshops organized by textbook publishers. S11 School's teachers said their school always encouraged teachers to attend workshops organized by both governmental and private institutions. The school also supported teachers who wanted to take an online class to gain more knowledge about teaching English. P1 School was also willing to provide financial support for their teachers to attend workshops and related training. S15 School did something different: the school invited guest speakers to lead workshops on curriculum design and development, writing lesson plans and teaching techniques.

Some schools developed their own learning resources for their teachers. For example, P7 School has an online classroom where their teachers and students can use the internet to facilitate their teaching and learning. P3 School provided Smart Classrooms. P1 School supported their English language teachers by providing supplementary teaching materials; the school had a budget for these purchases. Another issue relating to teaching resources and professional development needs was funding. Not all institutions always provided funding support for their teachers to attend workshops or for other professional development opportunities. Sometimes teachers had to pay out of their own pockets. S14 School's teachers said this was a major problem at their school.

Lastly, some teachers mentioned that they also needed to keep themselves up-to-date with current teaching theories and practices. However, while they thought this was important, they admitted that it was really difficult to find time to read, given their workload and other obligations. For example, the teachers at S14 School noted that their committee work and other administrative responsibilities exhausted them. This result echoes what was found in previous studies of Thai English language teachers where participants expressed that their 'overloaded teaching' (Noom-ura, 2013: 144) and other administrative tasks were causes of problems with teaching English in secondary schools.

Discussion and Conclusion

The findings from the present study, utilizing the case of primary and secondary schools in Thailand, demonstrate that writing instruction is one part of integrated four-skills English classrooms. What is found in the context of primary and secondary schools in Thailand echoes the teaching and learning of English in other EFL settings (e.g. Reichelt, 2005; You, 2004). Where writing instruction is concerned, the participating teachers associated grammar and students' vocabulary knowledge with their teaching of writing. In other words, the teachers found grammar and vocabulary important for the students' ability to write well in English. This could be possibly explained as follows. The teacher participants considered themselves to be language teachers; this meant the ways they addressed student writing and approached their teaching of writing were based on their academic backgrounds and training. What is found here also echoes what language teachers in Lee's (2010) study expressed about their teaching of writing. When teachers are not specifically trained in teaching L2 writing, it makes sense that they would approach their teaching of English writing by drawing from their own academic training. To help these language teachers broaden and expand their teaching repertoire, resources and professional development opportunities related to the teaching of L2 writing should be encouraged and provided. While the participating schools did provide some resources and professional development opportunities for their teachers, what was made available to the teacher participants was not directly related to the teaching of writing. A follow-up question to my own argument here is: Who should be responsible for this circumstance? And I do not have a clear answer. Apparently, the participating schools and their teachers have been trying their best.

While some teachers incorporated writing processes including freewriting, brainstorming, drafting and peer review into their teaching of writing, other teachers still used controlled composition and stated that it worked really well with their students. This was mainly because their students did not have enough vocabulary to compose their own writing. Additionally, accuracy and correctness seem to be the primary focus of the teaching of English writing. As the findings of the study demonstrated, the teacher participants felt more comfortable marking and correcting errors in student writing.

Looking closely at Thailand's different educational policies related to learning EFL, particularly the 2008 BECC, provides a more complete picture and gives a better understanding of teaching English writing at the primary and secondary levels in the country. Specifically, speaking has been valued as the most important communication skill. While writing is included in the EFL curriculum, it is not as important as speaking. This, in turn, has impacted how writing is valued in the English classroom. From a teacher perspective, teaching English means teaching students to be able to speak, listen, read, and lastly write. Writing is always the last communication skill teachers cover. What was found in the context of primary and secondary schools in Thailand resonates with what EFL teachers from China, Mexico and Poland in a recent study by Ene and Hryniuk (2018) perceived about English writing skills. To be more specific, these teachers' perceptions of English writing skills, like in Thailand, were influenced by their respective countries' educational policies.

Building on my discussion above, I conclude with some final thoughts, utilizing three major relevant questions for us teacher trainers/educators and teaching programs or writing teacher programs, if available, to consider. First, should a practicum in teaching L2/EFL writing be included in teacher education programs, like TESOL and other language-related programs like rhetoric and composition and applied linguistics? While this question is easy to answer with 'yes,' not all of these programs are able to offer such classes, mainly because teacher educators do not always have a background in teaching L2/EFL writing. To illustrate this, I use the case of teacher education in my current situation as an example. At my institution, a teacher education program is housed in the College of Education. Graduate students who concentrate on ESL education and who want to teach writing in different locations, including ESL and EFL contexts, will take a practicum in teaching L2 writing offered by the English Department. Given my expertise in L2 writing, I have taught this class over the past five years. This case of my own institution raises another important issue related to teacher education and preparation. Collaboration and communication between teacher education programs across campuses should be encouraged.

Secondly, should a writing class be separated at the primary and secondary levels? If so, who will teach these classes? This major question and its follow-up are based on what was discovered in the study. In the participating primary and secondary schools, except for one school that provided an intensive English program, the teaching of writing was combined in an integrated English classroom. These two related questions have to do with staffing and teacher training issues. As found in the study, the majority of English language teachers were not trained to teach writing. These questions appear difficult to answer productively. If offering a separate writing class seems impossible, valuing English writing skills and restructuring a class could be considered. As learned from the context of this study, a country's educational policy plays a significant role in how English is valued; this has impacted the status of English writing instruction.

Thirdly, should collaboration between universities and schools be encouraged in EFL contexts? If so, who should initiate this collaboration? These two related questions are not too difficult to answer. This partnership among universities and schools is for the purpose of teacher training and teachers' professional development opportunities. These two questions and the 'yes' answer were based on what was found in the study. To illustrate, S12 School, which provided the intensive English program, invited university professors/lecturers who specialized in teaching English writing to teach writing to their Grade 12 students. In my view, in addition to inviting these university professors to teach writing to their students, schools should invite these professors to be guest speakers leading workshops on techniques and strategies for teaching writing. If we can make this collaboration/partnership happen, students are the ones who benefit from it. Definitely, this kind of collaboration should be encouraged.

Appendix: Interview Protocol

(1) Please describe the English-language curriculums in your institution.
(2) How is English-language writing taught in your institution?

(3) Please describe the purposes/goals/objectives of English-language writing instruction.

(4) How is an English language-writing curriculum designed and/or developed?

(5) What are the methods used to teach English-language writing?

(6) What are the teaching materials used in English-language writing instruction?

(7) What are the textbooks used in teaching English-language writing?

(8) Who makes decisions about textbooks?

(9) What types of writing assignments are given?

(10) What types of writing feedback do students receive?

(11) How often do students receive writing feedback?

(12) How is students' English-language writing evaluated?

(13) Please describe students who take or who are required to take English-language writing classes in your institution.

(14) Where do students write?

(15) What particular difficulties do students have with their English writing?

(16) How is English-language writing instruction different from Thai-language writing instruction?

(17) Who teaches English language classes?

(18) Who teaches English-language writing classes?

(19) What are the educational backgrounds of the English language teachers and English-language writing teachers?

(20) How are English teachers prepared? How are they prepared to teach writing?

(21) What particular difficulties do English-language writing teachers encounter?

(22) Do the institution's English language curriculums outline the goals of English language instruction and English-language writing instruction?

(23) What kinds of support and resources are provided for English-language writing instructors?

(24) What are the plans, if any, for developing English-language writing instruction in your institution?

(25) Do you have any other thoughts you would like to share?

Acknowledgements

This study, which is part of an ongoing research project examining English writing education in Thailand, was supported by the 2016–2017 Summer Hodges Research Grants from the Department of English, University of Tennessee, Knoxville, TN. I would like to extend my sincere thanks to the participating teachers and schools for their time and help with this study. I am grateful to my friends, Hemmanwan Khanmanee,

Nattaya Pilangam, Chayanoot Veerasarn and Yata Ketchai, for their help with interview arrangements in Thailand. I would also like to thank the editors of this edited volume and reviewers for their helpful feedback.

Notes

(1) All the quotations from policy documents cited in this chapter were originally written in English. I directly quoted from the original texts.
(2) It is my intention to limit the scope of the literature review to work and studies examining English education in primary and secondary schools. Post-secondary writing and writing in the workplace are not included in the literature review, because they are not the focus of the current study.
(3) In the context of this study, the country is divided into four regions, and this system is used in administrative contexts. In the other system, the country is divided into six regions based on geographical locations: central, northern, northeastern, western, eastern, and southern.

References

Bautista, M.L. and Gonzalez, A.B. (2006) Southeast Asian Englishes. In B. Krachu, Y. Krachu and C. Nelson (eds) *The Handbook of World Englishes* (pp. 130–144). Malden, MA: Blackwell.

Casanave, C.P. (2009) Training for writing or training for reality? Challenges facing EFL writing teachers and students in language teacher education programs. In R. Manchón (ed.) *Writing in Foreign Language Contexts: Learning, Teaching, and Research* (pp. 256–277). Bristol: Multilingual Matters.

Chamcharatsri, P.B. (2013) Perception of Thai English. *Journal of English as an International Language* 8 (1), 21–36.

Dhanasobhon, S. (2006) English language teaching dilemma in Thailand. See http://www.curriculumandinstruction.org/index.php?lay=show&ac=article&Id=539134523&Ntype=7.

Dörnyei, Z (2007) *Research Methods in Applied Linguistics*. Oxford: Oxford University Press.

Ene, E. and Hryniuk, K. (2018) Worlds apart but in the same boat: How macro-level policy influences EFL writing pedagogy in China, Mexico, and Poland. In D. Crusan and T. Ruecker (eds) *International Political Contexts of Second Language Writing Assessment* (pp. 15–28). New York: Routledge.

Ene, E. and Mitrea, A. (2013) EFL writing teacher training, beliefs, and practices in Romania: A tale of adaptation. *European Journal of Applied Linguistics and TEFL* 4, 117–137.

Foley, J.A. (2005) English in ... Thailand. *RELC Journal* 36 (2), 223–234.

Hirvela, A. and Belcher, D. (2007) Writing scholars as teacher educators: Exploring writing teacher education. *Journal of Second Language Writing* 16 (3), 125–128.

Khamkhien, A. (2010) Teaching English speaking and English speaking tests in the Thai context: A reflection from Thai perspectives. *English Language Teaching* 3 (1), 184–190.

Lee, I. (2010) Writing teacher education and teacher learning: Testimonies of four EFL teachers. *Journal of Second Language Writing* 19 (3), 143–157.

Mackenzie, A.S. (2015) EFL curriculum reform in Thailand (blog). See https://alansmackenzie.wordpress.com/2011/06/06/efl-curriculum-reform-in-thailand/.

Manchón, R. (ed.) (2009) *Writing in Foreign Language Contexts: Learning, Teaching, and Research*. Bristol: Multilingual Matters.

Matsuda, P.K. (2003) Second-language writing in the twentieth century: A situated historical perspective. In B. Kroll (ed.) *Exploring the Dynamics of Second Language Writing* (pp. 15–34). New York: Cambridge University Press.

Methitham, P. and Chamcharatsri, P.B. (2011) Critiquing ELT in Thailand: A reflection from history to practice. *Journal of Humanities, Naresuan University* 8 (2), 57–68.

Noom-ura, S. (2013) English-teaching problems in Thailand and Thai teachers' professional development needs. *English Language Teaching* 6 (11), 139–147.

OBEC (Office of the Basic Education Commission) (2008) *2008 Basic Education Core Curriculum*. Bangkok: Agricultural Co-operative Federation of Thailand.

Reichelt, M. (2005) English-language instruction in Poland. *Journal of Second Language Writing* 14 (4), 215–232.

Samudvanijja, C. (2008) Preface. In *2008 Basic Education Core Curriculum*. Bangkok: Agricultural Co-operative Federation of Thailand.

Silva, T. (2013) Second language writing: Talking points. *Journal of Second Language Writing* 22 (4), 432–434.

Teng, B. and Sinwongsuwat, K. (2015) Teaching and learning English in Thailand and the integration of conversation analysis (CA) into the classroom. *English Language Teaching* 8 (3), 13–23.

Wiriyachitra, A. (2002) English language teaching and learning in Thailand in this decade. *Thai TESOL Focus* 15 (1), 4–9.

Wongsothorn, A. (2004) Thailand. In H.W. Kam and R. Wong (eds) *Language Policies and Language Education: The Impact in East Asian Countries in the Next Decade* (pp. 307–320). Singapore: Cavendish Square Publishing.

Wongsothorn, A., Hiranburana, K. and Chinnawongs, S. (2004) English language teaching in Thailand today. In H.W. Kam and R. Wong (eds) *English Language Teaching in East Asia Today: Changing Policies and Practices* (pp. 441–453). Singapore: Time Academic Press.

You, X. (2004) New directions in EFL writing: A report from China. *Journal of Second Language Writing* 13 (4), 253–256.

7 Writing Pedagogy and Practice in South Asia: A Case of English Language Teachers and Teacher Trainers in Nepal

Sarah Henderson Lee and Shyam B. Pandey

Introduction

Like English language teaching (ELT) in many international contexts, English writing instruction in Nepal does not stand alone. Rather, students receive second language (L2) writing instruction alongside L2 reading, speaking and listening instruction in an integrated skills class taught by an English teacher. Similarly, the training required of English teachers in Nepal does not specifically include an L2 writing pedagogy course. Given these realities, this chapter seeks to shed light on the experiences of primary, secondary and post-secondary Nepali English teachers and teacher trainers regarding L2 writing instruction. The findings presented here highlight the complexities of English writing instruction in the diverse educational contexts of Nepal in terms of preparation and continued development, pedagogical challenges and resources and support systems. By discussing these areas through the lens of postmethod pedagogy, this chapter aims to inform English language teacher education programs and professional development organizations at the local level.

Nepal, a small Himalayan country, is linguistically and culturally rich, with over 100 languages spoken as mother tongues. While Nepali is the official language and lingua franca among the country's diverse ethnic groups, English has in recent years become an integral part of life in Nepal, outgrowing the 'foreign language' label it has had within the education system since its 1950s adoption (Giri, 2015). The teaching of English in Nepal post-democracy (i.e. 1951) has largely been guided by policy that views English as a subject rather than a language. Here, policy makers have often overlooked contextual limitations, such as inadequate teacher training, the low English language proficiency of teachers and insufficient instructional materials and resources, and have implemented policy against the recommendation of language specialists and researchers, including the start of English instruction at Grade 1 and the implementation of a communicative language teaching approach.

Currently, Nepal has nine universities and 35,222 Grade 1–12 schools, of which 29,207 are public and 6015 are private (Government of Nepal MOE, 2016). Whereas private schools use English as the language of instruction in all grades, the majority of public schools still use Nepali as the language of instruction, including in the English language classroom. The student–teacher ratio in such Grade 1–12 classes is 39.9:1 (Government of Nepal MOE, 2016), with class sizes exceeding 60 students in some public schools and 40 students in some private schools (Aryal *et al.*, 2016). These realities of ELT in Nepal, similar to those across South Asia, contribute to students' academic difficulties, resulting in the disappointing national exam pass rate of 36.37% for Grade 12 (Government of Nepal MOE, 2016).

Despite the prioritization of the English language in Nepal's educational system, the preparation of Nepali English teachers is lacking. The Ministry of Education (MOE) is responsible for in-service teacher training programs specific to Grades 1–12. Giri (2010) attributes the ineffectiveness of this training to its 'ritualistic' nature and notes the limited qualifications of the trainers themselves (Giri, 2010: 66). Although largely autonomous from the MOE, universities' training programs for preservice teachers are not without problems. Many have questioned the theory–practice imbalance of such programs, noting a disconnect between the training content and the needs of the local teaching contexts (Aryal *et al.*, 2016; Giri, 2010; Negi, 2016). With the rise of organizations such as the Nepal English Language Teachers' Association (NELTA), however, positive change in the quality of professional development for the country's English language teachers is evident (Gnawali, 2016).

Review of Literature

While research on writing in additional languages has increased significantly in recent decades, it has largely focused on second rather than foreign language contexts and on learners rather than teachers (Leki *et al.*, 2008). Since Hirvela and Belcher's *Journal of Second Language Writing* special issue, where they 'initiate a process of drawing attention to the teacher education realm of the L2 writing field' (Hirvela & Belcher, 2007: 126), more research has been conducted on the needs and experiences of L2 writing teachers in diverse contexts. This includes the underrepresented context of English as a foreign language (EFL) writing instruction, where related methods, materials and motivations, as well as teacher preparation and training, can be notably different from English-dominant contexts (e.g. Cimasko & Reichelt, 2011; Lee, 2010; Manchón, 2009; Manchón & de Haan, 2008; Reichelt, 2005). Such differences are critical to understanding the local pedagogical and curricular realities of EFL writing instruction but remain largely unexplored in many contexts, including Nepal. Here, research on local English language instruction, while not specific to the teaching of writing, provides a snapshot of the current educational climate in the country. Additionally, recent research on the role of criticality in Nepali English teacher development highlights the success of reflective EFL teachers (re)negotiating the relationship between pedagogical ideals and realities.

Aryal *et al.* (2016) provide a detailed historical overview of ELT in Nepal and discuss several current related issues, many of which have been identified as challenges in other EFL contexts. These include large class sizes, limited funding and resources, low teacher and learner motivation, teachers' use of more traditional methods (e.g. lecture, chorus drill, rote memorization) and training not specific to teachers' grade level or individual language domains. Similar to earlier calls made by Bhattarai (2006) and Bhattarai and Gautam (2007), Aryal *et al.* (2016) stress the need for a large-scale survey on the status of English and ELT practices in Nepal, noting the importance of such data in bridging the gap between government-related polices (i.e. ideals) and local realities, and better preparing the country's English language teachers. When surveyed about their instructional practices, 120 Grade 8–10 English teachers identified many high-need training areas related to the existing gap, including classroom management of large classes, increasing student motivation beyond exams, modifying classroom language for a variety of learner backgrounds and levels, incorporating technology in spaces with limited access and providing effective and manageable feedback (Negi, 2016).

The linguistic diversity of Nepal adds to the complexity of ELT, as is evident in Poudel's (2010) work. Here, analysis of university teacher and student questionnaires and English classroom observation notes sheds light on the effects of multilingualism on English language instruction. Findings include the use of Nepali by the majority of students and teachers for both in- and out-of-class interactions, teachers' difficulty with content delivery due to varied language backgrounds and a clear disadvantage for non-Nepali speaking students. Also 'far removed from the "ideal" context, which often forms the basis of many "centre" approaches,' is the daily reality of students and teachers (Tin, 2014: 414). Using ethnographic observations and interviews, Tin (2014) seeks to understand the local pedagogical practices emerging from the contextual particularities of an English language class at a public university in Nepal. These particularities include limited and interrupted instructional time and resources, as well as the demanding and unpredictable family and job commitments of both students and teachers. Within such realities, Tin (2014) describes the contextually appropriate pedagogical practices of classroom teacher talk supporting active student engagement at home and material use balancing both product- and process-oriented approaches. To legitimize local teaching and learning, Tin (2014: 415) calls for teacher education programs to provide 'more space … for articulating and reconstructing local, peripheral voices and practices.'

Sharma and Phyak's (2017) case study of how Nepali English teachers develop criticality through a materials development activity and subsequent workshop and dialogue is representative of such space. Here, criticality refers to 'a dialogic process in which teachers develop alternative ideas that support the inclusion of social justice and other critical sociopolitical issues in second-language pedagogies' (Sharma & Phyak, 2017: 212). The focus on communicative methods in teacher professional development, according to Sharma and Phyak (2017), fails to consider local sociopolitical issues and, in turn, limits teachers' critical awareness of the inequalities their students may encounter. Instead, they argue for the incorporation of such issues into language content, especially given the country's caste system. The prepared critical materials were used to show support for the existing curriculum and the workshop and dialogue were designed to raise teachers' awareness of local social issues and to support the development of their alternative teaching ideologies by helping them prepare and demonstrate critical literacy lessons. Teachers' post-dialogue reflections highlighted the potential effectiveness of critical pedagogy within an exam-driven EFL context through teachers' ideological growth. By reconceptualizing teacher professional development in this way, the theory–practice disconnect noted in Paudel's (2014) study, where teachers' affirmative attitudes towards critical pedagogy in ELT did not translate into actual classroom practice, can be avoided.

While the above research on local English language instruction and the role of criticality in Nepali English teacher development highlights the current realities of ELT in Nepal and how teachers navigate such realities, L2 writing instruction is not the primary focus. In fact, L2 writing instruction and training in Nepal remain unexplored as research areas. To address this gap, this chapter explores the L2 writing instructional experiences of in-service English teachers and teacher trainers in Nepal. The related areas of preparation and continued development, pedagogical challenges and resources and support systems emphasize the complexities of English writing instruction in Nepal and, when discussed through a postmethod pedagogical lens, offer English language teacher education programs and professional development organizations context-sensitive suggestions for positive change.

Methodology

Both teacher and teacher trainer participants were recruited through NELTA. Teacher participants were recruited from a week-long professional development workshop organized by NELTA in Spring 2017. Forty Nepali English teachers participated in this training, and 36 teachers from nine different districts of the country consented to participate in this study. Teacher participants represented primary, secondary and post-secondary teaching contexts in both public and private institutions. Their years of teaching experience averaged 11 years and ranged from three to 35 years. Additionally, 30 of the teacher participants held a master's degree and six held a bachelor's degree, predominantly in the discipline of English education. Teacher trainer participants were recruited from a list of current NELTA trainers, and 12 out of 14 trainers consented to participate in this study. Teacher trainer participants, who served all districts of Nepal, averaged 12 years of training experience ranging from five to 20 years. Eleven of the teacher trainer participants held a master's degree and one held a doctoral degree. Table 7.1 further details participant information.

A single case study design (Yin, 2009) allowed for multiple data sources to capture the complexities of a commonplace situation. To better understand the lived experience of Nepali English teachers and teacher trainers regarding L2 writing instruction, as well as the meaning they make of their experience, questionnaires and interviews were used with participants. Both teacher and teacher trainer questionnaires (Appendices A and B, respectively) were submitted electronically and consisted of six largely background-related questions on English language teaching/training experience, educational background, professional development opportunities, preparation to teach L2 writing/train L2 writing teachers and classroom challenges related to the teaching of L2 writing. Regarding the interviews, Rubin and Rubin's (2005: 30–36) responsive interviewing model was employed, which: (1) obtains interviewees' interpretations of their own experiences; (2) considers the personality, style and beliefs of the interviewer; (3) generates ethical obligations for the interviewer; (4) allows for breadth in interviewees' answers; and (5) is flexible and adaptive in its design. After completing the questionnaire, all participants were invited to participate in an optional follow-up interview to elaborate on their questionnaire responses and reflect more critically on their

Table 7.1 Participant information

	Gender		Highest degree			Years of teaching experience					Years of training experience				
	M	F	BA	MA, MEd, MPhil	PhD	0–5	6–10	11–15	16–20	21+	0–5	6–10	11–15	16–20	21+
Teacher participants	21	15	6	30	–	6	17	8	2	3	–	–	–	–	–
Trainer participants	10	2	–	11	1	–	–	–	–	–	1	6	1	4	–

experiences with L2 writing instruction. Twenty-five of the teacher participants elected to be interviewed in a focus group corresponding to their teaching region; a total of six focus group interviews were conducted with these teacher participants. All 12 teacher trainer participants volunteered to be interviewed; eight were interviewed individually and four were interviewed in two pair groups. Interviews ranged in time from 27 minutes to one hour and 34 minutes.

Content analysis, referring to 'any qualitative data reduction and sense-making effort that takes a volume of qualitative material and attempts to identify core consistencies and meanings' (Patton, 2002: 453), was used recursively throughout the data collection process. Kumaravadivelu's (2001) postmethod pedagogy framework consisting of parameters of particularity, practicality and possibility, moreover, provided a lens through which to further categorize and contextualize the data sources. Here, a pedagogy of particularity stems from a heightened awareness of local exigencies, a pedagogy of practicality values teachers as reflective producers of context-sensitive pedagogic knowledge (i.e. practicing theory) and a pedagogy of possibility empowers both teachers and students by tapping into the lived experiences they bring to the learning/teaching context. Such a lens magnified the context-specific needs of Nepali English teachers in terms of teaching L2 writers, how they negotiate those needs with their current English language curricular and classroom realities and how they themselves connect to their L2 writing instructional practice.

Findings

The findings of this study highlight the complexity of teaching writing in Nepal from the perspectives of both Nepali English teachers and teacher trainers. To represent this complexity, the findings are organized by: (1) preparation and continued development; (2) pedagogical challenges; and (3) resources and support systems.

Preparation and continued development

The following themes were identified from the data regarding participants' preparation and continued development to teach writing: (1) a disconnect between pre-service training and in-service practice; and (2) top-down professional development.

A disconnect between pre-service training and in-service practice

Both teacher and teacher trainer participants highlighted the gap between teachers' university preparation and classroom teaching. One trainer, for example, recalled a lack of theoretical application: '[As pre-service teachers] we talked about communicative language teaching, we talked about suggestopedia, GT [grammar translation] method, audiolingual method, everything, but my professors never taught me how to develop materials on the basis of those theories' (Bandhu, Interview, 16 July 2017). Regarding the teaching of writing, both teacher and trainer participants noted teacher education programs' focus on theoretical knowledge specific to process writing. Although teachers were clearly confident in their knowledge of process writing, they expressed frustration regarding the fact that this knowledge did not support their classroom realities, which included serious time, space and resource limitations, as well as the added pressure to teach to the national exams. The teachers craved practical writing knowledge suited for their contexts, as voiced below:

> I want to learn something to teach writing practically but not theoretically because it encourages students to be motivated in writing. Sometimes the theoretical knowledge cannot work practically. If we learn something practically, it is easy to apply too. For example, the theoretical ideas that I learned during my university degree do not work well when I try to apply them in my class. (Indira, Interview, 30 May 2017)

Because their university experience prepared them theoretically but not practically, teachers turned to various professional development opportunities, including conferences, workshops and webinars, to acquire practical knowledge about the teaching of writing and language teaching in general. The majority of them did so, not because it was required of them, but because they wanted to be successful teachers of writing. Several teacher participants associated such success with keeping current on writing pedagogies. Indira, for example, emphasized, 'A good teacher always needs to be update[d]' (Indira, Interview, 30 May 2017). Such a positive attitude towards continued learning and advancement of practice was common among the teacher participants, regardless of whether their school context was public or private.

Trainer participants also saw a disconnect between their educational background and their work as teacher trainers. Teaching experience, according to Kiran, played an important role in his preparation to become a teacher trainer:

> Actually, my degrees and certificates did not only help me prepare English teachers to teach writing. My own teaching experience and action research helped me a lot. My practical work and experience have supported a lot in my training career. (Kiran, Questionnaire)

The context specificity of action research was highlighted by other trainers who noted the importance of teachers making decisions about their writing instruction based on data from their own classrooms. Not all trainer participants, however, were familiar and/or comfortable with action research.

Similar to teacher participants who turned to professional development organizations to bridge the gap between pre-service and in-service knowledge, many trainer participants credited such organizations with preparing them to do the in-service work of teacher trainers, including building in them the necessary confidence.

> Being a female and a mother it took me years to have courage to be a trainer. It is NELTA that has given a platform for me to come out of the shell and be a trainer. I think degrees are for getting a secure job and recognition in the society but the most important thing is the opportunity and confidence teachers must have to be a trainer. The trainer has to manage odd time schedules, leave approval, and other social, cultural obligations. If I were not in NELTA I would not be a trainer, just a job holder in a school. (Sarima, Questionnaire)

All participants, including teachers and trainers, associated university degrees and training with securing a job, as well as social status. They saw professional development, on the other hand, as critical to preparing them to do the in-service work of both English language teaching and training. No participant described their pre-service training as positively connected to their in-service practice.

Top-down professional development

Although the majority of teacher participants reported recent professional development participation, many of them expressed dissatisfaction with the focus content which, according to the teachers, often prioritized communicative language teaching approaches and the language domain of speaking as stated below:

> I have been attending several trainings but I rarely see the training sessions focused on writing specifically. But the shift now should go into the writing. Though speaking skill matters a lot, writing skill also should be the concern in the seminars and workshops. Writing skill is inevitable to us. Our focus should go in writing. (Nirmal, Interview, 30 May 2017)

For many participants, this prioritization of speaking in teacher training was related to the fact that native-like spoken English was still associated with a higher socioeconomic status in Nepal. Additionally, the role of the country's oral culture was noted.

Similar to their reflections on pre-service teacher training, teacher participants noted that professional development specific to the teaching of writing often favored theory over practice. For teachers, like the one below, this meant the continued lack of potentially effective, practical and engaging writing strategies in their pedagogical toolkits.

> I'd like to be trained in effective activities to teach writing. Actually, we have got many theoretical knowledges but we lack some teaching tips kind of ideas to teach writing. I want to teach the idea of unity, coherence, cohesion, and thesis statement practically but not theoretically. There must be some engaging activities. (Punya, Interview, 31 May 2017)

To the teachers, this theory–practice imbalance supported the disconnect between teacher training and teaching, causing some to question whether or not professional development organizers considered teachers' classroom realities at all. Trainers were, however, aware of the problem. One trainer, in fact, used the analogy of a driving class to describe the focus on writing theory in pre- and in-service teacher training:

> I've been given very good driving classes. I know what everything of the part of the car has been fixed and safely turn but I've never been given an opportunity to just sit in the seat of the driver and just experience it. (Ashish, Interview, 16 July 2017)

He continued the analogy to highlight the fact that trainers are not prepared to train English teachers in how to teach writing because they have limited or no real experience in doing so:

> Even though I'm expert at the theory how can I drive a car and how can I teach another guy to drive the car? I just can't give him the theory. So I don't dare to take him into the road as instructor. (Ashish, Interview, 16 July 2017)

The majority of trainers also referenced the critical role of local contexts in developing professional development for teachers but recognized that professional development organizations and trainers were not, in fact, considering local realities when planning professional development sessions. This, according to one trainer, was largely due to the missing needs analysis:

> Ok, basically what happens is the needs assessment. The needs assessment part has largely been neglected. We have a kind of essentially top-down process and practice. Whatever we do we do top-down. Top-down means we design the training with our perception. (Hem, Interview, 17 July 2017)

To address this problematic approach to professional development, several trainer participants called for more specialized English language teacher trainers with expertise in particular language domains and pedagogies, as well as familiarity with unique local contexts. Such positive change to professional development would address the current disconnect between in-service training and classroom practice, which nearly all participants identified.

Pedagogical challenges

Analysis of the data revealed three themes in terms of the challenges Nepali English teachers face in teaching writing: (1) teachers as non-writers; (2) students' low motivation and varied linguistic ability; and (3) space, class size and time constraints.

Teachers as non-writers

The fact that teachers did not write in English themselves was identified by both teacher and trainer participants as a primary pedagogical challenge. Here, teacher participants detailed this challenge specifically in connection to a lack of interest, time and linguistic knowledge. Milan, for example, highlighted teachers' limited interest in and experience with writing: 'It's very true that teachers also don't feel interested in writing. Many teachers don't have the writing experience. They themselves don't write much' (Milan, Interview, 30 May 2017). Manasi, on the other hand, emphasized teachers' lack of time and language skills in connection to this pedagogical challenge, noting the absence of writing practice in teacher education programs:

> Writing is least favorite language skill to us. Writing cannot be developed unless we write. There comes the difficulty. For this language skill, we need to sit down, time to think. You should have the vocabulary knowledge or you need to research something. Writing takes a time. That's why writing [is] least favorite. We teachers don't involve much in writing. During our university education, we just talk about the different phases of writing but don't actually experience them. (Manasi, Interview, 11 July 2017)

In addition to highlighting teachers' lack of interest, time and linguistic knowledge for writing in English, several trainer participants reflected on the effect of teachers as non-writers on students during writing instruction. Here, the direct relationship between teacher writers and student writers was especially noted in terms of motivation and confidence. Trainers, including Hem below, questioned why students would be motivated to start writing or be confident to engage in the writing process if their teacher never modeled this.

> However, the challenge is the teachers and the students both find it very difficult to start writing and normally teachers do not write and they ask students to write. Either teachers are not writing and they are not able to produce any sample of their writing for the students. That is the big missing part because it's very difficult to convince the students, you know if the teacher has not written anything and in the class probably the teacher is not presenting any sample of his or her writing. (Hem, Interview, 17 July 2017)

All trainer participants were in agreement that teacher education programs should work towards increasing teachers' writing skills while preparing them to actually teach writing, but only one participant knew of an existing example.

> One of the challenges that we face in Nepal is that teachers do not have a culture of reading and writing themselves. Therefore, through this blog project we are trying to develop a habit of reading and writing profession materials in the pre-service teachers. The student teachers are supposed to collaborate in a group of three and write blog entries on a regular basis. They also comment on the blog posts by other participants. This way, they are learning three skills – ICT [information and communications technology], writing and collaboration. We believe that these teachers

will be able to reflect the process they have gone through to write blog entries later in their class while they will be teaching writing to their students. Since they are engaged in the process of writing – where they need to collect ideas, prepare draft, share with peers and get feedback, revise and edit before they produce the final draft – we believe that they will be able to replicate their experience as a writers while supporting their students to develop writing skills. (Lal, Questionnaire)

Students' low motivation and varied linguistic ability

Teacher participants consistently raised students' lack of motivation and varied language proficiencies as real obstacles to their English writing instruction. Regarding the former, several teacher participants discussed students' low motivation for writing in relation to other language domains. Karishma, for example, stated: 'In our context, to teach writing as a second language is very challenging to us because the students are not motivated to participate in writing skills in comparison to other three language skills' (Karishma, Questionnaire). According to Binod, this was a result of the curriculum prioritizing other language skills and, in turn, teachers not providing in-class writing tasks for the students:

> Writing is the last language skill that comes in priority because it's done after other three language skills. But these language skills are interconnected. Mostly in public schools, students do get opportunities to practice the three other language skills but not writing. (Binod, Interview, 11 July 2017)

Similarly, trainer participants linked students' low motivation for English writing to the preferred domains of reading and speaking. This, according to Lal, was connected to teachers' ineffectiveness in providing engaging and interactive writing instruction:

> Students ... do not have as much interest in writing as they have in reading and speaking and this affects the level of commitment they demonstrate in writing projects. Besides most of the teachers in our context do not know the effective technique to teach writing. Most of them ask the students to produce a written text without involving the students in various activities to develop their writing skill. After giving the writing task, the students and teacher do not have any interaction and the final product is graded/marked. There is virtually no support provided to the students to help them in the writing process. (Lal, Questionnaire)

Teacher participants also identified the students' varied linguistic ability as a serious challenge to their teaching of English writing. The majority of teachers discussed this in terms of Nepal's unique linguistic and cultural diversity. For example, Baruni said, 'Teaching writing skills in English is a very challenging job in the context of our country. We have already known that our country is multicultural, multilingual and multiethnic country. While teaching English, our mother languages interfere' (Baruni, Questionnaire). Dhiren, like many others, referenced his ongoing attempt to address the challenges presented by such a classroom context: 'I am trying my best to change the teaching pedagogy according to these diverse conditions but it's very difficult in our context because students come from multiple linguistic backgrounds' (Dhiren, Interview, 7 June 2017). Although no teacher participant detailed such pedagogical change, many, like Prem, recognized the importance of providing accessible content to all learners and increasing the students' lexicon in the heterogeneous educational contexts of their country:

> The first challenge that we face while teaching is the learners with mixed ability. When you instruct them for [writing], some learners understand it and some others don't. It creates great problem in the classroom. Secondly, the vocabulary knowledge becomes an issue. Most of the learners do not have the habit of learning English and they don't have enough exposure in English language [to express themselves via writing]. (Prem, Interview, 20 July 2017)

Space, class size and time constraints

For most teacher participants, classroom management challenges stemmed primarily from space limitations and large class sizes. Such constraints had a direct effect on classroom writing activities, particularly those that required group work, and teachers' willingness to try many of the strategies learned in professional development sessions. Bir noted:

> We always talk about the ideal classrooms but things are not like that in reality. Crowded class with large number of students. No proper lighting. Not spacious classroom to conduct the group work activities. If these things are available … they'd help us to make our lessons more effective. (Bir, Interview, 20 July 2017)

Prem added:

> The classroom management is another challenge for us. When we try to do some group work, we don't have enough space in our classroom. Because of the infrastructural issue or let's say classroom space issue, we can't conduct the different activities that suit to our heterogeneous student population. (Prem, Interview, 20 July 2017)

Additionally, some teachers acknowledged that their lower proficient and struggling students were most negatively affected by this classroom reality. Gita shared:

> There are issues of physical management of the classroom where the furniture are not moveable and the number of students is very high. In every class, there are almost 50 or 55 students. We cannot pay attention to all the students who are below average. They cannot have active participation. They get lost somewhere. (Gita, Interview, 20 July 2017)

The trainer participants focused mostly on the contextual constraints of class size and time, especially in connection to process writing at the university level, as represented by Mahima below:

> We have to be very careful about time because ... we have to finish our courses. Because of the time concern also we cannot give [students] sufficient practices about the writing in the classroom. So that's why we want to give theory. We ask them to write but nobody will do the homework because we don't have much time to follow up that. And teachers don't have enough time to check more than 200 students in one class. It's a challenge in teaching in this kind of public colleges and schools or universities. So we don't have much time to follow that writing process because writing cannot be achieved in one day. (Mahima, Interview, 17 July 2017)

Even though the trainers expressed frustrations similar to those of the teachers in terms of contextual constraints, they did not reference consideration of these realities when planning professional development events.

Resources and support systems

Regarding resources and support systems related to the teaching of writing, the following data themes were found: (1) limited access to materials and technology; and (2) the absence of a teacher mentor program.

Limited access to materials and technology

Teacher participants from both public and private teaching contexts spoke about the pedagogical value of accessible materials and technology for writing instruction thanks to their professional development participation. This, however, was not their reality, as is evident from the two teacher voices below:

> We as teachers should encourage [students] to visit to the library regularly. If we also utilize the technology for instance the mobile phone or utilize the Internet and online resources, it can yield a productive result as well. Unfortunately, we don't have any of these resources. (Prem, Questionnaire)

> Actually there is the problem of essential teaching materials for teaching writing. Though we can find all of the things from Internet and the local level, it's not possible in our school. Internet is not available at all. Same problem is existing to students too. (Supriti, Questionnaire)

The teachers from contexts where internet access is not yet available and updated school libraries are a rare luxury returned home from professional development training often unable to implement any of the shared pedagogical ideas and strategies. Additionally, they did not have access to many teaching materials, especially those specific to the teaching of writing. Students faced similar challenges in that they struggled to obtain required course texts on time or at all and could not afford supplemental study materials.

The absence of a teacher mentor program

A few teacher participants described peer collaboration in terms of idea sharing and brainstorming.

> [My colleague and I] also collaborate before the class session and discuss about the teaching ideas and teaching materials. We do it most often. We do collaborate even while teaching other language skills. Two heads are always better than one. (Manish, Interview, 31 May 2017)

Heavy teaching loads and a lack of designated time and space for in-house professional development, however, often hampered the teachers' participation in such informal collaboration. Additionally, a lack of administrative support prevented the transition to a more formal mentoring program for teachers. In fact, many of the public teacher participants reported not being observed by a supervisor. For the public teachers who had experienced formal supervision, inconsistent and ineffective documentation and follow-ups were common. Private teacher participants, on the other hand, experienced frequent supervision by administrators, but this supervision was largely top-down with little space for teachers to participate in the corresponding meeting.

Discussion and Conclusion

The findings of the current study, a case study of English language teachers and teacher trainers in Nepal, shed further light on the complexities of EFL writing pedagogy and practice. While many of the pedagogical and curricular realities of Nepal mirror other EFL contexts, including large class sizes, insufficient materials and exam-driven curricula, the unique experiences of the teacher and trainer participants offer insight into the particularities of teachers' preparation and development to teach English writing in the linguistically and culturally diverse context of Nepal.

Teacher participants noticed a serious imbalance between writing theory and practice in their teacher education programs. Although confident in their theoretical knowledge of process writing, teachers were disappointed that such knowledge did not successfully transfer to their local practice. Eager to fill this gap in their training, many teachers turned to training opportunities sponsored by various professional development organizations. Here, they largely found more of the same in terms of the prioritization of theory over practice. When such professional development events focused on practice, it was rarely specific to writing. Teachers also struggled to implement the learned pedagogical strategies in their classrooms, often giving up and falling back on the more familiar teacher-centered, traditional methods.

From these findings it is clear that both teacher education programs and professional development organizations are out of touch with teachers' local realities in Nepal. In addition to echoing past calls for a government-sponsored needs analysis (Aryal *et al.*, 2016; Bhattarai, 2006; Bhattarai & Gautam, 2007), teacher educators and trainers need to have more of a presence in the classrooms of English language teachers. Teacher education programs, for example, could require participant-observation of writing instruction in connection to related university coursework. Similarly, teacher trainers affiliated with professional development organizations could explore the possibilities of training extensions in local classrooms. Expertise in writing was also minimal in both teacher preparation and development contexts where teacher educators and trainers were general language specialists and not writing specialists. This points to the fact that writing-specific training is needed for teacher educators and trainers, as well as for teachers. Additionally, larger professional development organizations such as NELTA could consider the creation of special interest groups (SIGs), perhaps in collaboration with the MOE, to support the development of more contextually sensitive trainings. Recognizing the primary roles of reading and speaking in current EFL curricula, trainers via SIGs could, for example, design workshops for teachers on the reading–writing and/or speaking–writing connection.

The addition of SIGs would also facilitate more professional networking between teachers and trainers, who together could tackle challenges in teaching English writing at the local level. While a few teacher participants experienced informal collaboration with peers at their institutions, the majority of them described collaboration as desired but unrealistic given their heavy workloads and the lack of administrative support. Finding time and space for teachers to reflect and work together could benefit the professional development of teachers and, in turn, the academic growth of students. Such collaboration could, for example, come in the form of MOE-backed teacher participation in SIGs, shared planning time for teachers before, during or after the school day or as a more formal mentoring program. In line with Pandey's (2009) findings, no teacher participant in this study reported participation in a formal mentoring program. Several teachers, however, noted that such a program would have been especially beneficial during their early teaching years. To strengthen the relationship between teacher education programs and schools, as well as between administrators and teachers, (re)conceptualization of mentorship and supervision is needed. How might senior teachers and administrators better meet the needs of novice and mid-career teachers by implementing a participant-observation model followed by an interactive dialogue? Relatedly, exploring how teacher trainers could extend professional development workshops through the observation of teachers' related practice could address one of the teacher participants' concerns about current professional development (i.e. the absence of any type of follow-up) and promote mentorship.

In addition to teacher education programs and professional development initiatives increasing their focus on writing in connection to teachers' local practice, they need to contribute to the writing development of individual teachers and help them 'see themselves as writers' (Casanave, 2009: 274). Both teacher and trainer participants in this study recognized the negative effect of non-writing teachers on writing instruction. To address the lack of interest, time and linguistic knowledge, as identified by the teachers, English teacher education programs could consider requiring both an academic writing course and a writing pedagogy course. In the first, teacher candidates develop their own English writing by experiencing the L2 writing instructional methods they will develop in the second, methods-specific course. Additionally, pre- and in-service teacher training programs could incorporate writing practice for teachers. Similar to the blogging example shared by one of the trainers in the 'Findings' section, teacher education programs could require pre-service teachers to use reflective journals to connect to learned pedagogical theories and methods and to continually improve their English writing skills and confidence. Such journaling could easily extend into in-service teachers' practice, possibly in connection to mentoring programs. In-service teachers could also explore writing possibilities for their students and increase their enthusiasm for writing by participating in writing workshops offered by professional development organizations.

Lastly, English language teachers and trainers in Nepal need access to more research on writing in their unique multilingual and multicultural context. Since Ortega's (2009) corpus of EFL writing studies, research specific to writing in Nepal has remained sparse. More longitudinal, ethnographic studies, for example, could shed light on the experiences of student writers and their teachers, helping to inform the practice of both teachers and trainers in the country. Additionally, since no participant identified as a teacher-scholar, professional development specific to action research is recommended. Here, reflective teachers become local agents of change by critically reflecting on data from their own writing instruction.

Appendix A: Teacher Questionnaire

Directions: Please respond to each of the below questions in as much detail as possible. Feel free to use more than one page if needed. Once you complete the document, save it and email it back to us as an attachment. Thank you!

(1) How long have you been teaching English and in what capacity (e.g. grade level, type of school)?

(2) What academic degrees and certificates have you obtained for your teaching career?

(3) How did the above degrees and certificates prepare you to teach writing in English?

(4) What professional development programs have you participated in since becoming an English language teacher?

(5) How did these professional development programs advance your ability to teach writing in English?

(6) What current challenges do you face in terms of teaching writing in English?

Appendix B: Teacher Trainer Questionnaire

Directions: Please respond to each of the below questions in as much detail as possible. Feel free to use more than one page if needed. Once you complete the document, save it and email it back to us as an attachment. Thank you!

(1) How long have you been training English language teachers and in what contexts (e.g. regions, levels, training types)?

(2) What academic degrees and certificates have you obtained for your teacher training career?

(3) How did the above degrees and certificates prepare you to train English language teachers to teach writing?

(4) What professional development programs for English language teachers have you developed and/or led?

(5) How did these professional development programs advance English language teachers' ability to teach writing?

(6) What current challenges do you think English language teachers face in terms of teaching writing?

Appendix C: Sample Interview Questions

For teacher participants:

- What aspects of English writing do you feel most confident teaching and why?
- What recent successes and challenges have you experienced in teaching English writing? How have you addressed any challenges?
- What content knowledge from your past education and training have you applied in your teaching of English writing and how effective has it been?
- What types of teacher collaboration have you experienced that support the teaching of English writing?
- What areas of second language (English) writing pedagogy would you like to see included in future professional development trainings and why?

For trainer participants:

- What observations have you made regarding the teaching of English writing in Nepal?
- How has second language (English) writing pedagogy been covered in recent professional development trainings for teachers in your region?
- Have you developed and/or led a training session focused on the teaching of English writing? If so, how effective do you think it was for participating teachers? If not, would you be comfortable offering such a training in the future? Why or why not?
- How might teacher education programs and professional development organizations better prepare Nepali teachers of English to teach writing?

Acknowledgements

A special thank you to NELTA for connecting us to so many great teachers and trainers in Nepal and to the teacher and trainer participants for so honestly sharing their voices.

References

Aryal, A., Short, M., Fan, S. and Kember, D. (2016) Issues in English language teaching in Nepal. In S. Fan and J. Fielding-Wells (eds) *What is Next in Educational Research?* (pp. 141–155). Rotterdam: Sense.

Bhattarai, G.R. (2006) English teaching situation in Nepal: Elaboration of the theme for panel discussion in the 40th TESOL conference. *Journal of NELTA* 11 (1–2), 11–16.

Bhattarai, G.R. and Gautam, G.R. (2007) The proposed ELT survey: Redefining status and role of English in Nepal. *Journal of NELTA* 12 (1–2), 32–35.

Casanave, C.P. (2009) Training for writing or training for reality? Challenges facing EFL writing teachers and students in language teacher education programs. In R. Manchón (ed.) *Writing in Foreign Language Contexts: Learning, Teaching, and Research* (pp. 256–277). Bristol: Multilingual Matters.

Cimasko, T. and Reichelt, M. (eds) (2011) *Foreign Language Writing Instruction: Principles and Practices*. Anderson, SC: Parlor Press.

Giri, R.A. (2010) English language teachers' resource centre: A model for developing contexts. *Journal of NELTA* 15 (1–2), 64–76.

Giri, R.A. (2015) The many faces of English in Nepal. *Asian Englishes* 17 (2), 94–115.

Gnawali, L. (2016) English language teacher development through teacher associations: The case of NELTA. *ELT Journal* 70 (2), 170–179.

Government of Nepal MOE (Ministry of Education) (2016) *Education in Figures* [data file]. See http://www.moe.gov.np/assets/uploads/files/Nepal_Education_in_Figures_2016.pdf.

Hirvela, A. and Belcher, D. (2007) Writing scholars as teacher educators: Exploring writing teacher education. *Journal of Second Language Writing* 16 (3), 125–128.

Kumaravadivelu, B. (2001) Towards a postmethod pedagogy. *TESOL Quarterly* 35 (4), 537–560.

Lee, I. (2010) Writing teacher education and teacher learning: Testimonies of four EFL teachers. *Journal of Second Language Writing* 19 (3), 143–157.

Leki, I., Cumming, A. and Silva, T. (2008) *A Synthesis of Research on Second Language Writing in English*. New York: Routledge.

Manchón, R. (ed.) (2009) *Writing in Foreign Language Contexts: Learning, Teaching, and Research*. Bristol: Multilingual Matters.

Manchón, R.M. and de Haan, P. (2008) Writing in foreign language contexts: An introduction. *Journal of Second Language Writing* 17 (1), 1–6.

Negi, J.S. (2016) Teachers' professional development to enhance ELT: Needs analysis for developing teacher training program in an EFL context. *Journal of NELTA* 21 (1–2), 40–53.

Ortega, L. (2009) Studying writing across EFL contexts: Looking back and moving forward. In R. Manchón (ed.) *Writing in Foreign Language Contexts: Learning, Teaching, and Research* (pp. 232–255). Bristol: Multilingual Matters.

Pandey, S.B. (2009) Mentoring for teachers' professional development in Nepal: A status study of Kathmandu district. Unpublished master's thesis, Kathmandu University.

Patton, M.Q. (2002) *Qualitative Research and Evaluation Methods*. Thousand Oaks, CA: Sage.

Paudel, J. (2014) Teachers' attitudes towards critical pedagogy and its practice in ELT classrooms. *Journal of NELTA* 19 (1–2), 132–146.

Poudel, P.P. (2010) Teaching English in multilingual classrooms of higher education: The present scenario. *Journal of NELTA* 15 (1–2), 121–133.

Reichelt, M. (2005) English-language instruction in Poland. *Journal of Second Language Writing* 14 (4), 215–232.

Rubin, H.J. and Rubin, I.S. (2005) *Qualitative Interviewing: The Art of Hearing Data*. Thousand Oaks, CA: Sage.

Sharma, B.K. and Phyak, P. (2017) Criticality as ideological becoming: Developing English teachers for critical pedagogy in Nepal. *Critical Inquiry in Language Studies* 14 (2–3), 210–238.

Tin, T.B. (2014) A look into the local pedagogy of an English language classroom in Nepal. *Language Teaching Research* 18 (3), 397–417.

Yin, R.K. (2009) *Case Study Research: Design and Methods* (4th edn). Thousand Oaks, CA: Sage.

8 Scaffolding Second Language Disciplinary Writing in Qatar: A Case Study of a Design Teacher's Development

Thomas D. Mitchell and Silvia Pessoa

Challenges in the Teaching of Writing at Branch Campuses

A recent trend in higher education has been the establishment of English-medium branch campuses of Western universities worldwide (Wilkins & Huisman, 2012). In these contexts, academic language, particularly writing, has been found to be challenging for students (Doiz *et al.*, 2013), who are mostly instructed by disciplinary faculty who may have had little training in pedagogical methods, let alone in second language (L2) writing pedagogy. Despite the increasing prevalence of international branch campuses, there is little research documenting teaching practices, teacher development and student outcomes in these institutions, particularly as it relates to writing (Altbach, 2007).

This chapter describes teacher development in L2 disciplinary writing instruction at an English-medium American university's branch campus in Qatar, where most students are L2 writers. We focus on the teacher development of a design professor who collaborated with us (writing professors with training in linguistics) to revise the guidelines of his writing assignments to better scaffold student writing. With this focus, our chapter differs from others in this volume that discuss the preparation of pre-service and in-service *language* teachers for teaching L2 writing. We take an expanded view of preparation for teaching L2 writing with our focus on disciplinary faculty in higher education.

Disciplinary faculty often ask their students to display learning through writing. However, without training in writing pedagogies, many disciplinary faculty rely on their own writing experiences as former students and professionals in their field for the design and assessment of writing. This is an area that deserves more attention because most L2 university students do the majority of their writing in courses that are taught by disciplinary teachers, not *language* teachers. We suggest that collaboration with writing teachers can help disciplinary teachers develop L2 writing expertise to better scaffold student writing. Such collaborations, although limited in higher education, have resulted in positive outcomes (Brisk, 2014; Dreyfus *et al.*, 2016; Fenton-Smith & Humphreys, 2015; Humphrey, 2016; Humphrey & Macnaught, 2016; Mitchell & Pessoa, 2017; Pessoa, 2017; Pessoa *et al.*, 2018, in press).

The branch campus where our collaboration took place follows the same curriculum as the main campus in a co-educational environment. The university has been in operation since 2004 and approximately 700 students have graduated there, majoring in five disciplines. The students come mostly from Qatar, the greater Middle East, Pakistan, India and Bangladesh, and have been educated in various educational settings, including Arabic-medium public schools, English-medium private schools and local 'national' schools (e.g. the Indian educational system in Qatar). While some arrive well prepared, many students struggle in the transition to college, in large part due to their limited experience in reading and writing academic texts in English (see, for example, Miller & Pessoa, 2016, 2017; Miller *et al.*, 2014, 2016; Pessoa *et al.*, 2014, 2017, 2018). Students who come from local government schools seem to be the least prepared, as recent educational reform has created conflicts and confusion as to whether subject matter should best be taught and learned in Arabic or English. Much of the curriculum in government schools was in Arabic before the Education for a New Era reform (2001–2004). This educational reform mandated much of the curriculum to be taught in English. Recently, however, there has been a move to go back to Arabic instruction for educational, administrative and cultural reasons. Thus, in this context, the teaching of academic L2 writing in the local schools has suffered tremendously and many students come unprepared to meet the high academic demands of writing at our English-medium university.

Our campus has several types of language support resources. There is an academic bridge program which provides EAP coursework for students who are not quite ready for the university. Our institution has an Academic Resource Center (ARC) with three full-time staff members and peer tutors who provide tutoring support to students not only in academic reading and writing but also in math and programming. Many faculty members request or require their students to visit the ARC for language support that faculty feel is beyond the scope of their course content or the faculty member's own expertise. Many courses also have student teaching assistants who support student learning in a variety of ways, including assistance with language.

It is not just these students who are challenged in this new context; it can be quite daunting for faculty to teach these students. At our institution, some faculty come directly from the main campus while others are recruited regionally and internationally. As reported in our previous work (Miller & Pessoa, 2017), many faculty coming from the United States arrive at this international context with a set of expectations based on their previous experiences in English-dominant contexts. However, their methods and materials may not be equally effective in this new context, and these teachers may not anticipate the challenges they will face when assigning writing to L2 English learners. Even when professors anticipate challenges stemming from differences in the international classroom, they do not always know how to adjust. Consequently, they may adopt a range of strategies, including 'dumbing down the curriculum' by eliminating or reducing writing assignments (see Wilkins & Huisman, 2012) or adjusting their expectations for such assignments. For example, some faculty report that they continue to have the same writing requirements, but change their expectations for language; whereas on the main campus they would judge grammatical errors to reflect a lack of precision and deduct points, on the branch campus they adjust by focusing more on ideas and less on grammar and linguistic connections to avoid giving most students low grades (Miller & Pessoa, 2017).

While there are professors in this institution who are satisfied with adjusting the expectations reflected in their academic reading and writing assignments, some are not. However, even when attempting to maintain the same standard for these multilingual students, many professors lack the language and writing expertise necessary to help L2 writers meet such expectations. This chapter discusses our collaboration with one such faculty member, a design professor who approached us to help him better scaffold student writing. Our chapter offers a model of writing collaboration between language experts and disciplinary faculty that can be used to improve the teaching of writing in the disciplines. Such a model is important because university students mostly write for courses taught by disciplinary instructors who may have little experience with teaching writing.

The Case Study

Robert,[1] the design professor, completed his MA in design at the home campus before joining the faculty at our branch campus. He sought our collaboration to support writing in one of his courses after he had been teaching for three years at the branch campus. He stated two main motivations for working with us. First, he was familiar with the course goals of the first year writing classes that we (the authors) teach and knew that he had a similar set of goals for argumentative writing. He wanted to strengthen the alignment between our courses so the students would know they were being evaluated in the same way. He commented that it was important to support student writing development across the four years, not just in an individual class, so using common vocabulary and approaches to the writing process could reinforce that development. Secondly, he was interested in improving student outcomes because he was adamant about the importance of strong written communication skills for designers. He commented, 'There are a lot of designers out there, but the best ones are those who can argue for the power and value of design.' He was concerned that the writing that the students produced in his course could be stronger, and he thought our expertise in supporting disciplinary writing would be valuable in helping students not only in his class, but also in preparation for their future professional lives. Throughout our collaboration, he was an enthusiastic and active participant.

The course we supported, 'The Designed World: A Liberal Inquiry into Design and Human Experience,' is for second through fourth year students, required for majors in information systems and available as an elective to others. Robert created the course himself, and he taught one section of 20–30 students per year. He described it as a reading-intensive and discussion-driven course that introduces students to design history, theory and criticism. The course comprises four units: communication (visual design), construction (industrial design), interaction (design for experience) and integration (using design principles from the first three units to address complex systems/problems). For each unit, the students are required to write an argumentative paper in which they apply one or more theoretical frameworks from the course to critique the design of real-world objects, spaces, experiences or systems. These papers range from 1000 to 2400 words. Several of the course objectives stated in the syllabus are directly related to these papers: to study and apply a set of design frameworks to approach ideas, design products and systems; to develop and strengthen skills in analysis and critical thinking of and about the built world; to develop and strengthen skills in academic reading and interpretation; and to develop and strengthen skills in argument and scholarly writing.

For Assignment 1, the students apply the concept of *noise*, as described by Warren Weaver (1949), to communication design. Weaver's article was not about communication design, so Robert wanted the students to demonstrate their understanding of it and how it could be used to critique design decisions in real-world examples, such as posters or signage. For Assignment 2, the students use a design heuristic – the useful/useable/ desirable framework (UUD) – to critique design decisions of our campus. For Assignment 3, the students explicate John Dewey's (1934) theory of experience through an example of a designed experience of their choosing, such as air travel or a visit to a hospital. The students then apply Kenneth Burke's (1969) five acts of dramatism to critique the design decisions of this experience. For Assignment 4, the students explicate the concept of 'wicked' problems (Rittel & Webber, 1973) through an example of their choosing (e.g. pollution), and then argue for the value of a human-centered, holistic design perspective. This requires the students to draw on multiple theoretical frameworks from the semester to show how such a perspective could help address the problem.

The Process of Collaboration

We began our collaboration with Robert with several research questions in mind. The first two are about Robert's course and the assignment guidelines; the second two are about features of student writing in the course:

(1) How can alignment between Robert's course and our first year writing courses be strengthened, both in terms of expectations and learning goals for written assignments? How can alignment between Robert's four writing assignments be made more explicit?
(2) What are Robert's tacit expectations for effective writing, and how can they be made explicit in the assignment guidelines?
(3) What is the main purpose and what are the functional stages (parts) of each writing assignment?
(4) What language resources allow students to meet the genre expectations of each assignment (namely, creating an effective evaluative stance as they incorporate source text material and support their claims)?

Our data sources included: student writing from Robert's course, both from the semesters when we collaborated and from previous iterations of the course; Robert's classroom materials, including the original assignment guidelines and their multiple revisions, his syllabus and grading rubric, course readings and lecture slides; and audio-recorded sessions with Robert, including interviews about the assignment guidelines and their revisions, and think-aloud protocols as he read student writing.

We analyzed our multiple data sets in various ways. We used qualitative methods to analyze interview data and think-aloud protocols and text analysis methods to analyze student writing. Our text analysis methods comprised both corpus analysis and detailed qualitative analysis. For the corpus analysis, we used a software tool called DocuScope (Kaufer & Butler, 1996, 2000). DocuScope is based on a theory of composition which holds that the rhetorical effects a reader perceives are the result of the author's linguistic choices. DocuScope has a built-in dictionary that automatically identifies, classifies and stores word strings into 112 categories of rhetorical experience that are arranged into groups, which are further divided into clusters.

After the collaboration, the expectations for each assignment became clear to us, so we were able to develop materials to scaffold the assignments which we then used to qualitatively analyze student writing. A detailed description of our analysis is beyond the scope of this chapter. However, briefly, we can say that our analysis focused on whether the students had an introduction framed as problem, issue or solution (discussed below) with a clear overarching claim that indicated an evaluative stance towards the subject matter. We also focused on whether the students achieved the expected parts of the assignments, in particular the analysis part of each assignment. This analysis had to be grounded in the disciplinary framework that was the focus of each assignment (e.g. *noise* for Assignment 1) and had to be framed using design concepts (e.g. typography, visual hierarchy, symbols for Assignment 1).

Briefly, in linguistic terms, we focused on the discourse patterns of argument and analysis from a systemic functional linguistics perspective, as discussed by Humphrey and Economou (2015). In addition to examining texts for an explicit tempered (nuanced and balanced) evaluation that stayed consistent throughout the text, we also looked for patterns of language discourse that indicated that the students were presenting and arranging their information for the analytical and argumentative purposes of the text. This involved using the disciplinary framework and the design concepts to present and organize the students' ideas. We also looked for patterns in which the students effectively incorporated course materials, using phrases such as *According to, Author X argues*, and effectively commented on the course material and linked it to their own examples. We also examined how the students showed how their descriptions of their examples supported the claims being made with phrases such as *This shows that, this confirms*. Finally, we looked for instances in which the student anticipated or acknowledged other perspectives, and countered them with more evidence with the use of phrases such as *even, might, seem, although this … that, while this … that*. For a more detailed description of our work analyzing student writing using this framework, see Pessoa *et al.* (2017, 2018).

Our initial collaboration with Robert took place from May 2015 to November 2015 as we developed materials to scaffold student writing in his course in fall 2015. We helped him revise his writing assignments and conducted writing workshops prior to each of the four assignments. We later revised the materials to conduct the workshops with a new group of students in fall 2016. What we report here is our first collaboration.

This collaboration can be described as a three-part process. First, we tried to understand what Robert valued in student writing by analyzing papers written by his former students. We then interviewed him and asked him to perform think-aloud protocols with the student papers. All of this helped us unpack his expectations for writing beyond what was explicit in his assignment descriptions. The second part involved collaborative rewriting of the assignment descriptions and developing materials for the workshops. In these workshops, we co-taught with the professor to explain the assignment guidelines for each major paper and guide the students through brainstorming activities to generate strategies for executing the essay's structure, functional moves and connections to course material. The third part involved a follow-up interview with the professor to reflect upon the collaboration and its outcomes, short interviews with the students at the end of the semester, and analysis of student writing after the collaboration.

Next, we describe the first two parts of the collaboration in more detail. We discuss preliminary insights from the outcomes of the collaboration in the conclusion.

Unpacking writing expectations

To understand Robert's writing expectations, we read his guidelines for each assignment and reviewed two higher graded student papers and two lower graded student papers for the first three assignments (a total of six student papers). We read the student papers looking for features of analysis and argumentation called for by the guidelines. We found that while the higher graded papers included some strong analysis, integrated supporting sources, applied theoretical frameworks and tended to be argumentative in nature, they were not consistent. More importantly, many of these higher graded papers did not advance a strong central argument early in the paper to create a consistent position and overall cohesiveness. The lower graded papers also lacked a central argument, but were weaker in their analyses, as they often relied heavily on description and narration, and did not apply theoretical frameworks effectively.

We then used the corpus software tool DocuScope to analyze a total of 69 papers (39 higher graded papers and 30 lower graded papers, divided across four assignments). DocuScope found differences between these essays in various categories and this confirmed much of what we had found in our small-scale analysis. The higher graded essays had more features of academic language, institutional register and reasoning than the lower graded essays. More specifically, the higher graded essays used more abstract thought, citations and reporting processes. This suggests that the higher graded essays used the analytical frameworks from the course and cited the course readings. The higher graded essays also had more negative relations, indicating that their analysis of designed objects and experiences was more critical (included both positive and negative evaluations). On the other hand, the lower graded essays relied more on narrative, reporting events and space movement (physical movement within or across spaces, typical of fiction writing and storytelling). These features indicate that the lower graded essays were more descriptive than analytical.

In our first interview with Robert, we learned that these findings were closely aligned with his expectations for strong writing. He indicated that in strong papers, he would hope to find that:

> the central argument is very clear right at the beginning. It's original thought or at least it's like something that we worked on together and then they were able to back it up. If they can't back it up then it's like, were you [the students] here [in class]? [...] Did you [the students] really grasp what the authors are saying to support what you're writing?'

However, our review of the six former papers indicated that even some higher graded papers did not have the valued features of a fronted central argument supported by effective use of class material.

After this initial interview, we conducted a 1.5-hour think-aloud protocol where Robert read the six papers that we had reviewed, commenting on strong and weak features. This process further confirmed many of our interpretations from the analysis. First, similar to his interview, when reviewing a paper that did not have a clear central argument, Robert read the first section and expressed frustration: 'I don't know where this is going.' Secondly, Robert articulated the need to explicate the appropriate theoretical framework early in the paper. For example, when reviewing a sample from Assignment 2, Robert commented, 'This paper should have had something about "useful/useable/desirable," definitely upfront,' in reference to the aforementioned UUD framework the students were to apply to that paper's analysis.

Thirdly, Robert's review of these papers confirmed that he expected the students to use key 'concepts' and the 'specific terminology' from the course to anchor their critical analysis. For example, while reviewing the higher graded Assignment 1 about how communication design can overcome noise, Robert positively evaluated the students' use of course concepts such as 'typography, hierarchy, and emotional imagery' to critique the poster design. Fourthly, Robert expected the students to clearly show their understanding of the appropriate frameworks by explaining them in their own words and focusing on them throughout the analysis. Fifthly, when noticing the use of references and citations in student papers, Robert made positive evaluations such as, 'it's good that the student brought in the author' or 'excellent reference,' and negative evaluations like, 'this is an obvious place to bring in Rams, I don't know why she didn't do it.' Robert also commented on the importance of nuance and complexity in the students' evaluation of designed objects and experiences, stating: 'It does not all have to be positive or negative.' Finally, he confirmed our findings about the importance of going beyond description when reading a lower graded Assignment 3: 'You have to tell a story to write this paper. That is part of the requirement. But in this one, that is pretty much all we get. The student needed to do something with this story.' The student was apparently unaware of the need to use description in the service of, or as a set up for, analysis.

We told Robert that the findings of our analysis aligned with his evaluations in the think-aloud, namely that he seemed to value a clear argument from the beginning, carefully applied frameworks to enable critical analysis, and meaningful citation of sources. We then discussed how these features aligned with the objectives of our first year writing courses, an alignment Robert had been interested in strengthening. Similar to what Robert values, in our writing courses we emphasize fronting a central argument at the beginning with a clear preview of supporting claims, clear ties to the main claim throughout the text, and effectively integrated information from source texts as support. We told Robert how our students learn to use the issue/problem/solution heuristic (Charney *et al.*, 2006) to structure introductions as a possible tool for strengthening alignment and improving his students' writing. Briefly, this heuristic allows the writer to introduce the topic to be discussed by creating a shared context with the reader, articulate a problem that arises from this issue and propose a solution to the problem as a central claim for the paper.

Lastly, the three of us briefly reviewed his guidelines for the four assignments. Based on what we (the authors) had learned, we gave him some general ideas about how he could make his expectations more explicit to the students, as discussed in the previous paragraph. He used these suggestions for a first set of revisions of these guidelines prior to the beginning of the fall semester. We finished with a brief discussion of his rubric and how the rubric could more effectively capture the features he values.

Scaffolding writing in the disciplines

Following this initial stage in May 2015, we began to collaborate with Robert on multiple revisions of the assignments to provide the students with more explicit and detailed guidelines. Robert used our May 2015 feedback to revise each assignment independently. In August 2015, the second author reviewed these revisions and suggested that he more clearly articulate his expectations for applying the frameworks discussed in class and how to avoid letting description or narration overwhelm the analysis. Although Robert's next round of independent revisions made the assignments clearer, we still had uncertainties about his expectations and knew that students would benefit from much more explicit guidelines.

Throughout fall 2015 (August–November), we met with Robert for two hours to further unpack his expectations for each of the four assignments (six hours in total). In each meeting, we posed questions to Robert about the most current assignment guidelines to ensure we understood his goals and expectations. Robert often seemed confused about what he was asking of his students (especially for Assignments 2 and 4), and we all clarified our understanding significantly after much probing and questioning (in the next section, 'A Detailed Description of the Process of

Scaffolding One Assignment', we provide an detailed illustration of what this process looked like). We (the authors) used what we learned in our meeting with Robert to draft more explicit guidelines about the central argument, required analytical frameworks and potential organization.

Next, we developed scaffolding materials for the workshops which were then reviewed by Robert and revised accordingly. The writing workshops were delivered in his class approximately two weeks before the assignment was due. The scaffolding materials listed the purpose of the assignment in general terms (e.g. apply design frameworks to an analysis of visual communication), followed by a specific description of the assignment.

In the workshops, we read the assignment with the students and then asked them what they understood was expected of them. We provided them with an example of the general argument they were to make in the given paper. For example, in Assignment 1, where the students were to use the concept of noise to critique communication design, we told the students that the central argument could be: 'Noise is overcome by good communication design.' We then brainstormed the potential parts of the paper: the introduction, an explication of the key concept (e.g. noise), the analysis of objects/experiences/spaces, and a conclusion. To ensure that the students would front their argument, we asked them to brainstorm ideas for what to include in the introduction. For the four assignments, we suggested using the issue/problem/solution heuristic that the students were familiar with from their English classes. See Figure 8.1 for a breakdown of what the Issue, Problem and Solution could be for Paper 1.

We then discussed strategies for drafting the other parts of the paper with a focus on developing paragraphs that front the analytical framework, make claims about how it applies in a critique of a real-world object, and support these claims with details from the object and source texts. Robert provided the students with a list of concepts and authors from the unit and suggestions for how they might be relevant to different parts of the paper.

Issue:	Good communication design: What is it? Why is it important?
Problem:	Noise can get in the way of good communication design: What is noise, according to Weaver? How can you explain it in your own words to someone who is unfamiliar with this concept?
Solution:	Show how X different objects succeed/fail/attempt to overcome the problem of noise: To what degree are these objects successful in overcoming noise?

Figure 8.1 Issue, problem and solution in introduction to Paper 1

A Detailed Description of the Process of Scaffolding One Assignment

In this section, we describe the process of scaffolding the paper for the unit on industrial design (Assignment 2). It is important to note that this description is inevitably a simplification of the actual process. Our discussions with Robert were lengthy and included many faulty paths; they required lots of questions, hypothesizing and clarifications before we were able to successfully unpack his expectations and draft strong revisions. Figure 8.2 provides the original writing assignment for Paper 2.

When we first discussed this assignment with Robert, we wanted to learn more about the responses he was expecting and how students might respond with an argumentative thesis that could be supported consistently. Specifically, we wanted to begin our conversation with questions like: Which of the prompt's three questions should students prioritize? How can students write a unified, coherent argument, rather than three separate analyses about a building, an outdoor space and a repeated design element? Should the main argument be about the campus as a whole, with the smaller parts working to support that claim? Which frameworks are they supposed to use, and should each part of the analysis use a different one?

During our conversation, Robert acknowledged that even the higher graded papers were lacking a strong, clearly articulated central argument, and instead presented several discrete analyses. Based on what he pointed out during his think-aloud reading of the sample papers, we understood that the UUD framework was key to this paper; we learned that this was the key framework from this unit and had been the focus of much class discussion. He wanted the students to explicate this framework early in the paper and apply it throughout to critique the object or space. He wanted the students to move beyond description and engage in critical analysis that was supported by the authors the students had read in the course.

We observed that the prompt did not make it clear that the question about the UUD framework was the most important one and that the students would benefit from some explicit ideas about which resources from

> Use the frameworks from this section and in 1200–1400 words conduct a survey of campus. It's a comprehensively designed environment populated with factory-produced objects, buildings, and landscapes. Choose one building, one outdoor space, and one repeated design element like a piece of furniture. On what basis do we judge these things? How effective do they serve their purpose and place? How balanced are their useful, usable, and desirable qualities? Be fair and critical. Cite our authors and external sources.

Figure 8.2 The original writing assignment for Paper 2

the course would be helpful in specific parts of the paper. When we asked Robert how the students were going to be able to write a unified argument rather than three separate ones, he struggled to find an answer.

The most revealing moment of the conversation occurred when we asked Robert how he himself would write this paper. He responded, 'Well, I could tell you so much about the overall design language of this campus by critiquing that light switch or this chair.' He proceeded to provide a nuanced analysis of the aesthetics and functionality of the light switch, and explain how this critique is relevant to, and in fact may be seen to reverberate throughout the office where we sat, the building and the campus as a whole. This response helped us to see that he was interested in having the students apply the UUD framework at different scales. We suggested that this idea of scales would be useful for prompting the students to craft a more unified argument.

Based on our suggestions, Robert made revisions to the prompt over the summer. He made significant improvements by explicitly asking the students to move from the scale of a single object, to its immediate environment, to the building and to the campus as a whole. He clarified that the students should focus on the UUD framework. He generated some guiding questions to help them consider each scale and included some suggestions about how to use source texts to support specific parts of the argument. Figure 8.3 provides his first attempt at revision.

After reading this revision, the second author met with Robert briefly in August 2015 to provide feedback. Her main suggestion was to reinforce the importance of the UUD framework and the need for analytical critique. Robert made another revision, one that was not substantially different. The main addition was some language emphasizing the need to move beyond description (Figure 8.4).

Despite the improvements, the revised assignment still did not do enough to explicitly emphasize the need to apply the UUD framework at each scale, and we (the authors) still had not arrived at a complete understanding of how to help the students create a coherent central argument. Our understanding of how the students could craft the central argument was mostly based on the professor's response to the question about how he would write the paper. In other words, we were thinking that the students would have to use the UUD framework to create an argument about the object at the smallest scale, and carry that same argument through each scale, with the object being representative of the campus as a whole.

We expressed our concern that such a task might be too challenging for the students when we met with Robert in October 2015 to finalize revisions to the prompt and plan the writing workshop. After multiple probing questions, he commented:

> Well, they don't necessarily have to make the same evaluation for the object as they do for the other scales. A table might be very useful or

useable for a specific purpose, such as collaboration, but the room that it is in might be very useful or useable for another purpose, such as studying.

This was another revelatory moment, as we understood for the first time that the students could narrow their application of the UUD framework by focusing on a single purpose. We asked the professor to generate a list of other purposes he would be interested in seeing the students consider

> For this paper, conduct a survey of campus. It's a comprehensively designed environment filled with objects, buildings, and environments of all scales, employing a wide range of materials, all serving different purposes. Choose one repeated, mass-produced object. How effectively does it embody useful, useable, and desirable qualities? Gather as much information about it as you can, like who designed it and for what original purpose and context. Consider its materials, ergonomics, and structural integrity. Second, where does the object live? How well does it fit, both aesthetically and functionally, within the architectural space? Critique the building space (e.g. atrium, classroom, gym) for how well it serves its purpose and community of use. Spend time in the space observing. Third, present and critique the building as a whole. Who was the architect? What are the building's aesthetic and functional aspects and how successful is it in that regard? What are its materials, pathways, and space allocations? Finally, consider the building as part of the broader Education City campus. How well does the building fit in, aesthetically and functionally? What is its relationship to its neighboring buildings and landscapes? How well is the movement of people encouraged? How pleasant are the spaces to be in? Cite our authors, frameworks, and external sources to support your critique. I would expect to hear from authors like Norman or Rams when critiquing the objects and Goldberger when critiquing architecture. Helpful resources: experts on campus, long-time inhabitants, and 4ddoha.

Figure 8.3 Robert's first revision of the assignment guidelines for Paper 2

> These various analyses should help you construct your evaluation of how effectively the object embodies useful, useable, and desirable qualities. In other words, don't lose sight of your evaluation/argument by just describing the object or the building. Your descriptions, critiques, and analyses should be presented as support for your main argument about the design qualities of the object. Use your description, critiques, and analyses to support the points you want to make.

Figure 8.4 The new text Robert added in his second revision of the guidelines for Paper 2

in their analyses. While the idea of applying the UUD framework using one of these purposes was helpful, we were concerned that the students still might write separate analyses for each scale, rather than one coherent argument. Finally, we arrived at the idea of having them select one single purpose and use the UUD framework to critique the campus at each scale with only that purpose in mind, thereby giving them both a unifying position for their paper and the flexibility to evaluate each scale on its own terms.

We (the authors) then revised the prompt and adjusted it based on Robert's feedback. In the final version (Figure 8.5), we made it explicit to the students from the beginning that they would use the UUD framework in their analysis of the four scales while focusing on a single purpose throughout. We re-emphasized this point multiple times. We provided a list of possible purposes that they could select from. We modeled a thesis that uses an evaluation of degree to create space for both positive and negative critiques. We listed questions for each scale to help the students generate ideas about what to consider as they applied the UUD framework to a particular scale.

The final step in scaffolding student writing for this assignment was the preparation and delivery of the workshop materials. We (the authors) drafted the materials and sent them to the professor for feedback. We began the workshop by reading the guidelines with the students, gauging their understanding by asking: 'Based on the assignment guidelines, what are the most important things the professor is interested in seeing you do in this paper?' During the conversation that followed, we explicitly showed the students how the sample thesis provided room for positive and negative evaluations. We underscored the importance of moving beyond description.

We then asked the students to brainstorm ideas about different objects they could use to start their analysis at the smallest scale, and how those objects relate to a specific purpose: 'Select a purpose from the list or a purpose you are interested in investigating and let's discuss what object and spaces you might analyze, critique, and how.' This activity helped the students understand what type of objects could set up a strong analysis and how the framework might apply to a variety of objects and spaces when considering a single purpose.

Next, we asked the students to generate ideas about how to structure the paper: 'Let's think about how we might organize this paper. What do you think will come first, second, third?' After discussing their responses, we provided the students with a sample, showing them how their ideas about the overall structure might work in a specific case (Figure 8.6). We showed them how they could structure their introduction with the issue/problem/solution heuristic, and how the argument could be supported through analysis at each scale. The professor provided a supplementary list of authors from the course that could be

Our campus is a comprehensively designed environment filled with objects, buildings, and spaces of all scales, employing a wide range of materials, all serving different purposes.

For this paper, you will choose **one purpose** to focus on and analyze how **useful, useable, and desirable** (UUD) the environment is for that purpose, from the smallest scale (an object) to the integrated campus of Education City as a whole. Possible purposes that you can choose might be: learning, studying, productivity, research, collaboration, social activities, physical and mental growth, expression of values, expression of grandeur, expression of Qatar's vision.

Your overarching claim for this paper should be something like:

The design of the Education City campus is **somewhat effective** in its purpose of encouraging collaboration. It is more effective in this regard at smaller scales, such as in the selection of furniture and arrangement of study spaces, and less so at larger ones, such the relationships between buildings.

You will analyze this environment with your selected purpose in mind. You will start by considering how useful, useable, desirable a single object (small scale) is for that purpose, how that object interacts with its immediate surroundings (medium scale), how this space is part of the entire building (large scale) and, finally, how the building is part of the campus as a whole (the integrated level). To carry out this analysis, you should carefully apply the useful, usable, desirable framework at each scale, always in terms of your selected purpose.

First, conduct a survey of campus objects and **choose one** repeated, mass-produced object. Gather as much information as you can about your chosen object, such as who designed it, and for what original purpose and context. Consider its materials, ergonomics, and structural integrity. Evaluate how effectively (or not) it embodies useful, useable, and desirable qualities for the purpose you have selected.

Second, consider where the object lives. How well does the object fit, both aesthetically and functionally, within the architectural space? Using the useful, usable, desirable framework, critique the building space (e.g. atrium, classroom, gym) for how well it serves the community of use for your selected purpose. Spend time in the space observing how it is used.

Third, consider this space as it relates to the building as a whole. How well suited is the building to your selected purpose in terms of the useful, useable, desirable framework? In considering the building as a whole, you can think about its aesthetic and functional aspects, its materials, pathways, and space allocations.

Figure 8.5 The final version of the writing assignment for Paper 2

Finally, consider the building as part of the broader Education City campus. Keep your selected purpose in mind and consider questions such as: How well does the building fit in, aesthetically and functionally? What is its relationship to its neighboring buildings and landscapes? How well is the movement of people and traffic mediated? How pleasant are the spaces to be in? How well considered are the public/private spaces and the flow between them? How well connected is the campus?

These various analyses should help you construct your evaluation of how effectively the object and the spaces embody useful, useable, and desirable qualities for a specific purpose. Don't lose sight of your evaluation/argument by just describing the object or the building.

Cite our authors, frameworks, and external sources to support your critique. I would expect to hear from authors like Norman or Rams when critiquing the objects, Goldberger when critiquing architectural space, and perhaps Ekuan when addressing scalar relationships and expression of values. Concepts and material from the class slides would also be good to consider.

External resources about objects and spaces include Legorreta books in the library, experts on campus, long-time inhabitants ('users'), the contemporary art catalogue at the reception desk, and 4ddoha.com.

Figure 8.5 (*Continued*)

helpful in supporting the analysis of each scale. We included some of these in the sample outline, and he gave them a more detailed list at the end of the workshop.

The workshop's final step was co-constructing a written analysis of one scale with the students. We used our sample, focusing on the smallest scale, and took ideas from the class about how to arrange an argumentative analysis of the chair's usefulness, usability and desirability for the purpose of productivity. As we took suggestions, we projected what we were composing so that everyone could see. We explicitly modeled the process of key strategies, such as establishing the relevance of the particular analysis of the chair to the overall claim and using the framework to establish a claim about the object early in the paragraph. We showed them valuable language for incorporating sources, how to balance description with analysis and how to arrange claims and support. This was the focus of our analysis of student writing, as detailed in the previous section on 'The Process of Collaboration'.

166 Second Language Writing Instruction in Global Contexts

1. Introduction: State your main claim based on your analysis of the object and spaces for your purpose. You might want to use the issue-problem-solution framework to structure your introduction and lead to your main claim. For example:

   Issue: You might not think that something as simple as the choice of an office chair could be indicative of the overall design language of an entire college campus.

   Problem: However, every design choice says something, and in a comprehensively designed environment like Education City, there are many different purposes that must be satisfied, and sometimes these are in tension with each other.

   Solution: In this paper, I argue that the design of the Education City campus is somewhat effective in its purpose of encouraging productivity. It is more effective in this regard at smaller scales, such as in the selection of furniture and arrangement of study spaces, and less so at larger ones, such the relationships between buildings.

2. The Aeron Chair as an example of industrial design and its UUD for your purpose (Outside Source like Herman Miller? Introduce the concepts of Rams, Ekuan)

3. The Aeron Chair as an element of an office; evaluating the office as space to meet your purpose of UUD (Who are its users? How well does it perform? How do people change their offices to suit different needs and functions? Ekuan? Goldberger?)

4–5. The building as a whole and how its UUD contributes (or not) to your purpose (How well does it perform its many, many functions? How does it express certain values or qualities? Outside Source? Goldberger?)

6. Our building in the context of campus and how the campus' UUD contributes (or not) to your purpose (Ekuan?)

7. Conclusion that reflects on that scaling-up. (Does what you observed in the Aeron Chair reflect something about Education City? Ekuan?)

Figure 8.6 Sample showing a possible way to organize Paper 2

Conclusions

This chapter has presented a model of collaboration between English faculty and disciplinary faculty for scaffolding multilingual learners' writing. In international branch campuses of English-medium universities, increasing numbers of multilingual students have to meet the writing demands and expectations of disciplinary teachers who may not have had any training in pedagogy, let alone L2 writing pedagogy. Thus, we argue that collaborations like the one presented in this chapter are needed to help disciplinary teachers scaffold L2 writing development. Such a model of collaboration can have a positive impact on teacher development and student writing outcomes, as we observed with our case study and as reported in the literature on interdisciplinary collaborations between language experts and teachers in the disciplines at the primary and secondary school levels (see, for example, Brisk, 2014; Humphrey, 2016; Humphrey & Macnaught, 2016) and to a lesser extent in higher education (see, for example, Dreyfus *et al.*, 2016; Mitchell & Pessoa, 2017; Pessoa *et al.*, 2018, in press).

Despite his great interest and enthusiasm in working with us and developing as a teacher, our case study Robert was in many ways no different from many other faculty in the disciplines. He had high expectations for his students' writing but did not make them explicit as these expectations were often not clear to him and he did not have the writing and language expertise to make them explicit. This is the situation for many faculty in the disciplines, as we and other researchers have documented extensively (see, for example, Coffin & Donohue, 2014; Miller & Pessoa, 2017). Many faculty members in the disciplines lack explicit knowledge of the rhetorical and linguistic features of disciplinary genres, limiting their ability to effectively teach these genres. Through the study of disciplinary genres, applied linguists and writing teachers can help faculty in the disciplines better scaffold student writing, as we aimed to do in this study.

Overall, Robert's trajectory can be summarized as a dedicated and committed faculty who started with high expectations but limited guidelines and developed into valuing explicit expectations. After our first semester of collaboration with Robert, we interviewed him about his insights on the redesigning of the assignments, the workshops and student writing. Robert was very positive about the collaboration and its outcomes. He reflected on how the detailed nature of the assignment guidelines made a difference in helping students better understand his expectations and how to meet them, in contrast to his first original short assignment guidelines:

> I guess I realized that sometimes an assignment prompt itself can be like a page long. I've always been under the assumption that a nice short, snappy, concise assignment prompt is good because it's clear, it's short and it will allow them [the students] leeway to go wherever they want with it. But, actually, that's not necessarily the best approach. I think I probably inherit that approach from pretty much every written assignment prompt I've ever gotten. All I ever got as a student was like, one or two sentences, write blah-blah-blah, include this and that. Having a nice expanded upon longer assignment prompt that allows you to communicate the faculty expectations will allow you to really encourage them to structure it in a specific way but still giving them freedom to fill out the essay as they see fit.

One aspect of the redesigning of the assignments that Robert alludes to is that the more detailed and structured guidelines of the assignments may compromise creativity. Although we (the authors) saw great value in providing structure, early conversations with Robert revealed that he valued writing that had a clear argument from the beginning, but that he also valued students' creativity in crafting their response. In explaining the concept of creativity, he talked about papers that made an unexpected turn in the argument, had unusual organization, and analyzed interesting objects and experiences in insightful ways. Initially, he was concerned about the more detailed assignments constraining such creativity. However, the post-collaboration interview showed his appreciation for the more detailed guidelines:

> I'm okay with them [the detailed assignments] because the papers are demonstrating more – like they're showing that they are making more connections between the authors, the in-class material. They're thinking about that material in critical ways and with the new prompts that we're giving them, it's so much more structured. Maybe for grad students [...], leaving these [the assignments] kind of open prompts would lead to more creativity. Okay, maybe we don't have that kind of freedom with our students, I could – maybe I'm just selling them short but I think I'm actually more interested in just making sure that they understand the content and demonstrate that. It might be drier but what are we here for, I guess? Why are they taking my class? [...] Yeah. I mean, honestly looking back over the years like how many really creative papers have I gotten that I really just love, you know, not that many, so I want to – are we losing anything? Probably not. Doing it in this new direction benefits everybody.

Robert may have received a few creative papers with the more concise guidelines he used before, but the more detailed guidelines seemed to be more appropriate to help the majority of his students better meet assignment expectations.

In addition to Robert's development in recognizing the importance of explicit writing guidelines, there were other positive outcomes from the collaboration. Although grade averages on the assignments did not drastically change from previous semesters, we have some indications of improved writing development. First, Robert commented, 'I think the papers got better.' Robert also briefly interviewed the students about the workshop in his individual meeting with them about Assignment 4 and Robert shared that 'everybody [the students] was grateful for the workshop.' Secondly, it seems that the collaboration allowed Robert to have a clearer understanding of his expectations and thus higher expectations for student work. In the post-collaboration interview, Robert compared assignments written by former students who did not receive our explicit instruction to the students who participated in our writing workshops. Reading through higher graded papers from a previous semester revealed that Robert was not as pleased with these papers as he once was. His expectations had changed and he indicated that he had held past students to a lower standard:

Why did I go easy on them? Because my prompts weren't clear enough. I had a different expectation like, well, okay, we asked them to do such and such, so grade them accordingly. That's my explanation for it. So, now I'm being really, I guess, intricate with the grading because we're giving them very clear expectations and we're getting a lot of support from those writing workshops. So, the papers better be good. [...] Like I said earlier, if I were to rate papers one and two [from a previous semester] based on [our new] expectations, I would have really pulled them down considerably.

When comparing papers from a previous semester to fall 2015 papers, Robert noticed improvements in the features we had determined he valued most: fronting a central argument; rooting the analysis on the frameworks from the course; citing the sources; and showing a nuanced and complex evaluation of designed objects, experiences and spaces. The collaboration gave Robert a principled approach for communicating his expectations for these features explicitly to his students, and a precise language through which to do so. Robert commented, 'At one time, I was sort of like self-conscious, having you guys read my comments because like, I'm not an English teacher but it's nice that there is some alignment [with what constitutes good argumentation].'

Thirdly, our preliminary analysis of student writing also reveals improvement in student writing compared to a previous semester. For example, DocuScope analysis of Paper 1 written in fall 2014 with Paper 1 from fall 2015 shows that the papers written in fall 2015 were more analytical, as they had more citations and relied less on the use of the DocuScope variables that are more associated with less critical and more narrative writing. In our preliminary small-scale qualitative discourse analysis of 2015 student writing, we have observed differences between Assignment 1's higher graded papers compared with fall 2014. For example, the higher graded papers from fall 2014 had features that are not valued by Robert: some lacked an explicit main claim; some either relied little or too much on source material to set up the argument; some did not frame the analysis using design theory and unifying concepts of analysis; some did not integrate the course material in the analysis; and in some the analysis tended to be more positive than nuanced. In contrast, the higher graded 2015 papers: consistently framed the introduction using the issue/problem/solution heuristic that we discussed in the workshops; effectively introduced the source material to set up the argument; had a focused and explicit main claim; used a unifying concept for analysis; framed the analysis using design theory; effectively integrated the course authors in the analysis; and highlighted both positive and negative features of communication design. Although there is still room for student writing improvement, particularly in the lower graded essays from fall 2015, our preliminary findings are promising.

The collaboration also contributed to our (the authors') growth as writing specialists. Every time we engage in disciplinary collaborations, we gain a deeper understanding of the writing expectations that our students encounter outside of our first year writing classes, and the language resources needed to meet these expectations. This allows us to be better writing teachers as we experiment with new ways of integrating our knowledge of our students' future rhetorical situations into the activities we use in our classes. Our collaboration with Robert, in particular, has shaped our understanding of how students are expected to apply analytical frameworks in the service of an overarching claim, and how students can effectively draw on source texts in ways that differ from disciplines like English or history. This understanding has informed our current collaborations with faculty in information systems, particularly as it relates to argumentative and analytical language in genres such as the case analysis.

In the future, we will analyze more student writing to, hopefully, further confirm the positive student outcomes from this collaboration and identify areas still requiring more explicit instruction. We have already identified several such areas, such as the use of analytical frameworks for analysis and crafting a balanced, critical stance. Overall, the interdisciplinary collaboration reported here has had a positive impact on teacher development and student outcomes. Analysis of former student writing, think-aloud protocols with the professor and continuing conversations with him have helped us all to understand his expectations and transmit them to the students in more explicit ways in order to better scaffold student writing. We are engaged in similar work with other faculty in the disciplines of history and information systems. Although this requires time commitment from all parties involved, the small size of our institution (we are all in the same building) and our light teaching load has allowed for these kinds of collaborations. We have been fortunate to work with highly engaged and committed faculty such as Robert, but we have also encountered less responsive faculty who see the value of the writing workshops we (the authors) offer to their students but who are somewhat resistant to changing their own pedagogical practices. Despite these challenges, our findings from writing outcomes in different disciplines suggest that this kind of collaboration can serve as a model for disciplinary teacher development in higher education.

Note

(1)   All names used are pseudonyms.

Acknowledgements

This paper was made possible by NPRP grant #8-1815-5-293 from the Qatar National Research Fund (a member of Qatar Foundation).

References

Altbach, P.G. (2007) Twinning and branch campuses: The professorial obstacle. *International Higher Education* 48, 2–3.

Brisk, M.E. (2014) *Engaging Students in Academic Literacies: Genre-based Pedagogy for k-5 Classrooms.* New York: Routledge.

Burke, K. (1969) *A Grammar of Motives.* Berkeley, CA: University of California Press.

Charney, D., Neuwirth, C.M., Kaufer, D.S. and Geisler, C. (2006) *Having your Say: Reading and Writing Public Arguments.* New York: Pearson/Longman.

Coffin, C. and Donohue, J. (2014) A language as social semiotic-based approach to teaching and learning in higher education. *Language Learning Monograph Series* 64 (1), 1–308.

Dewey, J. (1934) *Art as Experience.* New York: Minton, Balch & Company.

Doiz, A., Lasagabaster, D. and Sierra, J.M. (2013) *English-Medium Instruction at Universities: Global Challenges.* Bristol: Multilingual Matters.

Dreyfus, S., Humphrey, S., Mahboob, A. and Martin, J.M. (2016) *Genre Pedagogy in Higher Education. The SLATE Project.* London: Palgrave Macmillan.

Fenton-Smith, B. and Humphreys, P. (2015) Language specialists' views on academic language and learning support mechanisms for EAL postgraduate coursework students: The case for adjunct tutorials. *Journal of English for Academic Purposes* 20, 40–55.

Humphrey, S. (2016) *Academic Literacies in the Middle Years: A Framework for Enhancing Teacher Knowledge and Student Achievement.* New York: Routledge.

Humphrey, S. and Economou, D. (2015) Peeling the onion – a textual model of critical analysis. *Journal of English for Academic Purposes* 17, 37–50.

Humphrey, S. and Macnaught, L. (2016) Functional language instruction and the writing growth of English language learners in the middle years. *TESOL Quarterly* 50 (4), 792–816.

Kaufer, D. and Butler, B. (1996) *Rhetoric and the Arts of Design.* Mahwah, NJ: Lawrence Erlbaum.

Kaufer, D. and Butler, B. (2000) *Designing Interactive Worlds with Words: Principles of Writing as Representational Composition.* Mahwah, NJ: Lawrence Erlbaum.

Miller, R.T. and Pessoa, S. (2016) Role and genre expectations in undergraduate case analysis in information systems. *English for Specific Purposes* 44, 43–56.

Miller, R.T. and Pessoa, S. (2017) Integrating writing assignments at an American branch campus in Qatar: Challenges, adaptations, and recommendations. In L.R. Arnold, A. Nobel and L. Ronesi (eds) *Emerging Writing Research from the Middle East-North Africa Region* (pp. 175–200). Boulder, CO: University Press of Colorado.

Miller, R.T., Mitchell, T.D. and Pessoa, S. (2014) Valued voices: Students' use of engagement in argumentative history writing. *Linguistics and Education* 28, 107–120.

Miller, R.T., Mitchell, T.D. and Pessoa, S. (2016) Impact of source texts and prompts on students' genre uptake. *Journal of Second Language Writing* 31, 11–24.

Mitchell, T.D. and Pessoa, S. (2017) Scaffolding the writing development of the argumentative genre in history: The case of two novice writers. *Journal of English for Academic Purposes* 30, 26–37. doi:10.1016/j.jeap.2017.10.002

Pessoa, S. (2017) How SFL and explicit language instruction can enhance the teaching of argumentation in the disciplines. *Journal of Second Language Writing* 36, 77–78.

Pessoa, S., Miller, R.T. and Kaufer, D. (2014) Students' challenges and development in the transition to academic writing at an English-medium university in Qatar. *International Review of Applied Linguistics* 52 (2), 127–156.

Pessoa, S., Mitchell, T.D. and Miller, R.T. (2017) Emergent arguments: A functional approach to analyzing student challenges with the argument genre. *Journal of Second Language Writing* 38, 42–55.

Pessoa, S., Mitchell, T.D. and Miller, R.T. (2018) Scaffolding the argument genre in a multilingual university history classroom: Tracking the writing development of novice and experienced writers. *English for Specific Purposes* 50, 81–96. doi.10.1016/j. esp.2017.12.002

Pessoa, S., Mitchell, T.D. and Reilly, B. (in press) Scaffolding the writing of argumentative essays in history: A functional approach. *The History Teacher.*

Rittel, H. and Webber, M. (1973) Dilemmas in a general theory of planning. *Policy Sciences* 4, 155–169.

Weaver, W. (1949) The mathematics of communication. *Scientific American* 181, 11–15.

Wilkins, S. and Huisman, J. (2012) The international branch campus as transnational strategy in higher education. *Higher Education* 64, 627–645. doi:10.1007/ s10734-012-9516-5

9 The Role of Writing in an English as a Foreign Language Teacher Preparation Program in Turkey: Institutional Demands, Pedagogical Practices and Student Needs

Aylin Ünaldı, Lisya Seloni, Şebnem Yalçın and Nur Yiğitoğlu Aptoula

Introduction

As a lingua franca of scientific and academic communication, written English has an important role in professional and academic success in Turkey. Yet, similar to the nature of foreign language (FL) writing instruction in other non-English dominant contexts, writing instruction in Turkey, too, has been 'dependent upon a whole set of material conditions and social practices that do not necessarily coincide with those of [E]SL contexts' (Manchón, 2009: 2). In such contexts, learning and teaching writing is highly dependent on issues such as the language users' actual and perceived language proficiency, their prior L1 and L2 literacy experiences, and the sociolinguistic role of English (particularly English writing) in the local context (Manchón, 2009; Reichelt, this volume). Language learners in English-dominant settings usually learn how to develop certain approaches to writing mainly due to a necessity for writing in those settings. Yet, many EFL users are still on their way to developing language proficiency and hence see writing primarily as a tool to improve their general language skills, as described in Manchón's (2009) writing-to-learn, i.e. an additional language dimension. As in many English as a foreign language (EFL) settings, L2 writing is not taught as a separate subject area in the Turkish educational system. The only exception to this is those students who choose English as their primary area for university exams and take additional English classes, most of which usually focus on exam-based grammar activities. Even in these cases, the writing they do in these spaces is limited to and does not move beyond short language production through controlled writing such as paragraph and five-paragraph essay writing. Therefore, it is not usual for teacher candidates to engage in authentic writing before they start studying at an English-medium university and take discipline-specific courses.

The limited attention given to teachers' preparation for writing in EFL contexts (e.g. Casanave, 2009; Lee, 2010; Reichelt, 2009) is typically attributed to the lack of a need for L2 writing in the larger society. While this might also be true for the Turkish context, there is an increasing use of L2 writing even outside the school environment for many college students, including those who are training to be English teachers. In order to better understand some of the changing material conditions and practices of L2 writing instruction in Turkey, in this study we investigate teacher candidates' L2 writing experiences and perceptions of language proficiency in different areas of academic writing, as well as the mismatch between candidates' perceptions of writing assignments and the instructors' expectations of these assignments. More specifically, describing a first year writing sequence in a teacher training program at an English-medium university in Istanbul, we report on a survey study in which we discuss teacher candidates' general perceptions of and experiences with L2 writing, their experiences in the writing sequence, including the perceived transfer of writing skills they learned during their first year, and finally the perceived congruence of writing task expectations.

Through analyzing the first year writing curriculum and a survey conducted with first year teacher candidates, we address two research questions: (1) How is the first year writing curriculum for teacher candidates designed in an English-medium teacher training program at a Turkish university? and (2) What are the Turkish teacher candidates' perceptions of and experiences with writing during a new first year writing program? In what follows, we first provide some contextual information on the role of English and writing in the Turkish EFL teacher education context. We then give an overview of the first year writing curriculum at an English-medium (EMI) university, and finally we share the survey results on 98 first year teacher candidates' perceptions of writing as well as their experiences with writing-intensive courses. The chapter ends with a discussion on an ecological framework for writing instruction for the language development and L2 writing advancement of EFL teacher candidates.

Background

The role of English and writing in the Turkish educational system

English, the 'most studied foreign language and the most popular medium of education after Turkish' (Doğancay-Aktuna, 1998: 37), has been considered to be one of the most important foreign languages in Turkish society for various reasons. Atay and Ece (2009), for example, underline the importance of the acquisition of English language on the identity development of prospective teachers of English in Turkey. Similarly, Doğançay-Aktuna and Kızıltepe (2005) conclude that the role of English in the Turkish educational system shows a similar pattern to the role of English in European countries, in that English-Turkish bilingualism is usually an 'academically achieved type, instead of a naturally acquired one' (Doğançay-Aktuna & Kızıltepe, 2005: 264). However, as they argue, there is great variation in the quality and quantity of English language instruction among different socioeconomic and geographic groups, which prevents equal access to English language.

Turkey's English language teaching curriculum in the K-12 context has been greatly impacted by two educational reforms put forward by the Turkish Ministry of Education (MoNE). With the 1997 educational reform of MoNE, which expanded compulsory education from five to eight years, the number of hours dedicated to FL instruction increased considerably in both public and private school curricula. This change also encouraged the English language teaching curriculum to adopt highly communicative English language teaching methods. In alignment with the principles of communicative language teaching, schools adopted a highly performance-based assessment documenting students' language progress (Bayyurt & Akcan, 2016; Kırkgöz, 2017). In 2012, another educational reform was proposed and compulsory education increased to 12 years (named as '4 + 4 + 4', meaning four years of primary school, followed by four years of middle school and four years of high school). With this reform, two hours of FL instruction per week (predominantly English) is introduced in the second grade, and the number of hours increases to four hours in Grade 8. The English language curriculum for Grades 2 and 8 of MoNE, for instance, shows that speaking and listening are the primary language skills that are taught in the overall school curriculum. In Grade 9, on the other hand, English instruction increases to six hours per week, but in practice it decreases to four hours due to the time spent on university entrance exam preparation. Even though the curriculum says that all four skills are emphasized, we see that reading and writing are underemphasized.

In terms of L2 writing instruction, the curriculum established by the Turkish Ministry of Education contains limited writing instruction in Grades 2–4. The curriculum at these grades advises theme- and content-based instruction in which students should be given situation-based tasks targeting meaningful spoken interaction. Although spoken interaction is emphasized in the curriculum, the practice in classrooms rarely includes meaningful communication. On the other hand, as for the writing sequence, students should be exposed to three main types of texts between Grades 2 and 5: narrative materials (e.g. fairy tales, stories, cartoons, tongue twisters and fables); informative materials (e.g. lists, instructions, signs and posters) and interactive materials (e.g. postcards, conversations and formal and informal letters) (MoNE, 2018a). While the curriculum aims to familiarize students with a wide range of genres, the communicative functions these genres are used for are limited only to listening and sometimes short speaking tasks, again leaving writing at the periphery. The thematic organization of units continues in high school (Grades 9–12), focusing on 'experiential learning'. As stated in MoNE's curriculum, the units are created in accordance with the descriptors of the Common European Framework of Reference (CEFR) and include elements of functional and skill-based syllabus, mainly focusing on all four skills with an explicit emphasis on speaking and listening. The rationale behind favoring speaking and listening is that each lesson is 'sequenced to simulate the natural process of first language acquisition and start with listening and speaking activities and then proceed to reading and writing materials' (MoNE, 2018b, Curriculum for Grades Prep–12: 9). When we closely look at the curriculum, we see that the state does not mandate specific activities but makes recommendations on the skills and tasks that can be used for each grade level.

Parallel to these two major educational reforms, the teacher education departments at Turkish universities also went through major curricular changes. The curriculum of many ELT teacher training programs revolves around the following content areas: technical courses (e.g. linguistics, language acquisition, literary analysis and research methods), general FL courses (e.g. public speaking, vocabulary and advanced reading and writing), non-ELT compulsory courses (e.g. Ataturk's principles and the history of the Turkish Revolution, writing and speaking expression in Turkish) and pedagogical courses (e.g. teaching language skills, ELT methods and materials). These curriculum changes do not seem to leave much room for individual teacher education programs to specialize in a specific area of L2 teacher education. For instance, Selvi (2016) reports that critically oriented paradigms are usually missing from the L2 teacher education programs, disregarding the changing sociolinguistic needs of teacher candidates. As Selvi (2016: 261) states: 'individual programs preparing teacher work-force for a wide variety of levels, domains and contexts have almost no agency in shaping their curricula.' Although it is hard to exercise agency in restructuring content area courses due to top-down mandates, skills-based courses such as first year writing or pre-university language courses at English-medium universities can be regarded as important spaces in which to bring changes in the way we aim to develop teacher candidates' 21st century reading and writing skills.

Language teacher preparation programs and the teaching of L2 writing

Teacher education programs in Turkey are designed and supervised by the Council of Higher Education (CoHE) (Yuksek Ögretim Kurumu; YÖK). YÖK is an autonomous government-based institution which plans, coordinates and directs the higher education system in Turkey in accordance with the Turkish Constitution and the Higher Education Laws.[1] In 2006–2007, an English language teacher training program was structured and launched by YÖK, which proposed a curriculum framework and thus the knowledge base needed for EFL teacher education programs. As in other undergraduate degrees, a teacher training degree in the Turkish context is obtained through a public or private university, which requires a score from the Student Selection Examination – a central university entrance examination[2] administered by the Student Selection and Placement Center (ÖSYM). In the past, students who came from teacher training high schools such as Anatolian Teacher Preparatory Schools (which are no longer part of K-12 education due to recent changes) used to be awarded extra university entrance exam points so that they could be given priority in university placements. The presence of YÖK implies a centralized approach to university curricula in general and language teacher education programs in particular. However, as each university implements the central curriculum in its own unique way, language teacher programs might or might not offer writing courses that are crucial for a language teacher's language and content development. In fact, many of these programs lack writing focus. The decision to offer writing courses is influenced by the availability of faculty to teach these courses and reluctance to focus on one specific area of research while the curriculum demands are so high. Unlike the emphasis on writing we see in some of the teacher preparation programs or graduate programs in US institutions, very few language teacher training programs in Turkey make the teaching of writing a priority at any level of higher education. Most research published on pre-service English teachers in Turkey has been on areas such as their language proficiency (Altan, 2006; Çetinavcı & Yavuz, 2010), and writing teacher education programs have not received much attention.

As in many EFL contexts, teacher candidates in Turkey are still on their way to developing their English language abilities. In addition to developing language abilities, learning the content related to English language teaching in their L2 poses various academic challenges, including not being able to thoroughly comprehend the content or cohesively compose their ideas in written discourse. Due to curricular limitations, as well as the exam-laden education in the Turkish context, a large number of FL writers end up engaging in activities geared at improving language through writing rather than expressing content through writing. Coupled with many EFL teacher candidates' lack of practice with L1 and L2 writing, the lack of updated writing pedagogies, appropriate textbooks and other teaching materials also have a negative impact on student and teacher motivation.

The Study

Research questions and methods

The study reported in this chapter exemplifies an attempt to address the above-discussed problems within the context of an EFL teacher education program at an English-medium university in Turkey. It presents an effort to analyze the underlying problems, existing pedagogical practices and writing needs that are shaped by local social and educational conditions, in order to contrive a new first year writing sequence that would better serve teacher candidates both as language students and as prospective teachers. For the broader version of this study, data were collected from student and faculty interviews, participant observation, and artifacts such as assessment tasks including writing exams given to teacher candidates during their attendance at the first year writing sequence. In this chapter, we are primarily focusing on the survey data as well as the content of the current first year writing curriculum. This study focused on two research questions:

(1) How is the first year writing curriculum for teacher candidates designed in an English-medium teacher training program at a Turkish university?
(2) What are the Turkish teacher candidates' perceptions of and experiences with writing during a new first year writing program?

We answer the first question by describing the pedagogical practices, objectives of the first year writing sequence and conflicting institutional demands in our setting, and the second research question by analyzing responses from the end-of-the year questionnaires we collected from 98 students who attended two academic writing courses (English 103 and English 104). We report percentages from Likert-scale questions, and the responses from open-ended questions were grouped and analyzed according to emerging themes. Before reporting on these two aspects of the study, in the following part we cover the context in which these teacher candidates are trained to be EFL teachers in the Turkish context.

Context: The changing institutional expectations of L2 writing

The teacher candidates in the program discussed in this study have been accepted onto a prestigious university's EFL teaching training program in Turkey. As an English-medium higher education institution, this university receives the top 10% of the entire student population taking the university entrance exam. While the conditions pertaining to this university may not be generalizable to all other Turkish universities, the case is illustrative in showing the tensions between the pedagogical practices that shape students' learning of L2 writing prior to university and the institutional demands placed on teacher candidates upon their arrival in the department.

Each year approximately 90 students are placed in the program based on their nationwide university exam scores. In the Turkish context, high school graduates who would like to be placed in a teacher training program are assessed based on their knowledge of English, Turkish and the social sciences in this nationwide standardized exam taken by all Turkish students at the end of the last year of high school. The English exam, like all the other parts of the university examination, is a multiple-choice test and aims to assess the exam takers' skills in reading, grammar and vocabulary. Students prepare for this exam by dedicating at least the last two years of their secondary school life to practicing test questions, memorizing vocabulary lists and developing test-taking strategies, striving to achieve almost full scores in order to be placed in this program. As no writing production is required in the exam, writing can be seen as a disregarded area of the teaching and learning of the curricula in secondary schools during university exam preparation, demonstrating the formidable impact of a high-stakes multiple choice test. As a result, many language teacher candidates arrive at the university with some sharpened skills of test-taking in English, which are of almost no use in successfully navigating their coursework at university. Upon arrival, they also take the university's English Proficiency Test (EPT), which assesses academic reading, listening and writing skills with short answer questions and essay exams. The majority of the students cannot pass the EPT and have to attend language classes to improve their English in a year-long intensive pre-university English for academic purposes (EAP) program.

Contrary to the lack of writing emphasis during secondary education, writing is intensively practiced in the preparatory year. However, this writing instruction does not go beyond drilling on 'five-paragraph' expository and argumentative essays written independently of any source material. The L2 writing practice done in this context is solely based on personal knowledge and opinion, as is the case of how writing is presented in many EFL materials and assessed in FL proficiency tests, perhaps similar to what You (2004) refers to as the 'current-traditional' approach. It is not unusual to see students memorizing formulaic introductory and concluding sentences, sometimes whole paragraphs, in order to insert cue words picked up from the given task. Whereas at the lower language ability levels, teaching based on the textual features of certain essay types might function as a scaffolding technique, such survival skills become a hindrance for further development at higher stages of this institution. The proficiency test, as a high-stakes test for university prep students and teachers, leaves limited pedagogical space for alternative routes.

The idea and practice of the five-paragraph expository essay, on the other hand, similar to a multiple-choice language exam, is an EFL teaching and assessment artifact molding students into a language use condition that does not exist in real life. In academic settings, writing rarely occurs in isolation relying only on the writer's thoughts and ideas, but is practiced as a discourse synthesis process in which writers select, organize and connect information from multiple source texts as they compose their own texts (Spivey & King, 1989). Therefore, when language teacher candidates at this university start their program, they have usually gone through two disillusionary phases of language learning: one when they arrive at the prep year affected by the negative washback of the university exam; and the other when they pass the prep exam and see that the language demands at the department are quite different.

Some teacher candidates, sooner or later, feel the gap between the skills they have developed during preparatory year writing courses and those expected from them in the content courses, including the English literature and academic writing courses in the first and second semesters. For instance, they are usually reminded by content area teachers that retelling information from the sources and juxtaposing pieces of it is not enough to maintain academic discussion; they are expected to write purposefully and critically but with evidence from the learned material. A common piece of feedback we hear from teacher trainers to the candidates in the program is, 'Don't write as if you were writing for prep school.' Writing for prep school, on the other hand, is purportedly an important step for many teacher candidates who have had little or no exposure to any sort of meaningful L2 writing.

From a broader perspective, the gulf between the practices of secondary education and the prep year, and the gap between the institutional demands of the prep year and the content classes are not only a matter of writing instruction problems, but point towards a social and pedagogical incongruity among the layers of the educational system, which in turn translates to academic unpreparedness on the part of the students. It is known to MoNE teachers that large-scale secondary school educational policies have rarely emphasized higher order academic skills such as analytical thinking, ability to synthesize and evaluate information, and criticality beyond lip service. Students graduating from secondary schools, having spent long hours practicing English through multiple-choice language tasks but not having had the chance to deal actively with the cognitive challenges of thinking to write, lose a very important opportunity to develop themselves not only linguistically but also cognitively. Therefore, any attempt to design a curriculum to remedy the problems of incoming ELT teacher candidates should focus not only on developing writing abilities per se, but also primarily on improving the writing skills that are contextually relevant and immediately required of them, and concurrently on developing their English proficiency to an optimum level so that they can successfully face the demands of their content classes. More importantly, such courses should foster students' academic thinking skills so that they can cope with the demands of the academic writing tasks they have to deal with at the university, both in the departmental courses and in others.

Findings

In order to address our first research question on the first year writing curriculum for teacher candidates, we initially discuss the way our first year writing course sequence has been shaped over the years and go over some of the main theoretical underpinnings that guide the way these courses focus on academic writing and L2 writing instruction in general. The second research question, which deals with teacher candidates' experiences in these courses and their general perceptions of L2 writing, will be answered based on the exit survey results.

Curricular analysis: Theoretical underpinnings and objectives of the first year writing sequence

The curriculum of the first year writing sequence was primarily conceptualized with a two-year long effort of curricular revamping in order to make the content of the writing courses a better fit for teacher candidates' academic needs at the university level. This included streamlining the writing courses and incorporating our theoretical knowledge of L2 writing instruction and second language acquisition (SLA) theories to reshape the courses. We focused on the facets of *teacher candidates as writers* and *tasks and texts* as suggested by Hyland (2011) in order to delineate these needs. As a part of this curricular change, we conducted informal feedback sessions with former students and carried out needs analyses with lecturers from the Department of Western Languages and Literatures from which our students took several courses. As mentioned above, these revealed that our first year students continuously had difficulty with the writing tasks and exam papers, especially in literature-based courses, as they were not aware of the problem-solving, knowledge-transforming (Scardamalia & Bereiter, 1987) nature of writing demanded of them; they did not always understand the requirements of tasks and respond to them in alignment. That is to say, most students responded to the tasks with memorized knowledge even though the tasks required higher level analysis and synthesis of the necessary information for critical evaluation.

Designed to address the observed gaps in the curriculum, the writing sequence was prepared in order to meet Turkish EFL teacher candidates' writing needs by covering two higher levels of writing ability in Grabe's (2001) writing framework[3]:

(a) *writing to learn*: problem solving, summarizing complexity, synthesizing (composing and transforming, composing from multiple sources);
(b) *writing to critique*: persuading, interpreting (privileging perspectives and using evidence selectively but appropriately).

Based on these two principles, the program aimed to operationalize certain theoretical conceptualizations of teaching L2 writing. The major underlying principle in the renewed course, following Byrnes (2013), was to introduce writing as a meaning-making process. Byrnes (2013: 95) argues that 'writing is about meaning-making and the teaching of writing is, therefore, about assuring that a focus on meaning informs and guides the development of students' ability to become competent multilingual creators of written texts.' With this in mind, the first year writing sequence included reading tasks that required a careful analysis of intended messages in extended texts and building meaning relations across them for the evaluation and production of meaning. The reading and writing connection was made intentionally explicit (Hirvela, 2006) through exposing students to texts from a wide range of disciplines. Another indispensable component of the renewed first year writing sequence was providing recursive feedback in different forms to support teacher candidates through their developmental trajectories. Besides, task complexity would be carefully controlled and the candidates would be exposed to hierarchically increasing task demands (Robinson, 2011). We expected increasing complexity and accuracy in both language production and argumentation in the candidates' writing output with the increase in task complexity. Another principle to implement was clear task objectives. Task objectives were to be explicitly defined so that any disparity between the curriculum writers' and learners' expectations was prevented (Breen, 2009; Manchón, 2014). Last but not least, the skill of coherent argumentation was emphasized in the courses. This approach is based on the premise that academic writing at university requires managing complex ideas by identifying parallelisms and conflicts, establishing a voice and a stance, using textual evidence efficiently to support claims, and developing the ability to develop logical coherence between the parts of an argument (Stapleton & Wu, 2015; Wingate, 2012).

Shaped around these global principles, the two-semester composition sequence aimed, in particular, to first provide students with the necessary skills for basic essay writing and source use and, secondly, to enable students to evaluate ideas, claims and methods using external evidence or selected criteria substantiated by observations or informed rationalizations. Additionally, English 103 integrated evidence-based critical literary analysis to address the results of the needs analysis interview with the Department of Western Languages and Literatures. The second course in the sequence (English 104) focused on language and the processes of argumentation and persuasion. In particular, students were asked to analyze different kinds of evidence to support a claim; various kinds of evidence include observations, facts and statistics, expert opinion from diverse fields of study, outside sources such as newspaper articles, research papers, books and encyclopedias. This meant that students were expected to learn how to challenge their own and others' assumptions and assertions and to provide substantial evidence to explain and justify a position.

While the curriculum analysis and reflections we did on the first year writing sequence looked at the kinds of reading and writing skills the program required from the candidates, the survey findings focused on the kinds of skills that teacher candidates enrolled in this program brought with them and their experiences within the program. With this in mind, the next section addresses our second research question: *What are the Turkish teacher candidates' perceptions of and experiences with writing during a new first year writing program?*

Survey findings: Teacher candidates' perceptions and experiences of L2 writing

Teacher candidates' perceptions of their writing abilities as well as their experiences with L1 and L2 writing were investigated in the survey administered at the end of the students' first year in the program. More specifically, the questions elicited responses from teacher candidates ($N = 98$) on a range of writing-related issues such as the candidates' writing experiences with Turkish and English in both in-school and out-of-school contexts, their perceptions of English and Turkish writing proficiency and experiences with formal writing instruction. Due to the scope of this chapter, we will only report on three major trends that emerged in the survey: (i) teacher candidates' relationship with English and other foreign languages; (ii) teacher candidates' attitudes, perceived needs and perceptions of L2 writing; and (iii) the perceived congruence of writing task expectations in writing courses.

(i) Relationship with English and other foreign languages

The survey results indicate that the teacher candidates had been exposed to a considerable amount of English before coming to the teacher training program. Eighty-four percent of the candidates indicated that they had received English instruction for 8–12 years and 98% of them considered themselves to be speakers of more than one language, Turkish and English being the major languages reported (other primary foreign languages reported included Russian, German, French and Italian). Contrary to the common belief that Turkish students, like many EFL students around the world, do not have much exposure to English or impetus to use their literacy skills in English outside the classroom context, many of the students reported that they often used English in various communicative settings, such as videogames, networking, teaching English to family members, socializing with foreign friends, reading news websites and users' manuals, translating for jobs and watching movies (66.3% used English outside the school context). Additionally, many of them used English to travel abroad (42.9%), with the purposes for travel including completing school projects for a student organization, visiting relatives, pursuing language education and touristic reasons. The majority reported that they did not write much in Turkish (67% writing 0–1 page a week) and wrote slightly more in English (70% writing 2–5 pages a week).

(ii) Attitudes, perceived needs and perceptions of L2 writing skills

Despite considerable exposure to English, it seems that less than half of the students harbored positive attitudes towards writing in English: 46% reported positive perceptions of writing in English, 18% felt neutral and 36% reported negative feelings. The liking was slightly higher for Turkish: 54% positive, 24% neutral and 30% negative. No matter their attitude, 71% of candidates perceived writing as a necessary skill for their future professions, an important part of their lives.

Eighty-one per cent of the participants self-assessed their writing skills in English as good and above. This percentage was slightly higher in Turkish (89%). When asked about their strengths as student writers, among all the comments, 43% mentioned strengths related to argumentation, ideas, content generation and building up a coherent argument. Other comments can be categorized under the themes of reading and ability to use sources (11%), the ability to use language correctly and effectively (10%), and the ability to use creativity and imagination (8%). In 9% of the comments, the candidates openly said that they did not think they had any strengths (see Figure 9.1).

When asked to identify the areas in which they needed improvement, we see a variation of responses, ranging from a need to improve vocabulary (mentioned in 29% of all comments) and language use (18%), to support the generation of content and ideas (18%) and organization (16%) (see Figure 9.2).

The teacher candidates were also asked what they thought the main features of good writing in academic contexts are. Of 209 different comments made about the important features of good writing, the main

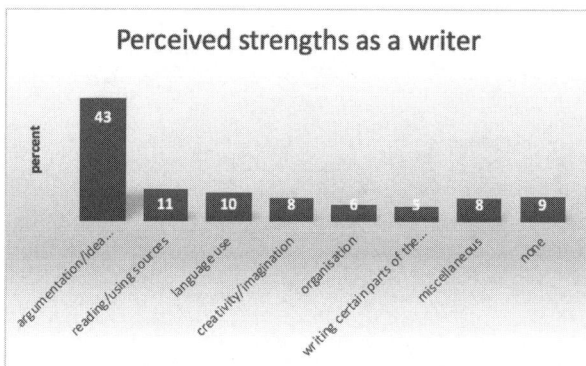

Figure 9.1 Perceived strengths as a second language writer

themes that occurred were strong argumentation (29%), good language use (26%) and creativity (21%). The candidates also thought being able to express one's opinions (14%) and knowing how to use sources (8%) were desirable skills (see Figure 9.3).

Another question was based on the text types the candidates most liked writing during the course of the two semesters (see Figure 9.4). Interestingly, of 104 comments made, argumentative essays were cited 35% of the time as the preferred text type. The teacher candidates reported that argumentative essays made them think critically, taught them to look at both sides of an issue and allowed them to express their ideas freely. Some found it easier to take a stance and write and some thought it was a worthwhile endeavor to try to convince the reader about a point of view. Sixteen percent of the candidates who said they liked writing story analyses reported that they liked reading stories. Some candidates mentioned that reading and analyzing stories was fun and it facilitated intellectual growth. The enjoyable side of uncovering implicit

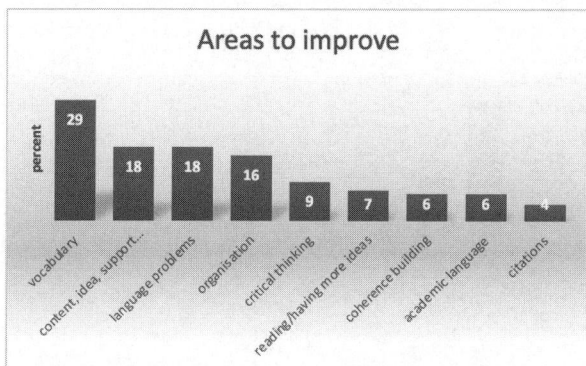

Figure 9.2 Areas to improve as a second language writer

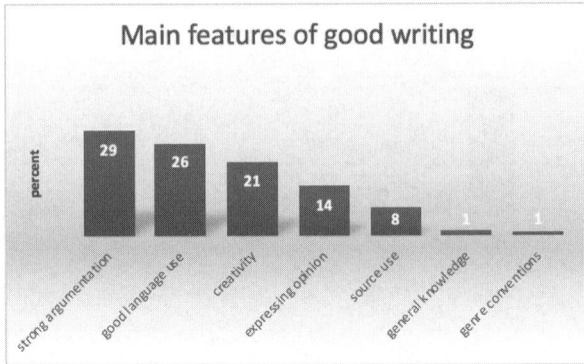

Figure 9.3 Perceived features of good academic writing

meaning in the stories was also mentioned as a reason. Thirteen percent of the candidates reported that they liked writing response papers best. They thought it was an opportunity to express thoughts and one's personal ideas. A candidate mentioned that 'evaluating something is more exciting than writing something from scratch' (Survey answer). Nine per cent of the candidates found writing essays based on the comparison of information from texts preferable. Some candidates said it gave them a chance to clarify arguments and counter-arguments and express their own ideas and that it encouraged the analysis and assessment of texts: '[I like] argumentative essays based on comparison of information from texts because I can reflect my ideas more efficiently', '[I like] argumentative essays and research paper because if you are writing these, you should do literature review and this helps you to improve your thinking skills.'; 'With argumentative writing, I have a chance to express myself clearly.'

When asked how much they thought they had improved in the writing-related skills emphasized in English 103 and 104, the candidates on

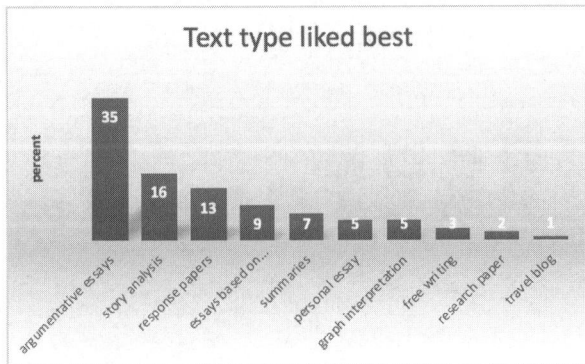

Figure 9.4 Preferred text-types

Table 9.1 Perceived academic writing skill improvement post-first year writing sequence

How much did you improve the following skills in English 103 and 104?	Score/10
Using citation conventions	7.51
Identifying useful information from sources	7.31
Incorporating sources	7.28
Organizing an essay into parts	7.09
Developing a logical argumentation	7.08
Connecting ideas with each other meaningfully	7.00
Thinking and writing critically	6.98
Paraphrasing	6.97
Following certain genre conventions (persuasive, analytical ...)	6.89
Summarizing	6.86
Synthesizing	6.84
Writing a thesis statement	6.84
Writing suitably for the audience	6.83

average thought they had improved in all skills satisfactorily (see Table 9.1). The highest proportions of perceived improvement were in source use and organization skills, whereas synthesizing, writing thesis statements and writing suitably for the audience were marked by slightly lower scores.

Finally, the whole writing sequence, English 103 and 104, was evaluated by the candidates in terms of the global objectives it aimed to achieve: improving students' writing skills; contributing to analytical and critical thinking; facilitating improvement in English; helping to write in other courses; and improving intellectual knowledge. Fostering creative writing was not conceived of as a component of the sequence; nevertheless, we included it among the questions in order to see the candidates' reactions (Table 9.2). The candidates scored both courses together on a scale of 1–10: 1 being 'not agree at all' and 10 being 'strongly agree'. To make more robust observations, we did not include the middle scores of 5–6 as positive but took them as neutral categories, neither on the positive nor negative side. It was encouraging to see that fewer than 20% of the group showed negative perceptions in any category. The majority of the candidates were on the positive side except for the last category on creativity (49%). The candidates found the writing instruction they received useful for other courses (67.3%) and helpful in terms of improving their writing skills (64.3%). They also reported that the first year writing courses were helpful in improving their English (63.3%) and also contributed to their critical thinking (63.3%) and intellectual knowledge (61.2%). Yet the highest negative evaluation the courses were rated with was for the support for intellectual knowledge (19.4%) and creativity (18.4%).

Table 9.2 Perceived benefits post-first year writing sequence

English 103 and 104	Negative (%) (1–4)	Neutral (%) (5–6)	Positive (%) (7–10)
Helped improve English	9.2	27.6	63.3
Useful for other courses	13.3	19.4	67.3
Improved intellectual knowledge	19.4	19.4	61.2
Helped use creative skills	18.4	32.6	49.0
Contributed to analytical and critical thinking	16.3	20.4	63.3
Helped improve as a writer	11.2	24.5	64.3

(iii) The perceived congruence and disparity of writing task expectations in writing courses

One of the important questions touched on in the survey was the perceived incongruity between how the writing tasks were conceptualized by the instructors and how the teacher candidates perceived these writing tasks. To the question as to whether there were any similarities or differences between what they and their professors expected from the assigned writing tasks, 43.6% of the students gave a positive response by saying there were 'no' differences between their expectations and the professors'. However, while 3.2% of the students declared that they did not have any idea, more than half of the students (53.2%) acknowledged perceived differences. Through content analysis, we could group the comments under two general headings. The candidates mentioned disparity in relation to (a) expectations about essay features (organization, coherence, content, language and style) and (b) task features.

(a) Expectations related to essay features

The candidates verbalized their thoughts on either what they had problems with – for example, essay features they struggled with – or what they did not find acceptable in the course. There were 22 comments in this category. The candidates seemed to have different perspectives on establishing coherence and clarity within essays; six candidates explained that they had not been able to satisfy the professors in that respect. Similarly, six candidates had problems in understanding what a strong thesis was. Five candidates commented that the degree of academic language expected from them was not appropriate for undergraduate level. Six students implied that the quality expectation was beyond their capacity. The candidates also mentioned that professors expected *strict organization* (3), *more criticality in idea evaluation* (2), *simplicity in language* (1), *unnecessarily formal language* (1), *the use of more citations* (1) and *more complex ideas than the candidate could produce* (1). A few exemplar comments are given below. For instance, one student commented: 'They want me to write extremely academically. I am an undergraduate student and I think that they all consider us as a master student. Come on!' Another student reflected on the professors' expectations on producing clear thesis statements: 'They seem be usually expecting a strict outline, such as too clear thesis statements that would not be interesting for the reader.'

(b) Task-related expectations

Several candidates mentioned the fact that they were expected to write on different topics and that the topics were difficult and alien to them (7). As one student commented: 'They want good arguments, but I cannot make good arguments especially when the topic is very distant to me.' Five students, on the other hand, mentioned that they were never clear about the task focus so their work was seen as irrelevant at times and that they did not understand the task requirements most of the time, which led them to prepare inaccurate assignments. For instance, one student stated: 'I think the problem is that I don't understand the instructions most of the time so almost everything becomes different than what my professors expected.'

Discussion

Closely analyzing the first year writing sequence of a language teacher training program at an English-medium university in Turkey and teacher candidates' perceptions of academic writing, our study reported on both macro and micro issues surrounding writing courses that aimed to improve teacher candidates' academic writing skills, particularly focusing on the development of argumentative writing. As explained earlier in the chapter, the pedagogical decision to prioritize critical thinking and argumentation in the first year writing sequence was given as a result of the needs analysis conducted with the Department of Western Languages and Literatures, where argumentation was found to be a prerequisite subskill in order for the teacher candidates to be confident in coping with the demands of academic writing requirements at the university. Given the candidates' limited exposure to L2 writing instruction during their pre-university years, this was a considerable step up from 'low-context writing prompts' (Ortmeier-Hooper, 2013), which predominantly require students to produce decontextualized writing such as compare-contrast essays or personal opinion style five-paragraph essays. Such survival genres in high school and preparatory school at university not only limited their opportunities to engage in authentic writing, but also rarely encouraged them to critically consider the content (e.g. source texts) and get involved in (e.g. respond to, synthesize) high-level thinking and decision making in writing. With this in mind, one of the promising outcomes of the writing sequence we spotlighted in this chapter was the move away from a standard writing template and the expectation that students act on more rhetorically complex texts. The array of writing prompts and texts to which students were exposed challenged them while providing them with the rich linguistic input necessary for their language development.

While the needs of our local context led us to primarily focus on argumentative writing, a close look at our current data also shows us that the overemphasis on argumentation as an academic skill comes with both advantages and disadvantages given the diverse language and writing skills that Turkish language teacher candidates bring with them to our classrooms. One of the beneficial effects as reported in the study is that candidates seem to acquire critical academic literacy skills such as supporting ideas with credible sources and discussing those sources critically in argumentative writing. Additionally, because the writing sequence aimed to support evidence-based critical argumentation skills, teacher candidates were more confident in the critical reading of diverse texts, developing a stance in the light of available information and supporting this stance by using coherent evidence-based argumentation with adequate use of sources. Yet this transformation and shift from controlled writing practices to higher level writing contexts did not come without challenges – neither for the teacher candidates nor for us as writing instructors with differing pedagogical training from non-Turkish contexts. For some teacher candidates, language problems, which derived from their low language proficiency, formed an insurmountable barrier in meaningfully engaging with high-level texts. Some of the revealing examples of these challenges were explicit in the survey data. The lack of vocabulary knowledge and their low language abilities created a range of challenges such as the inability to use source texts, adhering to the information presented in texts and the inability to cohesively organize their ideas, or even not being able to understand what the writing task asks them to do. We speculate that these challenges are a result of not only the teacher candidates' low language proficiency, but also their limited experience with higher order thinking skills in both Turkish and English writing. Similar findings were also observed by Alagözlü and Saraç-Süzer (2010), who explored 30 Turkish pre-service teachers' academic writing experiences and reported the challenges language teacher candidates face while writing argumentative essays. Their research indicates that, more than the language proficiency issue, the lack of training in the Turkish education system on critical thinking as well as the unfamiliarity of the argumentative essay genre made teacher candidates less confident about their writing experiences. While our survey results illustrate that students felt more confident about reading and producing argumentative genres, some teacher candidates also found this focus 'not enjoyable' and shared that these classes should, as the candidate puts it, 'not only try to teach us how to write, but also how to love writing.'

One of the challenges that we as writing instructors felt was the juggling of priorities. As we reflected on our writing instruction in this sequence, we constantly posed questions such as: How fair is it to expect a display of higher order thinking skills in L2 from candidates who have low language proficiency levels? What other genres and literacy practices can better prepare them for their teaching profession and beyond? How do we balance teaching the language skills that some candidates lack (e.g. vocabulary development through reading and writing), intellectual abilities related to critical thinking and written communication in multiple genres?

Conclusion: What's Next?

As written communication in English is increasingly becoming a significant part of everyday communication in non-English dominant contexts such as Turkey, the need for teacher preparation courses that focus on improving future teachers' L2 literacy should be a fundamental part of teacher education. In this context, we argue that a close examination of writing-oriented courses and candidates' experiences in such spaces is an important step to better understand the pedagogical tensions around L2 writing instruction and students' writing needs and experiences as future language teachers. Such courses also create opportunities for language candidates to see themselves as users of written communication, rather than as perpetual learners of a foreign language.

It is an undeniable fact that the high school curricula in the Turkish context provide limited writing instruction (Altinmakas, 2015; Yayli, 2011). However, this does not mean that this reality cannot be changed in higher levels of education. If we think that having good writing skills is an integral part of being a successful language teacher in an EFL context and a successful participant in the global society, then we might also want to start looking closely at both institutionalized and non-institutionalized writing spaces and examine the kinds of challenges and triumphs language teacher candidates seem to experience on their way to becoming language teachers and L2 writers.

Even though our writing sequence privileged academic writing, we think that writing sequences in language teacher preparation programs in EFL contexts can also benefit from including more diverse genres where students not only analyze research-based academic texts in order to learn argumentation, but also other kinds of texts such as historical narratives, comedy writing, satire, ethnographic writing, multi-genre essays or web-based texts. While there is merit in teaching academic writing within teacher training programs that are English medium, 21st century writing instruction should also reflect the realities of L2 writers' lives outside their academic contexts. For instance, many students we worked with also make meaningful and authentic use of multimedia reporting when they engage in written communication in online spaces such as quora, online video gaming, blogging or internship websites. The out-of-school literacy experiences of teacher candidates illustrate that literate knowledge is situated in everyday life. Future research inquiries into the writing preparation of teacher candidates can benefit from examining the multiple writing needs of candidates and drawing connections to a wider range of out-of-school genres and rhetorical situations (Ortmeier-Hooper, 2013; Yi, 2007, 2010). More localized and ecological writing pedagogies at all levels of education might mean that writing instructors and language teacher candidates are aware of the realities of English use in their local contexts and 'balance their local realities with an idealistic view of their work' (Casanave, 2009: 257). This might translate to a more language-based L2 writing curriculum which explicitly focuses on how language works in different writing situations and for different rhetorical purposes. This language-based approach to writing instruction (e.g. systemic-functional linguistics) can be beneficial for understanding how texts work in real life and the different kinds of choices L2 writers make across different writing situations, which in turn could increase both the linguistic and the writing competencies of the teacher candidates.

Finally, while such writing courses (e.g. the first year writing courses that we spotlighted in this chapter) give language teacher candidates abundant opportunities to improve as L2 writers, language teacher preparation programs in EFL contexts should also require more courses on L2 writing pedagogy where candidates reflexively think about various L2 writing issues as they apply to their own local contexts rather than focusing on the wholesale application of writing pedagogies imported from the Western world (Casanave, 2009; You, 2004).

Notes

(1) For further details, please visit the following website: https://www.yok.gov.tr/en.
(2) This standardized university examination in Turkey assesses exam takers' knowledge of various subject areas including history, Turkish literature and geography, and places the students into Turkish universities based on the scores they obtain. If students intend to be FL educators, in addition to Turkish and social sciences they need to take a multiple-choice FL proficiency test that assesses the candidates' FL abilities.
(3) It should be noted that this program did not attempt to cover Grabe's third level – writing to create as an esthetic and entertaining experience – as at the time of program revisions creative writing or leisure writing did not seem to be a writing practice that had immediate relevance to the teacher candidates' needs.

References

Alagözlü, N. and Saraç-Süzer, S. (2010) Language and cognition: Is critical thinking a myth in Turkish educational system? *Procedia Social and Behavioral Sciences* 2, 782–786.
Altan, M.Z. (2006) Beliefs about language learning of foreign language major university students. *Australian Journal of Teacher Education* 31, 45–52.
Altınmakas, D. (2015) Dynamic interaction of factors influencing Turkish university students' academic writing practices in English. Unpublished Master's thesis, Boğaziçi University.

Atay, D. and Ece, A. (2009) Multiple identities as reflected in English-language education: The Turkish perspective. *Journal of Language, Identity, and Education* 8, 21–34.

Bayyurt, Y. and Akcan, S. (2016) Türkiye'deki İngilizce Öğretmeni Yetiştirme Programları üzerine Düşünce ve Öneriler, 3. *Ulusal Yabancı Dil Eğitim Kurultayı* (pp. 3–9). Istanbul: Boğaziçi Üniversitesi.

Breen, M.P. (2009) Learner contributions to task design. In K. Van den Branden, M. Bygate and J.M. Norris (eds) *Task-based Language Teaching: A Reader* (pp. 333–356). Amsterdam: John Benjamins.

Byrnes, H. (2013) Positioning writing as meaning-making in writing research: An introduction. *Journal of Second Language Writing* 22, 95–106.

Casanave, C.P. (2009) Training for writing or training for reality? Challenges facing EFL writing teachers and students in language teacher education programs. In R. Manchón (ed.) *Writing in Foreign Language Contexts: Learning, Teaching, and Research* (pp. 256–277). Bristol: Multilingual Matters.

Çetinavcı, U.R. and Yavuz, A. (2010) Language proficiency level of English language teacher trainees in Turkey. *International Journal of Research in Teacher Education* 1, 26–54.

Doğancay-Aktuna, S. (1998) The spread of English in Turkey and its current sociolinguistic profile. *Journal of Multilingual and Multicultural Development* 19 (1), 24–39. doi:10.1080/01434639808666340

Doğancay-Aktuna, S. and Kızıltepe, Z. (2005) English in Turkey. *World Englishes* 24 (2), 253–265.

Grabe, W. (2001) Notes toward a theory of second language writing. In T. Silva and P.K. Matsuda (eds) *On Second Language Writing* (pp. 39–57). Mahwah, NJ: Lawrence Erlbaum.

Hirvela, A. (2006) Negotiating understanding in ESL teacher training. *ELT Journal* 60 (3), 233–242.

Hyland, K. (2011) Learning to write: Issues in theory, research, and pedagogy. In R.M. Manchón (ed.) *Learning-to-write and Writing-to-learn in an Additional Language* (pp. 17–35). Amsterdam: John Benjamins.

Kırkgöz, Y. (2017) English language education reforms and their effects on ELT in Turkish primary schools. In Y. Bayyurt and N.C. Sifakis (eds) *English Language Education Policies and Practices in the Mediterranean Countries and Beyond* (pp. 25–38). Frankfurt am Main: Peter Lang.

Lee, I. (2010) What about a feedback revolution in the writing classroom. *Modern English Teacher* 19 (2), 46–49.

Manchón, R.M. (ed.) (2009) *Writing in Foreign Language Contexts: Learning, Teaching, and Research*. Bristol: Multilingual Matters.

Manchón, R.M. (2014) The internal dimension of tasks: The interaction between task factors and learner factors in bringing about learning through writing. In H. Byrnes and R. Manchón (eds) *Task-based Language Learning: Insights to and from Writing* (pp. 27–52). Amsterdam: John Benjamins.

Ministry of National Education (2018a) English language curriculum for Grades 2-8. Retrieved from http://mufredat.meb.gov.tr/ProgramDetay.aspx?PID=327 (last accessed 10 June 2019).

Ministry of National Education (2018b) English language curriculum for Grades 9-12. Retrieved from http://mufredat.meb.gov.tr/ProgramDetay.aspx?PID=342 (last accessed 10 June 2019).

Ortmeier-Hooper, C. (2013) *The ELL Writer: Moving Beyond Basics in the Secondary Classroom*. New York: Teachers College Press.

Reichelt, M. (2009) A critical evaluation of writing teaching programmes in different foreign language settings. In R. Manchón (ed.) *Writing in Foreign Language Contexts: Learning, Teaching, and Research* (pp. 183–206). Bristol: Multilingual Matters.

Robinson, P. (ed.) (2011) *Second Language Task Complexity: Researching the Cognition Hypothesis of Language Learning and Performance*. Amsterdam: John Benjamins.

Scardamalia, M. and Bereiter, C. (1987) Knowledge telling and knowledge transforming in written composition. *Advances in Applied Psycholinguistics* 2, 142–175.

Selvi, A.F. (2016) English as the language of marketspeak. *English Today* 32, 33–39. doi:10.1017/S0266078416000286

Spivey, N.N. and King, J.R. (1989) Readers as writers composing from sources. *Reading Research Quarterly* 24, 7–26.

Stapleton, P. and Wu, Y. (2015) Assessing the quality of arguments in students' persuasive writing: A case study. *Journal of English for Academic Purposes* 17, 12–23.

Wingate, U. (2012) 'Argument!' helping students understand what essay writing is about. *Journal of Academic Purposes* 11, 154–154.

Yayli, D. (2011) From genre awareness to cross-genre awareness: A study in an EFL context. *Journal of English for Academic Purposes* 10 (3), 121–129.

Yi, Y. (2007) Engaging literacy: A biliterate student's composing practices beyond school. *Journal of Second Language Writing* 16, 23–39.

Yi, Y. (2010) Adolescent multilingual writers' transitions across in- and out-of-school writing contexts. *Journal of Second Language Writing* 19, 17–32.

You, X. (2004) 'The choice made from no choice': English writing instruction in a Chinese university. *Journal of Second Language Writing* 13, 97–110.

10 Opportunities and Resources for Pre-service English Teachers to Teach Writing: The Case of Northern Cyprus

Alev Özbilgin-Gezgin and Betil Eröz

Introduction

Writing is a skill that often develops later on in the process of foreign/second language learning, and it poses a challenge for language teachers, whether they are native or non-native writers of the target language. In teaching English as a foreign language (TEFL) contexts, language teacher education programs at undergraduate or graduate level generally have composition courses to help develop the writing skills of pre-service teachers as well as methodology courses that aim to teach these students how to teach writing. The way writing practices are used and valued influences the way writing is taught in various contexts (Lea, 2004; Silva & Leki, 2004).

The way writing practices are perceived affects the way writing is taught in different educational contexts (Kroll, 1990; Lea, 2004; Shi & Cumming, 1995). Literacy studies reveal that the way we attach values to reading and writing is not universal and that what we do with reading and writing is closely linked to how we socialize and how we use them in particular and situated contexts through literacy practices (Baynham, 1998; Gee, 1998; Özbilgin, 2004; Street, 1984). In a pre-service English teacher education program where students come to university with different linguistic competencies and with different understandings of writing due to their cultural upbringing/backgrounds, these factors are amplified. When the variety in student backgrounds and proficiency is paired with the variety in the educational, training and cultural backgrounds of instructors, some challenges and conflicts in the teacher education process are inevitable. With such understanding in mind, we wanted to explore the English as a foreign language (EFL) teacher education context in an English-medium university in Northern Cyprus, which is unique in the sense that it is an independent program housed in an overseas campus of the Middle East Technical University (METU) in Ankara, Turkey. Our aim in this chapter is to report on the experiences, perceptions and impressions of students in the writing skills courses as well as the approaches to teaching writing courses offered in this program.

One of our primary purposes in this study is to understand the needs and experiences of the pre-service teachers enrolled in the program with regard to learning and teaching writing in English, by exploring their notion of writing and whether it underwent any changes throughout their undergraduate studies, as well as their future plans for writing pedagogies in their own teaching. This knowledge will enable us to evaluate the effectiveness of our teaching writing pedagogies and practices. Furthermore, we will develop insights with regard to: (1) the perceptions of the faculty members and students (pre-service teachers) about the effectiveness of the writing-related courses offered in the program; and (2) the extent to which the writing courses in the TEFL program prepare students for their future teaching of writing. Such understanding of these two groups will help us, teacher educators working in this program, diagnose the values attached to learning and teaching writing in this particular context, leading us to revise our curriculum and approach(es) to writing instruction and practices.

Writing has not, historically, been central to the EFL education mission in Northern Cyprus and Turkey[1] (See Chapter 9 for further discussion on the role of writing in Turkish education). Both the preparation of novice teachers and the contexts in which they will work are understudied. Of course, more research alone is not the full answer. Teacher educators in Northern Cyprus and Turkey need opportunities to compare programs and research results in order to improve the writing education of their students. This chapter presents results of a qualitative case study at one public university in Northern Cyprus. The impact of globalization and the spread of the remix culture on communication has hastened the need for an examination of writing education programs as well as their pre-service teachers' subsequent teaching contexts (Evans-Tokaryk, 2014). Lee (2010: 43) observes that 'the Internet of today increasingly gives people the ability not to just consume content, but also remix it or interact with it in creations of their own.' With such a generation of young students coming to university equipped with era-specific experiences in which reading and writing mix in diverse ways, we need to know what teacher candidates feel about their development as writers and as teachers of writing.

Prospective teachers of writing enter TEFL programs at English-medium universities in Northern Cyprus and Turkey with certain conceptualizations of writing, arising from their previous learning experiences and cultures. Hence, we are interested in learning the notions both pre-service teachers and the faculty who teach writing bring to the program. Additionally, the study examines how the notions of writing change for both parties: for students from Years 1–4 and for the faculty after they teach a writing or writing-related course in the program. Lastly, we look into how pre-service teachers envision their future teaching of writing.

Literature Review

The importance of developing the writing skills of pre-service and in-service English teachers has been highlighted in language teaching literature (e.g. Altay, 2010; Ferris, 2007; Lee, 2011). It is crucial for English teacher education programs, both undergraduate and graduate, to have writing skills development courses (e.g. Ferris, 2007, 2014; Street & Stang, 2008) to help prospective and professional English teachers improve their language skills and writing abilities, because 'good writing instruction and writing teacher instruction are needed to improve student writing' (Lee, 2011: 154). Several studies suggest that former experiences of writing teachers shape their attitudes towards writing as a skill and their practices as writing teachers. For example, in Gallavan *et al.*'s study (2007), the teacher candidates emphasized the value of writing and the writing process, but they didn't always 'make clear connections between the assignments, themselves, and life' (2007: 64). They expressed uncertainty about how to 'teach writing effectively and how to integrate writing meaningfully across the curriculum' (2007: 67). They were also unsure of how writing might be beneficial in their own lives and in the lives of their future students. According to Street and Stang (2008), lack of confidence as writers; poor histories as writers; lack of meaningful professional development; and lack of time to teach writing pose challenges for teachers in teaching writing. In his case study of five pre-service teachers, Street (2003), found that the prospective teachers' writing abilities, experiences with writing, and self-perceptions as writers before entering the teacher education program had an impact on their writing teaching practices and attitudes. In this light, the impact of a writing-focused courses on the development of student teachers' writing skills and improvement of practices of teaching writing becomes a crucial element in teacher education programs (Street & Stang, 2008).

Various ways of helping prospective writing teachers to develop their writing skills have been proposed by scholars. Shin (2006) suggests that teaching writing through one-on-one tutoring of English as a second language (ESL) students and keeping writing journals about their experiences gives prospective teachers a satisfying experience which builds their confidence as teachers and increases their awareness of the challenges of the process of writing. Emphasizing the important role that the knowledge base plays in the efficacy of kindergarten writing teachers, Curtis (2017: 20) recommends explicit pre-writing activities, specific feedback and effective collaboration between teachers and students in order to increase teachers' competency in teaching specific writing skills. The positive effects of peer feedback (Ferris, 2010; Yu & Lee, 2016), coded teacher feedback (Kahraman, 2013), and a combination of rubrics and corrective feedback (Ene & Kosobucki, 2016; Ferris & Hedgcock, 2014; Hyland & Hyland, 2006) have also been reported to enhance the writing skills of second language (L2) writers of English. Certain pedagogical tools, such as scaffolding, process writing, peer feedback, and modeling, were also reported to play an important role in developing the perceptions of prospective teachers regarding how writing should be taught (Grossman et al., 2000).

In EFL contexts like Northern Cyprus and Turkey, it is crucial for English language teaching (ELT) programs to help prospective English teachers improve their language skills and writing abilities. While all faculties of education in Northern Cyprus and Turkey have followed a standardized curriculum prescribed by the Council of Higher Education (CHE) since 1998 (Şimşek & Yıldırım, 2001), there remains considerable variation from one program to the next. For example, the objective of a writing course can be defined in exactly the same way in the course catalogue in all pre-service teacher education departments. However, the design of each course might vary considerably. One course can be taught using the process-oriented approach (in which students are graded through multiple drafts and a portfolio), whereas the other might be taught using the product-oriented writing approach (in which students are graded through mid-terms and final exams generated in class). However, the frequent restructuring of teacher education systems since that time has led to diverse, and perhaps under-examined, approaches to teaching due to increased autonomy from CHE and the Ministry of National Education (MoNE) (Deniz & Şahin, 2006; see also Chapter 9). This diversity among teacher education programs calls for investigations of institutional philosophies of language teacher education (Arıkan, 2006; Erkılıç, 2008; Karakaş, 2012) as well as the practical and pedagogical knowledge delivered to teacher candidates.

Scholarly research in the Turkish context has mainly focused on individual program evaluations (Cosgun-Ogeyik, 2009; Karakas, 2012; Seferoğlu, 2006; Şallı-Çopur, 2008); comparison of pre-service ELT programs (Sanli, 2009); comparison of Turkish teacher education programs with programs around the world (Coşkun & Daloğlu, 2010; Grossman et al., 2007; Karamustafaoğlu, 2009); and analyzing specific aspects of and practices in the practicum course (Enginarlar, 1996; Eröz-Tuğa, 2003; Ismail & Çavusoğlu, 2017). Little attention has been given to investigating prospective teachers' writing ability and preparedness to teach writing, specifically.

Research studies conducted in pre-service teacher education contexts in Northern Cyprus have focused on a variety of learning and teaching related issues of prospective teachers. Some studies have focused on language proficiency and language skills development. For example, Erozan (2005) investigated the general language proficiency levels of teacher candidates and called for more research to be conducted in how teacher education programs deal with language proficiency. She claimed that programs experience similar difficulties in relation to the language improvement courses and the trainee teachers' language competence. Studies that followed this focused on the relationship between communication skills and attitudes towards the teaching profession (Yeşil, 2010); reading habits and interests (Pehlivan *et al.*, 2010); critical thinking skills (Serin, 2013); the relationship between vocabulary learning strategies and vocabulary size (Kalajahi & Pourshahian, 2012); and speaking anxiety (Tüm & Kunt, 2013) of pre-service teachers.

Other studies that had pre-service teacher education programs as their central context, examined various courses, practices, and curriculum elements of these programs. Kuter and Koç (2009) investigated the collaborative dimensions of the Internship partnership between an English-medium university in Northern Cyprus and four cooperating public schools. They suggested the establishment of a more formalized and reciprocal relationship between universities and cooperating schools in practicum. Debreli (2011, 2012) investigated the use of diaries to examine and track changes in pre-service teachers' beliefs about teaching and learning English as a foreign language. Similarly, Erkmen (2012) suggested various tools and tasks to uncover student teachers' beliefs, such as diary writing, observations, post-lesson reflection forms, and stimulated recall interviews. Selvi (2017) highlighted the importance of preparing teachers to teach English as an International Language and describes his classroom practices in an elective course offered in the teacher education program which was also the context of the study reported in this chapter.

With regards to research studies investigating the teaching of writing in the Northern Cyprus context, very few studies may be found in literature. Akçıl and Arap (2009) examined the attitudes and opinions of prospective teachers regarding their use of electronic portfolios and reported that teacher candidates had a positive attitude towards this technology for educational and learning purposes. Bostancı and Çavuşoğlu's (2018) recent study on the effectiveness of a writing course which uses the process genre approach (PGA) and a blended learning approach (BLA) for pre-service teachers underlined certain approaches that might help pre-service teachers generate better written products.

The current study is significant in the sense that it is the first project that specifically focuses on writing instruction in a teacher education program in Teaching English as a Foreign Language (TEFL) in the Northern Cyprus context. The study examined how teaching and learning writing was perceived by the faculty members and pre-service teachers in this program; the perceptions and experiences of both groups in relation to writing; and to what extent the writing courses prepared prospective teachers for their future teaching writing practices. In an attempt to provide an emic view of both students and faculty members by focusing on their reflections on the effectiveness of writing-related courses offered in the teacher education program, the following questions were addressed:

(1) What are the perceptions of the faculty members and students about the effectiveness of the writing-related courses offered in the English language teacher education program in Northern Cyprus? To what extent do the writing courses in the program prepare the students for their future teaching of writing?
(2) How do the faculty members approach the writing courses in the teacher education program in terms of goals and methodology?
(3) What are the expectations and experiences of the pre-service teachers about the writing courses in the teacher education?

Background

The setting of the study is an English teacher education program at the Northern Cyprus Campus (NCC) of Middle East Technical University (METU), located in Ankara, Turkey. The NCC is:

> ... the first overseas campus of a Turkish university, and was founded in accordance with an invitation conveyed to METU by the governments of the Republic of Turkey and Turkish Republic of Northern Cyprus in the year 2000 and the foundation law adopted in the year 2003. Located at the Güzelyurt district of North Cyprus, the Campus currently offers 15 undergraduate and 5 graduate programs providing the academic repertoire and quality maintained at the home campus in Ankara, Turkey. [This campus] is attached to the Middle East Technical University in all academic and administrative matters, and operates under the same educational standards and policies applied at its home campus. Thus, Northern Cyprus Campus provides yet another opportunity to study at a high ranking university, committed to the development of critical and creative thinking, self-discipline and motivation, leadership and confidence in students, and to graduate them with the ability to communicate and cooperate effectively and to adapt to new challenges and circumstances as well as with entrepreneurial skills and ethical standards... (METU, NCC website: https://ncc.metu.edu.tr/general-information)

The TEFL Program, which is an undergraduate English teacher education program, is the equivalent of the English Language Teaching undergraduate program at the School of Education, Department of Foreign Language Education at the main METU campus in Ankara, Turkey.

All language skill courses (reading, writing, listening and speaking), literature, translation, language teaching methodology and practicum courses are offered over a period of four years. Graduates of this particular program are expected to be competent to teach at primary, secondary and tertiary institutions in Northern Cyprus or Turkey. However, Turkish nationals are not legally allowed to teach at state schools in Northern Cyprus, and the same rule applies for Cypriot nationals for state schools in Turkey.

Political context

The political status of Cyprus influences writing teacher education because Cyprus is a divided and contested space. As a result of a dispute between Turkish and Cypriot communities in 1974, the island divided into two zones. In 1983 the Turkish Republic of Northern Cyprus (TRNC) was established but, due to restricted recognition, Turkish Cypriots became isolated and educationally disadvantaged. Politically, an international embargo is enforced and this situation has had a negative impact on the way teachers and students have access to education. Especially before the advent of the internet, ways to reach knowledge through books or through interaction in seminars or conferences were limited. With regard to teaching writing and writing teacher education, teachers are educated to teach the writing of essays for exams such as TOEFL or IELTS and writing is practiced to acquire/learn English.

In order to provide political and educational support, to compensate for the disadvantage of the embargo and also to reinforce high-quality education on the Northern side of the island, a major national university from Turkey opened a campus in Northern Cyprus in 2005 with the following mission:

> ... to lead social advancement at local, regional and global dimensions by providing education and carrying out research of universal standards in a multicultural environment following an approach that fosters innovation, entrepreneurship and sustainability. (METU website)

This mission is implemented in K-12 teacher education through the teaching English as a foreign language department, where language teachers are educated to have:

> ... a superior knowledge of English, critical teaching and thinking skills, and broad intellectual curiosity of languages and cultures. Graduates will have a near-perfect knowledge of English, including the rules and representations underlying the structure of English, Linguistics, Contrastive Turkish-English Structure, and teaching theories and methodologies. Additionally, the TEFL program at [this university] endeavors to provide students with literature and humanities courses to familiarize them with authentic texts, the best examples of written and spoken English, the social and historical contexts of the English language, and interdisciplinary literary and cultural experiences. (METU website)

The absence of any mention of writing or the education of writing teachers in the department's mission is noteworthy, although a more detailed inspection of the curriculum suggests the conscious provision of some preparation in writing.

Writing-focused courses in the curriculum

There are several writing-focused courses in this four-year teacher education program, with a small module on how to teach writing in one methodology-oriented course. In their first year, students take an integrated reading and writing course in which they read and write for academic purposes. They learn to generate their own topics, carry out related research in order to 'analyze, synthesize and evaluate information and react to readings in their compositions and develop basic research skills including library/internet searches and basic report writing skills, such as citing, paraphrasing, and referencing' (METU catalogue description). This course is supported by a grammar course which initially teaches how to write paragraphs and also focuses on form-meaning relations in creating meaning.

In the second year, the curriculum shifts from teachers as writers to the teaching of writing. In one methodology course, pre-service teachers focus on the history of EFL/ESL methods and how writing is emphasized (or not) in each method. In another, they learn about the current integration of writing and other language skills.

The third year pre-service course devoted to academic writing requires teachers to act as solitary authors conducting small-scale research and to write a traditional research paper. In addition, pre-service teachers conduct demo-teaching focused on the teaching of writing in a second integrated reading and writing course.

In their final year, pre-service teachers read and assess secondary school writing as part of their assigned practicum. This practicum also allows teacher candidates to observe some teaching of writing as well as practicing the provision of feedback on writing.

Over the course of four years, the curriculum for pre-service teachers contains a strand of writing and the teaching of writing with more emphasis on theory and a limited amount of study of teaching practice. However, it is noteworthy that in this specific program in their third year pre-service teachers are trained to teach writing, which makes this context unique in the North part of the island. In contrast, it has been found recently that in other teacher education contexts in Northern Cyprus, '... pre-service teachers focused mostly on their use of class activities, instructional materials, classroom management, and teaching methods in their reflections on their practice teaching sessions' (İsmail & Çavuşoğlu, 2017).

One explanation for such attention to educating pre-service teachers in teaching writing might be the fact that the faculty in this department are aware of the future demands with regard to teaching writing. First and foremost, many faculty members experienced writing as they studied at US or UK universities and had first-hand experience of how it works and, secondly, they are aware that teaching writing in L2 is an emerging field in its own right, educating teachers to become L2 writing specialists (Silva

& Matsuda, 2001). These factors might influence faculty's perspective in teaching writing in this particular teacher education program.

Methodology

This chapter presents the results of a case study exploring the perceptions of the faculty members and pre-service teachers about how effective the writing-related courses offered in the program were in preparing the prospective teachers to teach English writing. In addition to exploring the effectiveness of these courses, the chapter presents the useful practices employed by faculty members to help improve student writing.

Participants

The participants in this study were 12 pre-service teachers (four Turkish Cypriots and eight Turkish nationals) in their senior year in the program and four faculty members who taught writing or writing-related courses. The 12 senior students were taking or had taken writing courses offered in this program: 60% were female and 40% were male students with an age range of 19–24 years. One of the researchers taught writing to this cohort in their first year of university. She tracked those pre-service students who gave their consent to be a part of a research study in their senior year. In their first year and semester at university they practiced freewriting and journal writing, in-class writing, wrote a literacy autobiography, and generated a portfolio at the end of the semester. Thus it can be said that their experiences in the first year involved both process- and product-oriented writing. At the end of their last semester in the program they were approached by the researchers. Of the 19 students from the first year cohort, 12 of them agreed to read the writings they had generated and reflect on how they had changed over the years. They also shared their reflections on the way they taught writing in their fourth year in their practicum seminar.

In addition to the 12 senior students, four instructors who taught in the teacher education program (ranging from five to 10 years), three females and one male, participated in this study (see Table 10.1 for basic information about the faculty members). We had semi-structured

Table 10.1 Basic information about instructors

Teacher educator	Age	Gender	Years as teacher educator
Esin	30	F	5 years
Naz	32	F	7 years
Selim	35	M	8 years
Beyza	39	F	10 years

interviews with each instructor lasting for 25–30 minutes each; three of these interviews were held face-to-face and one of them over the phone. The four instructors specialized in various areas of ELT, namely teaching literature, teacher education, writing skills and global Englishes. All had received their graduate degrees abroad, in the UK or the US, where they were part of academic communities practicing academic writing. The fact that they themselves had experienced process, product and genre approaches to writing by writing in academia might have had an effect on the way they designed their syllabi and the way they approached teaching writing in their classes.

Design

In this qualitative case study, the data source included program and course documents and transcriptions of interviews with the pre-service teachers (i.e. trainee teachers in the teacher education program) and with the faculty members who have taught writing in this particular teacher education program. The program documents consisted of course descriptions, curricula, syllabi and lesson plans that the faculty members shared, as well as general program documents shared on the program website.

Semi-structured interviews with the pre-service teachers were conducted during feedback sessions as part of their writing class and in a focus group interview as a follow-up meeting at the end of the semester. As part of the focus group interview, the pre-service teachers were asked to do a comparative reflection and analysis of their own writing pieces from their freshman and senior years in the program. They reflected on whether and how they had developed as writers. They also projected how they might teach writing to their future students, elaborating on the writing teacher they aspired to be. Student interviews were conducted in English; however, they were allowed to switch to Turkish if they needed, in order to express themselves more comfortably.

Interviews with the faculty members were conducted in English. These interviews were semi-structured, face-to-face meetings, each of which lasted for about 50 minutes. The faculty members reflected on their experiences of teaching writing courses in the teacher education program. They started with an overview of the courses they taught. Then they discussed the assignments required and procedures followed for each course they taught, including feedback sessions, drafting processes and grading criteria.

All interviews were tape-recorded and were later transcribed by the researchers or a project assistant who was a senior student in the department. The Turkish segments in student interviews were translated by this project assistant and were then checked by one of the researchers for accuracy. The transcriptions were coded by both researchers to identify recurring themes which later formed the general categories of analysis. The interview transcriptions were shared with the participants for member checking; the parts they asked to remove were taken out of the database and were not included in the analysis. The database consisted of document analysis and semi-structured interviews with the pre-service teachers and the faculty members. Pseudonyms were assigned to all participants.

Findings and Discussion

In this section, we present the data from the interviews with the instructors and senior students, and the written documents, such as portfolios, from the students' first year at the university, as well as their practicum reflections.

Faculty perspectives on writing in the TEFL program

The data gathered from interviews with the faculty members who have taught writing courses in the TEFL teacher education program revealed two common themes: (1) the importance of learning to write well in order to become a competent writing teacher; and (2) the challenges they face and observe in the writing courses.

The significance of feedback on writing skills development

The four instructors who have taught writing courses or courses that involved assignments or tasks that required writing in the teacher education program agreed on the usefulness of the process approach to writing. They indicated that in order to become competent writing teachers, students first needed to be experienced writers. In the writing classes, instructors follow the process approach; they read multiple drafts of the same paper and work on the basics of writing. By giving regular feedback to students and helping them correct their mistakes on their own, the instructors try to enhance their writing skills. The faculty see the feedback sessions not only as a tool for helping students improve their writing, but also as a teacher training tool for preparing them to teach writing. The importance, necessity and usefulness of giving students individual feedback is highlighted by Naz:

> I did quite a lot of process approach. Because it is helpful especially when you have students who need to revise and work on their writing for a long time, process approach is helping them. ... [A]t the beginning it was challenging ... because they think that once they write, it is over, but then once they get used to it they are okay. I mean I didn't have any problem with that. ... I tried to give as much feedback as possible. One of the good things in the program was that there were fewer students and that was quite manageable. Now in [my new institution], I am teaching a course that is triple numbers of students, so those things, the amount of feedback

depends on the amount of time you have. But I feel like although the students' linguistic abilities are limited, they can get a lot of support from that. (Naz, Personal interview, 18 September 2017)

Yet another faculty member, Selim, emphasized the importance of the theoretical framework for teaching writing and the difficulty of implementing peer feedback:

I think that theoretical background is a particular area that certainly helps because there is something that I bring to the table, but there is always the other side of the equation: what students bring to the text as well. ... Because the whole idea of the feedback regardless of the content of the classroom or the language skill that we are talking about is a huge hot mass that I am still struggling with. (Selim, Personal interview, 25 September 2017)

Selim emphasized the need to create a feedback bridge among students to give an opportunity to critically reflect upon content and language. He added he noticed in different content classes the feedback ranged from surface comments like 'oh well done, good job' to completely irrelevant ones such as 'you had nice hair today.' He continued:

So on paper, it is based on theory and research and it uses the notion of feedback, but then how you back the concept with actual work is a big question mark. So to some extent I blame students, to some extent I don't, because [it is] working with individuals who have no training, let alone training who have probably had no exposure to peer feedback in their past eighteen years of schooling. (Selim, Personal interview, 25 September 2017)

This instructor acknowledged that even though in theory and in his own experience peer feedback was proven to be very useful, it was difficult to embed it in practice as students had not encountered such practice in their previous schooling. Thus, Selim rightfully voiced his concern for high quality written peer feedback although he provided the necessary conditions for it to take place in the classroom.

Challenges we face, challenges they face

One challenge that all faculty members emphasized, one that affected both the teaching and learning of writing in the program, was the low English proficiency of the students enrolled in this particular teacher education program. Due to the fact that the program is housed in a private university, the entry requirements are not as high as those of more competitive, public universities. The low scores expected of the incoming students becomes an indication of their English level, which is relatively lower than what would be expected of future English teachers. This necessitates a more basic, structured approach to teaching language skills on the part of the faculty members; that is, they find it necessary to go over very basic writing-related issues, such as paragraph writing, coherence, mechanics and grammar, before proceeding to more advanced issues, such as critical summary writing, free, creative writing, referencing and citation. Esin reflects on this as follows:

> I found it a bit difficult to teach the students how they should think about writing a long essay because as far as I have seen they couldn't perceive how different parts of the essay were speaking to each other. I was telling them if you are putting a sentence in a paragraph that sentence should be an essential part of that paragraph and if you take the sentence out the whole structure of the paragraph should collapse. In other words, I was trying to teach them how to write, you know, how to write in a coherent manner. Or similarly, on macro scale I found it a bit difficult to … they were having a hard time to write an essay in which each and every paragraph was an essential part of the whole body of essay but apart from that I was telling them you should create the structure of an essay in such a manner that each paragraph should necessitate the coming one. But for me this was an easy task, this was the essential thing about writing essays or paragraphs but as far as I saw then it was a really hard thing for my students so that was the main challenge I guess. (Esin, Personal interview, 28 August 2017)

Another common challenge that the faculty members highlighted was the lack of writing experience the students had prior to attending the teacher education program. Selim understands what pre-service teachers might go through:

> I teach 254 which is – as you know – second class in our second year continuation of methodology classes in which we introduce the idea of process, product, genre approaches to writing as their broader framework of what writing is. Looking at students, their backgrounds, partially I can sympathize with them because I am sort of product where they came from. We can understand although it has been so many years, we can still understand 'Oh this is still the same. Oh this still has not changed' in their pre-secondary education especially with regards to writing whether this is first language or second language. So it is one of those areas that is pretty much neglected. (Selim, Personal interview, 25 September 2017)

The faculty members were frustrated to find that the students were not experienced or skilled writers in their mother tongue, Turkish, either. In a way, they felt like they were working on the literacy skills of the students in Turkish in addition to their foreign language skills in English. Consequently, the early stages of the teacher education program followed a structural and mechanical process during which the students needed lots of guidance and were dependent on the faculty members in enhancing their productive skills. Beyza notes:

> Well, actually for the first year courses, for the grammar and composition courses, I actually expected them to know more about how to write a thesis statement or a topic sentence … But when I started teaching here

for the first time, I saw that students actually didn't know how to write paragraphs, and how to write essays … I noticed that our students here … they prefer to have more structured, or some kind of framework that they can follow … So I had to adapt myself to students' level and try to teach them how to write a paragraph. I remember the first time I taught it was difficult, but the second time I taught it was a lot easier because I knew how to respond their needs and interests as well. I remember for example choosing topics to write about was kind of difficult for me because I didn't really know the students' profiles. … I always encourage them to have autonomous writing, to do their own writing, but they seem to be dependent on each other or on the teacher. (Beyza, Personal interview, 28 September 2017)

The lack of emphasis on productive skills in their native language Turkish and their second language English during their K-12 education hindered the students' communication skills in oral and written forms. They were not even sure about how to address or compose a message to a professor to request something or ask a question. Beyza comments on this issue:

It is only about grammar. So they learn English. They don't look at those productive skills. There is no speaking, there is no writing of course in classes. And they just memorize the grammatical rules so that's why they can't produce once in high school, or even sometimes the university as well. So that's why they can't communicate. They can't even write emails because they don't know how to start, what to use. So … throughout their education, I think they just memorize those chunks and they are not very productive. (Beyza, Personal interview, 28 September 2017)

Getting these issues out of the way in the first year or two in the teacher education program delayed appropriate focus on skills-teaching approaches.

The faculty members, who had all received their graduate degrees abroad, used similar strategies and techniques to help prospective teachers improve their writing skills and become writing instructors. They started with the basics and moved onto advanced writing tasks using examples and samples whenever necessary, appropriate and possible. For example, while teaching essay writing, Esin started with an exercise on choosing and narrowing down a topic and Naz provided students with sample essays and papers for composition and research skills classes. Selim recreated his own writing learning process in the classroom by sharing his own experiences with the students and encouraging them to follow the steps he went through during his graduate studies when trying to improve as a writer. Both Esin and Selim supported the idea of having a Writing Center on campus. Beyza and Naz gave their students continuous feedback starting from the freshman courses, going from more structured and mechanics-oriented to more open and content-oriented types of feedback, observing the slow yet steady progress of the students.

All faculty members are dedicated to giving constructive, individual feedback that slowly leads to autonomous writing in many of the students. However, they unanimously agree that despite the progress the students make, some of them are still dependent, unconfident and unsure about their teaching skills in their senior year and pre-service teaching in practicum. The faculty members all consult their peers in the teacher education program where they work or colleagues in other institutions when they are unsure or stuck about an issue about their teaching in the program. Being open to suggestions and keeping their channels of communication open with other scholars provides them with new perspectives on skills development strategies as well as teacher education approaches.

Student perspectives on writing in the TEFL program

The data gathered from interviews with the pre-service teachers who had taken writing courses in the TEFL teacher education program revealed two themes: (1) a comparison of their previous (K-12) writing instruction with that in the TEFL program in terms of contribution to their writing development; and (2) how they envision themselves as future writing teachers.

From K-12 to college writing

During the interviews, the pre-service teachers described how writing was neglected in K-12. Therefore, when the pre-service teachers were asked to reflect on their writing they first noted their proficiency in writing, and immediately after commenting on it they attributed the lack of it to K-12. They simply did not have much experience in writing in English.

Bora, who discovered he enjoyed writing after starting the program, says:

> Well, as a first year student, I really wasn't into writing and I did very little of writing practice before university and I thought I wasn't a good writer. I didn't have the good qualifications for it. At first my thoughts about the course was like 'oh my god, I don't like writing; what am I going to do with this course?' And then, it wasn't actually that bad, I figured it out. It was adding something to me and I felt that I was getting stronger and stronger in the sense of writing. (Bora, Personal interview, 7 June 2017)

When Can compares his first year writing to his more recent work, he comments that his writing looks more sophisticated, and explains it like this:

> I notice my writing has become more sophisticated. When I took the first writing course, I felt like I came from kindergarten. I felt like I was illiterate. I thought I didn't know anything because of the education I had received. I was afraid that the tasks would be way beyond my knowledge. Now I feel I can write a 6000 word essay a day. Now, I feel, I can like the

idea of being called as a novice writer. (Can, Personal interview, 10 June 2017)

Orhan, similarly, reports that before preparatory school at university he did not know a lot about writing, because his teachers at K-12 schools did not have them practice writing in class. Ekin elaborates on her writing in English in her first year in some detail:

> Actually, in my first year I was not very serious and aware of that. … I was going to become a teacher someday. I was just enjoying the writing course; it was a whole new thing in English. I mean reading, I had some experience from high school but writing in English was a whole new concept. I was having some hard times, but it was fun. We were reading books and sharing our comments with each other. … Looking back, it feels like I have grown so much in terms of writing and reading because you know some words are just … strange. … I used some words like I definitely looked them up in the dictionary. These are not my words. (Ekin, Personal interview, 1 June 2017)

She continues by reflecting on teaching writing to 12-year-old elementary school students in her practicum:

> Apart from grammar teaching, I did writing assessment this week like the previous semester. I did not grade papers like 5, 10, but I ticked or wrote 'good' and 'very good' to minimize the competition among them. I used the back of the paper to write my comments. I did not say that 'this is wrong; it should be that', but of course gave the type of the mistake such as 'grm' or 'tens' to encourage process writing by self-correction. I think that not giving the right answers is a good way of challenging students in writing which also contributes to self-correction and work discipline in a positive way. When they see there is a mistake that they made, they wait for the corrected form of it. However, it is not different than a kind of spoon feeding. (Ekin, Personal interview, 1 June 2017)

Another participant, Ali, upon seeing the portfolio he wrote in his first year in the program, states that he was very naïve in the way he presented himself in his writing and adds:

> What I notice is my writing in this portfolio is like talking. Using a lot of spoken expressions but making lots of mistakes in using them. Portfolio title is 'Roll with Me' But I won't do it now … I learned language by watching TV serials and by playing games so I didn't know the grammatical structures required for academic writing. But after spending some time here I got basis for the grammar. We took many lessons and wrote papers and these first year writings are very different (naïve) when I look at them now. (Ali, Personal interview, 23 June 2017)

The comments of the pre-service teachers give us a hint about how their notions of writing have changed: in their own words, they have changed from 'the feeling of I don't know much about writing!' to 'I write academic papers.' They also attribute their initial state of development to their lack of prior writing experience at school, precisely where they themselves will teach writing.

All 12 pre-service teachers express disappointment due to not knowing much about writing, mainly because of their limited English proficiency level in their first year, which by their fourth year they can see. Without exception, they all commented on the growth in their proficiency level in English. Some also linked proficiency and intellectual growth when they were asked how they had changed over their undergraduate years. All referred to their acquisition of a new notion of writing. Ali describes growth as follows:

> We internalized the language in years. I used to use templates at the very beginning at preparatory intensive program. I think we improved both our language and the way we think. We can analyze and think deeply now. We can give clear examples so that our reader can understand us ... the idea we want to convey. We learned how we can express ourselves. (Ali, Personal interview, 23 June 2017)

Ayşe commented on the change, saying that she became more self-confident, especially about writing. She told us that she learned how to generate a topic, narrow it down, form a thesis statement and carry out a research project, which involved writing a paper complete with making citations and giving references. She also told us how liberated she felt when she wrote using her own words. Yet another student, Ebru, discussed the integration of researched information and her own commentary along with her improved speed of composition by saying:

> My first year writings are like prep school writings but may be not that structured. For example, I gave a reason here but I didn't give any background information. I wrote my observations ... I remember in my first semester I could write this page in half an hour but now I can write it in five minutes. ... We learned academic writing in year three. Relating ideas, our ideas, giving citations, using APA, referencing. ... I still have problems with those though. (Ebru, Personal interview, 3 June 2017)

Ebru's comment showed that she saw her work as still in progress and that she had learned how to reflect on her own writing skills development and her own learning.

The notion of what academic writing entails changed for these teacher candidates over their three years of study. The pre-service teachers learned through experience that they needed a focus in academic writing which they achieved through the use of a thesis statement. Further, they realized that in academic writing they were using other people's ideas. They understood how to synthesize their ideas with those of others. Finally, they learned how to use a style manual (APA) to code their academic writing for an academic audience.

When they were asked what contributed to their understanding of writing, they had different turning points. Many referred to their third year course in which they took research writing. They seemed to have appreciated the challenge and to recognize the experience as positive. Bora, for instance, said that reading peer papers in the classroom gave him perspective about what he should not do. He continued with some details:

> What should I avoid doing, like I was also looking at the feedback comments, and also the other people's writings. So I could have seen what other people's mistakes were, so that taught me as well. And I also gave feedback. At first, we didn't know how to give good feedback, but then we learned it. So that also improved my writing skills. Like I knew what to avoid. I understood that I have to avoid repetition in my writings and I have to stick to a point and follow that point. And also being appreciated … that is something that encourages me to write more; so being liked by peers, also helped me write more. (Bora, Personal interview, 7 June 2017)

In this cohort, only Bora saw the first year as a turning point. In addition to the growth of his critical awareness of his own grammar and rhetoric from feedback, he also became more confident about writing more and more regularly, as he says:

> This course (first writing course Advanced Reading & Writing) initiated my writing habit. I wasn't writing before in my free time. But then since I knew the basics from the first course, I did free writing on my own. So that was a plus for me because that was something that I had never done before. (Bora, Personal interview, 7 June 2017)

In the data excerpts presented above, the participants described how their notions of writing, especially academic writing, changed; that is, they transformed their way of thinking about their own writing while they were improving their writing of English.

The future writing teacher

The second theme that emerged from the data gathered from pre-service teachers focused on how they envisioned themselves as future teachers of writing. They projected the writing teacher they wanted to be by imagining what they would do in K-12 or university intensive English programs, contexts in which they might teach. All the pre-service teachers emphasized that they developed as writers to some extent as a result of taking the writing-related courses in the program. Each expressed the path they went through and envisioned what they would do in their future classes. They also explained why they would choose a certain approach or technique for their projected classroom practices. They reflected on their experiences in the writing classes they took in the teacher education program and integrated the ones they found to be useful and effective into their future teaching plans.

All pre-service teachers unanimously agreed on the challenges of learning academic writing, and therefore, imagined it to be a challenging teaching task for any English teacher. Bora expressed his reluctance in teaching academic writing and added his projected strategies to convey the importance of learning academic writing to his future students:

> I don't want to teach academic writing since it doesn't really get the attention of the students, but what I really like to teach what was essential for me. The first step to writing: make them like it. ... Because if you get people to like writing, they would continue, or at least it is what happened with me. So I would want to be the part of change of those students. I would ... I haven't thought of any ways but I would try to explain how writing could benefit their life, how it can improve their way of thinking and I would explain that writing isn't something mandatory, you can do it in your free time to just have a moment or for your own pleasure because writing like reading these days are perceived as mandatory. ... Writing should be encouraged rather than prioritizing grading. (Bora, Personal interview, 7 June 2017)

Bora's experience with writing changed from seeing it as an obligatory practice to learn his second language to perceiving it as a cognitively and socially engaging activity for him to employ. He could benefit from writing for both his personal and social domains of life. As he experienced this transformation in year one and used it all through four years of his education, he wanted his own students to experience it.

Ekin had strong feelings about academic writing too, but she also believed in the importance of teaching and learning academic skills:

> ... I don't like academic writing ... it is difficult. Because there is a framed vocabulary that you can use, everything is limited. ... You have to use . . . certain structures, or you know, abstract first and ... I cannot explain ... but I don't prefer writing. ... Because you have an audience first to write an academic ... in other kinds (of writing), I can choose my audience, my friends or my family with whom I want to share it. But in academic writing, there is a certain audience waiting for it . . . like give us something. (I want my students) to use writing to get familiar with their inner selves. Because when we are speaking, we are acting regarding the other ... how we are going to get heard. (Ekin, Personal interview, 1 June 2017)

Ekin found academic writing demanding both linguistically and socially. She especially disliked the idea of being read by a larger audience and yet she acknowledged the value of writing for her students.

The pre-service teachers had some creative and interesting suggestions for making academic writing more accessible for their students, especially for those learning English writing in elementary school. Orhan, for example, commented that if he had to teach K-12 students, he would try to make it enjoyable:

> I would find activities that would make them like/love writing. Academic writing can be boring. I would want to make it more fun. I would want to find ways to make it fun for them. The topics should interest them. I want them to write because they want to, not because it is mandatory. (Orhan, Personal interview, 20 May 2017)

Similarly, Ekin emphasized the social and fun aspects of writing and suggested using 'everyday things like billboards...campaigns, text messages or song lyrics, these kind of things to start with' (Ekin, Personal interview, 1 June 2017). Ebru also emphasized the importance of relating earlier writing tasks to daily life events and then moving on to more academic topics following the process approach (Ebru, Personal interview, 3 June 2017).

Pre-service teachers, who were more inclined towards working in tertiary institutions, expressed a preference for the process writing approach, because they had found it to be helpful for their own writing development. For example, Kiraz, who could imagine herself teaching at a university, seemed to appreciate the benefits of process writing and said:

> First, I would advise my students, I would suggest my students to check, to use Manchester's academic phrase bank. It's very useful for academic- writing. And in addition to that, I liked the approach you used like re-writing a text because normally like every time after I wrote a text, after I see the text I wrote, I look at the text and I see like did I write this? It's so you know, it's so bad. If I rewrite it, I know I can do (write) it in a better way. And sometimes, I see my grammar mistakes, and sometimes I don't see it as a text with high quality. I know if I rewrite it again . . . it will be much better. So, I think the approach (meaning process approach) we used in the first year was very useful. (Kiraz, Personal interview, 14 June 2017)

Sera, another student who believed in the importance of teaching academic writing in tertiary levels, insisted that free writing be part of the classroom practice in order to motivate students to write and enjoy the task:

> Actually, the first year's writing class (where we tried process writing) was I don't know how to define it but it was a utopic class that should be placed at every year of the university in my view...Because you know as students we do things and forget about them after the exam and in third year especially in third year...many people suffered because of heavy workload and because we couldn't have a way out of it. Free writings are like a way of therapy for the people like us who work, work, and work... it would relieve us. If I wanted them (my students) to write essays, I would show them some simple essays. So they would know, touch, and see the essay itself. So the definition would work for every single person in the classroom. Some exercises on imagining topics and then going through the semester like working on a structure: a topic sentence, a major support and everything, those structural things. And then one class would be

let's forget about it and write about your summer; it's not just this writing but anything you (want to) write. And then I would tell them we will have an idea in our mind, and I want you to tell me about your idea in the way I told you. (Sera, Personal interview, 2 September 2017)

Despite the fact that the participants didn't express a keen interest in academic writing, they had varying degrees of motivation to teach writing. They highlighted that they had achieved a difficult task with regards to writing, which gave them confidence as teacher candidates. As a result of their previous educational experience and individual endeavors regarding writing in the teacher education program, they were working out individual ways to make writing meaningful in their future classrooms. While one recognized the motivational value of relevant content to develop a positive attitude towards writing, the other saw the importance of revision and getting the academic register in writing. Similarly, while some felt that the teaching of subskills of writing, such as grammar, vocabulary and phraseology, needed to precede process writing, others suggested techniques like free writing to be therapeutic for students. Each, then, had an embryonic idea of how they wanted to go about their future teaching of writing.

Conclusion

In this study we examined how teaching and learning writing was perceived by the pre-service teachers and faculty members in the teacher program with regards to the writing focused courses offered in the program. We examined the perspectives of students and instructors regarding to what extent the writing courses prepared the prospective teachers for their future teaching writing practices and explored both stakeholders' reflections on the effectiveness of the writing-related courses offered in the teacher education program.

In terms of the perceptions of students and faculty members on the effectiveness of the writing-related courses offered, our findings indicated that the courses offered in the TEFL program were efficient in arousing curiosity and interest in the students about the writing process in two ways. First, certain aspects of these courses, especially those that included structural and organizational focus on texts, conveyed to prospective teachers what good writing looks like; how it should be structured and organized; and the mechanics of composition. The structural and technical elements of writing were well received and appreciated by the students because they did not have the chance to develop such basic skills in English courses during their primary and secondary education. Second, the courses that include meaningful use of writing were valued highly by the faculty members. As for the pre-service teachers, they were surprised at their gained ability in making use of both academic and personal writing. They valued the experience of free writing, journal writing and dialogic writing. Personalized writing tasks were also well received by the prospective teachers. The student group also appreciated creative and alternative approaches to writing, because these tasks gave them a chance to express their thoughts, ideas and feelings, which they discovered that they actually enjoyed despite their initial fear and dislike of writing.

The perceptions of the pre-service teachers in this study showed parallelism with findings in several other studies. Similar to the participants in Gallavan *et al.*'s study (2007), our participants entered the teacher education program unsure about the benefits of writing and disliked this practice initially. They also thought that writing should be taught more efficiently in elementary and secondary levels and highlighted the importance of developing writing skills in order to learn the content of program courses more effectively. They had anxiety about writing, but they blossomed as writers through meaningful writing practices in the program (Atay & Kurt, 2006). Clearly, their previous experiences as writers had an impact on their perceptions of writing-related tasks and writing-focused courses in the teacher education program (Street, 2003); students who were poor writers before found writing to be a very challenging task at the initial stages of the program (Street & Stang, 2008). Both the pre-service teachers and the faculty members in our study highlighted the usefulness of pedagogical tools, such as process writing and peer feedback, which was similar to the responses of the participants in Grossman *et al.*'s study (2000).

As for the extent to which the writing courses in the program prepared the pre-service teachers for their future teaching of writing, our findings indicated that emphasis needed to be given to the writing or writing-related courses pre-service teachers take, especially in their first year. It was clear from the reflections of both groups that students were not able to generate strong compositions in their first year or provide their peers with critical feedback in the given time frame and with their limited experience with process writing. The faculty members reported struggling with instructional challenges during the earlier years of the program, because of the low language proficiency of the students and the impossibility of moving outside the structural and mechanical basics of writing in class. They provided students with the basics of composition in English and had limited time and opportunity for unstructured, meaningful and creative writing tasks. Despite these obstacles, all the writing instructors tried to include tasks that might increase the motivation and eagerness of the students towards writing in general. Both groups highlighted the challenges of learning to write as a skill and teaching writing as an instructional activity. The pre-service teachers discovered during their practicum course that low English proficiency and scarcity of previous opportunities for free writing left them with no option but to concentrate on the very basics of structural composition in class. Similarly, the faculty members found themselves in a dilemma where they had to choose between lowering their standards and program expectations to meet the proficiency level of the students, and posing great challenges for the students and pushing them too hard, too soon.

In this study, the importance of having writing skills development courses for prospective teachers was confirmed (Altay, 2010; Ferris, 2007; Ferris & Hedgcock, 2014; Lee, 2011; Street & Stang, 2008). The teacher educators in our study reported using tasks and approaches suggested in literature for writing skills development of pre-service teachers. They showed individual attention to students in understanding and practicing with the writing tasks and also encouraged journal writing to build self-confidence (Shin, 2006). They also reported using explicit pre-writing activities (Curtis, 2017); peer feedback (Ferris, 2010; Yu & Lee, 2016); and corrective teacher feedback and rubrics (Ene & Kosobucki, 2016; Ferris & Hedgcock, 2014; Hyland & Hyland, 2006) as part of the process writing practice which was a common pedagogical choice for them. Similar to Lee (2011), the faculty members in our study believed in helping students improve their writing skills in order to become confident and effective writing instructors.

Appendix: Interview Questions for Pre-service Teachers and Faculty

Interview questions for pre-service teachers

(1) Before you started the program, what did you feel about being a teacher? What did it mean to you?
(2) What did you think of teaching?
(3) Will you please look at the texts you created in your first semester here at the program and say what you feel and think about this writing?
(4) How has your writing changed in years? Or your role as a writer or a writing teacher?
(5) How did you feel about being a writing teacher? Did you have any ideas about teaching writing?
(6) How would you teach writing to your students? What does a writing teacher do to teach writing in class, K-12 or at university (Intensive English Program)?

Interview questions for the faculty

(1) What writing courses have you taught? (To situate the context)
(2) What was the experience like? (To make the teacher remember her/his experience)
(3) What worked well with the students with regard to generating writing texts?
(4) Have you noticed any model/theory of writing as particularly successful? Any writing theories? Could you elaborate on them?
(5) What do you do in class with regard to:
grammar,
cohesion/coherence,

clarity,
revision,
feedback (peer/teacher),
referencing,
discourse (text type),
giving citations,
sharing writing with the wider audience (any publications)?

(6) What are the limitations of the program in preparing the students to teach writing later? Have any suggestions for improvement been offered by faculty members?
(7) Do teacher educators need special training to teach writing?
(8) If you, as a professor, wanted to advance your professional writing abilities/teaching writing what kind of opportunities would you want to be created?

Acknowledgements

We would like to thank Dan J. Tannacito for his insightful comments and helpful suggestions on an earlier drafts of this chapter.

Note

(1) For readers who may not be familiar with the relationship between Turkey and Northern Cyprus, some historical information might be relevant here. Since 1974 the island has been divided into two because of a political conflict and Civil War between Turkish and Greek Cypriots. In 1983 the Turkish Republic of Northern Cyprus (TRNC) was established. However, because of restricted recognition, Turkish Cypriots became isolated from the world. Turkey has close ties with Northern Cyprus in various aspects of life. With regard to education, there is a certain quota for Turkish Cypriots to become students at Turkish universities. In higher education, there is mutual intellectual exchange between the two nations. One other point is relevant to emphasize – since it gives information about the political status of universities in Turkey in general and the one under study in particular. In Turkey, currently all universities (state or private) are organized under the Council of Higher Education (CHG), deciding on the curriculum to be applied in all departments. Similarly, Northern Cyprus universities, in order to be able to receive an equivalence/accreditation for the diplomas they give, conform to rules and regulations set by CHG. The equivalent of this council in Northern Cyprus is titled the Higher Education Planning, Accreditation and Coordination Council (HEPACC).

References

Akçıl, U. and Arap, I. (2009) The opinions of education faculty students on learning processes involving e-portfolios. *Procedia Social and Behavioral Sciences* 1, 395–400.
Altan, M.Z. (2006) Preparation of foreign language teachers in Turkey: A challenge for the 21st century. *Dil Dergisi* 134, 49–54.
Atay, D. and Kurt, G. (2006) Prospective teachers and L2 writing anxiety. *Asian EFL Journal* 8 (4), 101–118.

Altay, I.F. (2010) A suggested syllabus for advanced writing skills at English language teaching departments. *Hacettepe University Journal of Education* 39, 20–31.

Arıkan, A. (2006) Postmethod condition and its implications for English teacher education. *Journal of Language and Linguistic Studies* 2 (1), 1–11.

Baynham, M. (1995) *Literacy Practices: Investigating Literacy in Social Contexts.* New York, NY: Longman.

Bostancı, B.B. and Çavuşoğlu, Ç. (2018) Pen-and-paper or online? An academic writing course to teacher-trainees. *Cogent Education.* doi:10.1080/2331186X.2018.1482606

Çetinavcı, U. and Yavuz, A. (2011) Language proficiency level of English language trainees in Turkey. *International Journal of Research in Teacher Education* 1, 26–54.

Cosgun-Ogeyik, M. (2009) Evaluation of English language teaching education curriculum by student teachers. *İnsan ve Toplum* 9 (1), 24–42.

Coşkun, A. and Daloğlu, A. (2010) Evaluating an English language teacher education program through Peacock's model. *Australian Journal of Teacher Education* 35 (6), 24–42.

Curtis, G. (2017) The impact of teacher efficacy and beliefs on writing instruction. *Delta Kappa Gamma Bulletin: International Journal for Professional Educators* 84 (1), 17–24.

Debreli, E. (2011) Use of diaries to investigate and track pre-service teachers' beliefs about teaching and learning English as a foreign language throughout a pre-service training program. *Procedia Social and Behavioral Sciences* 15, 60–65.

Debreli, E. (2012) Change in beliefs of pre-service teachers about teaching and learning English as a foreign language throughout an undergraduate pre-service teacher training program. *Procedia Social and Behavioral Sciences* 46, 367–373.

Deniz, S. and Şahin, N. (2006) The restructuring process of teacher training system in Turkey: A model of teacher training based on post-graduate education (PGCE). *Journal of Social Sciences* 2 (1), 21–26.

Ene, E. and Kosobucki, V. (2016) Rubrics and corrective feedback in ESL writing: A longitudinal case study of an L2 writer. *Assessing Writing* 30, 3–20.

Enginarlar, H. (1996) Practicum in ELT: Problems and prospects. *Dil Dergisi* 43, 92–99.

Erkılıç, T.A. (2008) Importance of educational philosophy in teacher education for educational sustainable development: *Middle East Journal of Scientific Research* 3 (1), 1–8.

Erkmen, B. (2012) Ways to uncover teachers' beliefs. *Procedia Social and Behavioral Sciences* 47, 141–146.

Erozan, F. (2005) Evaluating the language improvement courses in the undergraduate ELT curriculum at Eastern Mediterranean university: A case study. Unpublished dissertation, Eastern Mediterranean University, Gazimagosa.

Eröz-Tuğa, B. (2013) Reflective feedback sessions using video recordings. *ELT Journal* 67 (2), 175–183.

Evans-Tokaryk, T. (2014) Academic integrity, remix culture, globalization: A Canadian case study of student and faculty perceptions of plagiarism. *Across the Disciplines* 11 (2). See https://wac.colostate.edu/atd/articles/evans-tokaryk2014.cfm.

Ferris, D.R. (2007) Preparing teachers to respond to student writing. *Journal of Second Language Writing* 16, 165–193.

Ferris, D.R. (2010) Second language writing research and written corrective feedback in SLA. *Studies in Second Language Acquisition* 32 (2), 181–201.

Ferris, D.R. and Hedgcock, J.S. (2014) *Teaching L2 Composition. Purpose, Process, and Practice* (3rd edn). New York: Routledge.

Gallavan, N.P., Bowles, F.A. and Young, C.T. (2007) Learning to write and writing to learn: Insights from teacher candidates. *Action in Teacher Education* 29 (2), 61–69.

Gee, P.J. (1998) What is literacy? In *Negotiating Academic Literacies: Readings on Teaching and Learning across Cultures* (pp. 51–58). Mahwah, NJ: Erlbaum.

Grossman, P.L., Valencia, W.S., Evans, K., Thompson, C., Martin, S. and Place, N. (2000) Transitions into teaching: Learning to teach writing in teacher education and beyond. *Journal of Literacy Research* 32 (4), 631–662.

Grossman, G.M., Onkel, P.E. and Sands, M. (2007) Curriculum reform in Turkish teacher education: Attitudes of teacher educators towards change in an EU candidate nation. *International Journal of Educational Development* 27, 139–150.

Hyland, K. and Hyland, F. (eds) (2006) *Feedback in Second Language Writing: Contexts and Issues.* New York: Cambridge University Press.

Ismail, A.M. and Çavuşoğlu, C. (2017) Theory into practice: The content of pre-service teachers' reflections in Northern Cyprus. In I.H. Amzat and N.P. Valdez (eds) *Teacher Empowerment Toward Professional Development and Practices* (pp. 221–237). Cham: Springer International.

Kahraman, A. (2013) Affective and cognitive effects of coded teacher feedback on foreign language writing students. *Hacettepe University Journal of Education* 28 (1), 189–201.

Kalajahi, S.A.R. and Pourshahian, B. (2012) Vocabulary learning strategies and vocabulary size of ELT students at EMU in Northern Cyprus. *English Language Teaching* 5 (4), 138–149.

Karakas, A. (2012) Evaluation of the English language teacher education program in Turkey. *Novitas-ROYAL (Research on Youth and Language)* 7 (1), 64–83.

Karamustafaoğlu, O. (2009) A comparative analysis of the models of teacher education in terms of teaching practices in the USA, England, and Turkey. *Education* 130 (2), 172–183.

Kroll, B. (ed.) (1990) *Second Language Writing: Research Insights for the Classroom* (pp. 109–125). Cambridge: Cambridge University Press.

Kunt, N. and Tüm, D. (2010) Non-native student teachers' feelings of foreign language anxiety. *Procedia Social and Behavioral Sciences* 2, 4672–4676.

Kuter, S. and Koç, S. (2009) A multi-level analysis of the teacher education internship in terms of its collaborative dimension in Northern Cyprus. *International Journal of Educational Development* 29 (4), 415–425.

Lea, M.R. (2004) Academic literacies: A pedagogy for course design. *Studies in Higher Education* 29 (6), 739–756.

Lee, E. (2010) Remixing Lessig (reviewing Lawrence Lessig, Remix (2008)). *I/S: A Journal of Law and Policy for the Information Society* 6 (1), 41–66.

Lee, I. (2011) L2 writing teacher education for in-service teachers: Opportunities and challenges. *English in Australia* 46 (1), 31–39.

Özbilgin, A. (2004) Turkish and English literacy in an English medium university in Turkey: A qualitative study. Unpublished doctoral dissertation, Indiana University of Pennsylvania.

Pehlivan, A., Serin, O. and Bulut-Serin, N. (2010) Determining reading interests and habits of candidate teachers (TRNC Sample). *Procedia Social and Behavioral Sciences* 9, 869–873.

Şallı-Çopur, D.S. (2008) Teacher effectiveness in the initial years of service: A case study on the graduates of METU language education program. Unpublished doctoral dissertation, Middle East Technical University.

Sanli, S. (2009) Comparison of the English language teaching (ELT) departments' course curricula in Turkey's educational facilities. World Conference on Education Sciences. *Procedia Social and Behavioral Sciences* 1, 838–843.

Seferoğlu, G. (2006) Teacher candidates' reflections on some components of a pre-service English teacher education programme in Turkey. *Journal of Education for Teaching* 32 (4), 369–378.

Selvi, A.F. (2017) Preparing teachers to teach English as an International Language. Reflections from Northern Cyprus. In A. Matsuda (ed.) *Preparing Teachers to Teach English as an International Language* (pp. 114–128). Bristol: Multilingual Matters.

Serin, O. (2013) The critical thinking skills of teacher candidates. Turkish Republic of Northern Cyprus sampling. *Egitim Arastirmalari-Eurasian Journal of Educational Research* 53, 231–248.

Shi, L. and Cumming, A. (1995) Teachers' conceptions of second-language writing: Five case studies. *Journal of Second Language Writing* 4, 87–111.

Shin, S.J. (2006) Learning to teach writing through tutoring and journal writing. *Teachers and Teaching: Theory and Practice* 12 (3), 325–345.

Silva, T. and Leki, I. (2004) Family matters: The influence of applied linguistics and composition studies on second language writing studies – past, present, and future. *The Modern Language Journal* 88, 1–13.

Silva, T. and Matsuda, P. (2001) *On Second Language Writing*. West Lafayette, IN: Parlor Press/Routledge.

Şimşek, H. and Yıldırım, A. (2001) The reform of pre-service teacher education in Turkey. In R.G. Sultana (ed.) *Challenge and Change in the Euro-Mediterranean Region* (pp. 411–430). New York: Peter Lang.

Street, B.V. (1984) *Literacy in Theory and Practice*. New York, NY: Cambridge University Press. Thousand Oaks, CA: Sage.

Street, C. (2003) Pre-service teachers' attitudes about writing and learning to teach writing: Implications for teacher educators. *Teacher Education Quarterly* 30 (3), 33–50.

Street, C. and Stang, K. (2008) Improving the teaching of writing across the curriculum: A model for teaching in-service secondary teachers to write. *Action in Teacher Education* 30 (1), 37–49.

Tüm, D. and Kunt, N. (2013) Speaking anxiety among EFL student teachers. Hacettepe Üniversitesi Eğitim Fakültesi Dergisi 28 (3), 385–399.

Yeşil, H. (2010) The relationship between candidate teachers' communication skills and their attitudes towards teaching profession. *Procedia Social and Behavioral Sciences* 9, 919–922.

Yu, S. and Lee, I. (2016) Peer feedback in second language writing (2005–2014). *Language Teaching* 49 (4), 461–493.

11 English as a Foreign Language Writing Teacher Education and Development in Spain: The Relevance of a Focus on Second Language Writing as a Tool for Second Language Development

Lourdes Cerezo, Belén González-Cruz and José Ángel Mercader

Introduction

In the Spanish education system, English is the first foreign language (FL) from kindergarten to university, but particularly in primary, compulsory secondary and non-compulsory secondary education ($M = 97.4\%$), according to a report about FL teaching commissioned for the Office of Statistics and Reports by the Spanish Ministry of Education, Culture and Sport Government of Spain (2017). This report also establishes English as the instructional language of most bilingual programs implemented in the mentioned education levels (97.4%, 88.8% and 78.8%, respectively; $M = 88.3\%$).

Instruction in the English as a foreign language (EFL) class has traditionally centered on the study of language forms (i.e. grammatical rules and lexical items) and the development of the ability to understand oral and written language (i.e. listening and reading comprehension). Recent innovations in the EFL curriculum (see section below on 'Curricular

Guidelines for EFL Writing Instruction'), however, have shifted pedagogical attention onto the development of productive skills, which means that the overarching goal of EFL instruction is now the development of the ability to express oneself in and interact with other users of English, by means of both oral and written discourse.

On the other hand, the major expectation of bilingual programs in Spain is that learners acquire the subject matter taught in English while, almost inadvertently (i.e. without much explicit instruction in the forms of the language), also developing their English language skills.[1] This is clearly the case with grammar and pronunciation. In the bilingual subjects, teachers are not expected to provide students with explicit instruction in either area and, thus, any potential improvements can be considered the result of implicit teaching (Dalton-Puffer, 2008: 7). Vocabulary is a different matter: a large amount of instruction in the bilingual subjects focuses on helping students learn in both languages the vocabulary associated with the contents taught in English. Increasingly, schools are using textbooks that are purposefully designed for the implementation of this pedagogical approach with Spanish first language (L1) students. These materials are written in English and, most frequently, include appendices with bilingual lists of core vocabulary. As attested by empirical research on second language (L2) learning resulting from bilingual education, vocabulary is usually the only linguistic aspect that is explicitly treated in content and language integrated learning (CLIL) lessons (Matiasek, 2005, cited in Dalton-Puffer, 2008: 6). This instruction may include more monolingually oriented (in English) or more bilingually oriented (English-Spanish/Spanish-English) tasks but, ultimately, it is a *sine qua non* condition that students handle curricular subject matter in both languages. Regarding the language skills, most learning derives from materials that are addressed and dealt with receptively, while the productive skills are much less employed. If at all, the students are asked to reproduce curricular contents orally, but very rarely are they required to write.

The two dimensions that are commonly distinguished in the literature about L2 writing, *learning-to-write* and *writing-to-learn* (e.g. Manchón, 2011a), are clearly identifiable in the approach to writing instruction in the Spanish EFL classroom. Not so much, however, in the bilingual class, as educational authorities, material developers and/or classroom teachers do not seem to have understood the role of writing for the students to make sense of and acquire disciplinary knowledge (e.g. Hirvela, 2011). Writing can be considered as a tool for language learning (*writing-to-learn-language*; WLL) but, from a *writing-to-learn-content* (WLC) approach, it can also be regarded as a tool for discovery or negotiation of content (Hirvela, 2011). WLL posits that writing 'elicits attention to form-meaning relations that may prompt learners to refine their linguistic expressions – and hence to control over their linguistic knowledge' (Cumming, 1990: 483, cited in Manchón, 2011a). On the other hand, in a WLC approach, writing can contribute to content learning via written prompts such as 'note taking, organizing outlines, composing summaries, writing in journals, and conducting syntheses' (Hirvela, 2011: 39), which would enable learners to engage in language use in the manipulation of the content they are engaged with in other, non-linguistic subject areas. In fact, it is often through writing that learners 'will have to express what they know in the content areas as well as engage the content areas' (Hirvela, 2011: 41). WLC, hence, involves the learners in a heuristic process through which they have to transform content knowledge by using this content in writing. In this way, WLC can be used productively in three ways (Langer & Applebee, 1987: 136, cited in Hirvela, 2011: 40): (i) to gain relevant knowledge and experience in preparing for new activities; (ii) to review and consolidate what is known or has to be learned; and (iii) to reformulate and extend ideas and experiences. However, bilingual programs in Spain do not seem to be making the most of the learning potential of FL writing. Thus, because the English writing that primary and secondary students do is mostly circumscribed to the EFL class, the discussion about the role of FL writing in the Spanish education system will also be focused on how students learn to write in English and how they learn English by writing in English in the EFL class.

The remainder of this chapter proceeds as follows. After a brief explanation of our data-gathering procedures in the 'Methodology' section below, the role of EFL writing in the Spanish education system (namely, the curricular specifications that guide the teaching and learning of writing and a survey of the role of writing in instructional materials) is presented in the section 'Overview of EFL Writing Instruction'. Then, 'Writing in EFL Teacher Education and Professional Development' describes the type of education that student teachers receive in relation to EFL writing pedagogy. Here we also discuss the need to revise EFL teacher education programs and professional development courses to make room for writing pedagogy education that effectively trains EFL teachers in the language learning potential of writing, so that they can help their students learn to write in English (*learn-to-write dimension*; LW) but also, and very importantly in our EFL context, develop their knowledge of and competence in English through written output practice.

Methodology

Four main sources of information were drawn on in the preparation of the two focal sections of the chapter. For the 'Overview of EFL Writing Instruction' section, official documents produced by the central government and the governments of the Autonomous Communities were reviewed. These official documents are of three types: (i) the current law of education, a brief document which barely outlines the main features of the current education system; (ii) two royal decrees in which specific guidelines for each education level, year and subject are detailed; and (iii) a sample of the decrees and orders developed by the different administrative divisions of the country, in which the guidelines for the academic disciplines which had been only briefly outlined in the law and the royal decrees are then fully fleshed out (in essentially the same terms from one division to the other). Additionally, a total of 27 textbooks were scrutinized for information about writing pedagogy from the materials employed in Spanish EFL classrooms.

Another data source included is a questionnaire (Appendix 1) designed by the authors to gather EFL teachers' views on the suitability of their academic education and their pre- and in-service training to teach EFL writing. The information obtained through this questionnaire was used to complement the description of the type of education and training received by EFL teachers in terms of writing pedagogy. This description was elaborated after the authors' own (i) survey of first degrees in English studies and master's degrees in teacher training, information about which was gathered from the official websites of public and private universities, and (ii) our own knowledge about and experience with these two types of degree (see section on 'Writing in EFL Teacher Education and Professional Development').

With the questionnaire we aimed to triangulate our data by gathering information from EFL teachers, as we already had information from official documents (law, royal decrees and decrees, as well as official websites of Spanish universities) and pedagogical materials (textbooks). Primary, compulsory secondary and non-compulsory secondary education teachers from our own Autonomous Community were contacted initially to complete and have fellow teachers complete the questionnaire. Then we contacted teachers we knew in other communities to respond and have colleagues respond to the questionnaire. Finally, we randomly selected three schools from three communities and contacted the teachers in the English departments to complete the questionnaire. Thus, we managed to sample six different Autonomous Communities scattered across the national territory. Unfortunately, we only received nine completed questionnaires: two by primary education and compulsory secondary education teachers in our own community, two from two other communities, and then one from each of the other three communities.

The questionnaire is divided into six blocks. The questions in Block 1 were aimed at gathering information about the role of writing pedagogy in the academic education completed by the participating teachers. Similarly, Block 2 included questions to find out about the role of writing instruction in teacher training courses the participants might have completed. Blocks 3 and 4 sought to gather the teachers' perceptions about the adequacy of their own education and training in writing pedagogy. Block 5 aimed to collect information on how important writing was deemed by these teachers as opposed to other skills (e.g. speaking) and language aspects (grammar or vocabulary) in their own language teaching. Block 6 investigated the language learning potential of writing in the opinion of the participant teachers. Prior to these six blocks of questions, participant teachers had been asked about their age and gender, how many years of teaching experience they had, whether they were teaching in a public, private or semi-private school, the education level(s) and year(s) they were involved with and, finally, the type of course(s) they taught (EFL or bilingual subjects). The responses to this questionnaire will be summarized in the 'Writing in EFL Teacher Education and Professional Development' section.

Our last source of information corresponds to the websites of the Teachers and Resources Centers of the different Autonomous Communities (Appendix 2), which we surveyed to gather data about writing in professional development courses for EFL teachers.

Overview of EFL Writing Instruction in Spain

Curricular guidelines for EFL writing instruction

Current educational legislation in Spain (i.e. the *Organic Law on the Improvement of the Quality of Education*, known in Spanish as LOMCE, initially outlined in Law 8/2013 (Government of Spain, 2013) and fully developed in Royal Decrees 126/2014 and 1105/2014 (Government of Spain, 2014, 2015) establishes the organization of the FL curriculum across educational levels (i.e. primary education, compulsory secondary education and non-compulsory secondary education) around the four language skills of listening comprehension, speaking (production and interaction), reading comprehension, and writing (production and interaction), following the *Common European Framework of Reference for Languages: Learning, Teaching, Assessment* (Council of Europe, 2001, 2018; CEFR). Additionally, the development of a fifth, transversal skill is aimed for in both the oral and written modes of the language – intercultural awareness. Namely, students need to learn the forms of the language as well as and in direct relation to the norms which regulate their adequate use with interlocutors of different linguistic, social and/or cultural backgrounds. Ultimately, the goal is for the students to develop communicative competence in the FL, which will allow them to express themselves and interact with other users, whether native speakers or L2 users like themselves.

This five-block organization of the FL curriculum is comparable in virtually all Autonomous Communities across the national territory. Thus, while each community has its own curricular specifications for every level of education, developed in the respective Decree or Order, these are all based on the general guidelines delineated in Law 8/2013 and Royal Decrees 126/2014 (for primary education) and 1105/2014 (for compulsory and non-compulsory secondary education).

Regarding language provision, the mentioned royal decrees establish English, French, German, Italian and Portuguese as the languages that

Spanish children can choose to study as first and second FLs in primary, secondary and non-compulsory secondary education. The subject *first foreign language* (FL1) is compulsory in primary education and a large majority of primary schools decide to offer English for this subject. Pupils may add a *second foreign language* (FL2) in the last two years of primary education (Years 5 and 6, ages 10 and 11, respectively), and the language most commonly selected in this case is French, followed at a considerable distance by German and other FLs, according to the data published by the Ministry of Education, Culture and Sports for the academic year 2015–2016 (Government of Spain, 2017). The distribution of FL study in two subjects (FL1 and FL2) and the order of preference in terms of language (English, French and German as the most widely selected languages) is maintained in compulsory and non-compulsory secondary education across the Autonomous Communities, and it probably explains the fact that it is only for English, French and German that instructional guidelines are specified and developed in the curricula (referred to as 'syntactic-discursive contents').

FL instruction in primary education (and particularly in its early years) places the emphasis on the development of the oral-aural skills, that is, listening comprehension and speaking (production and interaction). Progressively, however, the written skills (reading comprehension and written production and interaction) are introduced to aid students in developing a more complete type of communicative competence (i.e. inclusive of all the skills) in the FL. This communicative competence must be necessarily developed in relation to the interests, needs and preferences of learners, which means that age, level of cognitive development and overall maturational development need to be considered in the selection of instructional methodologies and materials and in the development and application of language learning assessment procedures and instruments. In the next two levels – compulsory and non-compulsory secondary education – listening comprehension and speaking are still considered very important, but the overall distribution of instructional attention among the four skills is supposed to be much more even than in primary education.

The development of writing skills across education levels is organized in the curricular guidelines around the following aspects: writing process (pre-writing, writing, editing); communicative functions; use of learned linguistic elements (grammatical structures, lexical items and the rules of orthography and punctuation); and text types. The following section describes expected development in FL writing skills by the end of each education level (primary education, by age 12; compulsory secondary education, by age 16; and non-compulsory secondary education, by age 18).

Writing process

By the end of primary education, pupils are expected to have become aware (perhaps only implicitly) of the fact that writing involves the implementation of pre-writing strategies (planning), and must be followed by the editing of written output (e.g. self-correction) by means of available resources, whether internal (i.e. their own knowledge of the language elements and writing conventions) and/or external (e.g. a dictionary, on paper or online). Specifically, students are expected to realize that: (i) before writing they need to brainstorm, take notes and outline (even if at a very rudimentary level, in terms of text structure) what they are going to write about and select the linguistic elements that are necessary for text production (planning); and (ii) after writing they need to revise their written output for potential improvements before submission (editing).

These production strategies are further developed in compulsory and non-compulsory secondary education. Students are now (in compulsory secondary education) expected to plan their writing more effectively by drawing from their already developed overall linguistic competences (FL and L1). Hence, they become aware, perhaps more explicitly than in primary education, that planning involves thinking of what is already known about the topic and the type of text to be produced as well as what is not known and needs to be ascertained in relation to those two aspects for successful task accomplishment. In terms of the FL itself, this planning stage involves: (i) thinking of the communicative functions that the written assignment aims to fulfil; and (ii) retrieving the necessary linguistic elements (which include, although are not limited to, the necessary grammatical structures, lexical items, or knowledge of punctuation and orthographical rules, or text organization patterns). Then, in terms of actual writing, students realize that working on a writing task usually involves preparing an initial version which must be revised (i.e. self- or peer-edited) in search of errors or potential improvements of different types, after which it must be rewritten before submission. It is in non-compulsory secondary education that students are considered to become fully (i.e. explicitly) aware that there is both a process and a product to any writing task, and that an initial draft is usually not a finished product when it comes to writing (regardless of the language in which the writing is done).

Communicative functions

Writing, as speaking, is done to perform communicative functions, as the overall aim of FL instruction and learning along these education stages is not only that the students *learn the FL*, but that they develop the ability to *communicate in it*.

Hence, in primary education, students are expected to learn to: (i) provide basic personal information about themselves, their most immediate personal, academic and social environments (e.g. family members, schoolmates and friends) and their personal abilities; (ii) greet (in written texts as opposed to greeting people in oral discourse); (iii) introduce themselves and other people from their immediate personal, academic and social environments; (iv) describe themselves and other people, objects and places in their immediate environment; (v) provide personal opinions about topics which are ideationally not very complex and with which they are familiar; (vi) express their feelings (e.g. likes and dislikes, agreement and disagreement or apologies); (vii) narrate recent events and personal experiences; (viii) give and require assistance; or (ix) outline immediate future plans.

By the end of compulsory secondary education, students must demonstrate their ability to: (i) initiate and maintain personal relations through written interaction; (ii) narrate past (one-off or regular) events; (iii) describe current states and situations and future events; (iv) require and provide information, directions, opinions, advice, suggestions and warnings; (v) express knowledge (or lack thereof), certainty (or lack thereof) and probability; (vi) express will, intention and resolution (not) to do something; (vii) promise; (viii) indicate to others what (not) to do; (ix) allow and disallow; (x) express interest, approval, appreciation, sympathy, satisfaction, hope, trust, surprise and their opposites; (xi) formulate suggestions, wishes, conditions and hypotheses, and the overall ability to establish and maintain communication and organize the communicative event.

In non-compulsory secondary education, the ability acquired in compulsory secondary education to express the mentioned communicative functions is reinforced. It is also extended in that more complex aspects of certain functions partially acquired in compulsory secondary education and primary education are included in the curricular guidelines.

Use of learned linguistic forms

Students are explicitly instructed to use previously learned grammatical structures and lexical items in their written productions, usually with the aim of consolidating the correct spelling of commonly used, high-frequency words and the use of basic morphosyntactic patterns and structures in primary education. In compulsory and non-compulsory secondary education, this consolidation aim is still present; however, the main aim is now one of development or expansion of the L2 system. By requiring students to use, in their written output, previously learned linguistic elements, they are being encouraged to test their hypotheses about how the 'learned' morphosyntactic patterns and lexical items are used in written discourse, which is considered to assist in the consolidation of the known meanings or patterns of use of lexical items and grammatical structures, respectively, or to add new meanings and patterns of use. Clearly, writing is taught from a WLL perspective, especially in compulsory and non-compulsory secondary education.

Text types

Along these three stages of education, students are expected to become aware of the difference between the word, the sentence, the paragraph and the text, and to learn to produce different types of text, progressing from isolated words to phrases to simple sentences to short texts. This progress is commonly done with pedagogical scaffolding (i.e. previous oral practice or model texts), which becomes less and less structured as the students reach the end of their pre-university education.

Upon completion of primary education, students are expected to complete but also write texts, even if these are kept very short and simple, both from the linguistic and ideational points of view. Specifically, students must have learned to: (i) write notes, instructions, informal letters/emails, greetings, comics, and short and basic descriptions (of familiar places or personal likes), both in pen-and-paper and electronic formats; (ii) complete brief and simple forms (e.g. to sign up to social networks or to create an email account) or (iii) prepare simple forms to gather personal information from others; and (iv) write simple, personal correspondence about themselves and their most immediate environment (e.g. home or school) in the form of notes, postcards, emails, SMSs or instant messages using smartphone apps, in order to thank somebody for something, to congratulate somebody, to invite, to provide instructions, to provide information about themselves and their most familiar environment (family, friends, likes, everyday activities, objects and places), or to ask for information about these topics. When students finish compulsory secondary education, they are expected to: (i) write a detailed questionnaire with personal, academic and/or professional information (e.g. to apply for a study grant or to join an association); (ii) prepare their own résumé (on paper or in electronic format); (iii) take notes and messages with simple but relevant information about current events and specific details from the personal, academic and professional domains within their area of specialization or interest; (iv) write brief announcements and comments, pen-and-paper or electronic, requiring or providing information and opinions which are still kept simple but in which they can highlight important aspects, observing the corresponding writing and courtesy conventions, or the Netiquette when writing on the internet (e.g. to create or respond to a blog post); (v) write brief and simple reports to provide basic information about an academic or professional issue, or less common events (e.g. an accident), describing succinctly situations, persons, objects and places, narrating events in a clear linear sequence and explaining in simple but clear terms the reasons for certain types of actions; (vi) engage in different types of personal correspondence and participate in blogs, forums and chats to describe experiences, impressions and feelings, narrate in a linear and coherent sequence events related to their areas of interest, their daily activities and past experiences (e.g. recounting a trip, a special vacation or an important or interesting event, book or movie) or imaginary events, or exchange information and ideas about specific topics, indicating what is important and briefly justifying their opinions about them. The types of texts that students are expected to write by the end of non-compulsory secondary education are roughly the same as in compulsory secondary education, only now the students are expected to add more detail and increase the level of complexity of the texts produced.

Perhaps the greater instructional effort along the secondary education years is placed on instilling in the students the importance of learning to organize their ideas (also in their L1, which is done transversally, i.e. across the curriculum), given that the ability to organize thought contributes to the development of other competences of the overall curriculum. Students must realize that organization in the written text involves: (i) using complete and different types of sentences depending on their function within the text; (ii) grouping sentences appropriately according to their meaning and function within the text; and (iii) establishing clear connections among the sentences (and thus among ideas) through a variety of cohesive devices. They must then also realize that sentences must be coherently organized into paragraphs, and that a coherently and cohesively organized group of paragraphs constitutes a text. If textual structure is only hinted at in primary education, in compulsory and especially in non-compulsory secondary education students are expected to have become fully aware that writing, at an intermediate or 'independent' level, involves the ability to elaborate language beyond the level of the sentence (i.e. at text level).

Finally, two other dimensions cut across these five areas in the curricular guidelines for the development of writing skills: (a) textual authorship, whereby students learn that writing can be done as a solitary activity (individual writing) or with classmates (collaborative writing); and (b) text format (i.e. that texts can be written on paper or on the computer/tablet/smartphone). These dimensions are addressed in all three stages of education, as has already been indicated in the discussion about text types, communicative functions and the writing process above.

Materials for EFL writing instruction

The textbooks used in primary and secondary EFL classes in Spain are selected from among the English language teaching catalogues of leading publishing companies such as Cambridge University Press, Oxford University Press and Burlington Books. These publishers have a wide variety of EFL textbook suites from which schools select those that most adequately suit their pedagogical contexts, needs and preferences. In addition, in recent years, these publishers have started to produce textbooks specifically designed for Spanish learners of English which are purposefully designed to match the learning goals and methodological guidelines described in the curricula for primary, compulsory secondary and non-compulsory secondary education, as well as the CEFR descriptions of FL levels of ability that students must attain by the end of each education stage and upon which the mentioned guidelines have been elaborated. These levels are A1 for primary education, A2 for compulsory secondary education and B1 for non-compulsory secondary education.

These textbooks are normally designed to be completed over a nine-month course and are commonly organized around a series of thematic units within which the linguistic contents are conveniently sequenced. Specifically, very little attention is paid in these books (as in the curriculum) to the development of writing skills in 'lower' primary education (Years 1–3, ages 6–9): the focus is on the development of basic grammar, high-frequency vocabulary and the oral-aural skills, while the methodological approach is fundamentally one of learning-by-playing, as recommended in the curricular guidelines. The scarce writing practice that is done consists of the completion of sentences, short texts, tables or forms with (i) high-frequency lexical items related to the students' most immediate personal environment, and (ii) grammatical structures of the corresponding level of ability. This writing practice is mostly done in imitation of model texts and with the ultimate goals of practicing (i) and (ii) above, as well as reinforcing correct spelling and basic punctuation rules – hence again a WLL approach. Pupils also begin to write sentences and very short texts, in traditional (i.e. pen-and-paper) format or on the computer (on- or offline). On the other hand, textbooks for 'higher' primary education (Years 4–6) include a more balanced approach to the four language skills, and thus to the development of writing competence (here too reflecting curricular guidelines). Table 11.1 summarizes the typology of writing tasks for Years 5 and 6 of primary education as synthesized from the textbooks surveyed.

In compulsory and non-compulsory secondary education, textbooks include writing tasks whereby students continue to practice some text types learned in the previous stages as well as new types, as reflected in Table 11.2. The main difference of one stage with respect to the prior one is that students are expected to produce language that is gradually more and more: (i) fluent – i.e. flowing smoothly from word to word, sentence to sentence, paragraph to paragraph; (ii) complex (in morphological, syntactic and lexical terms); and (iii) accurate (i.e. containing fewer errors). It should not be forgotten that the curricular guidelines clearly indicate that students should develop their writing skills in terms of learning to write, i.e. the mechanics of text production as well as awareness of the different discourse demands of different text types, but also and very importantly that writing in the FL serves to practice and thus develop the students' knowledge of the FL forms (i.e. to learn the language).

From writing introductions and conclusions to complete essays (academic domain), to writing a biography or a narrative (personal domain), to writing applications and cover emails and letters (professional domain),

Table 11.1 Writing outcomes for primary education Years 5 and 6

Writing outcomes

Year 5 primary education	Year 6 primary education
Writing a **poem** using syllable counts and stresses	Completing a **story**
Completing a **play script**	Completing a **concept map** and using it to write a **leaflet**
Ending a **story**	Writing a **letter** to a friend
Writing an **information text**	Using a process diagram to **explain** how to ride a bike
Writing a **leaflet**	Writing a **bibliography**
Writing an **article**	Writing a **research project**
Writing a **newspaper report**	Writing a **personalized text**
Writing a **personal account**	Writing a **tourist information leaflet**
Writing up an **interview** from notes	Writing an **advice text**
Writing a **descriptive account**	Writing an **advert**
Writing a **film review**	Writing a **poem using similes**
Writing an **opinion text**	Writing an **essay**
Writing an **autobiography**	Writing a **playscript**
Writing about events **(factual recount)**	**Persuasive** writing
Writing an **adventure story**	Writing a **speech**
Writing a **narrative story**	Writing a **travel journal**
Taking **notes**	Writing an **extended narrative**
Writing a **cartoon strip story**	Writing a **character description**
Writing a **screenplay**	Writing a **personal travel recount**
Writing a **diary**	Writing a **story starter**
Writing a **narrative news story**	Writing a **letter** presenting arguments **in favor** and **against**
Writing a **suspense story**	Writing **instructions**
Writing a **traditional tale** or **legend**	Writing **interview questions**
Writing a **formal letter**	Writing an **information leaflet**

the textual typology included in the curricular guidelines for the EFL class in secondary education is clearly large and varied, as Table 11.2 shows. Given that writing courses are not included in the primary, compulsory secondary or non-compulsory secondary education curricula, students must learn to write in English in the context of the general EFL class, and writing instruction is commonly the responsibility of the general EFL teacher, not a writing specialist. The following section focuses on the type of academic education and professional training that teachers receive and with which they must learn to teach primary and secondary students to write in English.

Table 11.2 Writing outcomes for compulsory secondary education Year 4 and non-compulsory secondary education Year 2

Writing outcomes

Compulsory secondary education	Non-compulsory secondary education
Writing an opinion paragraph	Writing an argumentative (for/against) essay
Writing a film synopsis	Writing a letter (formal/informal)
Writing a book review	Writing an email (formal/informal)
Writing a biography	Writing an opinion (one-sided) essay
Writing a summary	Writing an argumentative (for/against) essay
Writing a personal narrative	Writing a description (place/person/event) essay
Writing a magazine article	Writing a personal narrative
Writing introduction paragraphs	Writing a summary
Writing conclusion paragraphs	Writing a personal narrative
Writing an argumentative (for/against) essay	Writing a covering email
Writing an opinion (one-sided) essay	Writing a biography
Writing a description (person/place/event) essay	Writing a news report
Writing a letter (formal/informal)	Writing a film review
Writing an email (formal/informal)	Writing a blog post

Writing in EFL Teacher Education and Professional Development

This section will initially and succinctly describe the types of academic programs that must be completed in order to become an EFL teacher in Spain, with a view to identifying the training (or lack thereof) provided to prospective teachers whereby they learn to teach their students to write in English. Then the suitability of educating and training prospective and in-service EFL teachers in the language learning potential of writing will be discussed, as it is crucial that FL teachers are aware of the double dimension of L2 writing – namely, the *learning-to-write* dimension, whereby students learn to write with the aim of developing writing skills specifically, and the *writing-to-learn-language* dimension, whereby overall ability in the FL is developed through the skill of writing (e.g. Manchón, 2011a), as already explained in the Introduction.

Writing pedagogy in teacher education programs and professional development courses

In order to become a primary education EFL teacher in Spain, a four-year degree must initially be completed. Most universities organize this degree on a 10 semester long, six credit courses per academic year basis, with one credit worth 10 contact hours. Instruction (i.e. pedagogical materials and classroom interaction) in 'Primary Education' degrees across the national territory has traditionally been conducted in Spanish (or/and the co-official languages in the bilingual Autonomous Communities); increasingly, however, public and private universities are also beginning to offer the 'English version' of the degree which, in terms of designation, is normally differentiated from its monolingual counterpart by the 'Mention in EFL' tag. Seventy-eight percent of all public universities in Spain offer the degree in primary education in Spanish, while only 23.07% of public universities offer the bilingual option (as well as the monolingual itinerary) in primary education. Private universities present similar figures: 70.37% offer a degree in primary education in Spanish, and 26.31% also give students the opportunity to study this degree bilingually. For the student teachers, opting for the 'Mention in EFL' degree involves completing content courses in English as well as the English language courses that are common to both modalities of the degree (monolingual and bilingual). The overall percentage of content courses offered in English may vary from one university to another, but very commonly more than half of them are offered in English, and the rest in Spanish (or/and the co-official languages, where it corresponds). As an example, the Faculty of Education at the University of Murcia offers a 'Primary Education' degree, with all its content courses in Spanish, as well as a 'Primary Education – Mention in EFL' degree, in which students must complete at least 60% of content courses in English. Completion of either modality of the degree alone grants access to teaching in private and semi-private primary schools. However, to teach in the public system it is necessary to sit a national competitive examination as well.

Both modalities of the degree include courses aimed at developing overall communicative competence in English, since a CEFR B2 level (roughly ACTFL 'Advanced Mid') is required to teach English but also to teach *in* English in primary education – i.e. to teach content subjects such as natural science or social science *in* English as part of the bilingual education programs currently offered in an increasingly large percentage of primary schools across the national territory. Then, also, both modalities normally include a semester-long course in ELT methodology.

To investigate how would-be primary education EFL teachers are effectively trained to (i) write in English and (ii) teach their future students to write in English, a review of the primary education degrees offered by the different public and private universities in Spain (respectively, 50 and 27 universities) was carried out. This analysis reveals that neither L2 writing nor L2 writing pedagogy are central concerns in the education of primary education teachers, as very few degrees offered by the Spanish universities include a complete course to learn to write in English or to learn to teach how to write in English. This finding of our review of degrees (see Methodology) is supported by the response of the primary education teacher who offered to complete the questionnaire introduced in the 'Methodology' section and whose answers are summarized below (see 'The Teachers' Voices' section). This teacher confirms that there is no subject in her bachelor's degree designed to instruct would-be teachers in writing pedagogy. At most, writing and the teaching of writing may constitute a part (e.g. one unit) of the contents of the methodology courses in the primary education degrees offered across the national territory. Most public and private universities (80% and 94.74%, respectively) include writing pedagogy contents as part of one semester-long subject within a four-year degree. The role of writing and writing pedagogy appears to be marginally more prominent in master's degrees specializing in TEFL, following our own survey of Spanish universities (although this finding was not confirmed by the results of the mentioned questionnaire). However, as already indicated, it is not necessary to hold a master's degree to teach in a public school, which means that the scarce training in writing and writing pedagogy that there might be in these degrees will not necessarily be part of every primary education teacher's qualifications, only of those who opt to specialize in TEFL by doing a master's degree.

To become a secondary education teacher, it is also necessary to complete a four-year degree, which in most universities is designated as 'Degree in *English Studies*' (although other degrees such as *Translation and Interpretation* and *Modern Languages* may also lead to a master's degree in TEFL). This degree presents a distribution of courses per academic year very similar to that of the previously described degree in primary education. The most significant differences, however, are that in *English Studies* (i) instruction is carried out in English virtually throughout the degree, and (ii) students are specifically trained to write in English – both in general language courses which aim to develop their communicative competence to CEFR level C1 or C2, and in academic writing courses included in the core contents of the degree. Writing pedagogy, however, is also very limited in the education of prospective secondary teachers, as it is mostly reduced to a small part of one methodology course included in the syllabus of the last year of the degree. Our findings are confirmed by the responses of eight of the nine teachers who completed the questionnaire (see 'The Teachers' Voices' section below). Another difference with primary education is that, to teach in the public sector, a master's degree in *Teacher Training* is compulsory. This degree, which can be completed in a large number of universities across the national territory (in 90% of public universities and 77.78% of private institutions), has a common core that all prospective secondary teachers must complete regardless of their area of specialization, and as many specialties as subjects in the curricula for compulsory and non-compulsory secondary education, one of which is TEFL. Students who specialize in TEFL complete a number of methodology courses,[2] in which, again, attention to writing pedagogy is minimum (indeed, only four of the eight secondary teachers who completed our questionnaire confirmed having had some instruction in writing pedagogy as a part of one of the courses included in their postgraduate degrees, as indicated in 'The Teachers' Voices' section below). As in primary education, after completion of this master's degree, it is also necessary to sit a national competitive examination to teach EFL in compulsory or non-compulsory secondary education in the public education system.

Very frequently, thus, primary and secondary teachers seeking further specialization in TEFL need to do so via professional development courses while they are preparing for the national examination or, more commonly perhaps, once they are already in service. These courses are normally organized by the Teachers and Resources Centers of the different Autonomous Communities. Our own survey of the training courses offered by the Teachers and Resources Centers together with the responses to the questionnaire reveal that these courses range from general courses such as English for EFL teachers, classroom management skills or ICTs for the EFL classroom, or more specific courses such as those aiming to develop teachers' oral skills in English or to educate them in the pedagogy of this skill: writing skills and writing pedagogy, however, are conspicuous by their almost total absence. Thus, four of the nine teachers who completed the questionnaire responded negatively to the question as to whether they had done any professional development course to train as EFL writing teachers, while the other five teachers responded that they had done one, two or three courses (only one of the teachers) to develop their overall English and English teaching skills, some of whose components had to do with how to teach writing in the EFL class.

In the following section, we briefly outline the main results of the answers provided by the teachers who responded to our questionnaire regarding writing pedagogy as part of the university and post-university training of EFL teachers in Spain.

The teachers' voices

The first part of the questionnaire aimed to gather information about teacher training received as part of university training (first degrees and MAs). Most teachers (77.7%) indicated that they had not completed any subject that was entirely or partially devoted to English writing pedagogy. The picture changed slightly in relation to postgraduate degrees, where 44.4% of the teachers indicated that they had completed one subject devoted to or including writing pedagogy training.

Regarding writing pedagogy as part of post-university, in-service language teacher development, 55.5% of the teachers indicated that they had completed training courses to improve their EFL writing pedagogy skills: most of these teachers (three out of five) completed one such course, and two of them completed two or more of these courses. These teachers also indicated that the duration of the writing pedagogy courses they had completed ranged from five to 30 hours. What is common to most participating teachers is that they claimed to have learned about writing pedagogy mainly on their own: (i) through professional practice (i.e. their own classroom instruction); (ii) consulting specialized manuals and webpages; (iii) following the assessment guidelines and models of various certifying bodies (e.g. Cambridge, Oxford); or (iv) discussing and sharing knowledge with other colleagues.

The questionnaire also aimed to gather information about the teachers' perceptions of the importance of being trained in how to teach writing and their awareness of the availability of this type of training. All the teachers but one (88.8%) indicated that writing pedagogy training is either *useful* (four out of nine), *very useful* (two out of nine) or *really useful* (two out of nine). In the same vein, 88.8% of them demonstrated with their answers that they were fully aware of the scarcity of training in writing pedagogy that is available to EFL teachers in Spain, both as part of university training (i.e. first degrees and MA degrees) and post-university, in-service professional development.

While all the participating teachers indicated that they considered writing pedagogy necessary for their training as EFL teachers, they differed as to when they believed this training should be received. Most teachers indicated that they should learn about how to teach writing as part of both their first degree and their MA degree, while only two respondents indicated that writing pedagogy should be provided exclusively as part of an MA degree in TEFL. Regarding writing pedagogy training in post-university, in-service EFL teacher development, 55.5% of the teachers considered that it should be mandatory to complete at least one 10-hour writing pedagogy course per year. Other teachers (three out of nine) considered that a 30- to 50-hour course every three years would be enough to prepare teachers to instruct learners in EFL writing.

Qualitatively, all teachers agreed that receiving training in *materials selection, adaptation and design* as well as in *lesson planning* for writing instruction would be the most beneficial. However, they seemed to attach less importance to *the use of ICTs, course design* and *error treatment* in the teaching of writing in the EFL class.

It is also interesting to discuss the information derived from questionnaire answers relating to the teachers' perceptions and beliefs about the importance of different aspects of the teaching of EFL, including writing. Most teachers (eight out of nine) considered grammar, speaking and listening comprehension more relevant than writing and reading. In addition, most teachers (five out of nine) concurred that the time that should be dedicated to writing is between 10% and 20% of the total EFL hours. The rest of the teachers considered that the percentage should be higher, between 20% and 40% of EFL hours.

Finally, when asked about the role of writing in EFL instruction, all of our respondents held that this skill is employed instrumentally, either to help learners develop their linguistic competence in English (hence, a WLL approach) or to assess their L2 competence or development. However, when comparing the relevance of using writing versus speaking for L2 development and assessment, only one of our participants favored writing over speaking. The reasons for this preference, however, were not provided.

As can be gathered from the above, the education of Spanish primary and secondary EFL teachers regarding writing pedagogy is deemed insufficient, more so after the recent curricular innovations discussed in the 'Curricular Guidelines for EFL Writing Instruction' section, whereby the development of the productive skills have gained prominence in the EFL classroom. These teachers are rather left to their own devices, as it were, regarding their qualifications to teach their future students to write in English. It is rather uncommon to find graduate (let alone undergraduate) programs which offer even a single complete subject aimed at developing their writing pedagogy skills, as confirmed by the survey of university degrees we carried out and the responses to our questionnaire.

The future of EFL writing teacher education and professional development: Focus on the language learning potential of L2 writing

The previous discussion has evidenced that curricular guidelines for EFL instruction in primary and secondary education widely provide for the language learning potential of writing. In those guidelines, writing instruction and practice is described (however implicitly) as a powerful pedagogical device that, conveniently implemented, has the potential to assist students in their acquisition and/or development of other L2 abilities (e.g. grammatical structures or lexical items) along with the development of their writing skills per se. In short, writing is acknowledged as a site for language learning (Manchón & Cerezo, 2018). The reason is that writing has been acknowledged to function 'as a psycholinguistic output condition wherein learners analyze and consolidate second language knowledge that they have previously (but not yet fully) acquired[;] writing elicits attention to form-meaning relations that may prompt learners to refine their linguistic expression – and hence their control over their linguistic knowledge – so that it is more accurately representative of their thoughts and of standard usage' (Cumming, 1990: 483, cited in Manchón, 2011a: 61). In other words, the approach to EFL instruction in the Spanish curriculum is primarily one in which a considerable emphasis is put on the use of writing practice for the students to acquire and/or develop their overall L2 competences. It must be remembered here that in the L2 writing literature, this approach is referred to as *writing-to-learn-language* and is opposed to a *learning-to-write* approach, whereby the emphasis is on the development of writing abilities per se and which may be more typical of *second* than *foreign* language contexts.

This language learning potential of writing rests on two theoretically and empirically grounded pillars: (i) the study of the different types of linguistic processes that take place while writing and how these may be beneficial in terms of language development; and (ii) the study of why and how the processing of written corrective feedback (WCF)[3] can aid L2 development. In both cases, the fundamental question for EFL writing instruction (and which any EFL teacher who wants to take advantage of this learning potential should know the answer to) is what is in writing and in the processing of WCF that can enhance L2 development.

Three main features of written output and WCF processing are considered beneficial for L2 development. The first is the offline nature of writing and feedback processing, which may afford learners *greater availability of time* for task completion (as opposed to the online nature of oral tasks and the immediacy of the feedback provision and processing these normally require). This slower pace of writing and WCF processing affords L2 writers more efficient control of their attentional capacities and linguistic resources which, accordingly, may lead to increased attention to incoming input (i.e. the WCF) and allow them to focus on language-related concerns during both writing and feedback processing. Secondly, writing and WCF are more *visible and permanent* than the language of oral tasks and oral feedback. The permanence of written output allows student writers to test their knowledge of the L2 by engaging in a process of 'cognitive comparison' between what they have written and their explicit knowledge of the L2, while its visibility can also motivate L2 writers to 'set up higher and more complex goals for themselves and to produce "pushed output", i.e. output that is not only accurate, but also precise, cohesive, and appropriate (Swain, 1995, 2005)' (Manchón & Vasylets, in press). As for WCF, its permanence and visibility make it easier for the student writer to notice the corrections and engage in the metalinguistic reflection and analysis of the L2 that is involved in the processing of such corrections (Manchón & Cerezo, 2018: 2–3). The third characteristic of writing and WCF processing is their problem-solving nature, which may potentially lead to a depth of processing of the L2 forms involved (in the production of written output but fundamentally in the processing of the corrections received on the errors made in the output) that may be conducive to language development when learners actively engage with it, i.e. provided they notice what is new in the input obtained (the corrections or WCF) and compare what is noticed in them with their own representation of the L2 (Manchón & Vasylets, in press).

Universities and Teachers and Resources Centers are responsible for the education and lifelong training of primary and secondary EFL teachers, which means that their study programs in the first case and training and development courses in the second should be aimed at providing EFL teachers with the most adequate competences to do their work. Their work, according to the education law and the curricular guidelines for EFL instruction and learning in primary, compulsory secondary and non-compulsory secondary education presented in this chapter, is to ensure that students finish their initial (pre-university) education knowing English and being able to use English for and in authentic communication purposes and contexts. With this aim, writing has an enormous learning potential that, to date, is not being sufficiently exploited. The current situation (almost total neglect of education and training in L2 writing pedagogy) needs to be reversed by universities and Teachers and Resources Centers equally, who should revise their catalogs of study programs and professional development courses or create new ones in which would-be or in-service teachers learn about the theoretical underpinnings of the language learning potential of L2 writing and the practical issues related to its implementation in the EFL classroom, including how writing processes and the provision of WCF can contribute to the development of other, non-writing abilities in the L2.

Conclusion

The propaedeutic value of instructing EFL teachers in the language learning potential of writing cannot be sufficiently stressed. Teachers who know (i) what it is exactly that they have to do with their L2 students to maximize their writing practice (i.e. learn to write and, through writing and feedback processing, develop other L2 competences) and (ii) the type L2 of development they can expect from their pedagogical interventions are at an advantage.

It is necessary that teachers are explicitly educated and trained in the language learning potential of L2 writing; namely, the initial education of both primary and secondary EFL teachers should include, at least, explicit writing instruction and practice to develop their own writing skills and linguistic knowledge. If not before, postgraduate education should be designed so that future EFL teachers learn about the double dimension of L2 writing and that, within the *writing-to-learn-language* dimension, writing and feedback processing have an unparalleled language learning potential that should be fully exploited in the EFL classroom. Teachers need to receive effective training into the language learning potential of L2 writing, which would allow them to be fully aware that L2 writing, in all its modalities (individual and collaborative) and conditions (time constrained and time unlimited), in all possible environments (pen-and-paper and computer mediated) and physical settings (within or outside the language classroom), with or without the availability of external sources (printed or electronic) together with different types of feedback provided along the composing process (Manchón, 2011b), may successfully mediate the development of the target language – i.e. as mentioned elsewhere, that writing can be an ideal site for language development.

Appendix 1

La enseñanza de la expresión escrita en inglés

Indica (con ✓):   Hombre   ☐   Mujer   ☐

Completa: Edad   ☐   años

Años de experiencia docente. (Indica con ✓)

Entre 1 y 3   ☐   Entre 3 y 5   ☐   Entre 5 y 10   ☐

Entre 10 y 15   ☐   Más de 15   ☐

Para Primaria y Secundaria: Centro en que desarrollas tu docencia. (Indica con ✓)

Público   ☐   Concertado   ☐   Privado   ☐

Indica con ✓ a) nivel educativo y b) curso o cursos que hayas impartido en los últimos tres años:

Primaria   4º   ☐   **ESO**   1º   ☐   **Bachillerato**   1º   ☐

5º   ☐   2º   ☐   2º   ☐

6º   ☐   3º   ☐

4º   ☐

Indica con ✓ la(s) asignatura(s) que impartes. Si no se corresponde(n) con las aquí indicadas, completa el apartado "Otra(s)".

Primera lengua extranjera, Inglés   ☐

Disciplina no lingüística en inglés:

PRIMARIA	Ciencias de la naturaleza	☐	Educación física	☐
	Ciencias sociales	☐	Educación artística	☐
	Matemáticas	☐	Valores sociales y cívicos	☐
	Otra(s):			
ESO	Geografía e Historia	☐	Física y Química	☐
	Biología y Geología	☐	Tecnología	☐
	Matemáticas	☐	Música	☐
	Educación Física	☐	Educación Plástica...	☐
	Otra(s):			
BACHILLERATO	Hª del M. Contemporáneo	☐	Física	☐
	Matemáticas	☐	Química	☐
	Cultura audiovisual	☐	Biología	☐
	Fundamentos del Arte	☐	Economía	☐
	Otra(s):			

Soy profesor(a) de **Escuela Oficial de Idiomas:**

Básico 1 – A1   ☐   Básico 2 – A2   ☐   C1   ☐

Intermedio 1 – B1.1   ☐   Intermedio 2 – B1.2   ☐

Avanzado 1 – B2.1   ☐   Avanzado 2 – B2.2   ☐

Formación universitaria

1 Completa a) y b), por favor. Responde en las casillas con letra azul y negrita.

    a) Formación **inicial**. Si tienes más de una titulación, indícalo.
       Ejemplos: *Licenciatura en Filología Inglesa, Grado en Educación Primaria (Bilingüe), etc.*
       Titulación 1:
       Titulación 2:
       Titulación 3:

    b) Formación de **postgrado**. Si tienes más de una titulación, indícalo.
       Ejemplos: *Certificado de Aptitud Pedagógica (CAP), Máster en Formación del Profesorado de Educación Secundaria...,* etc.
       Titulación 1:
       Titulación 2:
       Titulación 3:

2 En tu formación **inicial** (la que has indicado en 1.a), ¿cursaste alguna asignatura que tuviese como objetivo tu formación en la enseñanza de la expresión escrita en inglés?
No   ☐ (Indica con ✓ junto a "no")
Sí   ☐ (Indica con ✓ junto a "sí")
Si has marcado "sí", completa con el nombre o una breve descripción de la asignatura y la duración de la misma (con ✓):

    Asignatura 1:
    Anual   ☐   Cuatrimestral ☐   Trimestral ☐
    Asignatura 2:
    Anual   ☐   Cuatrimestral ☐   Trimestral ☐
    Asignatura 3:
    Anual   ☐   Cuatrimestral ☐   Trimestral ☐

3 En tu formación de **postgrado** (la que has indicado en 1.b), ¿cursaste alguna asignatura que tuviese como objetivo tu formación en la enseñanza de la expresión escrita en inglés?
No   ☐ (Indica con ✓ junto a "no")
Sí   ☐ (Indica con ✓ junto a "sí")
Si has marcado "sí", completa con el nombre o una breve descripción de la asignatura y la duración de la misma (con ✓):

    Asignatura 1:
    Anual   ☐   Cuatrimestral ☐   Trimestral ☐
    Asignatura 2:
    Anual   ☐   Cuatrimestral ☐   Trimestral ☐
    Asignatura 3:
    Anual   ☐   Cuatrimestral ☐   Trimestral ☐

4 Formación **inicial**. Si no realizaste ninguna asignatura completa cuyo objetivo fuese tu formación en enseñanza de la expresión escrita en inglés, ¿recuerdas si parte de alguna asignatura de tu programa de estudios tenía este objetivo?
No   ☐ (Indica con ✓ junto a "no")
Sí   ☐ (Indica con ✓ junto a "sí")
Si has marcado "sí", por favor, explica lo que recuerdes de esa asignatura:

5 Formación de **postgrado**. Si no realizaste ninguna asignatura completa cuyo objetivo fuese tu formación en enseñanza de la expresión escrita en inglés, ¿recuerdas si parte de alguna asignatura de tu programa de estudios tenía este objetivo?
No   ☐ (Indica con ✓ junto a "no")
Sí   ☐ (Indica con ✓ junto a "sí")
Si has marcado "sí", por favor, explica lo que recuerdes de esa asignatura:

Formación post-universitaria

6 ¿Has realizado algún curso que tenga como objetivo tu formación en la enseñanza de la expresión escrita en inglés?
No   ☐ (Indica con ✓ junto a "no")
Sí   ☐ (Indica con ✓ junto a "sí")

Si has marcado "sí", completa con una breve descripción del curso y, si lo recuerdas, el responsable de su organización e impartición (por ejemplo, CPR). Indica también la duración del curso en número de horas (con ✓):

Curso 1:
Menos de 5 horas
Entre 5 y 15 horas
Entre 15 y 30 horas
Más de 30 horas
Curso 2:
Menos de 5 horas
Entre 5 y 15 horas
Entre 15 y 30 horas
Más de 30 horas
Curso 3:
Menos de 5 horas
Entre 5 y 15 horas
Entre 15 y 30 horas
Más de 30 horas

7 Si no has realizado ningún curso sobre la enseñanza de la expresión escrita en inglés, pero te has formado en este aspecto de manera autodidacta, por favor, explícalo en las siguientes líneas. Formación autodidacta mediante...

Percepción de la adecuación de la formación en enseñanza de la expresión escrita en inglés

8 Consideras que, *en términos cuantitativos*, la preparación específica en enseñanza de la expresión escrita para el profesorado en formación (futuros profesores) y en servicio (profesores) es... (Selecciona sólo una casilla, con "✓")
    a) Muy insuficiente
    b) Insuficiente
    c) Suficiente
    d) Adecuada
    e) Excesiva

9 Consideras que, *en términos cualitativos*, la preparación específica en enseñanza de la expresión escrita para el profesorado en formación y en servicio es... (Selecciona sólo una casilla, con "✓")
    a) Totalmente inútil
    b) Muy poco útil
    c) Útil
    d) Muy útil
    e) Verdaderamente útil

10 ¿Crees que el profesorado (en formación y en servicio) debería recibir preparación específica en la enseñanza de la expresión escrita en inglés?
    No ☐ (Indica con ✓ junto a "no")
    Sí ☐ (Indica con ✓ junto a "sí")

11 ¿En *términos cuantitativos*, qué tipo de preparación específica en la enseñanza de la expresión escrita crees que debería recibir el *profesorado en formación*? (Selecciona sólo una casilla, con "✓")
    a) Ninguna.
    b) Una o dos asignaturas en la titulación inicial.
    c) Una o dos asignaturas en la titulación de postgrado.
    d) Una o dos asignaturas en la titulación inicial y otras tantas en la de postgrado.
    e) Más de dos asignaturas en la titulación de postgrado.
    f) Otros:

12 ¿En *términos cuantitativos*, qué tipo de preparación específica en la enseñanza de la expresión escrita crees que debería recibir el *profesorado en servicio*? (Selecciona sólo una casilla, con "✓")
    a) Ninguna.
    b) Un curso anual de 10 horas como mínimo.

c) Un curso anual de 10 horas como máximo.
d) Un curso de entre 15 y 30 horas cada 3 años.
e) Un curso de entre 30 y 50 horas cada 3 años.

13 ¿En *términos cualitativos*, en qué aspectos de la expresión escrita en inglés consideras que el profesorado se beneficiaría de recibir formación específica? Ordena de 1 a 5 según la importancia (1 máxima; 5 mínima), a menos que marques (con "✓") la opción "f".
    Si lo deseas, completa el apartado "g".
a) Diseño de cursos/asignaturas para enseñar expresión escrita
b) Planificación de clases para enseñar expresión escrita
c) Selección/Adaptación/Diseño de materiales para enseñar la expresión escrita
d) Utilización de las TICs para enseñar la expresión escrita
e) Tratamiento del error en la expresión escrita
f) Ninguno de estos aspectos
g) Otros aspectos:

La expresión escrita en el inglés como lengua extranjera

14 Indica el orden de importancia de los siguientes aspectos de la enseñanza del inglés como lengua extranjera, en tu opinión. (1, mayor importancia; 6, menor importancia)
a) Expresión oral (incl. pronunciación y entonación)
b) Expresión escrita
c) Comprensión oral
d) Comprensión escrita
e) Gramática
f) Vocabulario

15 En términos de horas lectivas, ¿qué porcentaje debe dedicarse a la enseñanza de la expresión escrita, en tu opinión? (Indica con ✓)
a) Menos de un 10%
b) Entre un 10 y un 20%
c) Entre un 20% y un 40%
d) Otros:
    Si lo deseas, completa o matiza tu respuesta:

16 ¿Qué tipos de texto practican los alumnos de las asignaturas que impartes? Selecciona tantos como corresponda (aunque se trata de asignaturas de cursos diferentes). (Indica con ✓)
a) Emails formales   f) Esquemas
b) Emails informales   g) Textos descriptivos
c) Cartas formales   h) Textos narrativos
d) Cartas informales   i) Textos argumentativos
e) Resúmenes   j) Textos expositivos

La expresión escrita en las disciplinas no lingüísticas

17 ¿Qué tipos de texto practican los alumnos de las asignaturas que impartes? Selecciona tantos como corresponda (aunque se trate de asignaturas de cursos diferentes). (Indica con ✓)
a) Resúmenes   f) Apuntes de clase
b) Esquemas   g) Textos descriptivos
c) Paráfrasis   h) Textos narrativos
d) Informes   i) Textos argumentativos
e) Instrucciones   j) Textos expositivos

    Otro(s):

18 ¿Con qué frecuencia utilizan tus alumnos la expresión escrita como instrumento para reforzar el aprendizaje de los contenidos de tu(s) asignatura(s) DNL? (Indica con ✓)
a) No la utilizan
b) Una vez a la semana, en clase
c) Una vez a la semana, como tarea de casa
d) Una vez al día, en clase
e) Una vez al día, como tarea de casa
f) La utilizan mucho, en clase y en casa, en distintos tipos de texto

Matiza o completa tu respuesta si lo deseas:

Percepción de la importancia de la expresión escrita en inglés

19 Responde a todos los ítems (a-d) con SÍ o NO. Consideras que la expresión escrita es...
a) un instrumento de evaluación de la competencia en L2.
b) una herramienta para el desarrollo de la competencia en L2.
c) un instrumento de evaluación de la competencia en L2 más adecuado que la expresión oral.

d) una herramienta para el desarrollo de la competencia en L2 más efectiva que la expresión oral.

20 Indica, por favor, qué aspectos relativos a la formación del profesorado en enseñanza de la expresión escrita en inglés no están recogidos en esta encuesta y consideras que son fundamentales para un profesor de inglés como lengua extranjera o de una DNL, según sea tu caso. Esta última pregunta te llevará más tiempo que las demás, pero es la más importante de la encuesta para poder reflejar la realidad de la enseñanza de la expresión escrita en inglés en nuestro país. Te agradezco enormemente este último esfuerzo.
La expresión escrita en la enseñanza del inglés como lengua extranjera:

La expresión escrita en la enseñanza de materias no lingüísticas en inglés:

Appendix 2

Andalucía	http://www.juntadeandalucia.es/educacion/portals/web/ced/actividades-formativas
Asturias	https://www.educastur.es/profesorado/formacion-e-innovacion
Cantabria	https://www.educantabria.es/centros-alv/566-nivel-1/nivel-2/nivel-3/plan-de-formacion-permanente-del-profesorado/39720329-plan-anual-de-formacion-de-profesorado.html
Castilla-La Mancha	http://centroformacionprofesorado.castillalamancha.es/comunidad/crfp/convocatoria
Castilla y León	https://www.educa.jcyl.es/profesorado/es/formacion-profesorado/plan-autonomico-formacion-permanente-profesorado
Cataluña	http://ensenyament.gencat.cat/ca/arees-actuacio/professors/formacio/
Ceuta	http://www.educacionyfp.gob.es/educacion-mecd/ba/ceuta-melilla/ceuta/portada.html
Comunidad Valenciana	http://cefire.edu.gva.es/sfp/index.php?seccion=ediciones&filtro_titulo=&filtro_ambito=001&filtro_nivel=&filtro_estado=inscripcion
Extremadura	https://formacion.educarex.es/cprsite
Galicia	https://www.edu.xunta.gal/portal/es/taxonomy/term/1289%2C1606/all/all
Islas Baleares	http://weib.caib.es/Formacio/distancia/activitats_.htm
Islas Canarias	http://www3.gobiernodecanarias.org/medusa/perfeccionamiento/areapersonal/
La Rioja	https://www.larioja.org/edu-innovacion-form/es/actividades-formacion/cursos
Madrid	http://crif.acacias.educa.madrid.org/index.php?option=com_content&view=article&id=10885:convocatoria-de-seminarios-grupos-de-trabajo-y-proyectos-de-formacion-en-el-centro&catid=11:certamenes&Itemid=25 https://formacion.educa.madrid.org/

Melilla	http://www.upeformacion.es/
Navarra	http://formacionprofesorado.educacion.navarra.es/web/2016/09/01/plan-de-formacion-2017-2018/
Región de Murcia	http://www.educarm.es/plancentrodeprofesores/

Notes

(1) For a discussion of the theoretical principles underlying content and language integrated learning (the name given in Europe to bilingual teaching of academic subject matter via a foreign language), see, for example, Ruiz de Zarobe and Jiménez Catalán (2009), Coyle *et al.* (2010) or, more recently, Genesee and Hamayan (2016).

(2) The number of methodology courses in the TEFL specialization of this master's degree may vary from university to university but, according to our own survey, it ranges from four to six courses, and the number of credits earned by the students range from 20 to 30, as each of these courses is normally worth four, five or six credits.

(3) Bitchener and Storch (2016: 1) define WCF as a 'written response to a linguistic error that has been made in the writing of a text by an L2 learner.' The corrections might address a variety of issues, but the focus of research on WCF has been placed on linguistic errors. Also, research has focused on the potential of the different types of WCF 'as a tool for language learning', from a *writing-to-learn* perspective (Manchón, 2011b: 61).

References

Baines, M. and Rodwell, S. (2014) *Trends 1. Student's Book*. Madrid: Burlington Books.

Bitchener, J. and Storch, N. (2016) *Written Corrective Feedback for L2 Development*. Bristol: Multilingual Matters.

Council of Europe (2001) *Common European Framework of Reference for Languages: Learning, Teaching, Assessment*. Cambridge: Cambridge University Press.

Council of Europe (2018) *Common European Framework of Reference for Languages: Learning, Teaching, Assessment. Companion Volume with New Descriptors*. Strasbourg: Council of Europe. See https://rm.coe.int/cefr-companion-volume-with-new-descriptors-2018/1680787989.

Coyle, D., Hood, P. and Marsh, D. (2010) *CLIL: Content and Language Integrated Learning*. Cambridge: Cambridge University Press.

Cumming, A. (1990) Metalinguistic and ideational thinking in second language composing. *Written Communication* 7 (4), 482–511.

Dalton-Puffer, C. (2008) Outcomes and processes in content and language integrated learning (CLIL): Current research from Europe. In W. Delanoy and L. Volkmann (eds) *Future Perspectives for English Language Teaching*. Heidelberg: Carl Winter.

Davies, P.A. and Falla, T. (2014a) *Solutions Pre-Intermediate. Student's Book*. Oxford: Oxford University Press.

Davies, P.A. and Falla, T. (2014b) *Solutions Upper-Intermediate. Student's Book*. Oxford: Oxford University Press.

Davies, P.A. and Falla, T. (2014c) *Solutions. Student's Book*. Oxford: Oxford University Press.

Dignen, S. (2013) *Over to You 1. Student's Book*. Oxford: Oxford University Press.

Genesee, F. and Hamayan, E. (2016) *CLIL in Context. Practical Guide for Educators*. Cambridge: Cambridge University Press.

Goldstein, B. and Jones, C. (2015a) *Smart Planet Level 1. Student's Book*. Cambridge: Cambridge University Press.

Goldstein, B. and Jones, C. (2015b) *Smart Planet Level 2. Student's Book*. Cambridge: Cambridge University Press.

Goldstein, B. and Jones, C. (2015c) *Smart Planet Level 3. Student's Book*. Cambridge: Cambridge University Press.

Goldstein, B. and Jones, C. (2015d) *Smart Planet Level 4. Student's Book*. Cambridge: Cambridge University Press.

Government of Spain (2013) Law No. 8. Ley Orgánica para la Mejora de la Calidad Educativa. *Boletín Oficial del Estado, Madrid*, 10 December. See https://www.boe.es.

Government of Spain (2014) Royal Decree No. 126. *Boletín Oficial del Estado, Madrid*, 1 March. See https://www.boe.es.

Government of Spain (2015) Royal Decree No. 1105. *Boletín Oficial del Estado, Madrid*, 3 January. See https://www.boe.es.

Government of Spain (2017) *Estadística de las Enseñanzas No Universitarias. Enseñanza de Lenguas Extranjeras, Curso 2015–2016*. Madrid: Subdirección General de Estadística y Estudios, Ministerio de Educación, Cultura y Deporte. See http://www.mecd.gob.es/servicios-al-ciudadano-mecd/estadisticas/educacion/no-universitaria/alumnado/lenguas-extranjeras/2015-2016.html.

Grant, E. and Payne, K. (2013a) *Viewpoints 1. Student's Book*. Madrid: Burlington Books.

Grant, E. and Payne, K. (2013b) *Viewpoints 2. Student's Book*. Madrid: Burlington Books.

Hancock, M. and McDonald, A. (2015a) *Out and About 1. Student's Book*. Cambridge: Cambridge University Press.

Hancock, M. and McDonald, A. (2015b) *Out and About 2. Student's Book*. Cambridge: Cambridge University Press.

Hirvela, A. (2011) Writing to learn in content areas: Research insights. In R.M. Manchón (ed.) *Learning-to-Write and Writing-to-Learn in an Additional Language* (pp. 37–59). Amsterdam: John Benjamins.

Kelly, P. (2015) *Mosaic 3. Student's Book*. Oxford: Oxford University Press.

Langer, J.A. and Applebee, A.N. (1987) *How Writing Shapes Thinking: A Study of Teaching and Learning*. Urbana, IL: National Council of Teachers of English.

Lewis-Jones, P., Puchta, H. and Stranks, J. (2012) *English in Mind 4. Student's Book*. Cambridge: Cambridge University Press.

Manchón, R.M. (2011a) Writing to learn the language: Issues in theory and research. In R.M. Manchón (ed.) *Learning to Write and Writing to Learn in an Additional Language* (pp. 61–80). Amsterdam: John Benjamins.

Manchón, R.M. (2011b) The language learning potential of writing in foreign language contexts. In T. Cimasko and M. Reichelt (eds) *Foreign Language Writing Instruction: Principles and Practices* (pp. 44–64). West Lafayette, IN: Parlor Press.

Manchón, R.M. and Cerezo, L. (2018) Writing as language learning. In J.I. Liontas (ed.) *The TESOL Encyclopedia of English Language Teaching* (pp. 1–6). Hoboken, NJ: John Wiley.

Manchón, R.M. and Vasylets, O. (in press) *Language Learning through Writing: Theoretical Perspectives and Empirical Evidence*. Cambridge: Cambridge University Press.

Matiasek, S. (2005) English as the Language of Instruction in Austrian Chemistry Lessons: Instance of Explicit Language Teaching. MA thesis, University of Vienna.

Pelteret, C. (2014) *Mosaic 1. Student's Book*. Oxford: Oxford University Press.

Puchta, H. and Stranks, J. (2010a) *English in Mind 1. Student's Book*. Cambridge: Cambridge University Press.

Puchta, H. and Stranks, J. (2010b) *English in Mind 2. Student's Book*. Cambridge: Cambridge University Press.

Puchta, H. and Stranks, J. (2010c) *English in Mind 3. Student's Book*. Cambridge: Cambridge University Press.

Puchta, H., Gerngross, G. and Lewis-Jones, P. (2015a) *Quick Minds 5. Pupil's Book*. Cambridge: Cambridge University Press.

Puchta, H., Gerngross, G. and Lewis-Jones, P. (2015b) *Quick Minds 6. Pupil's Book*. Cambridge: Cambridge University Press.

Reed, S., Bentley, K. and Koustaff, L. (2017a) *Guess What! Level 5. Pupil's Book*. Cambridge: Cambridge University Press.

Reed, S., Bentley, K. and Koustaff, L. (2017b) *Guess What! Level 6. Pupil's Book*. Cambridge: Cambridge University Press.

Ruiz de Zarobe, Y. and Jiménez Catalán, R.M. (2009) *Content and Language Integrated Learning: Evidence from Research in Europe*. Bristol: Multilingual Matters.

Simmons, N. (2014a) *Family and Friends 5. Class Book* (2nd edn). Oxford: Oxford University Press.

Simmons, N. (2014b) *Family and Friends 6. Class Book* (2nd edn). Oxford: Oxford University Press.

Swain, M. (1995) Three functions of output in second language learning. In G. Cook and B. Seidlhofer (eds) *For H. G. Widdowson: Principles and Practice in the Study of Language. A Festschrift on the Occasion of his 60th Birthday* (pp. 125–144). Oxford: Oxford University Press.

Swain, M. (2005) The output hypothesis: Theory and research. In E. Hinkel (ed.) *Handbook of Research in Second Language Teaching and Learning* (pp. 471–483). Mahwah, NJ: Erlbaum.

Wetz, B. (2014a) *Key to Bachillerato 1. Student's Book*. Oxford: Oxford University Press.

Wetz, B. (2014b) *Key to Bachillerato 2. Student's Book*. Oxford: Oxford University Press.

12 'Writing Makes Us Professional': Second Language Writing in Argentinian Teacher Education

Darío Luis Banegas, Marianela Herrera, Cristina Nieva, Luisina Doroñuk and Yanina Salgueiro

In Argentina, the context of this chapter, research on second language (L2) writing in initial English language teacher education (IELTE) has examined pre-service teachers' writing through case studies, corpus-based analysis, quasi-experiments and mixed methods. The focus has been on linguistic development evidenced in writing through individual and collaborative tasks informed by genre analysis and grammar. Nonetheless, there is a paucity of studies on pre-service teachers' perceptions on their motivation and identity in relation to L2 writing. Teacher educators and pre-service teachers may wonder about the impact of writing in IELTE and teaching as a profession. In this interest in impact, we believe that motivation and identity exert a significant influence on pre-service teachers' writing practices; thus, it is vital for teacher educators to understand the interplay between writing, motivation, identity and pre-service teachers' investment in their professional identity.

In this chapter, we first review studies on L2 writing in Argentinian IELTE. Secondly, we conceptualize identity, motivation, investment and the role of feedback in order to promote the inclusion of such key constructs among researchers in language teacher education in Argentina. Thirdly, we present our small-scale study carried out in an online IELTE program – the research methodology, findings and discussion in light of our research questions and theoretical background. Our study lends support to the need to include notions of motivation and identity in studies on L2 writing in IELTE programs in Argentina.

L2 Writing Teacher Education in Argentina

IELTE programs in Argentina are offered by state and private universities and tertiary institutions and they are usually between four and five years long (Banfi, 2017; Porto *et al.*, 2016). Their main goal is to prepare future teachers to teach English as another language in kindergarten, primary, secondary and higher education. IELTE programs are divided into three main areas: general pedagogy, professional practice and practicum, and subject-matter knowledge (Banegas, 2014). This latter area, delivered in English, includes knowledge of linguistics, specific didactics (e.g. how to teach grammar or writing within a communicative approach), literature, and English language improvement since pre-service teachers may still need to develop their L2 proficiency. Against this minimal description of IELTE in Argentina, in this section we summarize the topics on L2 writing in IELTE that have attracted the interest of teacher educators and researchers in Argentina between 2003 and 2017.

A brief glance at studies carried out in Argentina shows that one major research topic has often been understanding and improving pre-service teachers' writing through genre-based pedagogy and systemic functional linguistics (SFL). This overarching topic includes: understanding pre-service teachers' voice through appraisal theory in personal disclosure essays (Ibáñez, 2005); lexical resources to convey interpersonal meanings (Di Nardo, 2005); modality (Chiappero, 2006); formulaic sequences in academic texts (Zinkgraf & Verdú, 2015); theme-rheme organization in essays (Cangialosi, 2016); pre-service teachers' perceptions of genre-based pedagogies (Llaneza, 2015); and academic writing in regards to features, challenges and strategies (Camusso *et al.*, 2015). While such studies have yielded significant results for teacher educators, they solely focus on pre-service teachers as writers, disregarding the pedagogical element that defines IELTE programs.

Another important research topic has been error analysis and its impact on metalinguistic awareness. Studies have focused on the description and typification of errors to raise pre-service teachers' awareness of textual as well as broad communication strategies in essays (Ferreras *et al.*, 2005; Frigerio, 2005) and narratives (Tuero & Gómez Laich, 2008). While such studies encourage teacher educators to help pre-service teachers become aware of their own writing processes and accuracy, less is said about how error analysis and metalinguistic reflection impact pre-service teachers' understanding of teaching and learning writing.

Lastly, a third central research topic has been the development of pre-service teachers' collaboration and autonomy to enhance their writing skills. This topic includes: peer-feedback (Orgnero, 2005), self-monitoring and awareness of metacognitive strategies (Dalla Costa & Gava, 2015; González de Gatti *et al.*, 2012); use of information and communication technologies (ICT) to develop higher order thinking skills (Gava &

Anglada, 2015); and sociocognitive skills (Dalla Costa & Gava, 2016). In this regard, identity and motivation are missing, and such constructs could help understand how collaboration and autonomy operate in pre-service teachers' writing processes.

Drawing on the studies reviewed above, research on L2 writing in Argentinian IELTE shows a strong interest in pre-service teachers' writing practices. Notwithstanding, Balbi *et al.* (2003, 2005) have noted that IELTE programs only include the writing of summaries, narratives (short stories), letters, notes and short essays, while disregarding other academic genres, such as book reviews, which may prepare teachers to engage with the academic community as professionals.

It may be noted that while the studies above center their attention on pre-service teachers as L2 writers, overt attention to their motivations and identity not only as L2 users but also as future L2 teachers has not been evident in L2 writing research in Argentina. Thus, the guiding questions in this practitioner-based study were:

- How do pre-service teachers see writing in an online IELTE program in Argentina?
- How do motivation, identity and writing intersect among pre-service teachers?

Against this contextual framework and these guiding research questions, in the section below we review the concepts of identity, motivation, investment and language proficiency as strong features of professional development. Such interdependent constructs have been not fully embraced in L2 writing research in Argentina due to researchers' interests in investigating pre-service teachers as L2 users rather than as future teachers. Therefore this study seeks to contribute to that lacuna in the local literature.

Key Concepts

In this section we review identity, motivation, investment and language proficiency in the field of L2 writing. These concepts can contribute to understanding pre-service teachers' L2 writing practices not just as L2 writers but as future teachers of L2 writing.

L2 writing involves purposes, processes, products, principles, identity investment and creation, practices and techniques (Ferris & Hedgcock, 2014; Hinkel, 2015; Musanti & Rodríguez, 2017; Zhao, 2015). According to Hyland (2009), writing can be researched as a personal expression, as a cognitive process or as a situated act. In the context of our small-scale study, writing was explored as a cognitive process, i.e. writing as a non-linear, problem-solving activity for which writers employ different strategies to represent their own voice and identity while fulfilling the activity. This view helped us understand how pre-service teachers' engagement with writing may have an impact on their own beliefs and future practices as English as a foreign language (EFL) teachers (Yang & Gao, 2013).

Writing and identity are inseparable, as writing is one of the several manifestations of who we are. Identity, in the field of L2 studies, has been defined as 'the set of characteristics uniquely associated with that person. Identity is not singular or unitary but plural; a person has multiple identities, or identity facets (Cummins, 2011: 191), within a composite identity' (Pennington, 2015: 16).

As Pennington's words reveal, identity is fluctuating, in constant negotiation, and shaped by multiple factors, contexts and actors. In English language teaching (ELT), much has been written about language learning and identity (e.g. De Costa & Norton, 2017; Evans, 2015; Norton, 2013), language teacher identity (Barkhuizen, 2017; Gayton, 2016; Kiely, 2015; Pennington, 2015; Varghese *et al.*, 2005) and identity in L2 writing teachers (Hyland, 2007; Lee, 2013; Racelis & Matsuda, 2015). However, the case of pre-service teachers is also worth researching because they are still learners in higher education. They are learning English as an additional language and how to teach the language at the same time, and they aspire to become teachers so that they can teach what they have learnt. Through studies with pre-service teachers in Hong Kong, Trent (2011) observed that 'the trajectory of the pre-service teachers' identity formation relied not only on connecting past and future but also on their perceptions of current English language teaching practices' (Trent, 2011: 540). Trent (2013) adds that learning in teacher education programs plays a crucial role in pre-service teachers' identity and how that learning is coherent with professional practices in the school where they complete their practicum experience. In this process of professional identity formation, English language proficiency development is just as important as developing pedagogical knowledge. In a study with foreign language teachers, Richards *et al.* (2013) found that those teachers whose L2 proficiency level was higher developed more communicative lessons with rich input through their speech and delivered more effective teaching strategies including a greater focus on developing students' language awareness. In this landscape, pre-service teachers may be motivated to write proficiently, and this includes academic writing.

Pre-service teachers' process of L2 teacher identity construction may be influenced by their inner desires to become teachers and inspiring teachers they may have had in their trajectories as learners and as future teachers (Lamb, 2017). Depending on the possible selves pre-service teachers can construct, such as the teacher they want to be, the teacher they are expected to be and the teacher they are afraid of becoming (Hadfield & Dörnyei, 2013), their actions may be driven by numerous factors. Against these notions, we wonder: How much are pre-service teachers willing to do to achieve their sought professional identity? To what extent are pre-service teachers motivated to become the best teachers they can be? To answer these questions, we refer to Norton (2013), who points out that our understanding of identity and motivation cannot overlook the concept of investment. With reference to language learners, the author explains:

> If learners 'invest' in the target language, they do so with the understanding that they will acquire a wider range of symbolic resources (language, education, friendship) and material resources (capital goods, real estate, money) which will in turn increase the value of their cultural capital and social power. (Norton, 2013: 6)

By extension, pre-service teachers' investment in their English language proficiency through academic writing may allow them to acquire better grades in the present and develop a stronger professional identity as proficient language users in the future with greater possibilities for promotion. In this complex process, tutors' feedback acts as a powerful source of motivation. Several scholars in the area of writing in higher education (e.g. Ferris, 2014; Hyland, 2009; Hyland & Hyland, 2006; Lee, 2016; Ruegg, 2018) have extensively examined the role of feedback on L2 students' writing and suggest that tutors' feedback should be a combination of explicit (e.g. marking an error and supplying the correct form), indirect (e.g. asking a clarifying question), form-based and content-based comments, and include praise, criticism and suggestions. Nevertheless, while feedback can be motivating and a source of encouragement, the extent to which students will show active engagement with the feedback and work towards improving their written piece is up to them.

While scholars have focused on the importance of written corrective feedback to L2 writers, not much research has been done on the relationship between feedback and pre-service teachers' professional identity, motivation and investment when it comes to L2 writing. In this chapter, we examine the engagement of a group of Argentinian online pre-service teachers with academic writing in a module aimed at improving their English language proficiency. We explore the impact of the writing experience in their identity, motivation, investment and professional development.

The Study

This chapter is based on teacher research as the study reported was initiated by Darío, who was interested in understanding his pre-service teachers' L2 writing processes. On teacher research in writing, Hyland (2009) suggests:

> Small-scale practitioner studies have always been important in writing research. Often these originate in the desire of individual teachers or materials designers to understand something of the texts they present in

their classes, the writing processes of their students, or the textual practices of target communities. (Hyland, 2009: 140)

In this teacher research study, a group of pre-service teachers accepted
becoming both research participants and co-authors of this chapter. We
discuss this feature in the 'Conclusion' section of the chapter.

Research context

This study was carried out on one module, English Language IV,
which is part of an online distance IELTE program based in Bariloche,
southern Argentina (Banegas & Manzur Busleimán, 2014; Manzur &
Zemborain, 2017). English Language IV aimed to: (1) promote language
awareness; (2) develop critical thinking by approaching different text
genres and topics; and (3) develop reflective and academic writing of pre-
service ELT teachers. The syllabus was organized around six units with
the following topics: gender roles and interculturality through short stories; creativity and critical thinking in education; argumentation; reflective speaking and writing; features and types of academic writing (essays,
reviews); and literature in English lessons. Class activities included forum
participation around a question, a quote or a video, identification of textual features, summarizing and paraphrasing, identification of claims,
warrants, proofs and fallacies, assessing sample essays, process essay writing, process book review writing and reading a novel and writing an essay
based on a theme or character, among other activities. The module tutor's
role was to upload the materials for each unit, run online discussion
forums and provide written feedback on pre-service teachers' assignments. Table 12.1 shows the part devoted to writing development in the
module syllabus and illustrates some of the instructions provided to pre-
service teachers as the units developed. It shows that in terms of genres,
pre-service teachers moved from informal reactions and short texts (summaries) to argumentative texts (essays, reviews).

Participants

At the beginning of 2017, Darío, tutor of English Language IV, invited
45 pre-service teachers from the 2016 and 2017 cohorts to participate in a
study which would examine their perceptions regarding writing and
would include the writing of a text for publication. Twelve pre-service
teachers accepted his invitation. Thus, the study collected data from 12
pre-service teachers; however, for illustrative purposes, only six have been
included in the chapter, and four of those six are also co-authors of this
chapter. By the time they attended the English Language IV module, the
12 participants had completed modules on English language teaching
methodology for young and very young learners (for a complete list of
modules, see Banegas & Manzur Busleimán, 2014).

Table 12.1 Writing processes and products

Unit	Topic	Pre-writing task	Writing task
1	Gender roles and interculturality	Read stories by Chimamanda Adichie. Analyze plot summaries found online.	Choose one of such stories and write a plot summary of 150–250 words. Compare your summary with one already published.
2	Creativity and critical thinking in education	Ken Robinson on creativity. Watch his talks and read the book *The Element*. Discuss his ideas on a forum.	Choose one chapter from *The Element* by Ken Robinson. How is that chapter connected to the need of including creativity in formal education? Please provide a self-contained and well-organized answer.
		Watch videos on critical thinking (CT). Discuss teachers' experiences with teaching CT. Read a research article on CT.	Read an article on critical thinking. Do you think the article makes connections (explicit and/or implicit) between creative thinking and critical thinking?
3	Critical reading and listening	Identify facts and opinions in talks and essays. Summarize and paraphrase authors' ideas. Read and discuss short essays.	Read the research article by Rathert and Okan (2015). Do the authors distinguish facts from opinions? Is evidence used to support arguments? How good is the evidence?
4	Argumentation	Read essays and identify claims, proof, fallacies and warrants. Identify features of visual argumentation.	Choose a controversial picture or ad and analyze it following the features studied.

(Continued)

Table 12.1 (*Continued*)

Unit	Topic	Pre-writing task	Writing task
5	Genres in academic writing	Read reflective texts, book reviews and literature reviews. Identify features. Guided practice on academic vocabulary.	Based on the samples and features of book reviews, read the book *Teachers Research* (Bullock & Smith, 2015) and write a book review of 500–800 words.
6	Academic writing	Read and identify features of academic writing in essays and research articles. Guided practice on academic vocabulary.	Based on the different types of essays described above, write an essay (550–650 words) in which you discuss this question: Should teachers write academic texts and publish them?
7	Literature in the English lesson	Read and analyze essays. Read novels and discuss them through a forum. Read a book on literature in ELT and discuss it through a forum.	Write a short essay in which you explain how the novel of your choice has made an impact on you following the three models proposed by Carter and Long (word count: 600–700). Write a book review of either *Creative Ways* or the *Proceedings of the 1st International Conference: Teaching Literature in English for Young Learners* (word count: 600–700).

Data collection and analysis

The present study embraced an ecological perspective. By *ecological*, we mean that emphasis is placed on participants' relationships in their learning context and therefore data come from their interactions and regular tasks framed in specific teaching and learning processes (Arcidiacono *et al.*, 2009; Banegas & Consoli, forthcoming; Edwards & Burns, 2016). In this study, this perspective entailed collecting data from the regular tasks included in the English Language IV module delivered from March to November 2016 and 2017. Data sources included:

- *Pre-service teachers' samples of work.* In Unit 6, they wrote an essay on whether teachers should write academic texts and publish them. In Units 5 and 7, they wrote book reviews based on titles connected to the program (Table 12.1) with the aim of developing academic writing skills and critical thinking skills. Readers will notice that data focus more on book reviews; this is due to pre-service teachers' perceptions of book reviews as both challenging and motivating.
- *Pre-service teachers' participation in an online forum.* They had to share their reflections around two questions (Do you think that teachers should be proficient in academic writing in both Spanish and English? Do you think that we can benefit from being able to write reflective pieces, book reviews and literature reviews?).
- *One Skype-mediated individual interview carried out in Spanish by Darío with each pre-service teacher at the end of the academic year.* Selected questions included: Which texts did you find more challenging/easier? Did you follow any steps to write the book reviews? What kind of feedback did you find more helpful to improve your writing skills?

Drawing on grounded theory (Hawker & Kerr, 2015; Payne, 2015), the data analysis was an iterative process carried out first individually (each co-author alone) and then collaboratively (all co-authors together) to strengthen interpretation. The process included initial and open coding of the data collected, axial coding and core categories to understand the relationship between writing, identity, L2 proficiency, motivation and professional development. Furthermore, analysis on content and form was applied to examine pre-service teachers' assignments with tutors' feedback. Overall, the emerging core categories were: (a) writing as a stimulating skill that needs to be experienced; (b) teachers as becoming proficient L2 users through writing; (c) enhanced motivation from in-class writing tasks; (d) academic writing as a helpful aid to L2 proficiency; (e) writing book reviews as challenging practices; and (f) the benefits of balanced feedback.

Since there were no differences in the data gathered from both cohorts, the findings and discussions included in this chapter take the pre-service teachers involved as a whole unit of analysis. Six pre-service teachers' data have been included in this chapter as samples of the data obtained from the 12 participating pre-service teachers.

Findings

In this section, we present findings based on the data gathered through the online forum, pre-service teachers' samples of work, and interviews.

Online forum

After the pre-service teachers had read, analyzed and written different text types in Units 1–4 (Table 12.1), they participated in a forum to discuss teachers' language proficiency and the possible benefits of experiencing writing in the module. We identified three categories from their forum posts: (a) writing as a stimulating skill that needs to be experienced; (b) enhanced motivation from in-class writing tasks; and (c) teachers becoming proficient L2 users through writing.

Writing as a stimulating skill that needs to be experienced

The online forum interactions indicate that pre-service teachers believed that writing was a stimulating skill to develop and help develop but that they had to experience it themselves. In so doing, they would explore and reflect on the challenges and opportunities found through writing. For example, one pre-service teacher noted[1]:

> I do believe that teachers should be able to produce any of the previously mentioned pieces of writings for various reasons: 1- because in order to do so, you need to develop a number of skills that a teacher will eventually teach her/his own students 2- it is the best way to understand the process of writing such pieces, to learn how to do it by doing it. In that significative way of learning, teachers understand the steps and processes involved in writing and can therefore, teach them to others. (Ana, September 5, 2016)

Enhanced motivation from in-class writing tasks

The writing tasks included in the module proved to be a source of motivation even when they were assessed as challenging. The pre-service teachers invested (Norton, 2013) their time and energy in the writing tasks as they allowed them to develop their thinking skills. For instance, a pre-service teacher wrote:

> I personally like the challenge of doing some research on a given topic reading diverse authors and then reflect on it so as to develop my own critical idea about it. [...] I don't find writing any piece of academic

writing (essay, book review, critique, reflective writing, and so on) easy ... as I said before, they are always a challenge and time-consuming tasks, although I still enjoy writing them! ;) (Andy, September 7, 2016)

Teachers becoming proficient L2 users through writing

Proficiency in writing was perceived as a feature of effective teachers. In other words, teachers' professional identity seemed to be measured by their writing. In one forum post, a pre-service teacher wrote:

> I consider that as teachers we have to be proficient at academic writing because writing makes us professional and later we are going to teach our students how to write and we have to apply what we learnt. (Cel, September 9, 2017)

The three categories illustrated above are interdependent since they all refer to identity. Judging by the pre-service teachers' comments, the act of academic writing became a source of confidence raising as future professionals. In other words, the first-hand experience with writing, the in-class writing tasks and work on L2 proficiency contributed to their identity as future professionals since writing proficiency and ability to teach writing based on personal experiences was perceived as a manifestation of their professionalism. In this view, motivation and investment operated to help the pre-service teachers achieve that self-image of EFL teachers whose professionalism was measured by their L2 proficiency and teacher effectiveness for teaching writing.

The pre-service teachers perceived academic writing as a motivational drive in their identity construction (Hadfield & Dörnyei, 2013; Lamb, 2017), and it equipped them with further opportunities to achieve higher proficiency levels. The pre-service teachers wished to become their best version possible since they wished to be proficient users of English as it was their responsibility and their learners' right to have a good model in terms of language use. In addition, by experiencing writing themselves, these future teachers felt that they would be in a better position to help their learners with writing. In this regard, the pre-service teachers equated L2 proficiency with teacher effectiveness when teaching writing. This relationship resonates with Richards *et al.*'s (2013) study among L2 teachers, since they found that higher levels of L2 proficiency led to more successful teaching strategies for introducing content, supporting learners' language development and offering feedback. The pre-service teachers' interest in improving their L2 proficiency in writing was evidenced in their tasks. In the subsection below, such an improvement is illustrated.

Pre-service teachers' samples of work

Although the pre-service teachers wrote several text types (plot summaries, reflective pieces, essays and book reviews), attention is given

Teachers Research! is definitely a different book. It was eEdited by Deborah Bullock and Richard Smith in 2015, and it originated at the IATEFL Research SIG Teachers Research! Conference inon April 2014 in the U.K. I consider it may be taken as a resource book for teachers of English as it offers complete experiences focused on different concerns and situations we can usually find in our classrooms today.

Comentario [R1]: Move this to end of the review? Perhaps this could be part of your final recommendations.

The book begins with a short and clear presentation by Richard Smith stating the principles, organization and strategies of the conference itself. Then, an introduction of the nine stories in the book is presented by Deborah Bullock and R. Smith, who outlined the collection of experiences presented by different teacher researchers. They provide the reader with personal engaging experiences to reflect on, and inspiration to his/her own practice. The stories are numbered and presented as different chapters of in the book.

The first story is a research project conducted by Jessica Cobley and Becky Steven, teachers at the University of Western Australia. They explored ways to develop students' fluency through technology that included mobile applications to measure non-lexical fillers and a successful peer evaluation with interesting results.

Comentario [R2]: "research" is uncountable.

Figure 12.1 Celina's first book review

below to book reviews as samples of improvement in academic writing, since the pre-service teachers perceived writing book reviews as both challenging and motivating. This perception is explored in the following section.

In Unit 5 the pre-service teachers first read a guideline on how to write a book review and then compared the guideline with book reviews published in journals such as *ELT Journal* or *Language and Education*. After analyzing the genre of book reviews, they had to write, individually or in pairs, a short review between 500 and 800 words of a book called *Teachers Research!* (Bullock & Smith, 2015). Figures 12.1 and 12.2 illustrate extracts from two pre-service teachers' book reviews with Darío's feedback.

As can be seen in Figure 12.1, Celina struggled with prepositions, clause construction and textual organization at the level of information. Darío attempted to provide balanced feedback (Hyland, 2010), focusing on both form and content through explicit correction, indirect correction

concept the authors want to transmit which makes us think that as future teachers, we ourselves can develop our own TR programs in our local contexts. To conclude, the authors correctly argue that innovation in TR publications is needed; therefore the original presentations and narratives of teachers experiences in the educational research field as well as the editors' idea of providing links to the video recorded presentations encourages new genres of teacher-research publication. We definitely recommend this book to teachers interested in engaging in teacher research, teacher educators and future teachers who want to innovate in developing their own TR publications and share their educational experiences in order to explore new ways of teaching.

Comentario [R3]: This answers your opening questions partially. Good!

Comentario [R4]: New paragraph? This will help you highlight your concluding thoughts.

Comentario [R5]: Wonderful! I felt like I was reading a book review published in a journal. I am extremely happy with your use of cohesion and coherence, the use of subject specific vocab, academic register, and careful syntax.

Well done!!

Darío

Figure 12.2 Luna's first book review

Sections two and six are ~~quite~~ similar ~~in the way both~~as they are both concerned with images. Not only visual images, but the rest of the senses are involved to produce and appreciate similes and metaphors as tools to represent emotions. The activities presented in [chapter section]? two use the literary resources mentioned to create vivid descriptions and to make listeners appreciate interesting experiences. Similarly, in [chapter] six, students explore emotions and make others' emotions be reachable and connected to their own experiences.

Comentario [R3]: Be consistent.

Comentario [R4]: Same here. Either use "section" or "chapter" throughout the text.

Section three makes the teachers examine how the text affects the reader, which seems to be an original view of a literary work. That is to say, not to think about the possible "hidden meaning" of a text, but about the effect on the reader highlighting the concept of reading as a totally active process. The activities in this section are really implicated with creativity as their aims are related to the process of writing and to the understanding the choices a writer has to develop a particular purpose. These activities should be considered the richest and most advantageous as they approach Literature [actively.]

Comentario [R5]: Make this clearer?

Comentario [R6]: What do you mean?

Section Four deals with characters and characterisation. The activities developed in it make students put themselves in the shoes of the characters using a technique called hot-seating. Performing these tasks will allow students to see the world through the character's eyes.

Figure 12.3 Celina's second book review

through questions, and suggestions. In Luna's case (Figure 12.2) we did not observe any significant issues at the level of clause construction. Darío's feedback included suggestions about paragraph construction and praise about cohesion and coherence.

Finally, in Unit 7, the pre-service teachers could write either an essay or a book review of *Proceedings of the 1st International Conference: Teaching Literature in English for Young Learners* (Reyes Torres *et al.*, 2012). More than half of them chose to write a book review. Figures 12.3 and 12.4 show Celina's and Luna's performance.

Figures 12.3 and 12.4 show that Celina and Luna improved at the level of accuracy, paragraph construction and text organization. Darío's comments, framed as explicit corrections (e.g. 'Be consistent' in Figure 12.3) or questions (e.g. 'What do you mean?' in Figure 12.3) referred to aspects of style and clarity. These extracts are illustrative of what the whole group

Each section recommends a different approach to using creative writing in the classroom. To start with, section one focuses on the metaphor of weaving in the writing of a text, specifically a poem. Then section two deals with the use of images in terms of similes and metaphors. Here, the use of all senses and emotions ~~are~~ is emphasized to create a vivid impression in the reader's or listener's mind. Section three is concerned with working with beginnings and endings (and their effects) on narrative texts. In this part active and interactive activities that help to understand the creative processes authors undergo when composing their work [are provided.]

Comentario [R1]: Place this earlier in the sentence? The main verb is too "far away" from the noun activities.

Analytical and practical work is developed throughout the book. Regarding section four, it is related to characte[ri]sation and ways in which this can be explored. According to the writers, exploring characters outside the framework of the literary text by the acting technique of 'hotseating' enhances understanding of how they act and speak in the text. Section five concentrates on the construction of a text and how it can be de- and re-constructed. It is focused on the language of poems in this case and the elements poets use to create a variety of effects. Finally, section six examines the use of personal experiences both as a source and an approach to writing and reading. Here, some techniques explored in previous sections can also be applied in this context, for instance imagery and characterisation.

Comentario [R2]: Keep same spelling either BrE or AmE?

Figure 12.4 Luna's second book review

experienced: improvement in academic writing in terms of syntax, lexis and text development. For example, Figures 12.3 and 12.4 show that Celina and Luna did not find major issues with text organization as Darío's feedback did not refer to placing an idea elsewhere in the text; however, they still received suggestions regarding clause construction (e.g. 'Place this earlier in the sentence?' in Figure 12.4).

Interviews

At the end of the 2016 and 2017 academic years, the pre-service teachers were individually interviewed to reflect on the writing tasks and processes experienced in the module. They were asked about the texts they found challenging or easy to write, how they approached the tasks, and the tutor's guidance in the writing processes. Data analysis yielded three main categories: (a) academic writing as an aid to L2 proficiency; (b) writing book reviews as challenging practices; and (c) the benefits of balanced feedback.

Academic writing as a helpful aid to L2 proficiency

The pre-service teachers found that academic writing helped them improve their L2 proficiency because it motivated them to acquire new words and use syntactic constructions they were less comfortable with. For example, Andy, similarly to her forum post above, expressed:

> Because it's academic writing, then I feel I must use more complex sentences and more specific and sophisticated vocab. I need to sound different from other texts. So writing the book reviews made me pay more attention to accuracy. (Andy, November 20, 2016)

Andy's account above reveals that the writing task acted as a motivation source since it afforded the opportunity to enhance L2 accuracy. It also shows that pre-service teachers became aware of the differences between academic texts and other text types explored in the module.

Writing book reviews as challenging practices

While the pre-service teachers assessed writing book reviews as motivating and beneficial, they also acknowledged challenges which, as exemplified in Figures 12.3 and 12.4, they managed to overcome thanks to practice and feedback. They conceded that ensuring texture, i.e. that the book review was cohesive and coherent and responded to the textual features of a book review, was difficult to achieve. For example, one pre-service teacher commented:

> I had problems with paragraph writing in all my versions. Also cohesion was a problem. Like I had loose, dangling sentences here and there and there was no connection between one idea and the next. (Ana, November 19, 2016)

In Ana's case, she mentioned problems at the clause level, but her major difficulty seemed to be in relation to cohesion, not only within a paragraph but also from one paragraph to the next. While Ana illustrates the frustration reported by the pre-service teachers in relation to some aspects of writing development, other pre-service teachers signaled that the challenge was not language related but task driven as they seemed to lack the thinking skills (e.g. understanding and evaluation) involved in the task. In other words, the cognitive processes that precede and support the practice of writing were deemed as critical and necessary to succeed in the writing task:

> The initial problem was, ok, I have to read and understand the book. I had to make sure that my understanding was ok so that I could summarize it, analyze it and recommend it. (Cel, November 24, 2017)

The benefits of balanced feedback

All the pre-service teachers expressed that they valued being corrected through a combination of techniques, such as explicit correction and replacement or through questions that activated their language awareness. However, they stressed that feedback had to be constructive by including positive as well as negative aspects on both form and content. For example, a pre-service teacher said:

> I valued the corrections that made me reflect, those which said this is wrong and explain why, or say this is wrong, how could you change it? (Andy, November 20, 2016)

Andy's comment shows that explicit correction coupled with guiding questions or explanations promoted language awareness. In the case of Andy, and judging by other comments included in this chapter, sources of motivation to write and improve were triggered by the task, the tutor's feedback, and interest in becoming a proficient L2 teacher.

Feedback also proved to be a source of motivation for Celina. She valued balanced feedback as she could reflect on her strengths and weaknesses without frustration:

> Even though some of my texts came back with dozens of comments, they seemed to show that the tutor said, there's potential here, let's improve this. It was encouraging to see that there were good things as well as others which I had to work more on. (Celina, November 22, 2017)

Finally, feedback seemed to find traction when it focused on form not only at the word/phrase level but also at textual and content levels. The following extract illustrates this interpretation:

> Tutors tend to correct grammar, word choice, collocation, but to me it seems that they don't pay attention to the global text. Is it coherent? Is the content right? Corrections also have to be balanced in that respect. (Luna, November 18, 2017)

Overall, the pre-service teachers welcomed feedback that helped them capitalize on their strengths and reflect on their weaknesses not only at the surface level (word choice, syntax) but also at the textual (coherence, cohesion) and content levels. Such perceptions together with their views on academic writing reveal that this group of pre-service teachers saw academic writing as a springboard to reinforce their professional identity as teachers who (1) were proficient users of English, particularly in writing, and (2) were able to teach writing because they had experienced writing themselves. Such features of their desired identity motivated them to invest time and effort in order to succeed in completing tasks which proved to be both challenging and rewarding as they allowed them to develop professionally and linguistically.

What We Have Learnt

In this chapter we posed two questions:

- How do pre-service teachers see writing in an online IELTE program in Argentina?
- How do motivation, identity and writing intersect?

At first glance, we conclude that the way the pre-service teachers examined academic writing through their professional identities was under constant construction (Trent, 2011). They recognized themselves as future teachers and embraced the learning opportunities provided by learning academic writing as a bridge to achieve their ideal and possible teacher identities (Hadfield & Dörnyei, 2013; Lamb, 2017). In other words, we may advance the view that an IELTE pre-service teacher's identity is the combination of being a student as a future teacher and their professional future self, i.e. the teacher they want to become. Pre-service teachers wish to be highly proficient English language users as they feel that their own learning trajectories will better equip them with pedagogical tools to face their own professional lives. Therefore, IELTE programs need to ensure that pre-service teachers are provided with L2 writing tasks that help them construct their future professional selves. Yet, one new question surfaces: How do identity, motivation and writing intersect in the trajectory of EFL future teachers?

Figure 12.5 represents the synergies at play among the pre-service teachers in the online program under scrutiny. Based on the data analyzed, we advance that pre-service teacher identity, as a composite identity (Pennington, 2015), and with a focus on academic writing, shapes and is shaped by two interrelated factors: (a) pre-service teachers' present language proficiency; and (b) pre-service teachers' perception of future teacher development.

Without attempting to describe the pre-service teacher identity construction process as linear, the pre-service teachers in our study

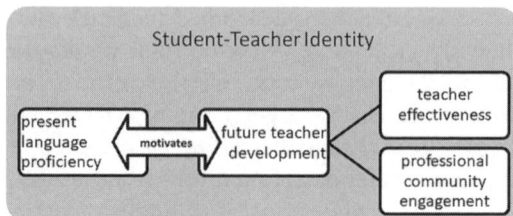

Figure 12.5 Pre-service teacher identity factors

highlighted the importance of language proficiency development as a starting point. It is called *present* because it is where their language practices are situated in their IELTE trajectories. The pre-service teachers' motivation to develop their English language proficiency refers to two aspects that position them as professional language users. On the one hand, their interest lies in being accurate language users in terms of syntax, vocabulary and textual management and, on the other hand, they need to have first-hand experience of writing skills development. Engagement with academic writing acted as a motivational force to achieve the present language proficiency factor in their identity development. Writing academic texts was envisioned and lived as a complex process, a challenge welcomed given their language-driven interests, which required becoming aware of and managing academic writing features not only read about but also found in published articles and book reviews. In the process, Darío's feedback exerted a motivational influence as discussed in Hyland and Hyland (2006). Dario's feedback was a combination of form-based and content-based comments, and included praise, criticism either through explicit corrections or questions, and suggestions encoded as questions, imperatives or assertions.

While language proficiency was part of their present identity as pre-service teachers, they also envisaged it as an aspect of their professional identity in relation to their future teacher development. Following Trent's (2011) conceptualization of the trajectory of pre-service teachers' identity, not only the past and future are influential; the present is key as well. Their past experiences as learners inform their present reflections and future possible selves. In this regard, their present and future visions, projections and selves enter into a symbiotic state through which they give feedback and motivate each other supported by their investment in the process of academic writing. According to our findings, language proficiency development through academic writing was assessed as an opportunity to develop and imagine pre-service teachers' future professional development. The notion of the ideal self in language education as discussed in Hadfield and Dörnyei (2013) is still prevalent among future teachers. As the participants expressed through the interviews and forum posts, being highly proficient in English evidenced through competence and performance is necessary for professional development because it is the foundation of two immanent dimensions in the process of becoming a teacher and being a teacher: (a) teacher effectiveness, and (b) professional community engagement. Pre-service teachers' perceptions of future professional development support the conclusions found in Richards *et al.* (2013). These authors concluded that language teachers proficient in the L2 they are teaching are more effective teachers as they provide learners with more varied vocabulary and balanced feedback on written and spoken tasks, scaffold learning through the use of paraphrasis and synonyms, and adjust their use of simple or complex structures and lexis according to the linguistic level of their learners. Similarly, the pre-service teachers in our study believed that the more proficient and experienced in writing they were, the more effective teachers they would be to scaffold learners' writing skills development, and the more ready to be part of the teaching community.

As discussed above, we suggest that future teacher development as part of the processual construction of teacher identity can be explained through two dimensions: (a) teacher effectiveness, and (b) professional community engagement. However, such dimensions may be seen as two goals placed at two different times in a teacher's career trajectory. In the first place, it could be suggested that the teacher effectiveness dimension is, chronologically speaking, an immediate goal to achieve given its impact on the first professional experiences of a novice teacher. In other words, a novice teacher may be first seen as an effective teacher. In the context of the pre-service teachers' perceptions in this study, teacher effectiveness referred to their capacity to teach writing through the deployment of successful teaching and writing strategies, this latter being made possible through their own prior experience with writing in IELTE. In the second place, the professional community engagement dimension, in contrast, could be considered a long-term goal through which teacher effectiveness and teaching experience can be capitalized, maximized and shared. Through their present interest and belief in the importance of teacher engagement with academic writing, pre-service teachers may develop their need to construct an identity that is rooted in the classroom but goes beyond to reach a wider community of practice. To some extent, being a teacher carries this interest in wanting to belong to a wider professional community of practice which may evaluate a teacher's biography and professionalism through their publications which, in turn, are evidence of a teacher's English language proficiency, teacher effectiveness and overall teacher development.

Despite the limitations of the small-scale nature of the study, our findings and discussions seem to portray Argentinian ELT pre-service teachers as future professionals who: (a) rank L2 proficiency as a dominant feature in their professional development; (b) approach academic writing as a distinctive means for professional development and identity construction; (c) correlate teacher effectiveness with their own L2 writing proficiency and first-hand experiences with skills development; (d) find motivation in challenging writing tasks because they contribute to their professional identity construction; and (e) are reflective and critical about their own writing development supported by balanced feedback. If we compare these features to our review of studies on L2 writing in Argentinian IELTE, it may be concluded that IELTE needs to include meaningful writing tasks which are coherent with strategies for L2 writing and which support pre-service teachers' future professional identity and language proficiency. In addition, further efforts should be invested in understanding pre-service teacher identity and perceptions with the aim of improving IELTE provision in Argentina.

The identity factors and their interplay as shown in Figure 12.5 should be included in IELTE programs in non-English dominant settings. Their presence should inform curricular decisions, syllabus design, material development and teacher educators' practices so that pre-service teachers' L2 writing development becomes a sustainable source of motivation and professional development.

Conclusion

This chapter was not only the result of teacher research but also of collaboration between a group of pre-service teachers and their tutor. On reflection of conducting the study and writing this chapter, including some of those pre-service teachers in the chapter write-up allowed them to expand their understanding of the topic as they learnt about academic writing in Argentinian IELTE and deepened their knowledge about motivation and identity as they made tighter connections between theory and practice from the data they had provided.

Throughout this chapter we have shown that in academic writing in IELTE, pre-service teachers can strengthen and (re)configure their present identity as pre-service teachers and language learners in relation to their imagined future identity as EFL teachers. Notions of identity in synergy with motivation and investment play a paramount role in the creation of needs, challenges and opportunities related to IELTE program enhancement and professional development in Argentina and, thus, should be acutely examined.

In terms of IELTE programs in Argentina and their pedagogical implications, this experience serves to illustrate that genre-specific writing tasks such as writing book reviews can initiate a long journey in a future teacher's trajectory and identity construction, as represented in Figure 12.5. Academic writing should not only be approached through writing long pieces of work such as articles or dissertations in postgraduate studies. Academic writing instantiated through a modest book review could show future teachers that they can engage with writing, improve their professional practice as practitioners and participate in a professional community of practice. Based on this experience, IELTE programs in the Argentinian context and other non-English dominant contexts should incorporate book reviews and reflective pieces and engage pre-service teachers in writing for publication. In this regard, it would be a real incentive, as Rathert and Okan (2015) suggest, for both pre-service teachers and tutors to see their products published and engage with a real audience outside the confines of a classroom. In this regard, collaboration could be explored not only at the level of writing but also at the level of examining writing practices and publishing reports on such examinations.

In terms of implications for future research in L2 writing in Argentina and elsewhere, studies could continue exploring motivation and identity with a focus on the identity factors represented in Figure 12.5, through longitudinal or cross-sectional studies with participants from both online and face-to-face IELTE programs. In addition, researchers could examine the extent to which pre-service teachers' identity as writing teachers is maintained and developed as they become full-time teachers and part of professional communities such as L2 teacher associations. Finally, if pre-service teachers' interest in academic writing and professional community engagement is strengthened in Argentinian IELTE, future research could explore the impact of pre-service teachers authoring articles or co-authoring with peers and IELTE tutors, and the extent to which their motivation is powerful enough to invest time and effort in writing for publication.

Note

(1) Forum posts have been included as unaltered responses to the module forum.

References

Arcidiacono, C., Procentese, F. and Di Napoli, I. (2009) Qualitative and quantitative research: An ecological approach. *International Journal of Multiple Research Approaches* 3 (2), 163–176.

Balbi, M.C., Lothringer, R. and Waigandt, D.M. (2003) Gris de ausencia: Los géneros académicos en la formación docente de grado en profesores de inglés. In M.I. Dorronzoro (ed.) *Enseñanza de lenguas extranjeras en el nivel superior: Balances y perspectivas en investigación y docencia* (pp. 179–181). Buenos Aires: Araucaria.

Balbi, M.C., Lothringer, R. and Waigandt, D.M. (2005) Academic genres in teacher education. In L. Anglada, M. López-Barrios and J. Williams (eds) *30th FAAPI Conference. Towards the Knowledge Society: Making EFL Education Relevant* (pp. 442–448). Santa Fé: ASPI.

Banegas, D.L. (2014) Initial English language teacher education: Processes and tensions towards a unifying curriculum in an Argentinian province. *English Teaching: Practice and Critique* 13 (1), 224–237.

Banegas, D.L. and Consoli, S. (forthcoming) Action research in language education. In H. Rose and J. McKinley (eds) *The Routledge Handbook of Research Methods in Applied Linguistics*. London/New York: Routledge.

Banegas, D.L. and Manzur Busleimán, G. (2014) Motivating factors in online language teacher education in southern Argentina. *Computers & Education* 76 (1), 131–142. doi:10.1016/j.compedu.2014.03.014

Banfi, C. (2017) English language teaching expansion in South America: Challenges and opportunities. In L.D. Kamhi-Stein, G. Díaz Maggioli and L.C. de Oliveira (eds) *English Language Teaching in South America: Policy, Preparation and Practices* (pp. 13–30). Bristol: Multilingual Matters.

Barkhuizen, G. (ed.) (2017) *Reflections on Language Teacher Identity Research.* New York/Abingdon: Routledge.

Bullock, D. and Smith, R.C. (eds) (2015) *Teachers Research!* Faversham: IATEFL.

Camusso, P., Somale, M. and Ziraldo, A. (2015) Academic writing: A key challenge for higher education students. In L. Anglada, N. Sapag, D.L. Banegas and M.A. Soto (eds) *EFL Classrooms in the New Millennium: Selected Papers from the 40th FAAPI Conference* (pp. 96–103). Córdoba: ACPI.

Cangialosi, F. (2016) Exploring the theme and rheme organization of articles written by EFL university students in Argentina. In D.L. Banegas, M. López-Barrios, M. Porto and M.A. Soto (eds) *ELT as a Multidisciplinary Endeavour: Growing through Collaboration. Selected Papers from the 41st FAAPI Conference* (pp. 73–83). San Juan: ASJPI.

Chiappero, M.C. (2006) Advanced literacy concerns: Modality in students' academic essays. In N. Séculi and M. Lembo (eds) *31st FAAPI Conference: Multiple Literacies – Beyond the Four Skills* (pp. 330–332). Rosario: APrIR.

Dalla Costa, N. and Gava, Y. (2015) Self-monitoring based on agreed-on assessment criteria in EFL writing. In L. Anglada, N. Sapag, D.L. Banegas and M.A. Soto (eds) *EFL Classrooms in the New Millennium: Selected Papers from the 40th FAAPI Conference* (pp. 185–193). Córdoba: ACPI.

Dalla Costa, N. and Gava, Y. (2016) The collaborative construction of knowledge through online forums for the development of sociocognitive writing skills. In D.L. Banegas, M. López-Barrios, M. Porto and M.A. Soto (eds) *ELT as a Multidisciplinary Endeavour: Growing through Collaboration. Selected Papers from the 41st FAAPI Conference* (pp. 18–28). San Juan: ASJPI.

De Costa, P.I. and Norton, B. (2017) Introduction: Identity, transdisciplinarity, and the good language teacher. *The Modern Language Journal* 101 (Suppl. 2017), 3–14.

Di Nardo, E.A. (2005) Writing in English: Evaluative resources to express interpersonal meanings. In L. Anglada, M. López-Barrios and J. Williams (eds) *30th FAAPI Conference. Towards the Knowledge Society: Making EFL Education Relevant* (pp. 107–113). Santa Fé: ASPI.

Edwards, E. and Burns, A. (2016) Language teacher–researcher identity negotiation: An ecological perspective. *TESOL Quarterly* 50 (3), 735–745.

Evans, D. (ed.) (2015) *Language and Identity.* London/New York: Bloomsbury.

Ferreras, C., Negrelli, F. and Portela, A. (2005) Error analysis as an interpretative tool: Correcting and evaluating mistakes in written production. In L. Anglada, M. López-Barrios and J. Williams (eds) *30th FAAPI Conference. Towards the Knowledge Society: Making EFL Education Relevant* (pp. 147–156). Santa Fé: ASPI.

Ferris, D.R. (2014) Responding to student writing: Teachers' philosophies and practices. *Assessing Writing* 19, 6–23.

Ferris, D. and Hedgcock, J. (2014) *Teaching L2 Composition: Purpose, Process, and Practice.* New York/Abingdon: Routledge.

Frigerio, I. (2005) Foreign language writing: Errors, communication strategies and interlanguage development. In L. Anglada, M. López-Barrios and J. Williams (eds) *30th FAAPI Conference. Towards the Knowledge Society: Making EFL Education Relevant* (pp. 492–498). Santa Fé: ASPI.

Gava, Y. and Anglada, L. (2015) B-learning in an EFL college class: Creativity, critical thinking and collaboration. In L. Anglada, N. Sapag, D.L. Banegas and M.A. Soto (eds) *EFL Classrooms in the New Millennium: Selected Papers from the 40th FAAPI Conference* (pp. 98–109). Córdoba: ACPI.

Gayton, A.M. (2016) Perceptions about the dominance of English as a global language: Impact on foreign-language teachers' professional identity. *Journal of Language, Identity & Education* 15 (4), 230–244.

González de Gatti, M.M., Dalla Costa, N., Gava, Y. and Kofman, G. (2012) Towards learner autonomy in EFL academic writing: Peer feedback and self-monitoring. In L. Anglada and D.L. Banegas (eds) *Views on Motivation and Autonomy in ELT: Selected Papers from the XXXVII FAAPI Conference* (pp. 96–103). Bariloche: APIZALS.

Hadfield, J. and Dörnyei, Z. (2013) *Motivating Learning.* Harlow: Pearson.

Hawker, S. and Kerr, C. (2016) Doing grounded theory. In E. Lyons and A. Coyle (eds) *Analysing Qualitative Data in Psychology* (2nd edn) (pp. 147–159). London: Sage.

Hinkel, E. (2015) *Effective Curriculum for Teaching L2 Writing: Principles and Techniques.* London/New York: Routledge.

Hyland, F. (2010) Future directions in feedback on second language writing: Overview and research agenda. *International Journal of English Studies* 10 (2), 171–182.

Hyland, K. (2007) Genre pedagogy: Language, literacy and L2 writing instruction. *Journal of Second Language Writing* 16, 148–164.

Hyland, K. (2009) *Teaching and Researching Writing* (2nd edn). London/New York: Routledge.

Hyland, K. and Hyland, F. (2006) Feedback on second language students' writing. *Language Teaching* 39 (1), 77–95.

Ibáñez, M.S. (2005) Entering the maze of academic writing: The role of personal statements. In L. Anglada, M. López-Barrios and J. Williams (eds) *30th FAAPI Conference. Towards the Knowledge Society: Making EFL Education Relevant* (pp. 236–243). Santa Fé: ASPI.

Kiely, R. (2015) English language teacher identity: A framework for teacher learning and professional development. In D. Evans (ed.) *Language and Identity* (pp. 207–228). London/New York: Bloomsbury.

Lamb, M. (2017) The motivational dimension of language teaching. *Language Teaching* 50 (3), 301–346.

Lee, I. (2013) Becoming a writing teacher: Using 'identity' as an analytic lens to understand EFL writing teachers' development. *Journal of Second Language Writing* 22 (3), 330–345.

Lee, I. (2016) Teacher education on feedback in EFL writing: Issues, challenges, and future directions. *TESOL Quarterly* 50 (2), 518–527.

Llaneza, G.A. (2015) Fractured tales for future teachers: Genre-based writing pedagogy in teacher training. In L. Anglada, N. Sapag, D.L. Banegas and M.A. Soto (eds) *EFL Classrooms in the New Millennium: Selected Papers from the 40th FAAPI Conference* (pp. 171–184). Córdoba: ACPI.

Manzur, G.I. and Zemborain, C. (2017) Exploring pre-service teachers' professional identity development through discourse in an online language teacher education programme. In D.L. Banegas (ed.) *Initial English Language Teacher Education: International Perspectives on Research, Curriculum and Practice* (pp. 105–119). London/ New York: Bloomsbury.

Musanti, S.I. and Rodríguez, A.D. (2017) Translanguaging in bilingual teacher preparation: Exploring pre-service bilingual teachers' academic writing. *Bilingual Research Journal* 40 (1), 38–54.

Norton, B. (2013) *Identity and Language Learning: Extending the Conversation* (2nd edn). Bristol: Multilingual Matters.

Orgnero, C. (2005) Peer review feedback: Emphasizing meaning in writing assignments. In L. Anglada, M. López-Barrios and J. Williams (eds) *30th FAAPI Conference. Towards the Knowledge Society: Making EFL Education Relevant* (pp. 91–98). Santa Fé: ASPI.

Payne, S. (2015) Grounded theory. In E. Lyons and A. Coyle (eds) *Analysing Qualitative Data in Psychology* (2nd edn) (pp. 119–146). London: Sage.

Pennington, M.C. (2015) Teacher identity in TESOL: A frames perspective. In Y.L. Cheung, S.B. Said and K. Park (eds) *Advances and Current Trends in Language Teacher Identity Research* (pp. 16–30). Abingdon/New York: Routledge.

Porto, M., Montemayor-Borsinger, A. and López-Barrios, M. (2016) Research on English language teaching and learning in Argentina (2007–2013). *Language Teaching* 49 (3), 356–389.

Racelis, J.V. and Matsuda, P.K. (2015) Exploring the multiple identities of L2 writing teachers. In Y.L. Cheung, S.B. Said and K. Park (eds) *Advances and Current Trends in Language Teacher Identity Research* (pp. 203–216). Abingdon/New York: Routledge.

Rathert, S. and Okan, Z. (2015) Writing for publication as a tool in teacher development. *ELT Journal* 69 (4), 363–372.

Reyes Torres, A., Villacañas de Castro, L.S. and Soler Pardo, B. (eds) (2012) *Proceedings of the 1st International Conference: Teaching Literature in English for Young Learners*. Valencia: Repoexpres.

Richards, H., Conway, C., Roskvist, A. and Harvey, S. (2013) Foreign language teachers' language proficiency and their language teaching practice. *Language Learning Journal* 41 (2), 231–246.

Ruegg, R. (2018) The effect of peer and teacher feedback on changes in EFL students' writing self-efficacy. *Language Learning Journal* 46 (2), 87–102.

Trent, J. (2011) 'Four years on, I'm ready to teach': Teacher education and the construction of teacher identities. *Teachers and Teaching* 17 (5), 529–543.

Trent, J. (2013) From learner to teacher: Practice, language, and identity in a teaching practicum. *Asia-Pacific Journal of Teacher Education* 41 (4), 426–440.

Tuero, S.B. and Gómez Laich, M.P. (2008) A comparative study of errors in EFL college majors' writing. In D. Fernández (ed.) *XXXIII FAAPI Conference: Using the Language to Learn – Learning to Use the Language* (pp. 154–159). Santiago del Estero: APISE.

Varghese, M., Morgan, B., Johnston, B. and Johnson, K. (2005) Theorizing language teacher identity: Three perspectives and beyond. *Journal of Language, Identity & Education* 4 (1), 21–44.

Yang, L. and Gao, S. (2013) Beliefs and practices of Chinese university teachers in EFL writing instruction. *Language, Culture and Curriculum* 26 (2), 128–145.

Zhao, Y. (2015) *Second Language Creative Writers: Identities and Writing Processes*. Bristol: Multilingual Matters.

Zinkgraf, M. and Verdú, M.A. (2015) Formulaic sequences involving 'fact' in EAP production: A corpus study. In L. Anglada, N. Sapag, D.L. Banegas and M.A. Soto (eds) *EFL Classrooms in the New Millennium: Selected Papers from the 40th FAAPI Conference* (pp. 58–69). Córdoba: ACPI.

13 Second Language Writing Teacher Education in Brazil

Solange Aranha and Luciana C. de Oliveira

Studies in the area of writing in Brazil have mainly focused on the teaching and learning of this skill, and not on teacher preparation to teach writing (Figueiredo, 2007). For example, studies have investigated learners, teachers, the effects of error correction, evaluation, instructional interventions, social and affective factors and the use of technology in writing classes (Figueiredo, 2007). Systematic investigations into writing teacher education are not available in research on English as a foreign language (EFL) writing in Brazil. Because of the lack of research in this area, we provide an overview of studies that have examined the teaching and learning of writing in order to contextualize the issues that this chapter explores.

Research that focuses on the teaching of writing in Brazil has mainly concentrated on the description and analysis of textbooks (Tenuta & Oliveira, 2012), tasks (Swiderski & Costa-Hübes, 2009) and teaching projects (Reis, 2012) at the elementary, middle and high school levels and in youth and adult education. Socio-discursive interactionism (Bronckart, 1999) and critical pedagogy (Freire, 1974) orient most investigations, since both theories guide Brazilian official documents. Studies focused on university levels, on the other hand, mostly concentrate on the description (Martins, 2014), the writing needs (Vieira, 2017) and the writing patterns (Silva, 2013) of specific discourse communities, based on socio-rhetoric theory (Swales, 2009) and/or systemic functional linguistics (Martin, 1997), or on the description and analysis of writing classes (Ferreira & Lousada, 2016) and of teachers' (Martins, 2005) and students' (Fiad, 2011) literacy, following the New Literacy Studies (Street, 1984). Works grounded in discourse analysis also investigate the teaching of writing in the academic environment, such as Almeida (2011), which is devoted to the writing practices of monographs, dissertations and theses.

In addition to analytical and descriptive works, Brazilian research also considers a variety of approaches for teaching writing. Most of them address genre writing for academic and scientific purposes by undergraduate and graduate students from different fields and disciplines. Machado *et al.* (2009), for example, based on their teaching and research practice in socio-discursive interactionism, designed didactic sequences for the production of academic genres such as reviews and abstracts. Their goal was to help readers develop specific language and writing skills. In their book, Motta-Roth and Hendges (2010) approach the academic genres *review* and *abstract* in addition to *scientific article*. Grounded on socio-rhetoric theory, the authors focus on their rhetorical organization, content, structure and linguistic features, evidencing how each of these aspects relates to the social and communicative purposes of the genres. While the aim of the book is to give basic orientation on how to produce academic texts, it is not directed at one specific academic discipline. Nonetheless, it is still a helpful source for novices, since the activities proposed in each unit invite readers to analyze and produce the genres in their field of study, giving them guidance in understanding the writing practice of their peers. Aranha (2009) has also worked at university level to discuss the items of a syllabus to be taught for specific areas and discusses how contextual issues influence teaching strategies and contents.

At the elementary and secondary levels, little research has been carried out. Souza (2017) studied the specificities and needs of her context and worked with the genre *school summary* with students in the second year of a technical high school. Because of the detailed curriculum presented by the author, her work serves as a methodological guide for teaching writing (and reading) at basic levels of education. Also working at this level, Teles (2010) proposed an educational sequence for the teaching of the genre *message* for fourth graders from an elementary school in northern Brazil. The goal was to investigate the writing process of the students and identify the nature of the difficulties they were encountering in order to work on ways to overcome them. Although the objective of the research was fulfilled, some methodological procedures contradicted the theory adopted by the author – socio-discursive interactionism. The obligatory use of an image in the textual production revealed a prescriptive rather than a descriptive teaching orientation of the genre. In addition, no didactic transposition of the genre was developed, and there was no educational model of the genre guiding the design of the educational sequence.

Eliminating the conflicts between theory and practice among pre-service teachers was the main goal of Tinoco (2008). The author proposed working with a literacy project for high school students from the Northeast of Brazil as a means of both developing students' agency and leadership through writing in their mother tongue and contributing to the preparation of pre-service teachers for the teaching of writing in light of New Literacy Studies. Her work is one of the few investigations in Brazil conducted in the context of teacher education. The literacy project was planned, conducted and evaluated by undergraduates in *Letras*, during the course *Estágio Supervisionado I* (Supervised Student Teaching I) under her supervision. Her findings show that literacy projects are pertinent to teacher education when teachers seek to widen their views on literacy aspects. However, due to the complexity of teaching one's mother tongue, in-service courses should follow the discussions presented during the pre-service phase.

One of the few research studies (Kleiman, 2009) that focuses on the preparation of pre-service teachers at university settings examines teacher educators' actions in pre-service teacher education. Kleiman's objectives were to understand how, when and why the teaching practices at the university prepare teachers, with their multiple literacy approaches, forms of reading and sharing of cultural tools. She investigates the identity of literacy teachers and professors in education and language teaching for undergraduate or continuing education.

According to a renowned Brazilian scholar, Professor Antonieta Alba Celani (2001), teachers must constantly educate themselves, focusing on learning more about effective practices and integrating theory and practice into their teaching. The foreign language teacher must be reflexive and critical. The author explains that it is the role of universities to educate these professionals, but the issue with the current educational system is that, in most universities, courses such as didactics, philosophy of education and psychology of education are not integrated. They also do not connect to the practicum courses that are part of the curriculum. Most students do not see any relevance in these courses, since these are taught from the perspective of teaching as transmission of knowledge. Teaching pre-service teachers how to teach writing appears to be part of this critical education and the pursuit of critical thinking and acting among teachers (Meurer *et al.*, 2005; Motta-Roth & Hendges, 2010).

In the Brazilian context, the teaching of academic writing is somewhat developed in graduate courses – not only the *Letras* ones – but little is known about initiatives that include other genres students may need in their lives, let alone those aimed at discussing writing theories future teachers may use in the classroom in junior and high schools.

Universities are responsible for preparing foreign language teachers (Volpi, 2001). Teacher education should include a good theoretical foundation, as well as the integration of theory and practice, with a supervised internship component that allows pre-service teachers to observe and discuss how theory is applied in the classroom. Pre-service teachers should also practice in the classroom, in order to familiarize themselves with the kind of school where they will be working. Volpi adds that training should also give emphasis to improving pre-service teachers' intercultural sensitivity, since they will act as bridges that connect different cultures.

The vast area of writing, teaching writing for specific purposes and preparing pre-service teachers to teach writing is crucial. Concerns about teacher preparation and the relevance of teachers in forming new citizens are present in many papers and projects. It seems that the lack of attention to research on writing teacher education in Brazil stems from the fact that the goal of universities is to prepare teachers for writing as a skill, rather than being concerned with preparing them to teach writing to their future students. In addition, attention to writing instruction is restricted to academic courses that have specific disciplines, guided by institutional practices and guidance. It seems relevant that the undergraduate courses consider including disciplines that discuss writing theories and theories of teaching writing in the *Letras* courses, as students will become teachers at different levels and will be required to teach different genres. However, Brazilian major universities do not appear to be aware of this need, since these aspects seem to be regarded as non-existent in the majority of well-known university syllabi.

The purpose of this chapter is to explore program sequences for the major entitled '*Letras*' (literally translated into English as 'Letters') in the main five macro-regions in Brazil to determine what kind of formal instruction pre-service teachers have to teach writing, if any. Our goal is to examine whether teacher education courses and language courses include teacher education for teaching writing. First, we contextualize the major *Letras* to show the complexities of the degree. Next, we present the methods for our selection of universities and how we examined each program sequence to explore to what extent each of these universities prepares pre-service teachers of EFL to teach writing in their future careers. Then we present recommendations for universities in Brazil to prepare teachers to teach writing.

Teacher Education in Languages and Literatures

The major *Letras*

Before we start to describe the specific major, we will discuss some major characteristics of the Brazilian higher education system. In order to be admitted to undergraduate programs in Brazil, students take entrance exams that are specific to each university system. When students register for these entrance exams they must indicate the major for which they are applying. Public universities receive the highest number of candidates due to their reputation for offering high-quality education free of charge. Competition depends on each major. Students take classes within their major from day one at the university.

The major *Letras* typically prepare students in Portuguese as a mother language (L1) and another modern language, such as English, Spanish and others. It is important to mention that students may apply for *Letras-Licenciatura* (licensure) to become teachers or *Letras-Bacharelado* (bachelor's) to become researchers or translators. According to a national website that informs the population about all the majors and their respective job markets (Guia do Estudante, 2017), aimed at students who are about to decide which one to pursue, students who major in *Letras* are dedicated to studying Portuguese and foreign languages and literature. Students usually specialize in a modern language but can also focus on a classical language such as Latin or Greek (Guia do Estudante, 2017). If students choose licensure, the main type of work is in public or private elementary or secondary schools as well as private language schools dedicated solely to the teaching of languages. Some of these licensed professionals choose to give private language classes, via Skype or other online platforms or face-to-face. They may also teach languages in factories that require Portuguese for international workers and English for Brazilian workers, for which language for specific purposes courses are designed. Other job opportunities include those with publishing companies so the professional may prepare original publications or revise and translate scientific and academic texts, and in industry where professionals may become interpreters and bilingual assistants. In addition, professionals may work as independent editors who do orthographic and grammatical revisions of texts. These professionals are also in demand to do movie subtitles for film production companies and software translations for computer companies. In this case, the students do *Letras-Bacharelado*, in order to become translators.

The major, in general, may include diverse content areas such as literary analysis, textual production, translation, and research on the evolution and use of languages. Theoretical subjects may include literary theory, phonology, morphology, semantics, Portuguese language, Brazilian literature and Portuguese literature. In some universities, as soon as students have taken the entrance exam, they may choose their preferred modern or classical language of specialization. In the majority of universities, students have to take Portuguese as a mother language and specialize in that language and are able to choose a modern or classical language in addition to Portuguese. In some universities, students only choose a modern or classical language after they have taken the main courses. The vast majority of universities have licensure programs to prepare teachers and a compulsory practicum experience and, in some, a final paper to conclude the program. The typical duration of the program is four years.

Issues with teacher education

The details above about the major show some difficulties in the preparation of professionals graduating with this degree. The fact that the program may not only be dedicated to teacher education and the necessity of opening new markets for graduates shows a complex scenario about the status of the profession. In addition, teacher education programs in general, not only within languages, have been systematically losing students, with spots not filled in many of them. Teachers are socially underestimated and low paid, in-service professional development is almost non-existent and violence in schools is rampant, among other elements of a scenario that is not promising for individuals who want to become teachers. A recent survey shows that the choice/search for licensure courses dropped 10% from 2010 to 2016 and 7.6% of students actually finished the majors they were enrolled in. The same survey shows that only 39.5% of graduate students are working in jobs related to their majors (Último Segundo, 2017).

A second and related issue relates to the politics of teacher education which have been downgraded systematically since the impeachment of former President Dilma Rousseff. In the second semester of 2017, the government announced a new approach to teacher education and proposed the 'Política Nacional de Formação de Professores' (National Policy of Teacher Education), which has encountered severe criticism from scholars and educators. In theory, the proposal aims at improving teacher education, but in practice, undergraduate students in different fields would be allowed to teach public school students as part of their studies. This proposal lacks clear guidelines for pre-service teachers and does not set clear standards for universities. Critics suggest that the government would save money in hiring teachers who graduated from a teacher education program, who would be replaced by undergraduate students of any field still taking courses. Nothing has been formally approved yet, but if we consider what has been happening in terms of laws after the impeachment, approval of a law that dismantles significant efforts in teacher education does not seem unlikely.

A common national curriculum seems, at a first glance, very tempting. However, critics argue that, due to the severe differences among regions and the diversity of needs related to the job market, social relationships and international communication, such a document would certainly deprive local communities.

Although the contexts are diverse in terms of students' social and economic levels and cultural and educational backgrounds, professors' qualifications (in the North region, for example, none of the professors responsible for educating teachers holds a PhD), and objectives (since each IES – Instituição de Ensino Superior – is relatively autonomous in proposing its syllabi), each and every course is organized around mandatory and elective subjects.

Method of Pedagogical Program Sequence and Syllabus Analysis

We selected the program sequences and official documents about the English language teaching of a university from each of the five macro-regions of Brazil. It is important to emphasize that the economic and social differences among the regions in Brazil are enormous. The Southeast represents the most developed region, whereas the North and Northeast represent the least developed. Representing the North region, we are analyzing the program from UFAC (Universidade Federal do Acre); in the South region, UFSM (Universidade Federal de Santa Maria); in the Northeast, UFPI (Universidade Federal do Piauí); in the Southeast, UNESP-IBILCE (Universidade Estadual Paulista, São José do Rio Preto Campus); and in the Middle-West, UFG (Universidade Estadual de Goiás). Except for the Southeast region (a state university), all the others are federal universities. UNESP and UFG hold a five-star category according to the Guia do Estudante (2017), UFSM holds four and UFAC and UFPI hold three. This star categorization is based on the Conceito Preliminar de Curso (CPC; Preliminary Course Concept), which is sort of x-ray of courses that considers quality indicators such as the grades students get at the Exame Nacional de Desempenho de Estudantes (ENADE; National Exam of Students' Performance), the academic profile of professors as well as their work regime, and how students evaluate the course's environment, infrastructure and quality of education. This categorization in the mentioned regions is predictable, as social and economic issues influence the quality of education. While the per capita income in São Paulo State, represented by UNESP, is R$1,516.21, it is R$744.67 in Rio Branco, represented by UFAC, and R$757.57 in Teresina, represented by UFPI (Terra, 2018).

In terms of student population, UNESP has 340 students in two shifts, divided into four foreign languages – Italian, English, French and Spanish, while UFAC opens 50 spots a year for each of the five languages offered – English, Portuguese, Spanish, French and Libras (Sign Language) – with a total of 250 students entering the courses per year. The number of graduate students, however, is almost half of those who enter. The difference is rampant in terms of structure: at UNESP the English course has 17 students in a class, whereas UFAC opens 50 places in the same class. The samples encompass different national categories and are representative of the country.

The selection used convenience sampling (Lavrakas, 2008) because the universities selected were convenient sources of data. We knew professors at each of these universities and so contacted them via email to request the sequences for the programs in which they taught. Our data analysis used the following procedure: after we received access to program sequences and the information contained in each, we searched for specific courses that focused on writing instruction and the teaching of writing. We were interested in the content of each course and how they addressed writing instruction, i.e. what aspects of writing the courses addressed.

First, we looked at each pedagogical program sequence, known in Brazil as Projeto Pedagógico de Curso (PPC), the official document that establishes which courses students are supposed to attend, the common core of each *Letras* course. This PPC is elaborated by a group of scholars from that university, respecting the context and the needs faced by that community. This analysis showed that many courses are present in just one university program; other courses are non-existent in certain universities. Secondly, except for the university in the Northeast, we analyzed the syllabi of disciplines that had something to say about English, teaching and writing. Under the same heading – English, for example – the content varied considerably.

Discussion

Our analysis of pedagogical program sequences revealed that most English courses are developed according to grammatical progressions, even though program sequences may provide a different picture. For example, at UFAC, English IX, which is offered during the last year of the course and the main objective of which is to 'deepen the structure of the language,' has the following syllabus in a 45 hour-course:

Thematic Units	Teaching hours
Thematic unit 1 – Morphology 1.1. Inflection and derivation 1.2. Closed and open Class of words	15h
Thematic unit 2 – Words: kinds and functions 2.1. Nouns and articles 2.2. Adjective phrases; adjective clauses 2.3. Relative adverbs; conjunctive adverbs	15h
Thematic unit 3 – Syntax 3.1. Syntactic structure 3.2. Phrases 3.3. Clauses 3.4. Sentences: structure and style	15h

Disciplines at UFSM, on the other hand, are not called 'English'. Each discipline related to the English licensure major is named according to its purpose: discourse and textual analysis in English, reading in English 1 and 2, and oral comprehension, to mention a few. No specific discipline is devoted to writing. Nonetheless, UFSM is the only one of the syllabi analyzed that is not organized around grammatical sequences.

Elective courses may be introduced/proposed in some universities to approach teaching and learning topics but, to our knowledge, teacher education for teaching particular macro-skills, and specifically writing, is not included. Electives may vary from children's literature in English to teaching through technologies, for instance.

UFG, in the Middle-West, has a specific discipline dedicated to writing, but the focus is writing production, not education for teaching writing. Its syllabus implies the development of the capacity to comprehend and express ideas and content through writing in the English language, discourse strategies and the production of various genres. UFSM, in the South, has a specific discipline whose main purpose is to critically reflect and expose the professional, ethical, social and political aspects of teaching EFL in national and international contexts; however, nothing is mentioned about teaching specific skills. Specific disciplines on English phonetics and phonology and functional grammar are also part of the language courses of most of the universities.

Well-elaborated course programs and syllabi can be found at most universities around the country, which employ diverse and updated theoretical references on linguistics, but none of the documents analyzed presents theories about how to teach and assess – skills that we consider crucial for language teachers. It is important to mention that at graduate level, UNESP (the university in the Southeast) has a specific discipline on writing approaches, but only graduate students on MA and PhD courses in applied linguistics have the opportunity to enroll.

Universities also state by law, from the second year onwards, that 25% of the time dedicated to foreign languages, among other disciplines, must be used for practice. The so-called Prática como Componente Curricular (PCC; Practice as Curricular Component) is an attempt to include teaching practice within language courses which, theoretically, would help students teach some of the content that they learn during the course. As mentioned before, each university is free to determine how the hours dedicated to PCC are used.

Following the guidelines for *Letras*, there are courses known as practicum during the third and fourth years. Each course usually lasts 60 hours a year. Each university approaches the course according to their projects and needs. Writing reports based on class observation during this course seems to be a common practice. Actual teaching practice in real classrooms appears to be less common.

According to Silva (2013), in the supervised internship reports, the underuse of reflective writing takes place when the pre-service teachers do not relate their experience in schools to the theoretical knowledge acquired throughout their undergraduate coursework. This is an area that needs to be further explored in universities throughout Brazil and faculty should help pre-service teachers make connections between theory and practice more explicit across the teacher education program.

Proposal to Incorporate Writing Teacher Education

As can be seen from the scenario of *Letras* courses, there is a strong need to incorporate disciplines dedicated to areas that discuss the teaching of the different skills, including writing. We now propose four areas of focus for writing teacher education programs in Brazil which could be embedded across several courses. We know this proposal will depend upon a national effort to change curricula around the country, but we hope this contribution may foster discussion around the theme.

A genre-based approach to writing instruction

Teacher education programs should expose pre-service teachers to the approach commonly known as 'genre-based,' as this influences the teaching of various genres and fundamentally guides the official documents in Brazil, although the approaches may (and should) vary. Since the publication of the National Curriculum Parameters in the late 1990s (Parâmetros Curriculares Nacionais; Brasil, 1997), the concept of genre has steered the teaching and learning of languages. These parameters have been the major guide for educational activities in Brazil. Genres have continued to influence the teaching of languages in Brazil, including Portuguese, English, Spanish and other foreign languages (Motta-Roth, 2008), since the establishment and publication of the Orientações Curriculares para o Ensino Médio (OCEM; Curricular Frameworks for High School Teaching; Brasil, 2006).

There are different orientations, often called 'schools', to genre-based approaches, including English for specific purposes (ESP), the New Rhetoric and the Sydney School (Meurer *et al.*, 2005). Although each school may emphasize different pedagogical emphases, what they have in common is summarized by Hyland (2007): 'Genre pedagogies promise very real benefits for learners as they pull together language, content and contexts, while offering teachers a means of presenting students with explicit systematic explanations of the ways writing works to communicate' (Hyland, 2007: 150).

The genre-based approach inspired by the Sydney School draws on systemic functional linguistics (SFL) (Halliday & Matthiessen, 2004). SFL is a theory of language which emphasizes how linguistic choices realize meanings. This approach uses the notion of the teaching-learning cycle (TLC) as a pedagogical tool for implementation in classrooms (Rothery, 1996).

The concept of a TLC is used to highlight the role of interaction and guidance in learning to read and write texts. The TLC is made up of three phases of activity: deconstruction, joint construction and independent construction (Rose & Martin, 2012). Guided by the principle 'guidance through interaction in the context of shared experience,' a genre-based approach is centered around the guidance provided by teachers in talking, reading and writing about a specific text in the context of a shared experience, such as a common text, movie or reading. Students write about something that they have shared as an activity – a shared experience – which is a critical component of writing. The TLC takes writers through the phases of deconstruction of mentor texts, joint construction and independent construction, allowing students different points of entry and enabling teachers to start at any one of these phases.

We believe that teaching EFL teachers this specific approach to writing instruction, and modeling for them how they would teach writing to their students, would enable them to provide the kind of guidance that students need in order to write different genres across the elementary and secondary grades. Pre-service teachers can learn to write and learn how to teach writing using this same approach. As program content may vary, this insertion could be carried out by either proposing a new discipline or including this approach in English language courses. In both cases, other approaches to teaching other skills are also likely to be included.

Designing, learning and practicing teaching writing

Another integral area for pre-service EFL teachers is practicing developing lesson plans and teaching writing within the teacher education program and during their practicum courses. Pre-service teachers would design lessons for different groups of students (beginners, intermediate, advanced) at different grade levels and contexts, focusing on the teaching of a variety of genres (see, for example, de Oliveira *et al.*, 2018, for some examples of genres to be taught at the secondary level in Brazil).

Ideally, when pre-service teachers take a course focused on developing their writing skills, they could also practice teaching within the course itself through mini-lessons to their classmates or in actual classrooms in local schools. Implementing writing instruction in local schools would be preferable, but we understand that this is not always possible due to pre-service teachers' conflicting work schedules (a lot of pre-service teachers already teach or work in other jobs while completing their licensure programs).

During the practicum course, at least one lesson to be delivered in local schools, where typically pre-service teachers will be teaching for their final year in the program, would focus on writing. This would enable teachers to practice teaching writing with actual students and further prepare them for their actual classrooms. We should consider, however, that the professor who teaches practicum is not necessarily an English teacher, as this discipline involves teaching every foreign language major. In many universities, the same professor teaches students whose major is English, Italian, French, Spanish, German, etc. Ideally, each practicum should be taught by a language professor specialized in the language students are majoring in, but unfortunately this is not the reality in many Brazilian universities.

Participation in the Programa Institucional de Bolsas de Iniciação à Docência (Pibid; Institutional Program of Grants for Initiation into Teaching)

The Ministry of Education (MEC) in Brazil has implemented a program entitled Programa Institucional de Bolsas de Iniciação à Docência (Pibid; Institutional Program of Grants for Initiation into Teaching) in order to encourage teacher education, with grants for pre-service teachers and supervisors in schools, supervised by a university professor. This program has received less attention under the current administration and very recently the government has proposed new directions for the program that are still rather obscure for universities and public schools. The focus of the original program, created in 2007, was to join efforts in teacher education for work in public schools. The program brings teachers who are currently teaching in public schools back to the universities to share experiences with pre-service teachers in different areas and to learn new approaches and methodologies for teaching. This drawing together of public schools, pre-service teachers and university professors is unprecedented in terms of public policies in Brazil.

Pre-service teachers may enroll in the program from the second year onwards, and may stay for three years. The program is present in most universities in the country. Our experience shows that the improvements pre-service teachers have made would not have been possible without this program (see Aranha & Cavalari, 2017).

Foreign language writing assessment

In addition to the areas related to teaching, key aspects for writing assessment should also be a focus of discussion and integrated in teacher education programs. As we have discussed elsewhere (see de Oliveira *et al.*, 2018), writing assessment has not been explored in current policy documents that guide the teaching of foreign languages in Brazil. However, we strongly believe that whenever we discuss and integrate writing instruction in teacher education, we also need to incorporate issues related to writing assessment.

Principles for foreign language writing assessment can be incorporated across courses that address the teaching and learning of writing. These principles, discussed in depth in de Oliveira *et al.* (2018), include:

(a) foreign language writing assessment should be ongoing;
(b) foreign language writing assessment should be authentic;
(c) foreign language writing assessment should be transparent;
(d) foreign language writing assessment should be an essential part of instruction;
(e) foreign language writing assessment should describe student progress over time.

Conclusion

This chapter has presented an overview of L2 writing teacher education in Brazil. We have presented the national politics for assessing *Letras* courses in Brazil, pinpointed information about the syllabi of public universities in the five macro-regions of the country, raised important issues related to majors and contents for teaching and presented a proposal for teaching writing at university level in Brazil. Our discussion of program sequences for public universities representing different regions in Brazil has shown the limited focus on writing teacher education, even in programs that focus on teaching writing as a macro-skill to pre-service teachers. Finally, we have included a proposal for universities that educate pre-service EFL teachers to include more of a focus on writing teacher education in four key areas: a genre-based approach to writing instruction; designing, learning and practicing teaching writing; participation in the institutional program of grants for initiation into teaching; and foreign language writing assessment.

We hope that this chapter serves as a starting point for other discussions of writing teacher education in Brazil and other countries alike. All of the issues highlighted here, especially in the discussion session, should be taken into consideration by programs wanting to incorporate writing teacher education into their programs.

Acknowledgements

The authors would like to thank Bruna Gabriela Vieira, PhD student at UNESP, São José do Rio Preto and Cristiane Rocha Vicentini, PhD student at the University of Miami, for helping with the literature review and references for this chapter. We would also like to thank the faculty members of the universities whose pedagogical program sequences and syllabi were analyzed here.

The authors contributed equally to the development and writing of this chapter.

References

Almeida, S. (2011) *Escrita no ensino superior: A singularidade em monografias, dissertações e teses [Writing in Higher Education: The Singularity of Monographs, Theses and Dissertations]*. São Paulo: Editora Paulistana.

Aranha, S. (2009) The development of a genre-based writing course for graduate students in two fields. In C. Bazerman, A. Bonini and D. Figueiredo (eds) *Genre in a Changing World* (pp. 465–482). Santa Barbara, CA: WAC Clearinghouse and Parlor Press.

Aranha, S. and Cavalari, S.M.S. (2017) PIBID/Letras-Inglês: O trabalho integrado com a escola e as propostas oficiais na UNESP/SJRP [PIBID-Letras English: Integrated work and official proposals at UNESP/SJRP]. *Revista Entretextos (UEL)* 17, 105–121.

Brasil (1997) *Parâmetros curriculares nacionais: Introdução aos parâmetros curriculares nacionais [National Curriculum Parameters: Introduction to the National Curriculum Parameters]*. Brasília: Ministry of Education of Brazil. See http://portal.mec.gov.br/seb/arquivos/pdf/livro01.pdf.

Brasil (2006) *Orientações Curriculares para o Ensino Médio – Linguagens, códigos e duas tecnologias [The Curricular Frameworks for High School Teaching – Languages, Codes and their Technologies]*. Brasilia: Ministério da Educação.

Bronckart, J.P. (1999) *Atividade de linguagem, textos e discursos: Por um interacionismo sociodiscursivo [Language, Texts, and Discourse Activities: Toward a Sociodiscursive Interactionism]*. São Paulo, EDUC.

Celani, M.A.A. (2001) Teaching foreign languages: Occupation or profession. In V.J. Leffa (ed.) *The Teacher of Foreign Languages: Building a Profession* (pp. 23–43). Pelotas: EDUCAT.

de Oliveira, L.C., Aranha, S. and Zolin Vez, F. (2018) Foreign language writing assessment and Brazilian educational policies. In T. Ruecker and D. Crusan (eds) *International Political Contexts of Second Language Writing Assessment*. New York: Routledge.

Ferreira, M.M. and Lousada, E.G. (2016) Ações do Laboratório de Letramento Acadêmico da USP: Promovendo a escrita acadêmica na graduação e na pós-graduação [Actions in the academic literacy lab at USP: Promoting academic writing in undergraduate and graduate courses]. *Ilha do Desterro: A Journal of English Language, Literatures in English and Cultural Studies* 69 (3), 125–140.

Fiad, R.S. (2011) A escrita na universidade [Writing at the university]. *Revista da ABRALIN* 10 (4), 357–369.

Figueiredo, F.J.Q. (2007) Pesquisas sobre a escrita em L2/LE: Algumas considerações temáticas e metodológicas [Research on writing in L2/FL: Some thematic and methodological considerations]. *Anais da ABRAPUI*. See http://www.leffa.pro.br/tela4/Textos/Textos/Anais/ABRAPUI_I_UFMG/language_pdf/lang32.pdf.

Freire, P. (1974) *Pedagogia do oprimido [Pedagogy of the Oppressed]*. Buenos Aires: Siglo Veinteuno.

Guia do Estudante (2017) Letras [Letters]. *Guia do Estudante*, 28 May. See https://guia-doestudante.abril.com.br/profissoes/letras/.

Halliday, M.A.K. and Matthiessen, C. (2004) *An Introduction to Functional Grammar* (3rd edn). London: Edward Arnold.

Hyland, K. (2007) Language, literacy, and writing instruction. *Journal of Second Language Writing* 16, 148–164.

Kleiman, A (2010) *Trajetórias de acesso ao mundo da escrita: relevâncias das práticas não-escolares de letramento para o letramento escolar* [Trajectories in acessessing the world of writing: relevance of everyday practices to school practices]. *Perspectiva, Florianópolis* 28 (2), 375–400.

Lavrakas, P.J. (2008) (ed.) Convenience sampling. In *Encyclopedia of Survey Research Methods* (pp. 149–150). Thousand Oaks, CA: Sage.

Machado, A.R., Lousada, E. and Abreu-Tardelli, L.S. (2009) *Planejar gêneros acadêmicos [Planning Academic Genres]*. São Paulo: Parábola Editorial.

Martin, J.R. (1997) Analysing genre: Functional parameters. In F. Christie and J.R. Martin (eds) *Genre and Institutions: Social Processes in the Workplace and School* (pp. 3–39). London: A. & C. Black.

Martins, A.A. (2005) Memórias de professores: Eventos e práticas de literacia/letramento [Teachers' memories: Events and practices in literacy]. *Revista Portuguesa de Educação* 18 (2), 185–213.

Martins, S.E.C. (2014) A comunicação na comunidade discursiva da Igreja Católica Apostólica Romana: Das Cartas dos Apóstolos a gêneros textuais atuais [Communication in the discourse community of the Roman Catholic Church: From the Apostles' letters to current textual genres]. Unpublished doctoral thesis, Universidade Federal de Uberlândia.

Meurer, J.L. and Motta-Roth, D. (2002) (eds) *Generos textuais: Subsidios para o ensino da linguagem [Textual Genres: Subsidies for the Teaching of Language]*. Bauru: EDUSC-Editora da Universidade do Sagrado Coração.

Meurer, J.L., Bonini, A. and Motta-Roth, D. (2005) (eds) *Generos: Teorias, metodos e debates [Genres: Theories, Methods, and Debates]*. São Paulo: Parabola Editorial.

Motta-Roth, D. (2008) Análise crítica de gêneros: contribuições para o ensino e a pesquisa de linguagem [Critical Analysis on genres: contributions to language teaching and research]. DELTA 24 (2), 341–383. See http://www.scielo.br/scielo.php?pid=S0102-44502008000200007&script=sci_abstract&tlng=pt

Motta-Roth, D. and Hendges, G.R. (2010) *Produção textual na universidade [Textual Production at the University]*. São Paulo: Parábola Editorial.

Reis, R.H. (2012) O discurso do Projeto Paranoá de Alfabetização de Jovens e Adultos – o alfabetizando e a alfabetizanda como sujeitos de poder, saber e amor [The discourse of the literacy development of young adults and adults of the district region of Paranoá]. In I. Magalhães (ed.) *Discurso e práticas de letramento: Pesquisa etnográfica e formação de professores [Discourse and Literacy Practices: Ethnographic Research and Teacher Education]* (pp. 289–312). São Paulo: Editora Mercado de Letras.

Rose, D. and Martin, J.R. (2012) *Learning to Write, Reading to Learn: Genre, Knowledge and Pedagogy in the Sydney School*. Sheffield and Bristol, TN: Equinox.

Rothery, J. (1996) Making changes: Developing an educational linguistics. In R. Hasan and G. Williams (eds) *Literacy in Society* (pp. 86–123). New York: Longman.

Silva, W.R. (2013) Escrita do gênero relatório de estágio supervisionado na formação inicial do professor brasileiro [Writing the supervised practicum report genre in the initial teacher education of Brazilian teachers]. *Revista Brasileira de Linguística Aplicada* 13 (1), 171–195.

Souza, R.R. (2017) Modelo de estrutura retórica para leitura e escrita de resumo escolar no ensino médio técnico [Rhetorical structure model for reading and writing school summaries in technical high school]. *Delta* 33 (3), 911–943.

Street, B.V. (1984) *Literacy in Theory and Practice*. London: Cambridge University Press.

Swales, J. (2009) Worlds of genre: Metaphors of genre. In C. Bazerman, A. Bonini and D. Figueiredo (eds) *Genre in a Changing World* (pp. 291–313). Santa Barbara, CA: WAC Clearinghouse and Parlor Press.

Swiderski, R.M.S. and Costa-Hübes, T.C. (2009) Abordagem sociointeracionista e sequência didática: Relato de uma experiência [Sociointeractionist approach and didactic sequence: Report of an experience]. *Línguas & Letras* 10 (18), 113–128.

Teles, R.S.A. (2010) O processo de produção de textos escritos dos alunos da 4ª série do E.M.E.F. Profa. Maria Nadir Figueira Valente [The process of written texts production by fourth grade students of the school Profa. Maria Nadir Figueira Valente]. In G.P. Silva and D.S. Rodrigues (eds) *Linguagem e educação na Amazônia: Faces e interfaces de pesquisas [Language and Education in the Amazon: Faces and Interfaces of Research]* (pp. 307–335). Tocantins: Cametá.

Tenuta, A.M. and Oliveira, A.L.A.M. (2012) Livros didáticos e ensino de línguas estrangeiras: A produção escrita no PNLD-2011/LEM [Pedagogical books and the teaching of foreign languages: Writing production in the PNLD-2011/LEM]. *Revista Linguagem & Ensino* 14 (2), 315–336.

Terra (2018) *Renda per capita de todas as cidades [Income per Person in All of the Cities]*. See http://economia.terra.com.br/infograficos/renda/.

Tinoco, G.M. (2008) Projetos de letramento: Ação e formação de professores de língua materna [Literacy projects: Action and teacher education of mother language teachers]. Unpublished doctoral thesis, Universidade Estadual de Campinas.

Último Segundo (2017) País terá 'apagão de professores', aponta pesquisa sobre cursos de licenciatura [Country will have 'teacher blackout', survey shows about licensure courses]. *Último Segundo*, 8 November. See http://ultimosegundo.ig.com.br/educacao/2017-11-08/cursos-de-licenciatura.html.

Vieira, B.G.A.M. (2017) Genre knowledge in the needs analysis process: Using a writing activity to assess present situation. *Trama* 13 (28), 29–53.

Volpi, M.T. (2001) Foreign language teacher training in view of new teaching approaches. In V.J. Leffa (ed.) *The Teacher of Foreign Languages: Building a Profession* (pp. 133–141). Pelotas: EDUCAT.

14 Preparing Teachers to Teach Writing in Various English as a Foreign Language Contexts

Melinda Reichelt

Introduction

For those preparing to be teachers of second language (L2) writing, it is important to understand how contextual factors influence writing instruction in various educational environments. This is especially crucial for those who teach or will teach in English as a foreign language (EFL) environments, because much of the research and pedagogical literature has an English as a second language (ESL) bias (Ortega, 2004), and because the parameters for teaching EFL writing differ significantly from those for teaching ESL writing. As Manchón (2009: 202) argues, 'the manner in which writing is learned and taught in FL contexts is dependent upon a whole set of material conditions and social practices that do not necessarily coincide with those of SL [second language] contexts.'

Leki (2001) describes the challenges frequently faced by teachers of writing in EFL contexts. These include common daily challenges, such as large class sizes, finding authentic purposes for writing, lack of resources, lack of teachers who are well prepared to teach writing, and students' lack of experience with L1 writing and lack of motivation for EFL writing. As writing becomes increasingly emphasized and tested in some EFL contexts, Leki notes, students with more resources may advance, while those with fewer resources may be left behind. Additionally, Leki argues, writing pedagogies stemming from English-dominant contexts, including process approaches, may not always be well received in various EFL contexts because they conflict with local pedagogical practices.

Future and current teachers of EFL can benefit from examining how circumstances that are specific to various EFL environments shape EFL writing instruction, in order to better tailor their teaching to the contexts in which they teach or will teach. This is important for teachers being trained in Inner Circle countries who may later teach in EFL environments as well as for teachers of EFL writing who are undergoing training in EFL contexts. Given their surroundings, members of the latter group are more likely to be sensitive to how local factors can influence writing instruction. However, even teachers being educated in EFL contexts will likely be reading research and pedagogical literature that stems from English-dominant countries; often these works advocate writing pedagogy that may or may not be suitable for EFL contexts. Teacher education programs can highlight possible mismatches between what the (primarily ESL writing focused) L2 writing literature advocates, and local pedagogical practices and circumstances that may run counter to these prescriptions.

Casanave (2009) argues convincingly that language teacher education programs do not prepare students well for teaching writing in EFL contexts, even when the teacher education programs themselves are located in EFL environments. She interviewed 12 Japanese master's and doctoral students in English language teacher education programs in Japan who were all working teachers, querying them about their background, coursework, beliefs about L2 writing, application of their beliefs and coursework to their teaching, and teaching practices. Most of Casanave's interviewees said they considered it important for their students to learn to write in English, but many felt constrained by local (Japanese) factors, such as: required curricula that focus on grammatical accuracy and correct translation; test-focused curricula; time constraints; and lack of authentic purposes for writing (which led to lack of student motivation). Many of the interviewees asserted that their master's programs 'did little or nothing to prepare them for the realities of their lives in the Japanese classroom' (Casanave, 2009: 268) because their training condemned traditional teaching in favor of communicative approaches, and because their training lacked relevance to the specifics of teaching in Japan. Many of Casanave's interviewees indicated that they hoped the program would focus more attention on local circumstances and would help them grapple with issues related to purposes, attitudes and motivations regarding writing. Similarly, Lee (2013: 343) argues that 'teacher education programs could focus on helping teachers examine decision-making within the ecology of their work context and consider how they could cope with the conflicting aspects of their work.'

In order to help address a need for teacher education for EFL writing that attends to local circumstances, this chapter highlights how contextual factors shape EFL writing instruction in various contexts throughout the world. It then offers suggestions for educating instructors about these issues.

Contextual Factors Shaping EFL Writing Instruction

A range of contextual factors shape ESL writing instruction in teaching environments around the world. Some of these factors include: local and institutional practices, beliefs and circumstances; availability of resources for teaching EFL writing; the sociolinguistic status of English in the teaching context; and the purposes and motivation for writing, especially in contexts where students have relatively low English proficiency and/or little experience with writing (Al-Jarrah & Al-Ahmad, 2013; Casanave, 2009; Cumming, 2003; Leki, 2001; Manchón, 2009; Reichelt, 2005b, 2009a, 2009b, 2011, 2013; Reichelt *et al.*, 2013; Ruecker *et al.*, 2014; You, 2010). The section below provides examples of how these factors shape EFL writing instruction in a range of different environments.

Local practices and beliefs about writing

Local and institutional practices and conditions related to writing instruction in EFL contexts can vary significantly from those of Inner Circle countries (Kachru, 1992; Kachru *et al.*, 2009). One relevant issue relates to what instruction students have received in writing in their first language (L1). Is L1 writing taught explicitly, or as part of other subjects, or not at all? In some EFL contexts, L1 writing may not be taught per se, and thus explicit writing instruction in the L2 might seem particularly foreign. For example, in Reichelt's (1996) research in Germany, some high school teachers of German indicated that they did not teach writing in the higher grades of secondary education. Writing instruction was, in fact, so intricately interwoven into the curriculum that teachers did not consider it writing instruction, but rather a natural part of text analysis. In the case of the research Reichelt reported in Germany, a strong but implicit focus on L1 writing instruction transferred to strong L2 English writing instruction.

Instructors interviewed in Reichelt's (2005b) research in Poland indicated that a strong tradition of L1 Polish writing instruction does not exist there. In the L1 curriculum, writing is taught explicitly only at the primary level. Later, in secondary school, when Polish students write papers about literature, they write their papers at home and do not receive feedback on intermediate drafts. On final drafts, they receive corrections, a grade and minimal commentary. Hatasa (2011) writes that, similarly, composition does not receive much attention in L1 Japanese instruction in Japan, where the focus moves from the (complex) Japanese writing system and vocabulary in primary school to literature and reading comprehension, with writing serving primarily as a follow-up activity. In contexts where L1 composition instruction has not received attention, L2 writing instructors may not have their own experiences of L1 (or L2) composition instruction to draw on in teaching L2 writing. In such cases, unless a curriculum for L2 writing instruction has been developed that is suitable for that particular context, L2 writing instructors may feel at a loss. They may avoid teaching writing altogether, if possible, or draw on L2 writing pedagogy from English-dominant contexts that may or may not be appropriate for their particular sociolinguistic and educational environment, and that may seem foreign and unfamiliar to students.

Additionally, EFL writing instruction is impacted by the writing traditions, styles and genres that are valued in L1 discourse in the particular teaching environment; in some cases, significant differences exist between local writing values and common practices related to teaching English language writing. For example, Clachar (2000) describes conflicts related to EFL writing instruction at the university level in Turkey. In Clachar's study, some of the instructors she interviewed resented the imposition of Western approaches to writing instruction, including Western rhetorical forms, which they saw as conflicting with students' own styles of writing. They indicated that Turkish writing culture involves understanding, respecting and preserving the knowledge embedded in texts rather than criticizing texts, and that Turkish writing allows for contradiction, subtlety, digression and indirectness. They also argued that if students didn't master grammar and spelling, this would reflect more negatively on the students' perceived literacy skills than would a lack of mastery of Western rhetorical forms. It is important to note that only some instructors in Clachar's study voiced these concerns. Others, she writes, expressed an 'accommodative ambivalence' (Clachar, 2000: 76) towards teaching Western rhetorical forms, sharing some of the above-mentioned worries of their colleagues but also seeing advantages for students in learning Western rhetorical forms, ones related to international communication and socioeconomic advancement.

Similarly, Hargan (1995) describes ways in which local writing practices and values in Italy conflict with the expectations of the typically native English speaking teachers who oversee a thesis-like project written in English by fourth year students in a small Italian university. The EFL writing faculty often complained that the students' work was difficult to read, full of plagiarism or excessive summarization and lacking in explicit argument structures, evidence, originality and voice. Hargan argues that instructors' expectations do not align with students' educational experiences, in which oral exams are more frequent than essay writing, and students lack experience with academic research writing altogether.

Clachar (2000) and Hargan (1995) outline conflicts between genres valued in English-dominant contexts and the genres that are valued and that students have experience with in their specific contexts. Such conflicts can lead to resistance on teachers' and students' parts, or to adaptation to the norms and writing pedagogies of English-dominant contexts, whether or not those norms and writing pedagogies are appropriate in the given context.

Writing instruction is also impacted by local policies related to writing instruction, such as policies regarding error correction. For example, Lee (2013) notes that the in-service secondary school teachers she worked with in Hong Kong experienced tension between their preference for selective, focused error feedback and the school's practice of requiring comprehensive error marking. In some cases, school policies may lead teachers to focus on form in their pedagogy more than they believe is appropriate. More broadly, EFL writing instruction is affected in general by students' expectations and experiences with writing instruction, both in L1 and L2. This includes whether students typically write multiple drafts of a piece, receiving feedback and revising before turning in a final draft. It also relates to whether students know how to engage in peer review. In many EFL contexts, students write only a single draft of a piece of writing. Reichelt (2009b) found in her research in Germany, for example, that most of the heavily weighted writing in secondary school, in both German and English, was undertaken in class, under time pressure. In China, because of large class sizes and heavy teacher workloads, teachers are usually unable to provide individual feedback on intermediate drafts of students' work. However, some instructors in China are experimenting with process approaches to EFL writing instruction, including conducting peer review (Yang *et al.*, 2006). At the university level in Iran, only English majors receive English language writing instruction. They typically do not use pre-writing activities, multi-drafting, collaborative writing, portfolio writing or engage in reading-to-write activities such as summarizing and paraphrasing. Students' low levels of English proficiency, combined with teachers' heavy workloads, make such activities difficult to implement (Naghdipour, 2016).

Availability of resources for teaching EFL writing

In many EFL contexts, there are not enough well-qualified teachers to teach English language writing. In fact, in some EFL contexts, there is a general lack of English teachers, and most have little training related to teaching writing. Additionally, instructor time and energy are in short supply, due to large class sizes and heavy workloads (Leki, 2001). In some contexts, lack of access to technological resources also poses challenges. Besides this, teachers may also have difficulty in finding instructional materials that are appropriate for their students' (often low) level of English proficiency and that appeal to their students.

Class size and teacher workload can significantly affect the implementation of EFL writing instruction. In many EFL contexts, instructors teach multiple sections of large classes, which presents various challenges when it comes to writing instruction. First of all, of course, is the matter of responding to student writing, which can be time-consuming and overwhelming even with smaller numbers of students. Instructors with large numbers of students must consider their workload when assigning writing and may be reluctant to assign significant amounts of writing. Large class sizes can also make it challenging for instructors to implement some activities that are common in ESL writing classrooms, such as collaborative work or peer review.

According to Naghdipour (2016), university classes in Iran can be as large as 50 or more students, and instructors carry a heavy teaching load. Teachers in Iran often feel underprepared to teach writing and have few opportunities to attend conferences or participate in other professional development, which also keeps teachers from experimenting with new ways of teaching writing. Because they receive low pay, teachers often work overtime for extra pay and undertake private tutoring. They are thus reluctant to increase their out-of-class workload by assigning additional writing that must be responded to. Lee (2011) notes that secondary-level English teachers in Hong Kong teach 25–30 English lessons per week, face large class sizes and must adhere to strict deadlines in returning graded compositions to their students. Additionally, they undertake significant other duties beyond the classroom. Elqobai (2011) writes of crowded English language classrooms in Morocco, where there may be more than 40 students in a class. Elqobai explains that imported, competency-based standards for teaching English, including English language writing, conflict with local Moroccan conditions, making the new standards ineffective. She writes that, due to large class sizes, lack of teacher training, inappropriate materials and lack of technological resources, the new standards are unsuccessful. Teachers in many other EFL contexts, including China (You, 2004, 2010) and Jordan (Al-Jarrah & Al-Ahmad, 2013) also face large classes and heavy workloads in teaching EFL. All of this, of course, affects what kind of writing instruction is feasible.

Sociolinguistic status of English

The sociolinguistic status of the target language in a given context affects EFL writing instruction because it impacts learners' perception of the language, and thus students' ideas about the importance (or lack of importance) of learning to write. Relevant sociolinguistic issues include: the role English plays in the broader societal context and in the educational institution where English is being taught; the history of English in this context; the attitudes students and others in this context have towards English; and the role EFL writing plays in the broader societal context and in the institutional setting. For example, Naghdipour (2016) writes that in Iran, although young people are highly motivated to learn English, the Cultural Revolution (following the Islamic Revolution in 1979) led to an insufficient lack of support for and development in English language teaching, which has adversely affected English language writing instruction, making the teaching of writing especially challenging. Elqobai (2011) describes the complex sociolinguistic landscape of Morocco where, when writing in English, her students often first translate word-for-word from Arabic into French (their first foreign language), and then from French into English, which severely constrains their ability to write in English.

In many places in the world, English is used for international communication in research and business as well as for interpersonal contact with people from all over the globe, many (probably most) of whom are not native English speakers themselves. Al-Jarrah and Al-Ahmad (2013) write that in Jordan, English has become the medium of instruction in many university disciplines, including medicine, engineering, science and economics. These authors note that learning to write in English increases students' professional opportunities because of the many roles English plays in the world, including in international organizations and conferences, banking, advertising, tourism and online communication. Thus, because of the global status of English and the roles it plays in the world, writing instruction in some contexts focuses on writing in English for specific purposes and in specific disciplines.

Purposes and motivation for writing in English

In any given EFL context, the sociolinguistic role that English plays is related to the purposes for EFL writing and students' motivation (or lack of motivation) for writing. The purpose(s) of L2 writing and writing instruction exert significant influence on students' views of EFL writing and on what types of writing assignments/genres are appropriate. In L2 English writing undertaken in L2 environments, where students may need to write to further their academic or professional goals, target language writing is seen as a legitimate end in itself (Yiğitoğlu & Reichelt, 2019). That is, since there is a clear need for students to write in English, there are clear purposes for writing instruction and writing. In contrast, in foreign language environments, it may be more difficult for students and instructors to find immediate purposes and real audiences for writing in English, especially for students who are not English majors or who are not studying in an English-medium program. Instead, in many EFL contexts, a primary role of English language writing instruction is to provide students with opportunities to practice newly learned vocabulary and grammatical structures; writing is thus seen as supporting overall target language development (Hatasa, 2011; see also Chapters 9 and 11 of this volume).

In many EFL contexts, one of the most salient purposes for writing instruction may be preparation for standardized exams that test writing. Often, those exams focus on grammatical proficiency, and thus students, teachers and administrators may see fostering grammatical accuracy as a key component of writing instruction (Lee, 2011, 2013). In other contexts, students may see English language writing as an important skill for their future. For example, Tarnopolsky (2000) writes about students in Ukraine who wanted an English language writing class that focused on helping them gain basic writing skills that they could later develop for their own purposes, in their studies and professions. He noted that the students wanted writing assignments to be enjoyable, interesting and fun, valuing assignments that allowed for self-expression and creativity.

The situation, of course, is different for students who are studying at an English-medium university or who are majoring in English. Naghdipour (2016) writes that in Iran, English majors and graduate students in English need English language writing for demanding assignments and exams, other graduate students and professors need English for publishing, and many students need to do well in the writing portions of exams such as the IELTS and TOEFL in order to study abroad and gain more opportunities. Additionally, English language writing is becoming an important skill for Iranians in doing business with the outside world. However, despite these functions of English language writing, Naghdipour notes that students are often more interested in improving their spoken English than their written English. The instructors that Naghdipour interviewed said that in writing assignments, students are typically more interested in improving their grammar than in focusing on more global concerns such as content, audience issues and other rhetorical concerns.

Suggestions for Preparing Teachers to Teach EFL Writing

Given the significant differences between ESL and EFL writing instructional contexts and considering how profoundly local factors can shape writing instruction, future and in-service teachers must be prepared to be sensitive to local factors and able to adapt their writing instruction to them. Although some teacher education programs have courses devoted to preparing students to teach L2 writing, many teacher educators will need to find innovative ways to integrate L2 writing related readings and activities into various courses in the teacher education program (or into staff meetings for in-service teachers). Below are descriptions of activities that can be used to prepare pre-service and in-service teachers for teaching EFL writing. Realistically, very few teacher educators will be able to implement all or even a majority of these suggestions. Instead, teacher educators can determine which activities suit their own program and can be feasibly implemented, and what kind of adaptations are necessary for the local context.

Learning from participating in writing activities

One way to educate pre-service teachers about EFL writing pedagogy is to demonstrate different L2 writing activities in classes where the future teachers themselves engage in English language writing. For example, in a teaching methodology class, students might write an L2 writing autobiography, an L2 learning autobiography, summaries or responses to assigned reading, or research projects. As part of that work, students can be taught strategies for generating ideas, planning their writing, engaging in peer review, and revising based on teacher or peer feedback. Instead of presenting these process approach related writing activities as something all teachers in all contexts should aspire to, teacher educators can analyze the activities in terms of how suitable they are for various EFL contexts, noting how factors such as class size, teacher workload, curricular require-ments, and the attitudes of teachers, administrators and perhaps parents might affect whether and how such activities can be adapted for EFL con-texts. Of course, if the teacher education program is itself situated in an EFL context, discussion can focus on the suitability of these activities for that particular context.

Additionally, as the content for course readings in a methodology class, teacher educators might incorporate readings related to teaching writing in EFL contexts. Teacher educators might find chapters in this book to be helpful for this purpose, as well as sources cited in this and other chapters in this volume.

Writing and discussing case study scenarios

Pre-service and in-service teachers can write and discuss case study scenarios in order to explore responses to the many challenges EFL instructors encounter in teaching writing. Lee (2013: 343) argues that case studies can be used 'to illuminate successful experience of writing teachers and help them negotiate responses to the dilemmas they face in their work.' Future and in-service teachers can be given example case studies as starting points (see Reichelt, 2000) and be asked to write case studies in the form of a story, using the present tense and giving the characters names. The case studies should include dialogue, realistic details and a clear chronology. Case studies should provide enough information that participants can understand the situation, but should also be left open enough to arouse interest and elicit discussion (Owenby, 1992). Then the case studies the participants have written can be copied and distributed in teacher preparation classes or staff meetings. Participants can work in small groups to read and discuss the case studies, later reporting back on their ideas to the larger group.

Investigating the sociolinguistic status of English

Teachers and future teachers can also benefit from learning about the roles English plays in various EFL contexts. If the teacher education pro-gram is itself located in a non-English dominant context, then it is highly desirable for teacher educators to focus on the roles English plays in that specific teaching context. However, even future teachers enrolled in teacher education programs in English-dominant environments would benefit from learning about the role that English plays around the world so that they can be attuned to their future students' needs, desires and attitudes regarding English, English language learning and English language writing. If there is time to treat this topic extensively, e.g. in a course devoted to sociolinguistics, students might read works related to World Englishes (e.g. Kachru, 1992; Kachru *et al.*, 2009), including pedagogical issues related to World Englishes (e.g. D'Angelo, 2012; Matsuda, 2012; Matsuda & Matsuda, 2010). Students might also read sociolinguistic profiles of English in various contexts (e.g. Abouelhassan & Meyer, 2016; Reichelt, 2005a, 2006). They can also conduct research to create a sociolinguistic profile of English in a given EFL context, highlighting the role of English language writing and writing instruction there. In so doing, they can review any relevant published scholarship or online material about that context and can also conduct interviews and/or surveys (via Skype and email, if necessary) with students, instructors and administrators from that context. When conducting this research, they might take inspiration from published sources that focus on the role of English language writing instruction in various EFL contexts, such as Al-Jarrah and Al-Ahmad (2013), Elqobai (2011), Lee (2011), Reichelt (2005b, 2009b) or Tarnopolsky (2000). In their work, students might pursue the following questions, along with others they devise:

(1) What role does English play in the broader societal context and in the educational institution where English is being taught?
(2) What is the history of English in this context, and what attitudes do students and others in this context have towards English?
(3) What role does EFL writing play in the societal context and in the institutional setting?

Finding purposes for writing

In many EFL writing instructional contexts, it is difficult for teachers to find real purposes for writing that students find interesting, relevant and challenging. This stands to some degree in contrast to writing instruction in many ESL contexts, where often students must learn to write in English in order to survive in their studies, the workplace or daily life. Thus, importing writing tasks from ESL writing contexts into EFL environments can in some cases be counterproductive, since the role that English language writing plays in EFL students' lives may be minimal compared to the role it plays in the lives of ESL learners. Careful consideration must be given to choosing, first of all, whether to teach writing at all in EFL contexts and, if writing is taught, choosing tasks that are meaningful to the students in some way. The issue of purposes for writing is an important topic for exploration in teacher preparation courses in EFL contexts.

In some cases, L2 writing specialists have critiqued FL writing instruction for making grammar study the focus of writing instruction (e.g. Heilenmann, 1991). However, in EFL writing environments, where there may be no clear, immediate purpose for writing to an audience of readers, it may be legitimate to use writing as a means of practicing vocabulary and language structures introduced in the class, assuming that students find such work meaningful.

Beyond using writing as a means of reinforcing overall EFL learning, instructors can consider other possible purposes for assigning EFL writing tasks. For example, students might enjoy writing in English as a means of personal expression, writing descriptions of themselves, their hobbies, their families, their studies and other aspects of their lives, perhaps in journal or blog form, sharing with their classmates or others as appropriate. Lo and Hyland (2007) describe a six-week experimental writing program they implemented in an English-medium primary school in Hong Kong. They write that 'the potential of English as a creative and personally expressive medium has been neglected in the primary classroom' (Lo & Hyland, 2007: 221), and set out to increase the students' motivation and engagement by assigning meaningful, interesting tasks that gave the students a chance to express themselves and interact socially. These included the students writing about their most memorable gift or photo, writing a letter to a recipient of their choice and writing a piece about what they do and don't like about their school. Students shared their work by creating booklets, sending their letters if they wished, and having their writing posted for others to see.

Students might also find motivation in writing creative works such as poems or short stories. They might find writing such pieces from scratch overwhelming and so can be given starting points. For example, students could be given a list of words to incorporate into a story, or be asked to write the ending to a story whose beginning is given to them. They might also work in groups to make the tasks more enjoyable. Teachers can use their creativity to develop many possibilities within the field of creative writing (see Reichelt, 1999: 27–28), or what Tarnopolsky (2000: 217) calls 'writing for fun.' Students can also be given opportunities to write for instrumental purposes, if teachers can identify any authentic reasons for students to write in English. Possibilities include email communication, blogs, social media or writing resumes, assuming these are relevant tasks in the teaching context.

Additionally, advanced students, including those whose main field of study is English, might gain knowledge about a field of interest or area of study through reading in English and then writing (in English) summaries and/or responses to what they have read. This can help students learn vocabulary and language structures relevant to that topic, as well as genres and ways of constructing knowledge in the chosen area (see Leki, 1991–1992, for using sequenced writing assignments on the same topic to build content and language expertise). Students might work individually, in groups or as a class to focus on topic that is locally relevant, such as the environment, sports, a local controversy, music, local cinema, endangered animals, water quality, internet security or food safety issues. Students can share their findings with each other and/or share them in an online forum so that they are available to a broader (English speaking) readership. Of course, teachers must always be sensitive to the political and social environment when guiding students in the choice of topics to pursue. Teachers must also be cognizant of their own time limitations when assigning such work, given the labor-intensive nature of responding to student work.

Pre-service and in-service teachers can discuss the difficulty of finding appropriate writing tasks for students in EFL contexts and might then discuss which of the following purposes are appropriate for writing instruction in the EFL context(s) they are familiar with:

- grammar and vocabulary practice;
- self-expression;
- creativity;
- instrumental purposes;
- online communication;
- knowledge-building purposes.

After discussion of appropriate writing tasks for various EFL teaching environments, students might develop a curriculum involving writing for a particular EFL writing context. They could determine what kinds of writing (or reading-writing) tasks and genres would be appropriate for that context. They might also design learning activities appropriate for the educational context, e.g. deciding whether and how to implement multiple drafts and peer feedback, and designating practical ways for teachers to assign meaningful writing without overburdening themselves with responding to student assignments. Such curriculum development work might be undertaken by one or more students in a curriculum design course, for example, if no course exists that focuses solely on teaching L2 writing.

Exploring local practices, beliefs and circumstances regarding writing instruction

In addition to exploring the broader sociolinguistic landscapes in which EFL writing takes place, pre-service and in-service teachers can benefit from exploring local practices, beliefs and circumstances regarding writing instruction. How can teacher educators help their students to understand and adapt to teaching writing in a context where practices and beliefs about writing may be different from those advocated by much of the literature on L2 writing? Teachers and future teachers of EFL might be asked to engage in some of the following.

With a specific EFL context in mind, pre-service and in-service teachers might research local L1 writing traditions and compare them with what they know of writing instruction in L1 English and ESL writing, perhaps consulting sources such as Ferris and Hedgcock (2013). As inspiration, they might examine Clachar (2000) or Hargan (1995), who discuss conflicts between the writing pedagogies of English-dominant countries and local writing practices in Turkey and in Italy, respectively. Pre-service and in-service teachers might extend this line of inquiry by choosing one or more specific EFL environments and analyzing the suitability of implementing various popular techniques associated with ESL writing pedagogy, such as the use of multiple drafts, peer review and collaborative writing. They can be urged to avoid framing EFL writing contexts in terms of deficit and can instead be asked to highlight situations in which ESL writing pedagogical recommendations are unsuitable for particular EFL contexts (see Leki's discussion of 'when it is appropriate to resist the hegemony of English-dominant countries'; Leki, 2001: 204).

Additionally, through discussion, questionnaires and/or interviews, pre-service and in-service teachers might explore the experiences of those who have learned or taught EFL writing, including class members, students in ESL/EFL classes and individuals they might interview through Skype. This can take place out of class or in class, with students reporting back to the group during class. It can also take the form of an in-class discussion roundtable with invited guests who have relevant experience. Students can act as moderators, asking relevant questions about EFL writing instruction that they have prepared in advance. These questions can relate to teaching practices as well as the beliefs that inform those practices.

Pre-service and in-service teachers can also discuss the fact that in many EFL contexts there is a lack of locally produced, locally relevant materials for teaching EFL writing (Tarnopolsky, 2000). Since devising one's own materials is very time-consuming, teachers may be cautioned to move slowly and incrementally in developing and introducing relevant, motivating, writing-related instructional materials.

Dealing with large class sizes

In many EFL environments, classes are large, which affects various aspects of instruction, particularly writing, given the time-consuming nature of responding to student work. Teacher educators can suggest strategies for teaching writing to large classes, such as: assigning frequent, short, ungraded writing that teachers respond to with brief comments; discussing with the entire class the strengths and weaknesses of only a few representative samples of student writing, hoping students can learn from the feedback teachers give on their peers' writing; or occasionally assigning group writing tasks in order to have fewer papers to respond to (Reichelt, 2005b).

Additionally, teacher educators might suggest that teachers of large classes experiment with peer review, preparing and guiding their students, especially through the modeling of peer-review practices – since many students are unfamiliar with the purposes and procedures for peer review. Highly structured peer-review checklists can be helpful for students inexperienced with peer review, who can benefit from guided peer-review activities (Ferris & Hedgcock, 2013). Additionally, large group peer review, in which a student paper is presented to the whole class and the teacher guides students in responding, can be useful in modeling good peer-review practices (see Naghdipour, 2016). Of course, not only can teacher educators describe these types of peer-review activities, but they can also implement and demonstrate the activities when the teachers-in-training themselves undertake writing. It is important to note, however, that in many EFL environments, grammatical accuracy in writing is emphasized over other aspects (Heilenmann, 1991; Lee, 2013); students may have limited ability to provide one another with feedback on language issues, and they may not trust one another's feedback in this area. These issues of the suitability of peer review for EFL contexts can be discussed frankly and openly, so that those teaching or preparing to teach in EFL contexts have a realistic idea of the potential as well as the challenges and drawbacks of implementing peer review.

Although many of us are not fond of the idea of machine response to student writing (Chen & Cheng, 2008; Li et al., 2015), this is also an issue worth exploring with current and future EFL writing instructors, given the extreme demands that responding to student writing places on teachers even with small class sizes. Future teachers might first investigate what such computer programs do and don't do, and read Chen and Cheng's description of the implementation of such a program in an EFL class in Taiwan. Future teachers can then debate the merits and drawbacks of using these programs and consider how the implementation of such programs might play out in one or two specific EFL contexts that class members are familiar with.

Besides making recommendations to in-service and pre-service teachers about teaching writing to large classes, teacher educators can also ask one or more class members to present information from articles about teaching large classes (e.g. Anderson, 2016) and finding appropriate ways to apply the information to the teaching of EFL writing. Class members can also be asked to interview (or correspond via email with) instructors who have experience in teaching writing to large classes. In-service and pre-service teachers can report back to the larger group about the challenges posed by large classes, as well as the strategies teachers use to cope when teaching writing to large numbers of students.

Conclusion

Scholars have recognized the significant differences between teaching ESL writing and teaching EFL writing (Leki, 2001; Ortega, 2004). And, of course, various EFL contexts differ in important ways from each other, based on specific local factors. Teacher educators who work with in-service and pre-service EFL teachers can prepare them for teaching writing by helping them understand and explore how various local contextual features impact how EFL writing is taught and can be taught in various contexts.

References

Abouelhassan, R.S.M. and Meyer, L.M. (2016) Economy, modernity, Islam, and English in Egypt. *World Englishes* 35, 147–159.

Al-Jarrah, R.S. and Al-Ahmad, S. (2013) Writing instruction in Jordan: Past, present, and future trends. *System* 41, 84–94.

Anderson, J. (2016) What to consider when teaching English in large classes. *Voices*, 10 November. See britishcouncil.org (accessed 17 June 2017).

Casanave, C. (2009) Training for writing or training for reality? Challenges facing EFL writing teachers and students in language teacher education programs. In R. Manchón (ed.) *Writing in Foreign Language Contexts: Learning, Teaching, and Research* (pp. 256–277). Bristol: Multilingual Matters.

Chen, C.F.E. and Cheng, W.Y.E. (2008) Beyond the design of automated writing evaluation: Pedagogical practices and perceived learning effectiveness in EFL writing classes. *Language Learning & Technology* 12, 94–112.

Clachar, A. (2000) Opposition and accommodation: An examination of Turkish teachers' attitudes toward western approaches to the teaching of writing. *Research in the Teaching of English* 35, 67–100.

Cumming, A. (2003) Experienced ESL/EFL instructors' conceptualizations of their teaching: Curriculum options and implications. In B. Kroll (ed.) *Exploring the Dynamics of Second Language Writing* (pp. 71–92). New York: Cambridge University Press.

D'Angelo, J. (2012) WE-informed EIL curriculum at Chukyo: Towards a functional, educated, multilingual outcome. In A. Matsuda (ed.) *Principles and Practices of Teaching English as an International Language* (pp. 121–139). Bristol: Multilingual Matters.

Elqobai, R. (2011) EFL class in Morocco: The role of writing. In T. Cimasko and M. Reichelt (eds) *Foreign Language Writing Instruction: Principles and Practices* (pp. 83–97). Anderson, SC: Parlor Press.

Ferris, D. and Hedgcock, J. (2013) *Teaching L2 Composition: Purpose, Process, and Practice*. New York: Routledge.

Hargan, N. (1995) Misguided expectations: ESL teachers' attitudes towards Italian university students' written work. *Language and Education* 9, 223–232.

Hatasa, Y.A. (2011) L2 writing instruction in Japanese as a foreign language. In T. Cimasko and M. Reichelt (eds) *Foreign Language Writing Instruction: Principles and Practices* (pp. 98–117). Anderson, SC: Parlor Press.

Heilenmann, L. (1991) Writing in foreign language classrooms: Process and reality. In J. Alatis (ed.) *Georgetown University Roundtable on Language and Linguistics* (pp. 273–288). Washington, DC: Georgetown University Press.

Kachru, B.B. (1992) *The Other Tongue: English across Cultures*. Champaign, IL: University of Illinois Press.

Kachru, B., Kachru, Y. and Nelson, C. (eds) (2009) *The Handbook of World Englishes*. Hoboken, NJ: John Wiley.

Lee, I. (2011) Issues and challenges in teaching and learning EFL writing: The case of Hong Kong. In T. Cimasko and M. Reichelt (eds) *Foreign Language Writing Instruction: Principles and Practices* (pp. 118–137). Anderson, SC: Parlor Press.

Lee, I. (2013) Becoming a writing teacher: Using 'identity' as an analytic lens to understand EFL writing teachers' development. *Journal of Second Language Writing* 22, 330–345.

Leki, I. (1991–1992) Building expertise through sequenced writing assignments. *TESOL Journal* 1, 19–23.

Leki, I. (2001) Material, educational, and ideological challenges of teaching EFL writing at the turn of the century. *International Journal of English Studies* 1, 197–209.

Li, J., Link, S. and Hegelheimer, V. (2015) Rethinking the role of automated writing evaluation (AWE) feedback in ESL writing instruction. *Journal of Second Language Writing* 27, 1–18.

Lo, J. and Hyland, F. (2007) Enhancing students' engagement and motivation in writing: The case of primary students in Hong Kong. *Journal of Second Language Writing* 16, 219–237.

Manchón, R. (ed.) (2009) *Writing in Foreign Language Contexts: Learning, Teaching, and Research.* Bristol: Multilingual Matters.

Matsuda, A. (ed.) (2012) *Principles and Practices of Teaching English as an International Language.* Bristol: Multilingual Matters.

Matsuda, A. and Matsuda, P.K. (2010) World Englishes and the teaching of writing. *TESOL Quarterly* 44 (2), 369–374.

Naghdipour, B. (2016) English writing instruction in Iran: Implications for second language writing curriculum and pedagogy. *Journal of Second Language Writing* 32, 81–87.

Ortega, L. (2004) L2 writing research in EFL contexts: Some challenges and opportunities for EFL researchers. *Applied Linguistics Association of Korea Newsletter*, Spring.

Owenby, P. (1992) Making case studies come alive. *Training* 29, 43–46.

Reichelt, M. (1996) An investigation of first and second language (English) composition theory and pedagogy at the secondary level in Germany. Unpublished doctoral dissertation, Purdue University.

Reichelt, M. (1999) A cross-cultural perspective on writing curricula. *International Education* 29, 16–42.

Reichelt, M. (2000) Using case studies in L2 teacher education. *ELT Journal* 54, 346–353.

Reichelt, M. (2005a) English in Poland. *World Englishes* 24, 217–225.

Reichelt, M. (2005b) English language writing instruction in Poland. *Journal of Second Language Writing* 14, 215–232.

Reichelt, M. (2006) English in a multilingual Spain. *English Today* 22, 3–9.

Reichelt, M. (2009a) A critical evaluation of writing teaching programmes in different foreign language settings. In R. Manchón (ed.) *Writing in Foreign Language Contexts: Learning, Teaching, and Research* (pp. 183–206). Bristol: Multilingual Matters.

Reichelt, M. (2009b) Learning content in another context: English-language writing instruction in Germany. *Issues in Writing* 18, 25–52.

Reichelt, M. (2011) Foreign language writing: An overview. In T. Cimasko and M. Reichelt (eds) *Foreign Language Writing Instruction: Principles and Practices* (pp. 3–21). Anderson, SC: Parlor Press.

Reichelt, M. (2013) English-language writing instruction in Poland: Adapting to the local EFL context. In O. Majchrzak (ed.) *PLEJ2: Psycholinguistic Explorations* (pp. 23–42). Łódź: University of Łódź Press.

Reichelt, M., Salski, L., Andres, J. *et al.* (2013) 'A table and two chairs': Starting a writing center in Łódź, Poland. *Journal of Second Language Writing* 22, 277–285.

Ruecker, T., Shapiro, S., Johnson, E. and Tardy, C. (2014) Exploring the linguistic and institutional contexts of writing instruction in TESOL. *TESOL Quarterly* 48, 401–412.

Tarnopolsky, O. (2000) Writing English as a foreign language: A report from Ukraine. *Journal of Second Language Writing* 9, 209–226.

Yang, M., Badger, R. and Yu, Z. (2006) A comparative study of peer and teacher feedback in a Chinese EFL writing class. *Journal of Second Language Writing* 15, 179–200.

Yiğitoğlu, N. and Reichelt, M. (2019) *L2 Writing Beyond English*. Bristol: Multilingual Matters.

You, X. (2004) 'The choice made from no choice': English writing instruction in a Chinese university. *Journal of Second Language Writing* 13, 97–110.

You, X. (2010) *Writing in the Devil's Tongue: A History of English Composition in China*. Carbondale, IL: Southern Illinois University/Edwardsville Press.

Index

Note: References in *italics* are to figures, those in **bold** to tables; 'n' refers to chapter notes.

adaptive teaching 20–22
  see also expertise of writing teachers
Akçıl, U. 199
Al-Ahmad, S. 294, 297
Al-Jarrah, R.S. 294, 297
Alagözlü, N. 190
Andrews, R. 85
Aranha, S. 274
Arap, I. 199
Argentina: L2 writing teacher education
  7, 250–252
  identity 250, 252–254
  key concepts 252–254
Argentina: research study 254–255
  data collection and analysis
    258–259
  ecological perspective 258
  feedback 254, 255, 261–262, 264–265,
    266
  findings 259–265
  interviews 263–264
  online forum 259–260
  participants 255
  pre-service teachers' samples of work
    260–263, *261*, *262*
  professional community
    engagement 267
  professional development 266–268
  research context 255, **256–257**
  teacher effectiveness 260, 267–268
  teacher identity 265–266, *266*
  what we have learnt 265–268, *266*
  conclusion 268–269
Arshavskaya, E. 64
Aryal, A. *et al*. 133
Atay, D. 175
Athanases, S.Z. *et al*. 20–21

Bailey, R. 36
Balbi, M.C. *et al*. 252
Bautista, A. *et al*. 95
Belcher, D. xx, 2, 13, 31, 53, 132
Benesse Educational Research and
  Development Institute 72, 73, 78
Bereiter, C. 19–20
Berliner, D.C. 18–19, 22, 25–26
Bhattarai, G.R. 133
Bitchener, J. 247n3
Blanton, L.L. 15
Borg, M. 66
Bostancı, B.B. 199
Brazil: proposal to incorporate writing
  teacher education 281
  designing, learning and practicing
    teaching writing 283
  foreign language writing
    assessment 284
  genre-based approach to writing
    instruction 281–283
  participation in Pibid (Institutional
    Program of Grants for Initiation
    into Teaching) 283–284
  see also Brazil: teaching of writing
Brazil: teaching of writing 7–8,
    273–276
  discussion 280–281
  issues with teacher education
    277–278
  major *Letras* 276–278
  pedagogical program sequence and
    syllabus analysis 278–280
  conclusion 284–285
  see also Brazil: proposal to
    incorporate writing teacher
    education

Brown, G.T.L. 49
Browne, C. 77–78
Browne, C.M. 77
Bullock, D. 261
Burke, K. 153–154
Byrnes, H. 182

Casanave, C.P. xix, xx, 10, 82, 146, 289
Çavuşoğlu, Ç 199, 202
CEFR *see* Common European
    Framework of Reference
Celani, M.A.A. 275
Chen, C.F.E. 301
Cheng, W.Y.E. 301
China: concept development xx, 52–53
    academic conferences 58
    concept formation in writing
        pedagogies: interview findings 61–65
    convergence of everyday and
        scientific concepts 63–64
    critical thinking 63–64
    disjunction between everyday and
        scientific concepts 64–65, **65**
    everyday (spontaneous) concepts 53,
        54, 61–63
    feedback 292
    journal articles 57–58
    National Excellent Courses 59–61, 62
    research design 55–56, **56**
    resources: survey results 56–61
    scientific concepts 53, 54
    sociocultural theory of concept
        development 53–55
    teacher development workshops 53,
        58–59
    teacher workload 293
    discussion and implications 65–68
China National Knowledge
    Infrastructure (CNKI) database 57
Chinese Social Sciences Citation Index
    (CSSCI) 57, 64
Cimasko, T. 2, 3, 11n1
Clachar, A. 291, 300
class size 292–293
    China 292
    Japan 81, 84, 122
    Nepal 132, 142–143
    strategies 300–301
    Thailand 116, 122
CNKI (China National Knowledge
    Infrastructure) database 57

Common European Framework of
    Reference (CEFR) 83–84, 176
    descriptors for writing assessment
        proficiency 84
communicative language teaching
    (CLT)
    Japan 75–76, 78
    Nepal 132, 136, 138
    Turkey 175
computer evaluation programs 301
concept development *see* China:
    concept development
contextual factors 8, 288–289, 290, 302
    availability of resources for EFL
        instruction 292–293
    local practices and beliefs about
        writing 290–292
    purposes and motivation for writing
        in English 294–295, 297–299
    sociolinguistic status of English
        293–294
Cook, M. 82
Corno, L. 20
creative writing 99, 105, 108, 187, 207,
    216, 298
Crusan, D. *et al.* 31
CSSCI *see* Chinese Social Sciences
    Citation Index
Cumming, A. 223, 239
Curtis, G. 197–198

Darling-Hammond, L. 91, 109
de Haan, P. 1–2
Debreli, E. 199
Desimone, L.M. 94
Dewey, J. 153
Dhanasobhon, S. 116
Ding, Y. 57
disciplinary writing *see* Qatar: second
    language disciplinary writing
Dismuke, S. 91
DocuScope 154, 156, 169
Doğancay-Aktuna, S. 175
Dörnyei, Z. 117, 266
Dreyfus, H.L. 19, 23, 24
Dreyfus, S.E. 19, 23, 24

Ece, A. 175
ecologically responsible teacher
    education 10–11, 258, 289
Economou, D. 155

Educational Testing Service 72
Elbow, P. 94
Elqobai, R. 293–294, 297
Ene, E. 126
English as a Foreign Language (EFL)
    see contextual factors; Japan: EFL
    writing instruction; Spain: EFL
    writing instruction; Spain: EFL
    writing teacher education; teacher
    preparation for teaching EFL
    writing; Turkey: role of writing in
    EFL teacher preparation
English as an International Language
    95, 199
English for Academic Purposes (EAP)
    Japan 83–84
    Thailand 122
Erkmen, B. 199
Erozan, F. 199
error analysis 251
error correction 292
expertise of writing teachers xx, 3, 13–14
    adaptive expertise 14, 20–22
    application of routine–adaptive
        expertise framework 22–25
    defined 17–18
    growth points 24–25
    L2 writing teacher education research
        14–17
    progression from novices to experts
        19, 19–20
    propositions 18, 18–19
    research questions 27
    routine experts 21, 22
    and teaching 17–20
    conclusion 25–27

Fang, Y. 94
feedback 17
    written corrective feedback (WCF)
        240, 247n3
    see also Argentina: research study;
        Hong Kong: feedback literacy
        development; Northern Cyprus:
        case study
Ferris, D. 300
Ferris, D.R. 26
Flower, L. 94
FLTRP 59
foreign language writing:
    terminology 11n1

Freeman, D. 13
Furlong, J. et al. 91, 107

Gallavan, N.P. et al. 197, 216
Garner, M. 36
Gautam, G.R. 133
GDUFS see Guangdong University of
    Foreign Studies
Geisler, C. 17
genre-based approach 65, 67, 104, 251,
    281–283, 291, 298–299
Geoghegan, C. 92
Germany: writing instruction 290, 292
Giri, R.A. 132
Glaser, R. 20
Goh, R. 94
Golombek, P. 24–25
Golombek, P.R. 54–55
Gopinathan, S. et al. 93
Gorsuch, G.J. 77
Grabe, W. 182
Grossman, P.L. et al. 216
Guangdong University of Foreign
    Studies (GDUFS) 60, 64
Guénette, D. 36

Hadfield, J. 266
Hamada, Y. 82
Hanington, L.M. 94–95
Hargan, N. 291, 300
Hatano, G. 21
Hatasa, Y.A. 290
Hayden, H.E. et al. 21
Hayes, J.R. 94
Hedgcock, J. 300
Hedgcock, J.S. 23, 26
Hendges, G.R. 274
Higano Inagaki 86 26
Hirose, K. 74, 85
Hirvela, A. xx, 2, 13, 31, 53, 132, 224
Hong Kong
    primary school writing 298
    teacher workload 293
Hong Kong: feedback literacy
    development 31–32
    classroom experimentation 40–41,
        44–45
    effective feedback in general 34–35
    effective written corrective feedback
        (WCF) 35
    error correction 292

Hong Kong: feedback literacy
    development (*Continued*)
    impact of WTE 41–42, 45–47
    Joyce's feedback literacy development
        37, 38–43
    realities of feedback in L2 writing 36
    role of writing 32
    Susan's feedback literacy
        development 37, 43–48
    writing teacher education 32–33
    writing teacher education (WTE)
        course 33, 36–37, 39–40, 43–44
    conclusions 48–49
Howe, A.C. 54
Hryniuk, K. 126
Humphrey, S. 155
Hyland, F. 266, 298
Hyland, K. 65, 181, 252, 254–255,
    266, 282

identity 7, 9, **16**, 175, 250, 252–254,
    265–266, 266
Inagaki, K. 21
investment 254
Iran: English writing instruction 292,
    293, 295
İsmail, A.M. 202
issues and perspectives 1–2
    ecologically responsible teacher
        education 10–11
    moving forward 8–11
    overview of book 2–8
    reflexivity xx, 10–11
Italy: local writing practices and values
    291, 300

Japan: EFL writing instruction 71–72
    assistant language teachers (ALTs) 87
    communicative language teaching
        (CLT) 75–76, 78
    English education and English
        writing 72–74
    key influencing factors 71–72, 72
    see also Japan: MEXT Course
        of Study; Japan: other local
        constraints; Japan: university
        entrance examination system;
        Japan: university entrance
        examination system proposed
        changes
Japan: MEXT Course of Study 71, 74–75

course of study for English
    education 75–76
guidelines and textbooks for English
    writing 76–77
inconsistencies between guidelines
    and writing instruction 77–78
Japan: other local constraints 81, 289
    class size and time management 81,
        84, 122
    JTE teaching and learning culture
        81–82
    L1 writing instruction 290
    student motivation towards English
        learning 82–83
Japan: university entrance examination
    system 78–79
    English examinations 79
    examination washback on English
        teaching and learning 79–80
Japan: university entrance examination
    system proposed changes 83
    implications for teacher education
        86–87
    JTE teacher training 85–86
    proposed English writing tests
        83–85, **84**
    test of English for Academic
        Purposes (TEAP) 83–84
Johnson, K.E. 24–25, 54–55, 64, 68, 86
Jordan: English as medium of
    instruction 294
*Journal of Second Language Writing
    (JSLW)* 1–2, 13, 111, 132

Kamimura, T. 85
Khamkhien, A. 116
Kikuchi, K. 77–78, 82
Kızıltepe, Z. 175
Kleiman, A. 275
Kleinsasser, R. 81–82
Kobayakawa, M. 77
Koç, S. 199
Koike, I. *et al.* 73
Kowata, T. 80, 81
Kroll, B. 15
Kumaravadivelu, B. 136
Kuter, S. 199

L2 writing teacher education research
    14–15
    chronology 15

experienced teachers **16**, 16–17
pre-service teachers 16
teacher populations studied 15
topics **16**, 16–17
L2 writing: terminology 11n1
Lalande, J. F. 35
Lantolf, J.P. 67
Larsen, D. 24
learning-to-write 9, 224, 234
Lee, E. 196
Lee, H. 23
Lee, I. 31, 36, 126, 197, 217, 289, 292, 293, 296, 297
Leki, I. *et al.* xvii, xviii, 24–25, 80, 288, 300
Liu, H. 57
Lo, J. 298
Lockhart, C. 58
Long, M.H. 17, 18
Lortie, D. 66
Lyster, R. 36

McCarthey, S.J. 92
Machado, A.R. *et al.* 273–274
Mackenzie, A.S. 113
McNeil, D. 24
Manchón, R.M. xvii, 1–2, 3, 9, 173, 174, 240, 288
Martin, S. 91
Matsuda, P.K. 14
Morocco: English writing instruction 293, 294
Motta-Roth, D. 274

Naghdipour, B. 292, 293, 295
National Commission on Writing 03 91
NELTA *see* Nepal English Language Teachers' Association
Nepal 5, 131–132
absence of teacher mentor program 144
English as language of instruction 132
findings 136–144
literature review 132–134
methodology 134–136, **135**
pedagogical challenges 139–143
pre-service training/in-service practice disconnect 136–138
preparation and continued development 136–139
questionnaires 135, 146–148
resources and support systems 143–144
space, class size, time constraints 132, 142–143
students' low motivation/varied linguistic ability 141–142
teacher development xix
teacher training 132
teachers as non-writers 139–141
top-down professional development 138–139
discussion and conclusion 144–146
Nepal English Language Teachers' Association (NELTA) 132, 134–135, 145
Newell, G.E. *et al.* 21
Nishino, T. 78
Noom-ura, S. 116–117, 123, 125
Northern Cyprus: case study 203
design: interviews 204–205, 217–218
English proficiency of students 206–207
faculty perspectives on writing in TEFL program 205–209
findings and discussion 205–215
participants **203**, 203–204
significance of feedback on writing skills development 205–206, 209
student perspectives on writing in TEFL program 209–215
students' communication skills 208
students' writing experience 207–208, 209–212
conclusion 215–217
see also Northern Cyprus: resources for pre-service English teachers
Northern Cyprus: resources for pre-service English teachers 6–7, 195–197, 202
background 200–203
Council of Higher Education (CHE) 198, 218n1
literature review 197–200
methodology 203–205
Ministry of National Education (MoNE) 198
Northern Cyprus Campus TEFL Program 200–201
political context 201, 218n1
writing-focused courses in the curriculum 202–203

Northern Cyprus: resources for
    pre-service English teachers
    (*Continued*)
  see also Northern Cyprus: case study;
    Turkey: role of writing in EFL
    teacher preparation
Norton, B. 254

Okan, Z. 269
Organisation for Economic
    Cooperation and Development
    2015 Global School Ranking 92
Ortega, L. 1, 9, 146
Ortmeier-Hooper, C. 189

Pandey, S.B. 145
Parsons, S.A. 20
Patton, M.Q. 136
Paudel, J. 134
pedagogical content knowledge 23
peer review 54, 60, 64, 122, 292, 301
Pennington, M.C. 253
Pennycook, A. 52
Pessoa, S. *et al.* 155
Phyak, P. 134
Pillai, A.D. 94–95
Poland: L1 writing instruction 290
Poudel, P.P. 133
pre-service English teachers *see*
    Northern Cyprus: resources for
    pre-service English teachers
procedural knowledge 23
purposes and motivation for writing in
    English 294–295, 297–299

Qatar: case study 152–154
  process of collaboration 154–159
  scaffolding one assignment *160*,
    160–165, *162*, *164–165*, *166*
  scaffolding writing in the disciplines
    158–159, *159*
  unpacking writing expectations
    156–158
  conclusions 166–170
Qatar: second language disciplinary
    writing 6
  challenges teaching writing at branch
    campuses 150–152
  Education for a New Era
    reform 151
  see also Qatar: case study

Rathert, S. 269
reflexivity xx, 10–11
Reichelt, M. 2, 3, 11n1, 61, 290, 292,
    296, 297
resources
  availability of for EFL instruction
    292–293
  China: concept development 56–61
  Nepal 143–144
  Spain Teachers and Resources
    Centers 226, 246–247
  see also Northern Cyprus:
    resources for pre-service English
    teachers
Reyes Torres, A. *et al.* 262
Richards, H. *et al.* 253, 267
Richards, J.C. 17, 58
Rittel, H. 154
Rousseff, D. 278
Rubin, H.J. 135
Rubin, I.S. 135
Ruecker, T. 52

Sage, K. 80
Sampson, G.P. 52
Samudvanijja, C. 113
Saraç-Süzer, S. 190
Sato, K. 81–82
Scardamalia, M. 19–20
Scarino, A. 49
second language writing: terminology
    11n1
Selvi, A.F. 176–177, 199
SFL *see* systemic functional linguistics
Sharma, B.K. 134
Shin, S.J. 197
Shintani, N. *et al.* 35
Silva, T. 111
Silva, W.R. 281
Singapore: teacher preparation 4–5,
    91–92
  Academy of Singapore Teachers
    (AST) 93
  classroom contexts 97–98
  context 92–95
  English Language Institute of
    Singapore (ELIS) 93–94, 107, 109
  exams 98–100
  factors influencing teacher
    preparation 93, 96–100
  findings 96–107

language use 96–97
methods 95–96
National Institute of Education
    (NIE) 93, 94, 96, 104–105, 108, 109
preparing pre-service teachers to
    teach writing 101–104
professional development 93–95
professional development to support
    writing instruction 104–107
research projects 105–107
Syllabus 97
discussion and implications 107–109
Sinwongsuwat, K. 116
Smith, R.C. 261
Snow, R.E. 20
sociolinguistic status of English
    293–294, 296–297
Souza, R.R. 274
Spain: EFL writing instruction 224
communicative functions 228–229
curricular guidelines 226–231
language provision 226–227
materials 231–233
oral-aural skills 227
text types 229–231
use of learned linguistic forms 229
writing outcomes 232–233, **233**, **234**
writing process 227–228
see also Spain: EFL writing teacher
    education
Spain: EFL writing teacher education 7,
    222–224, 234
bilingual programs 223, 224
language learning potential of L2
    writing 239–241
methodology 224–226
official documents 224–225
questionnaire 225–226, 237–239,
    242–246
Teachers and Resources Centers 226,
    246–247
teachers' voices 237–239
writing pedagogy 234–237, 239
conclusion 241–242
see also Spain: EFL writing
    instruction
Stang, K. 197
Storch, N. 247n3
Street, C. 197
student motivation 34, 36, 44, 73,
    82–83, 124, 141–142

subject matter knowledge 23
Swain, M. 240
Swales, J. 65
Symposium on Second Language
    Writing (SSLW) 13–14
systemic functional linguistics (SFL)
    151, 192, 251, 282

Tahira, M. 78
Taiwan: writing evaluation program
    301
Tanaka, N. 80
Tando, H. 85–86
Tarnopolsky, O. 294–295, 297, 298
Tay-Koay, S.L. 95
Tay May Yin 97
teacher effectiveness 260, 267–268
teacher identity 265–266, 266
teacher knowledge 23
teacher preparation for teaching EFL
    writing 295
creative writing 298
dealing with large class sizes 300–301
exploring local practices, beliefs,
    circumstances re writing
    instruction 299–300
finding purposes for writing
    297–299
genre writing 298–299
instructional materials 300
investigating sociolinguistic status of
    English 296–297
participation in writing activities
    295–296
writing/discussing case study
    scenarios 296
writing for instrumental purposes 298
teachers' instructional behavior 17
teaching-learning cycle (TLC) 282
teaching writing
as part of language teaching xviii
teacher preparation and education
    xviii–xix, 2, 3
Teles, R.S.A. 274
Teng, B. 116
Thailand 5, 111–112
Basic Education Core Curriculum
    (BECC) 113–114, 120, 126
Basic Education Curriculum (BEC)
    112–113
Course of study for languages 113

Thailand (*Continued*)
  English writing instruction in
    primary and secondary schools
    112–115
  literature review 115–117
  Ministry of Education Curriculum
    Reform Committee (CRC) 112
  National Economic and Social
    Development Plan (2007–2011) 113
  National Education Reform Act
    (1999) 112
  Office of the Basic education
    Commission (OBEC) 113–114
  see also Thailand: present study
Thailand: present study 111–112, 117
  data sources and data analysis 119,
    127–128
  interview protocol 119, 127–128
  participant selection 117–118, **118, 119**
  findings 119–125
  teachers' approaches to writing
    instruction 120–122
  teachers' perceived resource and
    professional development needs
    124–125
  teachers' preparedness to teach writing,
    issues and challenges 122–124
  discussion and conclusion 125–126
Tin, T.B. 133–134
Tinoco, G.M. 274–275
TLC (teaching-learning cycle) 282
Trent, J. 253, 266
Tsui, A.B.M. 17–18, 20, 27
Turkey: role of writing in EFL teacher
    preparation 6, 173–175
  Council of Higher Education (CoHE;
    YÖK) 177
  language teacher preparation
    programs xix, 177–178
  Middle East Technical University
    (METU) 196, 200, 201, 202
  Ministry of Education (MoNE)
    175–176
  role of English and writing in
    educational system 175–177, 291,
    300
  conclusion: what's next? 191–192
  see also Northern Cyprus: resources
    for pre-service English teachers;
    Turkey: study

Turkey: study
  context: changing institutional
    expectations of L2 writing 179–181
  curricular analysis 181–183
  English for academic purposes (EAP)
    program 179
  English Proficiency Test (EPT) 179
  findings 181–189
  research questions and methods
    178–179
  survey findings: teacher candidates'
    perceptions and experiences
    183–189, *185, 186,* **187, 188**
  discussion 189–191

Ukraine: English writing instruction
    294–295
United States
  National Writing Project 92, 107
  professional learning communities
    (PLCs) 92
  teacher professional development
    (PD) 91–92
Ur, P. 60

Vasylets, O. 240
Volpi, M.T. 275
Vygotsky, L.S. 53–54, 65

Wada, M. 77
Wang, C. *et al.* 57, 64
Watanabe, Y. 79–80
Weaver, W. 153
Webber, M. 154
Weir, C.J. 84
writing-to-learn 9, 174, 223
writing-to-learn-content (WLC) 223–224
writing-to-learn-language (WLL) 223,
    229, 234, 239, 241
written corrective feedback (WCF) 240,
    247n3

Xi'an International Studies University
    (XISU) 60–61, 62
Xu, Y. 49

Yasuda, S. 73
Yoshida, K. 83
You, X. 180